Mary Chesnut's Civil War Epic

Mary Chesnut's Civil War Epic

JULIA A. STERN

The University of Chicago Press   *Chicago and London*

JULIA A. STERN is associate professor of English and American studies at Northwestern University, where she is also director of undergraduate studies and the Charles Deering McCormick Professor of Teaching Excellence. She is the author of *The Plight of Feeling: Sympathy and Dissent in the Early American Novel* (1997), published by the University of Chicago Press.

The University of Chicago Press, Chicago 60637
The University of Chicago Press, Ltd., London
© 2010 by The University of Chicago
All rights reserved. Published 2010
Printed in the United States of America

19 18 17 16 15 14 13 12 11 10   2 3 4 5

ISBN-13: 978-0-226-77328-5 (cloth)
ISBN-10: 0-226-77328-0 (cloth)

The Northwestern University Research Grants Committee has provided partial support for the publication of this book. The University of Chicago Press gratefully acknowledges this assistance.

Library of Congress Cataloging-in-Publication Data

Stern, Julia A.
Mary Chesnut's Civil War epic / Julia A. Stern.
p. cm.
Includes bibliographical references and index.
ISBN-13: 978-0-226-77328-5 (cloth : alk. paper)
ISBN-10: 0-226-77328-0 (cloth : alk. paper)
1. Chesnut, Mary Boykin Miller, 1823–1886. Diary from Dixie. 2. United States—History—Civil War, 1861–1865—Personal narratives, Confederate—History and criticism. 3. Women—Southern States—Diaries—History and criticism. 4. Southern States—Biography—History and criticism. 5. Confederate States of America—History—Sources. I. Title.
E487.C5237 2010
973.7'82092—dc22
[B]
2009022151

⊗ The paper used in this publication meets the minimum requirements of the American National Standard for Information Sciences—Permanence of Paper for Printed Library Materials, ANSI Z39.48-1992.

TO MY PARENTS,
   Janet Boshes Stern and Charles Arnold Stern,
AND TO MY BOYS,
   Michael Martin Myers and Nicholas Joseph Stern Myers

CONTENTS

List of Figures, ix. Acknowledgments, xi

ONE: *Introduction*, 1. TWO: *Walls* EPIC IN MINIATURE, 29. THREE: *Seeds* FERTILITY, FLOWERS, AND FRATRICIDE, 49. FOUR: *Seeds* FRUITS AND FAMINE, 79. FIVE: *Words* READING AND WRITING, 107. SIX: *Smells* THE STENCH OF SLAVERY AND SENTIMENT, 133. SEVEN: *Masks* THEATRICALS IN BLACK, 167. EIGHT: *Masks* THEATRICALS IN WHITE, 191. NINE: *Revolt* FAMILY TROUBLES IN THE HOUSE DIVIDED, 207. TEN: *Revolt* MORE FAMILY TROUBLES IN THE HOUSE DIVIDED, 231. ELEVEN: *Recognition* LOOKING DEFEAT IN THE FACE, 253

Notes, 267. Index, 311

FIGURES

1. James Johnston Pettigrew, Hector and Ajax from the *Iliad* (drawings, nineteenth century), 30

2. James Johnston Pettigrew, scenes from the *Iliad* (drawings, nineteenth century), 31

3. John Flaxman, "Andromache Fainting on the Wall" (engraving, eighteenth century), 38

4. Timothy O'Sullivan, "A Harvest of Death, Gettysburg, Pennsylvania" (photograph, 1863), 69

5. Mary Chesnut, "Annual Expense Book" (cover page, 1870–71), 99

6. Mary Chesnut, "Annual Expense Book" (entry, February 1870), 100

7. Mary Chesnut, "Annual Expense Book" (entry, January 1871), 101

8. Currier and Ives, "Washington's reception by the ladies . . ." (lithograph, ca. 1845), 157

9. "Mrs. Elizabeth Witherspoon of Society Hill, S.C." (clipping, *Charleston Courier,* September 1861), 222

10. Gallows bill for hanging Elizabeth Witherspoon's murderers (manuscript, 1861), 244

ACKNOWLEDGMENTS

From almost the moment the idea for this book crystallized into words, Robert A. Ferguson has believed in it. Teacher, mentor, and treasured friend, he has read every proposal and multiple drafts of chapters. His suggestion from Locke, that "slavery is a state of war," transformed my understanding of slave resistance. Mitchell Breitwieser supported this book as he has all my work since the mid-1990s. I continue to marvel that the magic of print could inspire such intellectual communion. Ann Douglas's writing and teaching remain central to everything I think about the connection between affect and narrative. Richard Sacks's graduate course on the epic converted Columbia's literature humanities curriculum into a source of lifelong pleasure. Carole Slade sent me a Virginia Woolf essay exploring women, illness, and creativity that enriched chapter 3.

Eric Sundquist, Northwestern's former dean, enthusiastically responded to early thoughts about the project. Daniel Linzer, Northwestern's provost, generously has supported my research and my teaching. S. Hollis Clayson, director of the Alice Berline Kaplan Institute for the Humanities at Northwestern, fellow Wellesley graduate, art historian, and dear friend, oversaw the year-long fellowship that allowed me to complete the manuscript. Enormous thanks to her and to the institute staff. Andrew Wachtel, dean of the graduate school and another dear friend, awarded me a university research grant that made possible an important trip to the archives in South Carolina and a subvention to defray the costs of publication. Mary Pat Doyle made his generosity material.

Helen Deutsch has been my inspiration and fellow traveler since December of 1990. It was she who convinced me to follow my intellectual passions and write an entire book about Chesnut's Civil War narrative, despite the unfashionability of "author" studies. Tim Spears, an early advocate and acute reader, was crucial in helping me conceptualize my imagined audience for this study. Christopher Castiglia suggested that the aesthetic was a key to understanding Chesnut's cultural project. Wendy Graham read with characteristic rigor and care. Eric Lott worked through early drafts on short notice. Cindy Weinstein gave me brilliant suggestions for chapter 6. Augusta Rohrbach, fellow Chesnut scholar, made marvelous suggestions on the first two chapters. Stephanie McCurry, Southern historian par excellence, answered esoteric questions; contending with this book was less arduous for her intellectual companionship.

Susan Herbst followed the progress of the project from various Olympian administrative locations with wit and empathy.

Robert S. Levine, dear friend and colleague extraordinaire, may be the most generous academic in American literary studies. He invited me to the University of Maryland to present a very early version of this book. Comments there from Leonard Cassuto, Mary Helen Washington, Carolyn Karcher, and Heather Nathans enriched my revisions over several years. Edward Larkin brought me to the University of Richmond the following year, and afforded me two terrific settings to present additional pieces of the project. Tom Allen and Elizabeth Barnes raised provocative questions, both of which found their ways into the final manuscript. And the members of the Fault Line History Reading Group, particularly Woody Holson, Douglas Winiarski, Mark Valeri, and Brent Tarter, offered important insight into historians' current thinking about the problem of slavery and resistance. Panels at the MLA, the M/MLA, the Melville/Douglass Conference, and the Narrative Conference, particularly Christopher Looby, Elizabeth Young, Ellen Weinauer, Teresa Goddu, Dale Bauer, Cindy Weinstein, Coleman Hutchison, and Kathleen Diffley, afforded delightful occasions for collaboration. Jana Argersinger's decade-long camaraderie has been a gift of the profession, and her readerly insight remains unmatched. Elizabeth Renker's friendship has elevated my at-times flagging spirits, helping me to remember that scholarship and motherhood sometimes make uneasy companions. Julia Adeney Thomas provided the historian's acuity and the friend's laying on of hands at crucial times.

Susan Manning, the friend who with open arms welcomed me to Evanston nearly two decades ago, did a brilliant reading of the proposal and both chapters on theatricality. Carl Smith read reams of pages and offered vital suggestions for clarifying my argument. Betsy Erkkila read a large chunk of the manuscript, raising questions that transformed how I addressed the connection between gender and textual production. Jay Grossman had a hunch about the significance of class in Chesnut's narrative that deepened my thinking in crucial ways. Christopher Herbert's vast knowledge of the Indian Mutiny illuminated important, unknown, territory. And Martin Mueller illuminated Greek masking.

Particular thanks go to friends and colleagues Mary Finn, Jeffrey Masten, Wendy Wall, Jules Law, Reg Gibbons, Blakey Vermeule, Page DuBois, Katy Breen, Susie Phillips, Christopher Lane, Tracy Davis, Bonnie Honig, Huey Copeland, Mike Sherry, and Doris Garraway. I am very grateful to them all. Thanks beyond words to those younger scholars in my classrooms, former and current graduate students Christopher Hager, Elizabeth Fekete Trubey, Marcy

Dinius, Hunt Howell, Coleman Hutchison, Ashley Byock, Katy Chiles, Peter Jaros, Sarah Mesle, Abram Van Engen, Sarah Turner Lahey, Melissa Daniels, Wendy Roberts, Greg Laski, Hugh McIntosh, and WanaLee Romero. I also thank my Chesnut-reading former and current undergraduates: Megan Glick, Jessica Jones, Elizabeth Wulff, Alison Ehrmann Hager, and most recently, Jamie Poslosky, Oren Ables, Jayne Kenney, and Tara Stringfellow.

Years after Christina Adkins wrote a prize-winning honors thesis on Chesnut, and while beginning a dissertation at Harvard, she tirelessly worked as my research assistant, a fount of energy when I flagged, and a genius in the archives. With unstinting commitment, she read every draft chapter of the manuscript; without her brilliant final suggestions for revision, this book would be a poorer thing indeed. Megan Glick, while completing her Ph.D. at Yale, did superb research on the history of nineteenth-century medicine. Matthew White did magisterial work on the pertinent nineteenth-century newspaper culture in which Chesnut was immersed. Kim Becnael found extraordinary documents pertaining to the execution of the slaves who murdered Betsey Witherspoon. Sarah Turner Lahey uncovered the eighteenth-century newspaper citations for Washington's return to Trenton and Willie Lincoln's death. My gratitude to you all.

Deepest thanks go to my readers for the University of Chicago Press. Elisabeth Muhlenfeld, president of Sweet Briar College and our most distinguished Chesnut scholar, had doubts about my organizational strategy and the adequacy of my amplification of the literary aspects of Chesnut's writing process. It is my hope that in my revisions I have sufficiently addressed these important concerns, and I thank her for her ongoing support of this project. Kathleen Diffley is my scholarly and professional ideal. Generous, demanding, imaginative, and deeply learned, she knows as much about the print culture of the Civil War and Reconstruction as anyone working today. My development of the manuscript would have been impossible without her insight and advice. Jane E. Schultz, a scholar whose work on Civil War nurses' narratives has transformed our understanding of gender in the war, was my other reader. Her intellectual embrace of my idiosyncratic interests, and her innumerable, imaginative, and thoughtful suggestions for expanding sections of the manuscript, enriched the ambition of the book.

In Camden, South Carolina, Chesnut's lineal descendants Martha Williams Daniels, who sadly died as this book went to press, and her daughter and namesake, "Marty" Williams Daniels, welcomed me with warmth and generosity. She devoted a day to showing me Mulberry Plantation, the Chesnut's library, the grounds, and even the private family cemetery located twenty miles away. Her intellectual hospitality was matched only by her culinary gifts. Marty's friend and colleague Barbara Falconroth became the other archival angel of my book, reproducing and sending me hundreds of pages of unpublished letters and documents from the Mulberry Plantation collection. I shared an extraordinary conversation with Martha the elder, who, despite significant health problems, agreed to talk with me about her Aunty. Her father was David R. Williams IV, son of Stephen Miller Williams, or Miller, Mary Chesnut's favorite nephew. Mrs. Daniels was the last link to Mary Chesnut's world, and our conversation was magical. Her son, Professor Christopher Williams Daniels, generously sent me his master's thesis on three generations of Chesnut men, which offered a treasure trove of analysis and copies of obscure archival documents pertaining to the family: work rolls for freedmen and -women in 1867, bills, and more. His immediate responses to my e-mail barrage of questions helped make this book better than it ever would have been without his interest and generosity. Profound thanks go to Henry Fulmer, chief manuscript archivist at the Caroliniana Library at the University of South Carolina. His expertise, kindness, and friendship across eight years have extended well beyond the archives; he is the finest in his field. Thanks as well to the South Carolina Department of History and Archives, the Camden Historical Society, the Darlington County Archives, and Bruce Brown, owner of Bloomsbury, the Chesnut "town" home in Camden, for his generous house tour and Chesnut family history. David Shields, eminent scholar, journal editor, and friend, and Lucia Shields hosted me in Columbia, concocting a superb, multicourse South Carolina dinner and sharing his knowledge of "Carolina Gold," the region's most famous rice. Judith Kalb and Alexander Ogden's hospitality made my inaugural visit to Columbia unforgettable. Thanks to you all.

Alan Thomas is my treasured editor and beloved friend. I still cannot believe that at his young age, it is he who makes the world turn for the University of Chicago Press. Deepest thanks to him for the sensitivity with which he escorted me through the publication process, again. Randy Petilos handled legalities with characteristic aplomb. Copyeditor Carlisle Rex-Waller made this writer's narrative dreams come true. And Greg Laski's brilliance makes indexing look easy.

As in all of my endeavors, my parents and siblings have been with me every step of the way. My mother, Janet Boshes Stern, has the unique distinction of being the first person to read the entire manuscript in draft. I bless her for that and for much else. My father, Charles A. Stern, a gentle-variety Civil War fiend, is in medias res with the manuscript. I thank him for that and for his ongoing support of the project, including sending me any tidbit he could find about the war or its cultural history. Richard Stern, Patricia Stern Smallacombe, Grace Morsberger, and James Smallacombe exemplify brotherly and sisterly love. Deborah Boxerman supported me and my project well before it began. She keeps the link between thought and feeling not only alive but electric.

My beloved boys, Michael Myers and Nicholas Myers, have lived with this project for nearly a decade. When Nicholas was six, he asked me what my book was about. I explained that Chesnut was a very smart Southern woman who wrote a book about living during the Civil War; her family had owned 450 slaves and, though she actually thought slavery was wrong, she wasn't able or willing to free those people. It took the South's losing the Civil War to make that happen. My book, I said, tried to understand how this lady felt about her slaves and former slaves, and how the black bondspeople felt about Mrs. Chesnut. "Mama!" he exclaimed, "let me draw the picture!" Minutes later, he handed me the image of a woman in a puffy skirt with a head and a hairdo and arms, and three shapes resembling acorns with berets. The skirt was Mrs. Chesnut; the bereted acorns stood for her slaves (acorns / chestnuts / Chesnut blacks). Over the bereted acorns, a cartoon bubble said: "We Chesnut's have feelings, too!" That a six-year-old could fathom the crux of my scholarly fascination gave me hope that this project would spark interest in a wider variety of readers than I might have imagined originally. During the summer in which I completed my first draft of the manuscript, now fourteen-year-old Nick spent hours a day with a group of boys who, though loud and zealous, always respected my need to write. His friends Harvey Penn and Jaren Walker deserve my special thanks for their interest. "You're writing a book!" they would exclaim. "Sweet!"

Twenty-seven years ago, I met the man I thought at the time would be an ideal intellectual interlocutor, a fact that, I'm privileged to say, remains true today. It was he who, having studied American literature with Leo Marx and epic poetry with David Halperin, urged me to go to graduate school in English; and it also was he who suggested that having an imaginative streak while doing serious scholarship might not be a bad thing. It is he who makes possible both love and work; and to him, I owe everything.

CHAPTER ONE

Introduction

"Justice without mercy," Mary Boykin Chesnut opined, invoking the witticism of the moment about the portraits her friends were having taken on the eve of the Civil War. Of her own image, recorded during this period, she noted: "Got my carte de visite. Mr. Chesnut very good—mine like a washerwoman."[1] In the spring of 1861, making one's photograph had become all the rage among Confederate cabinet members and their wives. Mary Chesnut was no exception: in late March of that year, she patronized a local Charleston photographer with her husband, presidential aide-de-camp James Chesnut Jr., presumptive heir of Colonel James Chesnut Sr., one of the wealthiest slaveowners in South Carolina.[2] Despite having lived a life of privilege, Mary Chesnut responded to the portrait produced that day in a fashion that scarcely accords with twenty-first-century notions about the language of refined Southern matrons. Nor does it correspond with our ideas about how such aging belles imagined their own personae. Well-born and brilliantly married, superbly educated and intensely intellectual, Mary Boykin Chesnut was not representative of Southern women of her class and era. While she conformed to genteel nineteenth-century social protocols, Chesnut simultaneously felt compelled to analyze, with withering rigor, her own behavior and that of her elite milieu, as well as to study the men and women from all walks of life she encountered during the war. The prescient Chesnut could detect in her carte de visite a washerwoman emerging from the image of the aristocratic matron. Moreover, she could understand the palimpsestic relation of lady to laundress as strata of the same self, overlapping incarnations captured by the magic of photography. This expansive vision applied to her own writing as well, allowing her to imagine how, under the pressure of martial conquest, the fortunes of Confederates high and low could resolve into one grim fate. Chesnut's double consciousness *avant la lettre* consequently enabled her to look defeat in the face and record its cultural implications as has no other nineteenth-century American writer working in the epic form and meditating on the subjects of race, slavery, and the house divided.

This book argues that Mary Boykin Chesnut composed one of the greatest epics in American letters, a work never read in its own century. Having drafted observations in diary form between 1861 and 1865, Chesnut reviewed the manuscript in 1866 and put it away until the late 1870s, when she began to transcribe the jottings of the bellum period into full sentences and complete thoughts. Departing at times from her original wartime musings and working imaginative elements into the story, the 1880s Chesnut came to reenvision the smoothed-over Civil War fragments with an eye toward creating a more ambitious account. In a final burst of creative energy between 1880 and 1883, the diarist of the 1860s fashioned herself into a literary writer, giving expression to the devastation of an entire society. Casting her book in diurnal form, Chesnut bequeathed a manuscript that, far from being an actual diary, was a consciously crafted work of art.

Scholars have speculated about just how "unfinished" her manuscript was. Had Chesnut lived another decade or more, she might have continued her revisionary efforts as long as such labor remained possible. Her extant correspondence reveals that Mary Chesnut of the mid-1880s still had much to say. The process of writing had long ago become a way of life, Chesnut's spiritual exercise in a shattered world. And the manuscript she left at her death was marked by a power and pathos, if not a polished introduction or stunning conclusion, that any doppelganger-self, writing into the 1890s, would have found difficult to surpass.

Drafts of the epic she had come to imagine were left unfinished when in 1884 her household was struck by what developed over the next year into mortal illness for her husband and her mother. The chronic afflictions that had plagued Chesnut herself since midcentury, meanwhile, had in no way abated. Relatively early in her life, Chesnut had begun to suffer from angina pectoris (hardening of the arteries), which caused chest pain and breathing problems. Somewhat regularly, she was attacked by recurring bouts of "gastric fever," or typhoid, as well. A semi-invalid for most of her adult life, Chesnut ultimately died of a heart attack, though not before her husband eventually succumbed to paralysis and death on February 1, 1885. A mere eight days later, on February 9, the aged Mary Boykin Miller expired as well, leaving Chesnut profoundly bereft and physically broken. Within twenty-one months, on November 22, 1886, she would be dead herself.

Martin-Avary Edition

Chesnut's most important twentieth-century editor, the late Yale University historian C. Vann Woodward, conjectured that having set aside the work to nurse her husband and mother, Chesnut never took it up again, though an extant letter to Mrs. Jefferson Davis suggests that she had not finished her reworkings, which needed "to be overhauled, again and again" during this period.[3] Chesnut's magisterial, highly literary, if unfinished account of experience at the center of the Confederacy was not published in its author's lifetime. The childless matron bequeathed the entirety of her writing to protégée Isabella Martin, a spinster schoolteacher who in her editorial capacity, collaborating with professional writer Myrta Lockett Avary, bowdlerized what ultimately was brought to print in 1905 by Appleton and Company of New York, after being excerpted in five numbers of the *Saturday Evening Post*.[4]

Among many other of their problematic interventions in Chesnut's work, Martin and Avary called the book *A Diary from Dixie: The Civil War's most celebrated journal, written 1861–1865 by the wife of James Chesnut, Jr., an aide to President Jefferson Davis and brigadier-general in the Confederate Army*, a title its creator never authorized and likely would have hated, as she did the Southern anthem from which her editors drew their inspiration. This first edition of Chesnut's Civil War narrative derived from the 1880s manuscripts, though Martin and Avary never indicated that what they had published was not a diary written to the moment between 1861 and 1865, but something rethought and reworked over difficult decades of poverty, chronic illness, spousal disenfranchisement, and narrowed opportunities. What Martin and Avary may not have recognized was that even in its unfinished state, the manuscript they took up had been crafted with an eye to epic significance.

Shaping her massive work into a triptych featuring three generations of flawed but heroic Chesnut men (the Colonel; his son James, her husband; and James's nephew Johnny), the literary writer of the 1880s animated the Confederate past and present while also foreshadowing her powerful intimation, glimpsed as early as late winter of 1865, that any postwar Southern future would be bleak indeed.[5] Chesnut inaugurated her narrative with an emphasis on the ninety-year-old James Sr., while the middle third of the manuscript focused on the wartime experience of her husband, Brevet Brigadier General James Chesnut Jr.[6] The final third of the book accented the adventures of young cavalry officer Captain Johnny Chesnut, grandson of James Sr. and nephew of James Jr. and the favorite of both, who served as father figures to the young man. Portraying her kin as multifaceted characters, the writer modeled their complexity on the rich personae crafted by her novelist-idol, George Eliot. But the real star of the production was Mary Boykin Chesnut herself, re-presented as a literary character in her 1860s diarist alter ego: Mrs. James Chesnut Jr., scribbling Confederate matron. It was this persona who became the protagonist—indeed, the heroine—of the 1880s narrative.

Both Woodward, who edited the authoritative 1981 volume of the 1880s book on which most of the following study is based, as well as distinguished biographer Elisabeth Muhlenfeld, who coedited with Woodward our only extant version of the original 1860s diary, have established that Chesnut did not write at all in 1863 or 1864. And in the 1880s book, she reported that she had burned thirteen months of 1860s diary-keeping: this represented the period beginning with a serious illness in August of 1862, when she was nursed by her beloved sister Kate (Katherine Miller Williams) in Flat Rock, North Carolina, and ending in early May 1863, when during the battle of Chancellorsville, the Union cavalry under General George Stoneman conducted a terrifying raid very near Richmond, where the Confederate cabinet and their families resided. In the literary work of the 1880s, Chesnut describes that this closest of calls moved her to destroy over a year's worth of her diary; she apparently feared that it could fall into enemy hands and perhaps expose the foibles of highly placed Confederates from her circle. No documents remain from the thirteen-month period during which she purportedly subjected her prose to the fire. It is possible that Chesnut crafted the image of artistic conflagration to make a larger point about the process of literary reconstruction itself. Whether her fire was historical or fictional, the literary artist of the 1880s used it to telegraph that her self-conception as a writer actually had begun to take form as early as midwar.

As Chesnut noted in the 1880s narrative, she decided to fill in those years from "memory," recreating this period from what she called "scraps" and from her collection of letters: "So this is no longer a journal but a narrative of all I cannot bear in mind which has occurred since August 1862" (September 23, 1863, 425). What had been unendurable emotionally thus took belated literary form in a creative act wrought from despair experienced two decades earlier. This portion of the 1880s book consequently is unhitched from the 1860s diary.

These "Memoirs" are organized around accounts of death and destruction: the decimation, member by member, of entire Southern families; the battle-related death of Cheves McCord, only son of Chesnut's dear friend, the writer and Confederate ideologue Louisa McCord; the mutilation (a saber cut across the face) and subsequent demise of her friend Frank Hampton, whose lifeless corpse and mangled visage she viewed when his remains lay in state at the capitol building; Chesnut's two epic journeys to the underworld, the death-haunted house of her sister Sally, who had lost to disease in less than fourteen days two of her three children; and the passing of the great Confederate general Stonewall Jackson from pneumonia, contracted after the amputation of an arm as a result of wounds received under friendly fire by a North Carolina unit following the battle of Chancellorsville. Many Confederate military prognosticators, including Chesnut in her self-ordained role of Cassandra, one persona among the several she crafted to represent her self of the 1860s, feared that the loss of Jackson would cripple "the Cause" irreparably. Some Civil War historians, working 140 years after the fact, would not have disagreed with what, in the summer of 1863, were dismissed as pessimistic lamentations.

Cassandra Wails

In adopting the fictional persona of Cassandra, her most dominant alter ego, the narrating Chesnut of the 1880s highlighted irony as the tone she preferred above all others. But in alluding to the beautiful Trojan princess whom a yearning Apollo had endowed with the gift of prophecy but, on being spurned, doomed to be disbelieved, Chesnut revealed the perilous nature of her endeavor as a writer. Reworking her fragmented Civil War diary into a coherent aesthetic achievement, Chesnut sought to convey the experiential and emotional truth of her own wartime years, during which she had enjoyed extraordinary access to the leading minds of the Confederacy.

Unlike Homer's prophetess, the self-consciously drawn alter ego of the 1860s, now a character in the 1880s book whom the narrating Chesnut called "Cassandra," often was incorrect or mistaken about the governmental and martial details she originally had recorded in her 1860s diary. Her social and cultural insights during the war, however, were nothing less than virtuosic, and the 1880s narrative captured that paradox. The literary-minded Chesnut of the 1880s was committed less to historical precision than to the accurate representation of how life *felt* to those living in the center of Rebel headquarters in the years 1861 to 1865. While the 1880s book is related by a narrator, no significant gap exists between the perceptions of this speaker and the represented consciousness of the 1860s persona Mary Chesnut, "scribbling woman." Transforming her book twenty years after surrender, the writer could have employed an omniscient narrative voice to tell this story of war and woe. But she rejected such a strategy, maintaining instead the fiction of a diurnal perspective, to breathtakingly realist effect.

So, for example, in the 1880s, Chesnut did not correct mistaken information from the 1860s diary, but let it stand in all its error. In that regard, she was less Cassandra than Delphic Oracle. The truth of her work lay not in its historical rigor, but in the astuteness of its judgments of the human nature playing out before her eyes. As for the ability to prophesy, Chesnut joked in the 1880s narrative about a moment two months before the end of the war in which Isabella Martin had no illusions about Chesnut's vatic powers. The passage unfolds the double vision of hindsight so crucial to the artist transforming historical material:

> Isabella has been reading my diaries. How we laugh. My sage ratiocinations—all come to naught. My famous insight into character—all utter folly. They were lying on the hearth, ready to be burned, but she told me to hold on—think of it a while. *Don't be rash.* (February 23, 1865, 724)

In *Confederates in the Attic,* his 1998 cultural history of Civil War memory, Tony Horwitz has shown that "the War of Northern Aggression" persisted, for Southerners at least, late into the twentieth century and beyond. Certainly, the war remained alive for inhabitants of the former Confederate states well after the failure of Reconstruction, the advent of Redemption (at the state level, the restoration of power to white elites), and the ubiquity of Jim Crow discrimination and violence against the millions of African Americans remaining in the region.[7]

The reality and ramifications of defeat continued to plague certain former Confederates living at the turn of the century. South Carolina literary scholar James Kibbler has speculated that most genteel Southern families around this moment would have owned or read a copy of the Martin-Avary *Diary from Dixie* or, at least, perused the excerpts from the *Saturday Evening Post.*[8] But what Martin-Avary's readers would have derived from *A Diary* exists at a huge distance from the narrative Chesnut labored over at the end of her life. In fact, her first editors omitted entire themes and events, particularly sections of text involving the subjects of slavery and cross-racial encounters. They also reworked the material from a decidedly un-Chesnut-like point of view, making her sentences decorous, regularizing and correcting punctuation, in ways that might have maddened their creator. Accordingly, it is fair to say that the book Chesnut was in the process of expanding and polishing in the years before her death largely has gone missing from literary histories of the latter nineteenth century.

Williams Edition

It is important to note that the only other, pre-1981-Woodward version of Chesnut's Civil War "diary," edited by novelist Ben Ames Williams and published in 1949, restored material crucial for understanding the book Chesnut left in manuscript.[9] Particularly significant are those pages concerning the murder by her own slaves of Chesnut's first cousin, the elderly Betsey Witherspoon. This event serves as the literary Chesnut's microcosm for exploring what she had come to feel were the mysteries of slave consciousness and black agency under bondage. Indeed, Chesnut's amplification of racial themes in her 1880s narrative marked a stark point of departure from her 1860s diary. Clearly, race was an issue about which she thought intensely in the two decades after the war. Thus Chesnut's elaboration of her experience at Mulberry's black church in 1861 from a passing incident into a central episode was the product of long literary gestation. The 1860s diary, in contrast, focused on the problem of faction, which seemed to plague Southern society from the pinnacle of the Confederate government and Rebel military to its local manifestations in the Chesnut and Boykin households. Despite Williams's willingness to include what we might consider Chesnut's darker 1880s materials, much remains missing, largely as the result of Williams's insistence on condensing the sheer volume of the manuscript(s) he found. The Woodward edition comes to 835 published pages, compared to Williams's own 547 and Martin and Avary's 404.

Williams also retains Martin and Avary's un-Chesnut-like title, another indication that the work's second editor was not much more in tune with the author than his predecessors had been. Indeed, he engages in his own subtle "smoothing over" of Chesnut's idiosyncratic punctuation and prose. And both the Martin-Avary and Williams editions tinker with her opening and closing entries, among other dimensions of the work's complex, unfinished literary form, although there exist four drafts of the introduction alone. (This perhaps is what drove Williams to offer his own "version.") Williams does explain to his readers that while the text had been drafted in the 1860s, its author "edited" and "transcribed" her manuscript in the 1880s. While this point of clarification goes some distance in illuminating the thorniness of the narrative's textual evolution from diary jottings to work of art unacknowledged in the Martin-Avary edition, it does not *quite* make clear that much of the 1880s labors involved the entire reinvention of small kernels from the 1860s diary.

Many possible explanations exist for the omission of Chesnut's 1880s book from standard accounts other than studies of Civil War writing per se, where the narrative is quoted reverentially but never read for its profound literariness. A primary concern involves the editorial status of the text(s), the question of which manuscript(s) of what era should be privileged—the "ur" 1860s diary fragments or the postwar 1880s narrative transformations? Such questions have been summarized best under the rubric that there is more than one *real* Chesnut narrative. Many scholars endorse the writer's so-called final intentions, the creative metamorphosis she was enacting through 1883 (itself unfinalized, and from which Martin and Avary culled their 1905 materials). Certain historians, devoted to the reading of primary source documents, authorize the unexpurgated thoughts revealed in dashed-off diary jottings in 1861, 1862, and 1865. These 1860s fragments are themselves often as cryptic as Emily Dickinson's poetic variants. Without the aid of the literary transformation of the manuscript in the 1880s as a sort of key, the value of the 1860s diary is limited; likewise, the reverse can be claimed about the full intelligibility of the creative metamorphosis of the 1880s without the benefit of the 1860s fragments. In his own edition of 1981, Woodward used excerpts from the 1860s to flesh out both 1880s lacunae and the fingerprints of Chesnut's editorial self-censorship in revision. But even for a historian as steeped in the bellum and postbellum Southern cultural milieu as was Woodward, the textual conundrums afforded by what remained of the writer's work produced their own dialectical interpretive problems for his edition.

Yale Edition

In fact, not just one but multiple manuscript portions exist for what Woodward called the journal and I term the 1880s literary narrative. In the late 1870s, Chesnut apparently recopied the 1860s diary fragments and began to massage them into a continuous account, work done in pencil. Then, she turned to novel writing, drafting "The Captain and the Colonel" and "Two Years; or, The Way We Lived Then." Approximately forty pages for a third work of fiction, tentatively titled "Manassas," also exist. It was in the early 1880s that Chesnut returned to her Civil War diary and undertook the massive project of imaginative reworking that she left at her death, and from which Woodward conducted his decade-long editorial work of excavation and restoration. In her final epoch of revisionary and imaginative production, Chesnut omitted some episodes from the 1860s diary and transformed many others from casual remarks to full-blown dramatic scenes, shifting person and voice, casting her own earlier, monologic commentary into the dialogue of newly added characters, amplifying into highly developed literary tableaux the symbolic valences she had glimpsed in events. As many as four drafts exist for certain portions of the 1880s revisions, including attempts at an introduction and the section known as "The Bright Side of Richmond" describing the amateur theatricals of winter 1864.[10]

Beyond the maze of multiple layers of revision, development, and new composition, further literary historical confusions pertain to generic provenance and periodization: some scholars have read Chesnut's 1880 narrative as a work of autobiography, others as a memoir, and a few as a volume of fiction. Arguments have erupted over whether the 1880s narrative really counts as a piece of Civil War writing. Many assert that Chesnut's 1880s "book" should be considered as a text springing from the post-Reconstruction South, exploring Confederate experience with historical double vision. Woodward's magnificent if palimpsestic 1981 version of what he titles *Mary Chesnut's Civil War* (*MCCW*) is the first complete edition of the 1880s revisions ever to see print. But evaluating the editorial interpolations of salacious or incriminating material from the 1860s diary that an increasingly cautious and self-conscious Chesnut excised during the revisions of the 1880s is a complicated endeavor. Chesnut's post-Reconstruction deletions speak for themselves: such passages belonged to the 1860s diary and had no place in the 1880s narrative. Nevertheless, the 1860s diary, in print only in Woodward and Elisabeth Muhlenfeld's 1984 edition, *The Private Mary Chesnut: The Unpublished Civil War Diaries* (*TPMC*), can be read in its gnomic entirety, as a freestanding volume, independent of the 1880s narrative. To do so, however, shuts the door on light shed by the 1880s transformations preserved exclusively in Woodward's Yale edition.

Woodward's Chesnut consists primarily of the literary efforts of the 1880s with the occasional interlarding in brackets of material from the 1860s diary that elaborates or explains confusions in the 1880s reworkings; that fills in names effaced in the 1880s for the sake of protecting the privacy of former friends and foes; or, in several very rare instances, that provides ur-versions of those passages that revisit and rework a point to very different political effect from its original articulation. Almost all such shifts involve Chesnut's accelerating racism after the Civil War, which likely was the product of economic resentment during decades of hardship and struggle in which once aristocratic planters came to endure poverty different in degree but not in kind from that suffered by their former slaves.[11]

The 1860s diary, in contrast, reveals that Chesnut's attitude toward African Americans often was sympathetic and that she was no advocate of black bondage. The writer had maintained this decidedly unpopular attitude since her early teens. In the face of her father's unexpected death on the Mississippi cotton plantation he had struggled to farm after giving up a congressional career, the Miller plantation slaves were sold at auction. Mary watched the shattering of the very black families with whom she had lived and played for two formative years and was turned against the institution, at least in principle. There is no record, however, that she made any effort to free her husband's slaves; her opposition was limited to ongoing conversations about the evils of slavery with younger friends like the Preston girls and their male Hampton cousins during the war, young people whose antislavery attitudes she documents in the literary narrative of the 1880s. Chesnut's hatred of slavery functioned in paradoxical concert with her inability to see blacks as equals and her guilty acknowledgment that she reveled in the comforts provided by the African Americans in her household.

In light of these considerations, taking on the textual problems of Mary Chesnut's Civil War narrative is not for the faint of heart, much less for the editorially untutored. Accordingly, this project follows a different strategy for approaching a nexus of texts veined with literary, cultural, and historical riches largely unmined by scholars in English and history departments alike. My method departs almost entirely from that of cultural critics like Edmund Wilson and Daniel Aaron, who reintroduced the Chesnut of the 1949 Williams *Diary from Dixie* to American letters, and from that of historians such as Eugene Genovese and Elizabeth Fox-Genovese, the latter of whom devoted an entire chapter to Woodward's 1981 Chesnut in her *In the Plantation Household,* a foundational feminist historical study of nineteenth-century Southern women's relations across the color line.[12] All admirers of Chesnut's writing, these scholars pluck and deploy quotations as if they constituted transparent documentary evidence of such disparate points as the existence of an inchoate feminism fomenting in the plantation mistress class and an innately aristocratic Southern loathing of or apology for slavery.

But far from documentary, Chesnut's 1880s passages are literary tableaux, in many cases born of original materials, but embellished, expanded, and reshaped. Historians who work with Chesnut's book have yet to grapple with this enormous complication of *genre:* what seems like the published version of a voluminous primary source in fact constitutes the literary transformation of original 1860s observations into a quasi-fictionalized narrative. Historians compare original 1860s diary scenes with those in the literary 1880s version, correctly arguing for a brutally candid, relatively tolerant middle-aged Chesnut over against a guarded, apologist, decidedly bigoted elderly one. But what they do not address is that far from offering a transparent window onto the 1860s, the writing left by Chesnut in the mid-1880s is informed by twenty years of creative marination and artistic transformation.

It makes perfect sense, then, that Wilson and Aaron, Chesnut's greatest literary champions prior to the scholarly advent of Woodward and Muhlenfeld twenty plus years later, call her the Tolstoy of nineteenth-century American letters. Yet these critics lament the generic no man's land into which her book falls. Methodologically simple and interpretively ambitious, my project plunges headlong into this morass of textual, historical, and generic dilemmas. I look in unprecedented exegetical detail at Chesnut's 1880s writing in the only published form inclusive of the range of her work—the Woodward edition, winner of the Pulitzer Prize for history in 1981—aided as well by *The Private Mary Chesnut* of 1984.

Thus, this study focuses on the Woodward edition, understanding that what this great Southern historian published in *Mary Chesnut's Civil War* does not correspond exactly to anything in the archive. In fact, when he could not establish their relevance to the surrounding narrative material, Woodward did not include long newspaper clippings that Chesnut had pasted into her copybook. He similarly decided against including pages in which the 1880s writer had transcribed long passages of poetry that did not echo the contiguous narrative. Fortuitously for Chesnut's literary-minded readers, however, he retained the majority of her commonplace-book quotations from volumes of verse, drama, and fiction, as well as passages from collections of philosophy, theology, and history, both ancient and contemporary. And in his footnotes, Woodward scrupulously accounted for his own editorial practices, documenting as fully as possible the information he had not included in his edition.

My study also is informed by Chesnut's other writings, including the novels and the unpublished memoirs featuring her sister as a young woman and her husband as a gentleman and soldier. Such materials afford a rich background against which to ponder those vital questions raised by Chesnut's unfinished Civil War epic, which unlike anything else in American letters offers a window onto mid- and late-nineteenth-century Confederate culture.

The slender archive of secondary historical and literary critical research on Chesnut's work only begins to parse out the significance of her representations of a society en route from apotheosis to defeat. Equally overlooked in the criticism and central to this project are Chesnut's recurring ruminations on slavery, freedom, racial difference, class struggle, gender politics, her own reading and writing, and most important from a literary historical point of view, her trenchant critique of *Uncle Tom's Cabin* and what she viewed as the perniciousness of sentimentalism, the dominant fictional mode of mid-nineteenth-century America.

In my effort to do justice to the untapped literary treasures contained in Chesnut's unfinished 1880s epic, I do not dwell, for example, on the aborted romance of Sally Campbell Buchanan "Buck" Preston and General John Bell "Sam" Hood, which has been the subject of much of the commentary Chesnut's book so far has enjoyed. Critics read Buck, the physically exquisite, intellectually accomplished, and universally sympathetic daughter of Chesnut's dearest friends, the aristocratic Carolinians General John and Caroline Hampton Preston, as an emblem of the Old South in all of its beauty and charm. In turn, they understand Hood, the lowborn, West Point–educated, self-made military hero, famous for risking himself and his men in perilous martial maneuvers, as a symbol of doomed Southern bravado.[13]

While the potential for class crossing in this romance appealed to the idealistic Buck, her traditional parents were horrified. After Hood ventured too far, it became clear that their fragile "engagement"—one he fervently sought and that violated the wishes of both General and Mrs. Preston—never could blossom into marriage.[14] Chesnut's imaginative treatment of a courtship that threatened the convention that elite Southern women marry within their class remains fascinating, both as character study and social allegory. But the romance of Buck and Hood has dominated the scholarship in ways that have eclipsed over eight hundred pages of equally fascinating episodes, including mistresses being murdered by slaves, amateur theatrical performances unfolding against a background of military crisis, the accidental death of Jefferson Davis's favorite child, and the food shortages suffered by women refugees from Columbia in the winter of 1865, to offer only several examples.

Intriguingly, the famous romance of Buck and Hood was not a prominent feature of the 1860s diary. Chesnut developed its significance only in her literary work of the 1880s. To be sure, the pages that follow explore a series of scenes and anecdotes that almost entirely involve Chesnut's 1880s amplifications and reinventions, and whose 1860s diary status often is negligible. Nevertheless, Buck and Hood do figure tangentially in these readings, for example when the wounded general makes a spectacle of himself during the amateur performance of Sheridan's *The Rivals*.

I also steer away from an aspect of "the house divided" theme that has intrigued many critics: the occasionally tempestuous state of Mary and James Chesnut Jr.'s marriage. In the 1880s narrative, Chesnut emphasized how her highly emotional and expressive, often sarcastic, temperament ill suited her stoic and reticent mate, a man for whom honor was all and display was anathema. The friction produced by their poor fit as a couple became exacerbated as they shared close quarters on the road with the Confederate cabinet. From the beginning of the war, various flirtatious colleagues of James began to shower Mary, by her own lights no great beauty, with inordinate attention. The 1880s author depicts James Jr.'s palpable jealousy and his interdiction of intimate walks and carriage rides with these potential "suitors."

The scant scholarly treatment of the 1880s book tends to cluster discussions of Chesnut's sui generis feminism, her critique of the way in which matrimony disenfranchised independent-minded women economically, their position at times akin to that of slaves. Even Woodward devoted several pages of his introduction to Chesnut's critique of marriage and women's legal subordination. My analysis departs from the marital dimension of Chesnut's domestic division theme, instead exploring the fragility of other intimate bonds the writer shared with members of her family-in-law: with her husband's mother, his niece (raised by her in-laws), and various others, as well as with her two maids and her husband's bondservant. These understudied relationships afford additional, necessary, insight into Chesnut's feminist critique of domesticity.

Epic

From individual psychological portraits to grand historical sweep, the epic reach of Chesnut's ambition has been noted by Wilson and Aaron, though little explored. In what follows, I argue that such classical aspirations extend beyond her numerous allusions to Homer, Troy, Sparta and Athens, Prometheus, Menelaus, Helen, Achilles, Ulysses, Dante, Milton, Byron, or her reference to herself throughout the narrative as a wailing Cassandra. Comparative literary scholar Richard Sacks claims that the epic form is, simultaneously, a culturally foundational and a self-consuming artifact. Epics involve representation of the project of founding a nation or culture—here, Confederate government and society. Chesnut memorializes her nation's traditions through mimetic attention to its domestic practices, including her own daily routines, evening soirees, hospital work, and rounds of visiting; its political and historical events, from secession and the inauguration of Davis to the murder of Lincoln and Lee's surrender; and its divinities or theology in depictions of Protestant worship, both white and black, Catholic landladies, Jewish friends, and political personalities.

Revealing encyclopedic ambition to catalogue the totality of a represented realm, epics weave a linguistic fabric that highlights the cultural traditions of oratory, poetry, and song. Thus, Chesnut records instances of slave music, nostalgic plantation ballads, Robert Burns's Scottish verses, Handel's "Dead March" from *Saul,* Confederate military airs, and varieties of dialect across the lines of race and class.[15] Epics also portray a requisite journey to the underworld, which, in the unusual case of Chesnut's book, happens at least twice. In short, these magisterial narratives offer a critical analysis of the culture in formation and are marked by a fault line that deconstructs the epic universe itself, as when the writer depicts herself rereading with pleasure and immediately thereafter burning old letters and potentially compromising passages from her diary. The fissures around which Chesnut's book seemingly undoes itself riddle the materiality of the written word: consider her burning of the diary in 1862, which she rematerializes in "Memoirs," crafted in the early 1880s; or contemplate the 1860s persona's perusal of old letters whose correspondents express eternal devotion but whose identities long ago have faded from the writer's memory. The 1880s narrator notes: "A painful raising of old ghosts—looking over and destroying letters all day. I see people writing to me as my dearest friends whose very names and existence I have long forgotten" (November 25, 1861, 242).

In its status as an American epic, Chesnut's narrative embraces numerous literary genres, though this study will not be able to explore them all: tragic drama, with Jefferson Davis as Shakespearian hero or mythic Greek sufferer, as his wife describes him at war's end, "my poor old Prometheus" (April 19, 1865, 787); Southwestern humor in the tall-tale tradition, involving the drunken Confederate cavalry officer who rides horseback into a bar and is celebrated for his equestrian prowess; Victorian domestic fiction, featuring the romantic delusion of Buck Preston and General Hood, whose rocky courtship mirrors the progress of the war; and military history, particularly Chesnut's incisive critiques of the once-celebrated General Beauregard as melancholic retreater and General Joseph E. Johnson, whom she faults for preserving the life of his army at the price of engagement with the enemy that could determine the outcome of a seemingly endless war.

The 1880s narrative also strikes a heroic tone in its treatment of the many dimensions of martial strife; here, the writer seems to have the *Iliad* in mind: she shows us her own vision of the fight for Fort Sumter; hears in detail conflicting firsthand accounts of the battle of First Manassas; and witnesses by proxy the strangulation of Richmond and attendant retreat of the Confederate armies and government in the winter of 1864–65. Most profound for the purposes of my inquiry is Chesnut's acuity regarding slavery and the problem of cross-racial recognition and misunderstanding; in this regard, I believe, she anticipates Faulkner's insights in *Absalom, Absalom!* (Indeed, if Kibbler's hypothesis is correct, Faulkner's family may have owned, and the aspiring modernist may have read, *A Diary from Dixie*.)[16]

Beset by racial prejudice, like many whites of her class and experience, Chesnut nevertheless captures something of the psychological complexities of her two maids and her husband's valet; these portraits of the 1880s are marked by affection and admiration. Thwarted by the ongoing illegibility of the slave "mask," Chesnut's recurring image for the inscrutability of black expression during the war, the literary Chesnut inadvertently gives voice to the subtle resistance of her own bondspeople; in doing so, she grants the reality and the power of slave consciousness itself.

As a woman's narrative, the 1880s work is as textured as *Clarissa* (if only half as long). Like Richardson's masterpiece, *Mary Chesnut's Civil War* inflects a wide panoply of issues relating to gender, from the author's painful allusions to her own infertility and the fecundity of female slaves to women's degraded status before the law and, most significant for Americanist criticism, her assault on all things sentimental and feminized.[17] The great irony, of course, is that Chesnut's obsession with Stowe and *Uncle Tom's Cabin* actually transformed the South Carolina writer's literary sensibility: a stalwart critic of all that was sentimental, the 1880s Chesnut found in Stowe an unacknowledgeable mentor when it came to her own imaginative ambition. Indeed, the literary Chesnut's commitment to creating an epic account of the Civil War was inspired, however unconsciously, by the book Stowe had conjured from her "feelings" about slavery (obviously underwritten by prodigious research). Put more simply, Stowe's best seller was the incubus that drove Chesnut's ambition; fanned by her own spark of Stowe-hating, the 1880s Chesnut's imaginative fires fueled the creation of her literary narrative. Such a conclusion might have shocked the revising author herself, but the anxiety of influence at work in Chesnut's reactivity to Stowe's great book is one of this study's central assertions.[18]

Chesnut's book of the 1880s is as searching on the subject of divided houses and fractured national families as *King Lear,* her proof text by the winter of 1865. In both the 1860s diary and the 1880s narrative, she meditates on the relation of politics to private life, concluding that the locus of maximum danger for a woman of her class and situation is not the public but the domestic sphere. Most abhorrent was rustication, isolation from her culture's conflicts, on the plantation among her in-laws. Expressed with characteristic economy, we hear her plaintive refrain on the subject of life in Camden. She tells her husband in an 1880 entry for December 10, 1863, in Richmond: "And you said you brought me here to enjoy one winter before you took me home and turned my face to a dead wall" (503). Only weeks after Confederate surrender, in an 1880s entry for April 23, 1865, James Jr. remarks: "Your sentence is pronounced—*Camden for life*" (796). Under Chesnut's razor-edged gaze, South Carolina relations and neighbors, as well as Richmond's political luminaries and military leaders, spring to life as both idiosyncratic, realistic characters and paradoxically powerful symbolic representations of ideas and dynamics at work in a nation riven by war.

Chesnut's Literary Critics

The literariness of *Mary Chesnut's Civil War* has yet to be fully appreciated or explored. With the exception of the editorial prefaces and follow-up essays of Woodward and Muhlenfeld, a scant handful of scholarly articles, and a fairly small assortment of doctoral dissertations devoted to or featuring Chesnut's 1880s literary narrative, research on both the book and its author is largely documentary and comparative.[19]

Ironically, beyond the indispensible work of Woodward and Muhlenfeld, the finest reading of Chesnut's 1880s book as a literary enterprise comes from an intellectual historian, Michael O'Brien. His superlative essay, "The Flight down the Middle Walk," approaches Chesnut's 1880s narrative with the imagination and acuity of the finest literary critic. O'Brien discusses the epigrammatic aspirations of Chesnut's 1880s work; her use of fractured and overheard voices; and the ways in which her revisions of the 1860s diary work toward dissolving or weakening coherence rather than focusing the narrative.[20] Though distinguished Civil War literary scholars such as Kathleen Diffley see the 1880s narrative operating in the tradition of the Victorian compendium, O'Brien contends that Chesnut's book more closely resembles the experiments of modernist writers of the 1920s and 1930s than it does the narrative forms of the nineteenth century. Or, as he puts it: "My argument is not that Chesnut is a modernist, but on the subtle and confused continuum that leads from the Anglo-American literary culture of 1860 to that of 1930, she is closer to the latter end than we have thought."[21]

O'Brien's most remarkable insight involves a hypothesis about the relation between Chesnut's wartime self-medication with opium, both for gastric fever (typhoid) and for what may have been chronic anxious depression, and the literary form she developed, the multiple voices she casts in the reworked 1880s narrative:

> Chesnut kept disorder out of the mind because she feared it, as well she might. Chesnut may have understood the instability of reason and madness, but she certainly refused to confront it, sometimes escaping by means of the oblivion of opium.... So Chesnut kept her voices out in the world, attached to flesh and blood, where they were safer. Indeed, she seems to have exported her own thoughts and attached them together.[22]

O'Brien's notion that Chesnut's book is built from the imaginative projection of "voices out in the world" helps clarify the ways in which the revising writer transformed what began as ad hoc diary jottings into a work of literary art. Certainly the self-conscious crafting of the former into the latter suggests that those who see the 1880s narrative as an autobiography, as much of the dissertation scholarship proposes, have not understood, fully, the difference between diurnal accounting and literary artistry.

In a chapter on Mary Boykin Chesnut in his book-length study of American life-writing, G. Thomas Couser offers perhaps the best noneditorial analysis of Chesnut's revision before the work of O'Brien. Couser characterizes Chesnut's revision as "a novelized chronicle in diary form." Most significant, he identifies the epic references that pepper the 1880s narrative. Still, by calling such allusions "mock heroic" comedy, Couser diminishes Chesnut's overwhelming ambition to craft a work that could stand next to that of Homer and Virgil, however presumptuous such aspirations would have appeared had they been articulated aloud by a nineteenth-century American woman.[23]

While Chesnut imagined an epic sweep for the overarching structure of her 1880s book, the complicated collection of manuscripts she left at her death actually were crafted from tiny structural units: the miniature and the fragment constituted Mary Chesnut's literary building blocks in the creation of the 1880s narrative. Thus, the formal paradox of the book, her invention of an epic out of a collection of anecdotal "scraps," as she called them in "Memoirs," had everything to do with her having been subject to "women's time": the expectation of constant interruption during her writing process, as she was the de facto head of household. Chesnut comanaged the postwar dairy business that provided half her total income, in addition to collecting rent on the couple's "Negro houses," which before 1865 functioned as Mulberry's slave cabins, built from bricks made on the plantation. Through these endeavors, she supported James Jr., her mother, and her extended family. In addition, the butter and eggs also provided a living for her former slave Molly, who in fact had initiated this dairy enterprise as a partnership with her then mistress in the second year of the war. Attending to cows and chickens, making butter and collecting eggs, selling these products to family members and friends in Camden, and after several years, assuming the care and raising of her sister Kate's son, David Williams III, thus came to replace the daily wartime rounds of socializing, hospital work, recuperation from sickness, and diary-writing between the years 1861 and 1865.

Because her attendant periods of solitude had become ever more fleeting by 1880, Chesnut's basic literary unit had to be small enough that it could be composed during her rare uninterrupted moments. According to biographical lore, Jane Austen scribbled away at a writing desk in the family sitting room in the evenings, but at an instant's notice was ready to secrete her drafts under the blotter. As if anticipating Virginia Woolf's injunction to women who would write, Chesnut actually did have a room of her own: the library at Sarsfield, the home her husband built for her from the same bricks that forty-five years earlier had been fired on the plantation and used to create some of Mulberry's outbuildings, which had become obsolete with the emancipation of the Chesnut slaves. The younger Mr. Chesnut was insistent on providing an independent dwelling place so that on his death, his widow could not be evicted from the family estates, which had been entailed to another generation. It is hard to imagine that the writer wasn't moved by the fact that this final home of her own had been constructed out of materials that no longer leant support to slavery, an institution under which she had lived in luxury and which, paradoxically, she also had hated.

But although she had a beautiful residence, Chesnut could not control the ways in which her time was parsed out: while dairy farming had its own regular rhythms, animals sickened, delivered calves (a recurring theme in her 1880s correspondence), and required extra attention in other unpredictable ways. Accordingly, as Chesnut had discovered during her wartime diary-keeping amid the flurry of the daily events enumerated above, the most expeditious strategy for constructing her ambitious 1880s book was to iterate large numbers of miniature pieces; over time, the many parts would accrue into an impressive totality. In this way, she transformed the nineteenth-century scrapbook collection of thoughts and clippings into a design that feels almost, if not quite, modern.

In trying to come to terms with the formal complexities of Chesnut's 1880s narrative, a range of theoretical articulations about the anecdote (from Joel

Fineman, Jane Gallop, and Helen Deutsch) and the anthology (from Leah Price) come to mind.[24] While extremely suggestive, none of these descriptions has quite accounted for the sui generis way in which Chesnut's literary miniatures function. Susan Stewart's notion of the souvenir may offer the most evocative figure for understanding Chesnut's goals as both historian and epic poet:

> The souvenir generates a narrative which reaches only "behind," spiraling in a continually inward movement rather than outward toward the future.
>
> The souvenir is by definition always incomplete. First, the object is metonymic to the scene of its original appropriation in the sense that it is a sample.
>
> The souvenir replica is an allusion and not a model; it comes after the fact and remains partial to and more expansive than the fact. It will not function without the supplementary narrative discourse that both attaches it to its origins and creates a myth with regard to those origins. What is this narrative of origins? It is a narrative of interiority and authenticity. It is not a narrative of the object; it is a narrative of the possessor.
>
> The double function of the souvenir is to authenticate a past or otherwise remote experience and, at the same time, to discredit the present. The present is either too impersonal, too looming, or too alienating compared to the intimate and direct experience of contact which the souvenir has as its referent. This referent is authenticity.[25]

If Chesnut's literary narrative of the 1880s is a product of what Diffley has called the South's "ugly crawl through Reconstruction and into the Jim Crow era and beyond,"[26] Stewart's notion that the souvenir has a double function, "to authenticate a past . . . and at the same time to discredit the present [which] is either too impersonal, too looming, or too alienating compared" to that past makes sense of the uncanny double time, double consciousness of Chesnut's vision as a "Civil War" writer. That the literary matron of the 1880s compiled her "souvenirs" into an enormous compendium marks the way she worked to transcend the miniature's necessary incompletion all the while honoring its fragmentariness at the level of the page. This is the brilliant paradox of Chesnut's artistic design.

In contemplating the nature of Chesnut's miniatures in a modern literary context, it is inevitable to invoke T.S. Eliot's "these fragments I have shored against my ruins," perhaps the most memorable lines expressed at the end of *The Waste Land*. Eliot's verse epic clearly speaks to a post–World War I universe: technological horrors new to the history of warfare had nearly annihilated a generation of young men and left participating nations, even the victors, stricken. The troops of the Confederacy, foreshadowing the decimation of the British and the French armies fifty years later, also sacrificed what seemed like an entire generation of men. A good number of those lost were no longer young or had barely left boyhood; the South's significantly smaller population mandated that, by the third year of the war, younger boys and older men had enlisted or had been drafted.[27] Eliot's attitudes obviously cannot be mapped congruently onto Chesnut's sense of the Civil War's devastations. Nevertheless, there are parallels.

Particularly salient is the idea that literary genres such as the novel, or even the old-fashioned Victorian commonplace book for Chesnut and the lyric for Eliot, could no longer account for the transformed world into which these particular (noncombatant) survivors had been thrust. In that regard, the fragment or the miniature, compiled into a massive compendium, offered nineteenth-century American literature a new way of attaining access to the disruptions and fractures of survival, all the while that the epic frame, particularly for the 1880s Chesnut, afforded the resulting work a place in an American literary tradition with powerful, authorizing, precursors.

An example of the way that the miniature could and did come to play a larger part in the epic context of the book comes in the episode of the slave Laurence's reaction to Mary Chesnut's sudden withholding of cash in response to the uncertainties of the times. Developed in the 1880s, the scene appeared for August of 1861, four months into the Civil War.

> Laurence [Mr. Chesnut's "golden" colored, plump, and elegant valet] does all of our shopping. All of his master's money was in his hands until now. I thought it injudicious when gold is at such a premium to leave it lying loose in the tray of a trunk. So I have sewed it up in a belt which I can wear upon an emergency. The cloth is wadded, and my diamonds [are] there, too. "Ticklish times," I say. "But then are you not late about it? Now there seems no need. Before Manassas we could see the sense of it." It has strong strings—can be tied under my hoops about my waist if the worst come to the worst, as the saying is. Laurence wears the same bronze mask. No sign of anything he may feel or think of my latest fancy. Only I know he asks for twice as much money now when he goes to buy things—at least twice as much as he used to take when it was lying in the tray, for him to do as he pleased with it. (August 5, 1861, 132)

Crafted twenty years on, and ostensibly a self-deprecating reflection on the measures Chesnut had taken in wartime to protect the couple's assets from potentially sticky-fingered slaves, this passage sheds fascinating light on the way in which Chesnut the literary artist had come to understand that her cross-racial encounters during the war often occurred according to an unspoken script. Apparently the mistress and Laurence had been engaged in a wordless power struggle, and just who was dominant at any given time happened to fluctuate, though Chesnut herself suggests that the valet often held sway. Since the start of the war, and perhaps earlier, when James Chesnut Jr. was a U.S. senator, accompanied to Washington by his wife and valet, Laurence apparently had enjoyed fiscal carte blanche. Accordingly, he clearly comprehended his wartime duties in Richmond as those of a majordomo as well as gentleman's gentleman, working in concert with the maid Molly, and for a brief period at the very end of the war, her substitute, Ellen, the mistress's maid and cook.

The 1880s narrative suggests that sometime in August of 1861, Chesnut apparently woke to the reality that her relations to her slaves required readjustment. While her justification for the change in attitude, that "gold is at such a premium," may have been accurate economically, the larger portrait she painted in her reworkings was that she had been sleepwalking through the role of authoritative mistress. Now, with a much anticipated war finally in progress, Chesnut felt impelled to reclaim her own authority over the domestic sphere, particularly the power of the purse. Laurence's responding salvo, the request for double the funds, expressed a potentially uncomfortable reality: that mistress and man had been operating according to an unarticulated but clear agreement: leave the marketing to Laurence, and he would make the family money go a long way. Also unspoken but apparently assumed, at least until the mistress changed the rules precipitously, he would continue to take for himself an appropriate "commission" for these services.

As a bound urban house servant at this historical moment, for Laurence to have money in his pocket seemed to assuage some of the sting of remaining unfree. Meanwhile, Chesnut could not deny that she had liked not having to think about gold coins loose in the trunk tray. The best slaves, she said in an 1880s entry for midwar, "think for you, they know your ways and your wants; they save you all responsibility, even in matters of your own ease and well-doing" (November 28, 1863, 488). This fantasy of black mental telepathy appears to have been operative chez Chesnut before 1861. Certainly by the epoch of the 1880s literary reworkings, Mary Chesnut had come to see her struggles with her (then) slaves as rich subject matter for her book. Her persona's dramatic expression of distrust surely had put a crimp in domestic relations across the color line, something the acutely sensitive Chesnut could not deny. Indeed,

Introduction 21

as the literary Chesnut implied, casting moral judgment on the character of her younger self, she had reason to regret her expressed distrust of Laurence, which clearly came to prick her conscience.

Even more remarkable than the dumb show she had conducted with her husband's valet was the wartime Chesnut's creation of the gold and diamond money belt, which in the case of a threatened encounter with Yankees, could be worn clandestinely, under her hoops. Given the thematic emphasis the writer placed on her own childlessness, the metaphorics of the money belt seem particularly poignant: tied under her hoops, secured at the very spot in which a baby might have grown but did not, Chesnut's "gold" and "jewels" remained cold and inert. Adding to the irony was the fact that she had been as absent-minded about the money belt as she had about the coins in the trunk tray: thoughtlessly tossing the belt over the bedstead, Chesnut's wartime persona relied on Molly to retrieve it, chide her mistress for her carelessness, and return the sash, clucking with disapproval. All the while, the maid faithfully left untouched and made no reference to its cache of hidden treasure. So, just as Laurence and Chesnut played their game with gold coins, Molly and her mistress carried on their own pantomime featuring hidden diamonds.[28] Reflecting on the delicate tug of war for domestic power she had struck up with her slaves in the early years of war, the self-conscious writer of the 1880s developed the kernels of two historical incidents into glittering literary miniatures.

The jewel-and-coin-filled sash thus embodied the actual wealth Chesnut possessed, but it decidedly did not make up for the child she lacked. As the belt circulated between herself and her slaves, however, a significant ritual of exchange unfolded, one that in all its weirdness attempted and, in the case of Laurence, failed to assuage her anxiety about the status of the bondspeople in her household who could glimpse the coming of freedom. Across four years of war—indeed until her death, for Molly and Ellen stayed on with Chesnut as wage workers—she and her servants danced a minuet of shifting dependencies, in which their overt social identities belied the reality that mistresses like Mary Chesnut would be diminished profoundly without the abiding care of their African American slaves.[29]

Meanwhile, Laurence maintained his "bronze mask," a less valuable counterpart to Chesnut's gold coins because it was figurative, but operating ultimately in the same register: Chesnut may have had the money, but Laurence had the occult (underground) knowledge from which issued his uncanny social power. Of all her bound servants as well as those of her friends, only Laurence seemed to know where, with enough money, ice could be procured in Richmond in high summer, for example. Securing nothing under his clothes, other than the permanent pass that James Jr. had drafted for his use in the city, a somewhat extraordinary privilege making possible occasional evenings of freedom (in the form of Negro dances and balls), Laurence's careful veneer of inexpressiveness was as plain as the nose on his face. Functioning in the 1880s narrative as an exquisite set piece, this miniature also bore vital relation to Chesnut's study of slave agency during the Civil War period, one of her great themes.

Additionally, as this reading of the symbolic richness of the money belt begins to suggest, Chesnut's 1880s narrative is composed of what often proves astonishingly lyrical language, complex imagery, and trenchant historical thematics. It is remarkable, as well, for the way in which Chesnut's narrating voice self-consciously meditates on its own procedures in passages literary scholars term "metanarrative" episodes. Such moments offer a window into those points in this long-revised and reconceived work in which the multiple fictive personae that dominate the narration—inquisitor general, explainer, matron and frump, ruined invalid, biting wit, as well as the imported tones of Buck Preston and Isabella Martin, all alter egos—step aside so that Cassandra, representing the writer of the 1860s diary, can speak.

Consider what perhaps is the most poignant example of a metanarrative meditation, one Chesnut actually excised from her 1880s revisions, though Woodward reinserted it, to important effect:

«[T]he 10 volumes of memoirs of the times I have written . . . still I write on, for if I have to burn—and here lie my treasures, ready for the blazing hearth—still they have served already to while away four days of agony.» (February 23, 1865, 724)

The sections of the manuscript to which she refers are ten of her original 1860s volumes, reduced to seven books by the time of Woodward and Muhlenfeld's editorial epoch. In the passage from the 1880s, the literary Chesnut is "writing on," against the dark of night, so to speak.[30] Remarkably, she alludes to what she has created as her treasures, a very rare attribution of value in comparison to earlier characterizations of a book she has been making from "scraps." It is as if, knowing in her heart that the war will end in Confederate defeat, the 1860s diarist finally recognizes that, in the midst of destruction, she has created something consequential. And, at the very least, scribbling has offered an antidote to despair.

Historically speaking, the narrative might prove useful as well, or so the literary Chesnut fancied in another passage crafted in the 1880s manuscript.

Introduction 23

In a moment very early in the war, she catechizes herself on the potential worth of her writerly enterprise:

> Congaree House. Second year. Confederate independence. I write daily for my own distraction. These *memoirs pour server* may, some future date, afford dates, facts, and prove useful to more important people than I am. I do not wish to harm or hurt anyone. If any scandalous stories creep in, they are easily burned. It is hard, in such a hurry as things are, to separate wheat from chaff.
>
> Now I have made my protest and written down my wishes. I can scribble on with a free will and free conscience. (March 10, 1862, 301)

What the 1880s writer called self-distraction, an activity ordinarily indulged in by the vain or the self-absorbed, had the redemptive advantage of benefiting the historians of the future. Surely Chesnut remembered the experience of having untangled the documentation for Beauregard's battle plan from the account her husband had shared with her in the wake of First Manassas, which she had inscribed in her original diary for July 1861. In that episode, the evidence Chesnut produced from her jottings definitively provided President Davis with the facts he had sought. For this service if even for no other, the diary (and its creator) had merited kudos.

As for potentially less profitable and more disreputable ruminations, the writer of the 1880s consoled herself with the notion that the 1860s persona facing any potentially problematic entry could edit it out with the strike of a match. Here she imagined her work reaching elevated political and military figures as, of course, it already had done in response to Jefferson Davis's call for the Manassas investigation. The wartime persona subsequently disclaimed the wish to cause harm with her prose. And she noted that in the heat of the moment of composition, it could be difficult to parse those fragments that could prove valuable to posterity from those that would not. Tellingly, the revising writer used language suggested by Matthew 3:12, drawing from words spoken by John the Baptist, who tells his auditors that he has come with the winnowing fork or fan. Accordingly, he enjoins, what is valuable must be preserved, while what is without worth must be consumed (by fire, Chesnut's most effective editorial technique). The 1880s writer concluded this remarkable passage by having her persona proclaim that, after having rigorously interrogated herself concerning her own creative intentions, she now is purged of guilt and can go forward with recording her impressions of life during the war.

So the literary Chesnut envisioned the potential efficacy of fire for a writer with a work in progress. But just as portions of her original diary text could be destroyed by flames, they also could be buried in the earth for the sake of preservation from marauding Yankees. These men were Sherman's "bummers," the Union troops who had marched from Atlanta to the sea and up through the Carolinas by 1865, who had sacked an entire half of Mulberry House in the spring of that year. The other half was spared only because Scipio, the old Colonel's body servant, convinced the enemy to desist out of respect for his master's great age. Leaving off their destruction of the architecture and furniture, Sherman's men stuffed large bags with books and papers from the family library and spewed them out along the very road on which only weeks later, the Chesnuts rattled their way home. The literary Chesnut composed this entry for earlier that spring, in Chester, South Carolina, her final refugee locale:

> This yellow Confederate quire [ream] of paper blotted by my journal has been buried these three days with the silver sugar dish, teapot, milk-jug, and a few spoons and forks that follow my fortunes as I wander. With these valuables was [General] Hood's silver cup, which was partially crushed when he was wounded at Chickamauga. (April 22, 1865, 791)

Here it is not the destruction of writing by burning, nor the casting of pages to the winds as Union soldiers did outside Mulberry, that is significant. Instead, the diary itself, temporarily interred in the ground, less like the burial of a corpse than the planting of a seed, makes possible the redemption of Chesnut's writing and the reimagining of her experience in the face of defeat. This episode thus affords in miniature the cultural work that the 1880s narrative itself might do: bring back to life, through its literary power, an entire world that its creator has observed and survived in the very course of its destruction.

To reprise, the literary Chesnut of the 1880s has pictured the potential cremation of compromising parts if not all of the 1860s diary, as well as imagining its potential rebirth from the ground. In fashioning this remarkable scene, then, Chesnut provides a metanarrative meditation on the process of creation itself. Additionally, letters figured in Chesnut's 1880s narrative, some noted as burned and others preserved and transcribed in revision. Nineteenth-century America was a profoundly epistolary culture, a collection of local communities threaded together by the letters that people exchanged by the reams. And in fact, much of my knowledge of Chesnut has been garnered through perusal of her extraordinary letters.

What interests me here, however, is what we might call the epistolary version of a road not taken: letters no longer extant, but composed, regretted, and ultimately burned, and then immediately alluded to in subsequent epistles penned by Chesnut's many friends in Columbia, who had endured Sherman's plundering of the city and the eventual conflagration that engulfed it. Local survivors were convinced that the Union army had initiated what was taken to be arson. In fact, raw cotton bales in one sector of the town somehow became doused with the runoff from the alcohol consumed, by the near gallons, by Rebel soldiers and Southern civilians alike. The two groups had broken into a local Confederate supply warehouse to "salvage" what they could of the medicinal liquor before the Yankees overtook them; and in their frenzy, spilling as they went, nearby cotton caught fire, to devastating result.[31]

Here is Chesnut's 1880s account of the spectral letters, composed, destroyed by burning, and then recounted in follow-up epistles, detailing an inferno that had been literally unspeakable:

> Without any concert of action, everybody in Columbia seems to have suppressed the first letters written by them after Sherman's fire, arson, burglary, called a "raid." Miss Middleton sent me a letter from Sally Rutledge, hardly alluding to Sherman. She said she had written a folio in the first red-hot wrath which consumed her—indignation, disgust, despair—but upon sober second thoughts, she had thrown it into the fire. Mrs. McCord's first letter reached me. It was like herself—cool and businesslike. In a postscript she said she had written a letter in her first futile rage at the senseless destruction &c&c, but that letter she thought it wisest to destroy. Mrs. St. Julien Ravenel's first letter which was received alluded to the burning of Columbia by saying the letter telling of it she did not send for reasons she would give someday. (April 3, 1865, 777)

Words penned in red hot wrath, conflagrations blazing in the streets and burning down the homes in the city, roaring inside citizens' fireplaces and, more deeply, within the very souls and bellies of its enraged inhabitants: fire appears to have been everywhere. In an uncanny moment of communion, everyone Chesnut knew in Columbia was on the same page, so to speak. Nearly all of her numerous friends seemed to have concluded that accounts penned in the immediate wake of the horror had to be consigned to the flames still burning. In this passage, the 1880s literary Chesnut thus immortalized an epoch in which trauma was experienced, expressed directly in letters, reconsidered, and the epistolary trace of it destroyed, reports of devastation themselves dematerialized by fire and then reconjured as twice-told tales in subsequent letters, this time offered in broad sketches rather than minute detail. Such are the fault lines along which epic accounts deconstruct themselves.

The epic and the miniature come together to create what becomes Chesnut's reworked literary narrative. By the time the Civil War had exploded into being, the figure of a "house divided" had become ubiquitous: in a famous speech by that name delivered in 1858, Lincoln himself had taken from Mark 3:25 this potent figure for the fracturing nation. Without ever employing the metaphor directly, Chesnut nevertheless breathed it in; and her genius was to craft a picture of the civic family under duress out of what she had observed of both the national and the Confederate political scene, the latter in all of its contentions and cabals. Conversely, when she imagined the machinations of those of her husband's family, whom she detested—particularly James Jr.'s orphaned niece Harriet Grant, as well as the daughters of his sister Mrs. Mary Cox Chesnut Reynolds, not to mention the younger siblings of beloved nephew Johnny Chesnut, the "Cool Captain," those nieces and nephews who lived in Florida and continually demanded money from the old Colonel—she described their grasping, aggressive behavior in terms of treason and faction.

In other words, the political, linked to the epic and the domestic, connected to the miniature, always already interanimated one another in Chesnut's vision of both her larger and smaller worlds. Perhaps she saw all family life as political and all governmental activity as domestic, but her ever circulating view of their interrelation allowed her to create what is our most astutely imaginative representation of the Confederate chain of being, from General Robert E. Lee and President Jefferson Davis through the children of her father-in-law's slaves. It is fitting, then, to consider a final metanarrative observation on the very issue of separate, as opposed to intersecting spheres, which Chesnut penned in the 1880s as an entry for October 25, 1861:

> [Trescott] wrote a state secret to my husband, and I answered the letter. He wrote a piece of society scandal to me—"strictly confidential"—and so in a business letter's postscript Mr. C alludes to it. He does not know how to deal with such a mixed up establishment. (225)

Critics and historians should be grateful indeed that the Chesnut household was so confused. As the artist of the 1880s implied in this remarkably nonchalant assertion of her agency as a woman writer, to her, the notion of separate spheres was anathema. Their collapse and eventual smudging during both the Civil War and its long and grueling aftermath offered Mary Boykin Chesnut an opportunity she otherwise might never have imagined, enabling not only her own survival, but the inspiration for her epic achievement, the transformation of her wartime diary into literary art.

CHAPTER TWO

Walls

EPIC IN MINIATURE

Mary Chesnut's 1880s narrative offers a kaleidoscopic vision of the Southern home front and the political command center of America's most murderous conflict, a conflict that seemed to demand treatment on a grand scale. Encyclopedic in scope and size, epics are built from repertoires of "type scenes," thematic staples revealing the breadth and depth of their creators' imaginative purchase on a represented universe: the woman surveying her city at war, the hero voyaging to the underworld, and the revelation of the protagonist's disguised identity are three keystones of the literary genre that inspired Mary Chesnut's transformation of her diary. The *Iliad* is sung by an unnamed narrator sympathetic to but never identified with Achilles or the Greeks; the *Aeneid* reveals how once-defeated Trojans ultimately become victors in their founding of Rome, achieving the greatest second act in classical literature. Chesnut's 1880s account of the American Civil War, originally conceived and drafted in the first person though largely recast in the third, adopts neither of these perspectives. It does not focus exclusively on the heroic deeds of President Jefferson Davis or her husband, Brevet Brigadier General James Chesnut Jr., though the *kleos* (glory) of both figures and of others, particularly Stonewall Jackson, Robert E. Lee, and John Bell Hood, comes in for abundant praise. Chesnut offers no redemptive alternative to the South's defeat—no Trojan-style finale for the Confederacy in Mexico, which undaunted Rebels such as Louis Wigfall had contrived in the wake of Lee's surrender. Instead, her

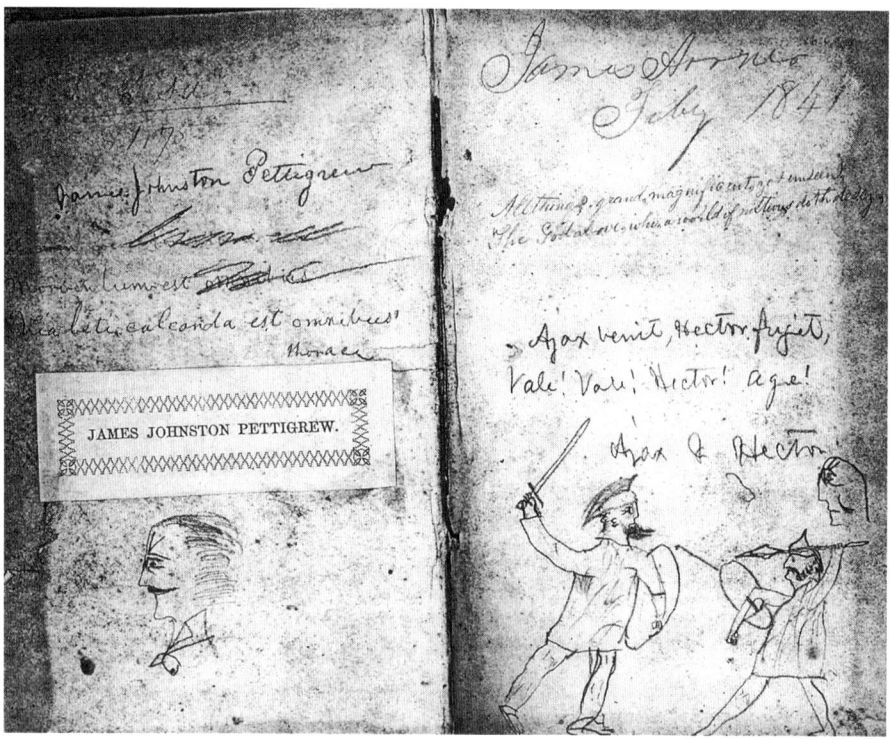

FIGURE 1. *James Johnston Pettigrew, Hector and Ajax from the* Iliad *(drawings, nineteenth century). Inside the endpapers of his schoolboy Greek reader, young Johnston Pettigrew depicts Hector and Ajax dueling in hand-to-hand combat, dressed in early-nineteenth-century Southern militia garb. Courtesy of Mulberry Plantation, Camden, South Carolina.*

---

epic narrative is a woman's story of war, conceived from the loser's vantage point. And its middle-aged civilian author is its unlikely heroine. In Chesnut's reworking, the destruction of Southern culture abides unredeemable, marking hers as an epic unique to the tradition that inspired it.

Most significant are Chesnut's use and transformation of two epic "type scenes," the presence of mournful women on the walls and the voyage to the land of the dead. I return in the final chapter to the third epic formula, the revelation of identity, focusing on Chesnut's crucial defacement of two episodes of recognition.[1] The 1880s writer borrows the motifs of the journey to the underworld and the revelation of identity from Homer's *Odyssey* and the theme of women on the walls from the *Iliad,* though characteristically, she makes all three topoi distinctively her own. Centering on the epic ambition of her 1880s narrative, this project takes up Chesnut's attention to domestic life in wartime, secessionist politics, Confederate military strategy, comparative world history,

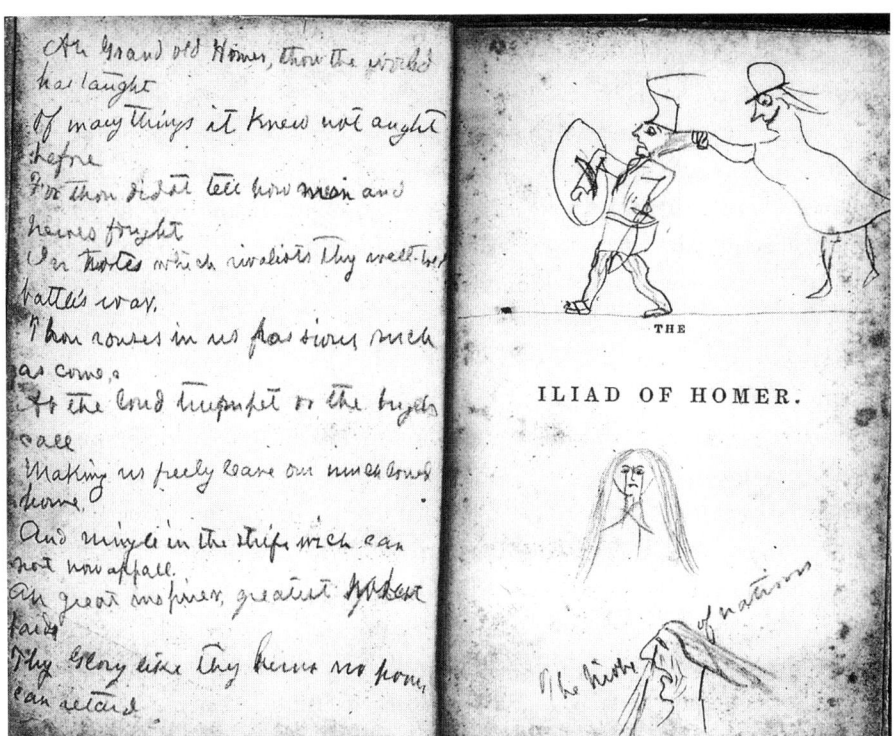

FIGURE 2. *James Johnston Pettigrew, scenes from the* Iliad *(drawings, nineteenth century).* In more endpaper doodles, Pettigrew imagines epic combat nineteenth-century Southern style. The Pettigrew family would join with the Chesnuts in Kate Miller Williams's children's generation: Stephen Miller Williams, Mary Chesnut's beloved nephew Miller, married Jane Pettigrew. Courtesy of Mulberry Plantation, Camden, South Carolina.

varieties of religion, and her culture's informing myths about African Americans, sandy-hillers (poor whites in the South Carolina countryside), white Confederate elites, the immigrant Irish, Southern Jews, and women.[2]

Chesnut deploys thematic building blocks used in the epic tradition since scribes first recorded Homer's songs hundreds of years after his moment, and her use and adaptation of type scenes offer insight into her vision of the martial world and its relation to her feelings about loss and death on the home front. I turn first to the epic type scene involving the soldier's wife or soldiers' wives surveying martial action (or in the Homeric case, a pause in the fighting) from a position high above the city at war. While book 6 of the *Iliad* gives female voices an opportunity to protest armed conflict, its tones are elegiac rather than antagonistic, with Andromache's prophetic fears for her husband and baby son, Hector and Astyanax, doomed princes of Troy. This episode is

Walls: Epic in Miniature 31

linked significantly to a final scene of a woman on the ramparts, at the end of book 22. After Andromache learns of Hector's death, she runs from her house and ascends the walls of the city; there, she witnesses Achilles dragging her husband's corpse behind his chariot. As she swoons in the arms of her attendants, Homer describes the widow's collapse in the exact epic formula he uses to narrate the death of heroes: "The darkness of night misted over the eyes of Andromache. / She fell backward, and gasped the life breath from her, and far off / threw from her head the shining gear that ordered her headdress" (*Iliad* 22.466–68).[3]

Classicist Richard Sacks has argued that Homer's unique use of language theretofore reserved exclusively for describing the battlefield demise of warriors accords Andromache an elevated status in the epic tradition. Though she will recover from fainting—her darkness of night is figurative—the poet has endowed her with the sort of greatness that lives on in Chesnut's own characterization of women who endure the horrors of war, including herself.

That said, the 1880s narrative contains a decidedly antic description of Chesnut's viewing of the attack on Fort Sumter, in which prior to Northern surrender, the sole casualty is a Federal horse. Remarkably brief, lacking blood and gore, and punctuated by digression, the report of the clash in the bay from a hotel roof in Charleston constitutes virtually the only "battle piece" of the war in her reworked manuscript. In that regard, her account of the women on the rooftop watching the spectacle of Fort Sumter serves as a surrogate history for manifold battles Chesnut does not witness and only obliquely or tersely notes, often days or months after their conclusion: Shiloh, Chancellorsville, Gettysburg, the Wilderness, Chickamauga, Atlanta, Franklin.[4]

She also provides a narrative treatment of First Manassas (Bull Run in Northern parlance), represented largely because her husband participated in its final hours and recounted his experiences to Chesnut the next day; she recorded details in her fragmentary 1861 diary and expanded them in the 1880s project. These writerly impulses proved particularly handy for "the Cause," as a political contretemps had been brewing in the Confederate capital over why General Beauregard, the Rebel commander, had not pursued fleeing Federal troops back to Washington. Reconstructing Beauregard's intended battle plan from his wife's diary record of the account he had given her, James Chesnut Jr. was able to respond to Jefferson Davis's request for documentation of Beauregard's objectives, despite the fact that the Creole general had been unable to execute them on the field.

Mrs. Chesnut's vivid description of how her writing helped Davis to unravel conflicting military reports marks just one instance of the 1880s narrative's self-consciousness of its own status as epic. Without articulating the triumph overtly, her words reveal that neither General Beauregard, nor the commander-in-chief who questioned his strategy, nor even her own husband, who served on Beauregard's staff but worked for President Davis, proved the hero of the day. Instead, kudos were owed to a person who was absent entirely from the fight at Manassas Junction: Mary Chesnut, the cabinet wife who also happened to keep a diary, and who deserved Confederate laurels when it came to sorting out what really seemed to have happened on the battlefield near the stream called Bull Run. Mary Boykin Chesnut had earned the *kleos* of the hour, Homer's word for the kind of glory that is worthy of poetic immortality, that is, inclusion in an epic.[5]

These two early encounters—one witnessed directly, the other twice told by her most reliable interlocutor—constitute the sum total of Chesnut's direct battlefield reportage. Nevertheless, historians such as Edmund Wilson and C. Vann Woodward believe the 1880s narrative comprises our most illuminating account of the Civil War, created by someone whose hands never held rifle or saber and who never donned military garb, save for her officer husband's standard-issue overcoat, which she took up in sartorial desperation, on a cold night in 1864.[6] Chesnut's 1880s chronicle records the political machinations leading up to battle and reports the devastating material aftereffects of the western army's forays, both of which—machinations and aftereffects—she witnessed firsthand: as a member by marriage of Davis's inner circle, a volunteer in local Confederate hospitals, with a husband fighting at the front, Chesnut occupied a situation typical for a woman of her class but extraordinary for a female writer whose subject was civil war.

Across the lines of gender, contemporary soldiers' accounts, both Northern and Southern, obviously afford more visceral and immediate images of the war than Chesnut possibly could provide. But however fascinating for their power and emotional connection to battlefield events, most such works lack Chesnut's panoramic vision of Confederate life on multiple fronts. And few possess the imaginative and intellectual reach of her 1880s narrative, much less the literary ambition to cast her work in epic mode.

I conclude the analysis of Mary Chesnut's epic form with two descents into hell, visits that her epic precursors make only once. In an 1880s entry for 1862, Chesnut renders her first trip to the underworld and communion with the "dead." Visiting her sister's fever-ridden frontier home, she invokes the bleak tones of Sophoclean drama in reporting what she has witnessed.[7] With nothing to relieve the vista of disease, mortality, and devastation overwhelming the family, Chesnut cannot avoid the ramifications of irrevocable loss. This inability to evade death, which she will later call looking defeat in the face, marks a turning point for her in the early years of the war.

Hundreds of pages later, in her 1880s account for May of 1865, the writer describes a second descent, this time figurative rather than literal: a retreat through South Carolina's ruins, registered in tones of benumbed irony. What Chesnut confronts at Mulberry in that final year of the war involves more than personal grief (her mother-in-law has only recently died; her father-in-law has less than a year to live). The shattered remnants of an entire way of life lie before her. This experience is different from her deathwatch in Alabama in 1862, and she records it in the 1880s narrative as a postmortem. Most significant for my argument, her deliberate repetition of the underworld motif, reserved in epic treatments of homecoming from war either for an essential chapter or for an extended passage of poetic lines (book 12 of the *Odyssey,* book 6 of the *Aeneid*), speaks volumes about the self-consciously literary nature and historical complexity of her writerly ambition.

Walls

Borrowing epic conventions, I begin in medias res to explore Chesnut's deployment of Homeric motifs, tropes, and type scenes in the 1880s revisions. She records her survey of the first battle of the Civil War, seen from the rooftop of her Charleston hotel. The fact that the Confederate firing on Fort Sumter was a deliberately provoked, choreographed exercise, the penultimate move in a confrontation orchestrated by Lincoln and reciprocated by Davis comes as something of a shock to readers not fully familiar with Civil War history.

Lincoln had issued an ultimatum to the Confederate government about what he saw as the equivocal status of the fort: though lying in Southern territory after the secession of South Carolina (the first state to leave the Union), Sumter remained in the hands of the remnant of the U.S. Army that had withdrawn there on South Carolina's departure. Its commander, Colonel Robert Anderson, had been unwilling to evacuate the fort and turn it over to the South, as the Confederate administration had stipulated. Instead, as supplies dwindled to near starvation levels, Anderson requested succor from the U.S. government.

Vowing not to fire the first shot of the impending conflict, Lincoln telegraphed Anderson that he was sending food and medical supplies; he added, however, that no arms or additional forces would be included in the relief mission. Davis saw this ambiguous gesture as a provocation and retorted that if the fort were not evacuated by midnight of April 12, General Beauregard's men would begin firing from the bay off Charleston harbor. Chesnut's husband was one of the Creole general's aides-de-camp dispatched to row out to secure Sumter's surrender. When all Confederate appeals for submission were rejected, the Rebels began shooting. It was 4 a.m. on April 12, 1861.

In the 1880s narrative, Chesnut describes what she had witnessed on that night twenty years earlier as a civilian spectator:

> The women were wild, there on the housetop. Prayers from the women and imprecations from the men, and then a shell would light up the scene. Tonight, they say, the forces are to attempt to land. (45)

In her original diary jottings of the 1860s, Chesnut makes only telegraphic mention of viewing the fray from her hotel roof. While many crucial tableaux in the 1880s narrative originate in rich kernels from the 1860s diary, it is rare that something this historically significant is not recorded in more detail than "I start up—dress & rush to my sisters in misery. We go on the housetop and see the shells bursting. They say our men are wasting ammunition." After noting that her husband is rowing in a boat in the harbor, she concludes: "[M]en & women rush in—prayers—imprecations. What scenes. Tonight a force will attempt to land" (*TPMC*, 59). In the 1860s diary, Chesnut describes her own anxious anticipation of the run-up to the deadline for surrender, as well as her jubilation over the success of the mission in the following days. But absent are anything more than forty-some terse words to describe what we know was a strategically scripted encounter, including the fact that visiting civilians like Chesnut had been apprised that they could view the mêlée from the rooftops of their lodgings.

The scene Chesnut developed for the 1880s narrative was inspired by her own experience on the roof, laconically noted in the 1860s diary, but it may have been amplified by having seen (obviously after the fact) an issue of *Harper's Weekly* for May 4, 1861, featuring an engraving titled "The Housetops in Charleston during the Bombardment of Fort Sumter." This tableau has become a classic of Civil War iconography. Indeed, so compellingly memorable is the image that Woodward and Muhlenfeld use it as the frontispiece to their edition of the 1860s diary, *The Private Mary Chesnut,* despite the fact that no narrative analogue for the illustration is to be found anywhere within the text.

In the 1880s revisions, Chesnut depicts frenetic activity, "prayers from the women and imprecations from the men" (46). The *Harper's Weekly* image, published shortly after the actual events, highlights an even more dramatic scene of despair, with women collapsing into each other's hoopskirts like deflated flamingos. Of the approximately seventeen spectators pictured in the engraving—and it is hard to decipher discrete bodies amid the confusion of drapery and hoops—at least seven are prostrate, hunched over the body of a companion, or sunk on bended knee, nearly flattened by what they are witnessing.

In addition to depicting female fright in the 1880s narrative, Chesnut describes one of her male housetop compatriots sneering in response to a shell burst, "waste of ammunition" (46). This remark reveals that Chesnut is capable of conjuring a complex scene in which, simultaneously, uninitiated women are terrified and more militarily savvy male observers are piqued over the strategic absurdity of what is unfolding. But how are we to understand the iconographic disparities pertaining between Chesnut's downplaying this "surveillance of the city at war" in her 1860s diary fragment, the *Harper's Weekly* 1861 representation of collective Southern terror and abjection over the scene in the harbor, and her later development of the episode into a major tableau for the 1880s narrative, which accords somewhat more with the *Harper's* image than with her original jottings?

Kathleen Diffley, a leading scholar of magazine literature published during the Civil War and Reconstruction, argues that the "engraving testifies more to art department imagination than to the documented euphoria of the city's crowds. What magazines made sense of was the anxiety of their readers, who were often far from reported events."[8] Diffley's hypothesis about the image reflecting the apprehension of the *Harper's Weekly* audience makes emotional sense: because this is the opening of a civil war, those figures on the roof could stand for any and all Americans, not only the inhabitants of Charleston. And it certainly is understandable that citizens witnessing the first battle of what would become a momentous catastrophe would respond with expressions and attitudes of terror.

But the image can be read less allegorically than historically and in a darker fashion. *Harper's Weekly* was, after all, a Northern publication. Propagandistic, pro-Union sentiments could have inspired the engraving. Spurred by Northern patriotism, the image's creator may have sought to portray Southerners as devastated and demoralized at the start of war, despite the fact that they won this particular fight. Though the picture captures the opening salvo of the engagement, in which the outcome remained unknown, the image was published nearly three weeks after the battle of Fort Sumter concluded in what was seen by both sides as Confederate victory.

Immediately focusing the viewer's gaze are the pair of women who have swooned in an interlocking heap of drapery in the foreground of the picture plane. The artist has organized his figures into a rough "X" formation, with a supine woman placed at the bottom and top of each leg of the X; the swooning female couple at the fore make up the X's left foot. Each of the outer flanks of the image reveals a solitary woman in collapse, balancing the composition with this emphasis on female prostration. But the homosocial pair entwined in the foreground constitute the picture's centerpiece, and I would argue that something from the history of art, the Western tradition's representations of war, can be read in the memorable iconography.

Lost to history is the name of the artist, let alone any information about his aesthetic training or referential repertoire. But to raise the issue of authorship about mid-nineteenth-century pictorial practice in a mass-cultural publication like *Harper's Weekly* presumes a romantic or postromantic conception of artistic originality that had not yet taken hold of bellum American culture. It was the practice of *Harper's Weekly* to employ a large staff of engravers, none of whom was credited in print; these craftsmen worked according to a "house style" that was uniform across issues.[9] It is not at all implausible, nevertheless, that art historical sources inform this drawing of female civilians responding to a city at war, for the theme is as old as Western culture's first poetic narrative. A truism of the neoclassicism that swept the Anglo-American world after the founding of the United States was that the eighteenth century harkened back to Roman models (Washington as Cincinnatus, the nation as a republic), whereas the nineteenth century was known for its interest in reprising Greek cultural themes (Daniel Webster as Demosthenes; and in his war against American civilization, Thoreau carrying the *Iliad* to Walden Pond). Thus, one inspiration for an artistic rendering of nineteenth-century women grieving over a city at war could be cognate scenes from Homer's *Iliad,* the classical tradition's proof text for this subject.

Perhaps in this case John Flaxman's engravings for Alexander Pope's translation of the *Iliad* (begun 1793) provided the iconographic prototype. The Flaxman illustrated edition was a late-eighteenth-century production; it was also, in its popularity and ubiquity as an Anglophone translation, read well into the late nineteenth century. It is possible that the *Harper's Weekly* artist's inspiration for "The Housetops in Charleston" came from Flaxman's plate 25, "Andromache Fainting on the Wall," which depicts the Trojan princess's dramatic response to the news that Hector has been slain (*Iliad* 22.466–74). If this art historical genealogy is credible, the Northern illustrator has depicted the early moments of what turned out to be a Southern victory—Fort Sumter—by conjuring an image that refers, synecdochally, to Trojan defeat.

FIGURE 3. John Flaxman, "Andromache Fainting on the Wall" (engraving, eighteenth century). It is likely that the English Iliad Chesnut would have used was the one translated by Alexander Pope and illustrated by John Flaxman. This eighteenth-century translation was read throughout the nineteenth century in England and America. In this engraving for book 22, Flaxman pictures Hector's widow, Andromache, swooning into the arms of her ladies in waiting after learning of his death.

According to the analogical thinking that spurs Chesnut to call herself Cassandra, the Confederate States of America is Troy and the United States is Greece. Perhaps this would explain the illustration's weirdly proleptic vision of the South losing the war at the very moment of that conflict's opening shots. Such a reading is encapsulated in the image's somewhat inaccurate picture of the civilian response to what the artist knew was a Confederate triumph. The fact that in the 1880s narrative Chesnut reports her male companion's dismissal of the battle's strategic significance suggests that he, at least (and obviously she as well), knew that the South would win this opening round at little human cost; thus he could deplore the waste of ordnance.

By taking up the *Harper's Weekly* image as inspiration for her 1880s account of the housetops, rather than excluding or minimizing the tableau of wild women in prayer, as she did in her 1860s diary, Chesnut would have been making a crucial narrative choice. The stark linearity of Flaxman's swooning Andromache, supported by her waiting women, may have served as the ur-text for the "Housetops in Charleston" engraving; if so, the mythological meaning of the allusion contradicted the manifest political content to which the image failed to refer accurately: civilians viewing what would become the Confederacy's first winning battle. Perhaps the engraving represented wish-fulfillment on the part of the Northern artist that Southern victory be pictured in the visual language of defeat, by way of reference to the epic tableau of Flaxman's plate 25 for Pope's *Iliad*.

The *Harper's* pictorial thus limns what Harold Bloom would call a moment of misprision, an illustrated misapprehension of reality, influenced in this case by propagandistic political impulses. But the fact that Chesnut might have remembered this image in the 1880s, identifying her rooftop self with Andromache, which would imply, figuratively, the death of "Hector"—insert whatever representative hero of the Confederacy one wishes, be it Albert Sidney Johnston, Stonewall Jackson, or J. E. B. Stuart, her nephew's cavalry commander, all of whom had died before 1865—suggests that she wants her reader to see this initial victory as a foreshadowing of eventual Confederate defeat.

Chesnut ends this scene with her 1861 persona inadvertently sitting on a working chimney and needing to be "put out." What plays here as a moment of comedy bordering on hysteria inaugurates a series of more pointed and ominous incendiary thematics that dapple the remainder of the 1880s narrative. It is important to consider what Chesnut, daughter of a South Carolina "Fire-Eater" (radical secessionist), has to say about the potential self-conflagration she faced on April 12, 1861. On the surface of things, her brush with serious injury seems to have had nothing to do with the shelling of Charleston harbor, other than the fact that Chesnut was so hypnotized by the battle that she lost her own bearings on the roof:

> Last night—or this morning, truly—up on the housetop I was so weak and weary I sat down on something that looked like a black stool. "Get up you foolish woman—your dress is on fire," cried a man. And he put me out. It was a chimney, and the sparks caught my clothes.... But my fire had been extinguished before it broke out into a regular blaze. (April 12, 1861, 46–47)

Realizing that Chesnut's ember-strewn garments could explode into flame, her unidentified rescuer himself erupts in derision, calling the matron names but also capturing the distracted Chesnut's attention and very possibly saving her from injury. Interestingly, his scornful tone also echoes the "imprecation" of her male compatriot, who earlier has cursed the South's "waste of ammunition" in this seeming pantomime of battle. Perhaps these two instances of male ire encountered at 4 a.m. are not significant as personal but as political effusions, expressive of frustration that a war is unfolding from which, at this opening moment, they are excluded.

Whatever the explanation for both men's crankiness, Chesnut's sardonic personification of herself as a brand plucked from burning is fraught with significance. The language emphasizes that what is afire is not her dress, but her self. Like an inexperienced Rebel volunteer, terrified by the sight of first battle and exhausted from the anxiety that preceded it, she carelessly mistakes the dangerous (a burning chimney) for the innocuous (a black stool), and only by seconds avoids suffering severe harm. However humorously told, the episode Chesnut includes in her 1880s narrative represents a paradigmatic moment found in many Civil War soldiers' accounts, the description of a close encounter with death.[10]

Had Chesnut been injured on April 12, she, like the Federal horse, would have been counted as "collateral damage," though the horse legitimately could be said to have lost its life in the line of duty. Chesnut, on the other hand, would have sustained her hurt in a freak moment of what might be seen as "friendly fire," if we consider that the chimney involved was heating a Confederate hostelry. This rumination on the proper classification of "battlefield" casualties is meant to suggest only that civilians in civil wars are, by definition, vulnerable, and that even moments of patriotic spectatorship can be fraught with danger. By 1865, the distinctions between domestic and military fronts had collapsed nearly entirely, as the roles of civilian and soldier, Rebel fighter and home guardsmen, military wife and partisan spy became hopelessly tangled.

But we can also discover in this episode of chimney-sitting a perhaps unwitting reflection of another theme vital to the 1880s narrative, Chesnut's infertility. With her hoopskirts deflated as she mounts the chimney — in fact, although Chesnut describes herself dressed in a "double gown," a nineteenth-century dressing gown crafted from two layers of cloth and involving no hoops at all, her image is clearly prompted by the *Harper's Weekly* illustration of women bedecked and behooped on the rooftops of Charleston — the weary Chesnut resembles some sort of giant female bird, roosting unknowingly on what proves to be a dangerous nest, one that fosters not future offspring but potential injury and ashes.[11]

Chesnut's rushing off a nest of flames may seem a long figurative distance from images of infertility. But the 1880s account of the episode on the rooftop is followed nearly immediately by references to the once-childless Louisa Hamilton and her "lately achieved baby" (47). In the third sentence of the subsequent entry, Chesnut writes: "Louisa Hamilton comes here now. This is a sort of news center. . . . She had no children during her first marriage. Hence the value of this lately achieved baby" (47). Significant is her emphasis on Mrs. Hamilton's reproductive success with a second mate; this happy actuality contradicts prevailing nineteenth-century gynecological theory, which wrongly (but not surprisingly) attributed cases of infertility to "female trouble." The entry may telegraph Chesnut's unconscious acquittal of her own feelings of culpability for the fact that she and James Chesnut have had no children; maybe she is not singularly responsible for the ashen nest on which she has rested for over twenty years.

But most significant is Chesnut's self-deprecating assertion that her "fire" has been extinguished before it has broken into a blaze. Though literally this is a life-saving moment, its figurative meaning is more equivocal. The sparks in question suggest the sort of female power that inspires the production of children. They also point to Chesnut's potential for illuminating the political field. An abiding irony of Chesnut's career is that the very infertility she bemoaned actually enabled the literary creativity from which female friends like Varina Davis were precluded by the demands of the social roles they filled. This paradox illuminates the scene under discussion: Chesnut's sparks are doused by an irate Southern male, one who finds her presence on the roof at the start of the war more incendiary than appropriate. This figure, whose identity is lost to history precisely because Mary Chesnut of the 1880s did not name him, obviously understood nothing about the internal fire and power of the woman whose dress he extinguished but whose imagination remained unquenched. I will return to the motif of spark and blaze, where fire takes on a second meaning beyond potential imaginative power to suggest something far more ominous and destructive. For now, however, I want to turn to the supernatural and epic connotations of this symbol.

Underworlds

From fire to hell: the Homeric dimensions of the path Mary Chesnut charts throughout the war, as recorded in the literary narrative crafted twenty years after defeat, seem particularly resonant in her figurative accounts of two voyages to the underworld. In the 1880s narrative, she reports what she encounters in Alabama in 1862 when, expecting to face the death of her elderly mother, she stumbles instead on a realm of unanticipated bereavement. Chesnut has received a telegram stating that her sole surviving parent, Mary Miller, is gravely ill at the frontier home of Chesnut's sister Sally. Responding to this bad news, James Jr. unequivocally forbids his wife to undertake the arduous steamboat and wagon journey to Alabama; and his objections come as no surprise to Chesnut, well aware of the fact that her chronic illnesses make any such travel perilous at best. Weighing her conflicting duties, Chesnut ignores her husband's orders and makes the punishing trip, accompanied only by her slave Molly. On arrival, this is what she sees:

> As we drew near the house it looked like a graveyard in a nightmare—so sad, so weird, so vague and phantomlike in its outlines. I found my mother ill in bed, feeble still, but better than I had hoped to see her. "I knew you would come" was her greeting, with outstretched hands. Then I went to bed in that silent house, a house of the dead, it felt. ("Memoirs," 462)

Chesnut has found the ailing Mrs. Miller en route to recovery. But she also has learned that two of her three young nieces have expired from the fever—the youngest succumbing before her aunt has even had a chance to meet her.

The unexpected deaths of these girls level Chesnut's spirits in ways that even the anticipated loss of a beloved mother might not have done. The 1880s narrative returns again and again to an abiding fact of Chesnut's life: she lives in a state of chronic, low-level melancholy over childlessness and the emotional and material future it forecloses for herself and her husband.[12] Chesnut acutely sympathizes with those mothers in her purview who have lost offspring, not only as a result of bayonets, bullets, and bombs in the years 1861–65, but also from consumption, childbed fever, and typhoid. The narrative brims with catalogues of these familiar dead, describing the context in which they lost their lives and the effect on their survivors of their passing. Employing such inventories of people and material objects is another key feature of the epic.

Certainly by the time she undertook her transformation of the narrative decades following Lee's surrender, Chesnut had become intimate with the ways that death itself had been denatured by the rhythms of war, claiming the young and strong more often than it did the unwell or the aged. Put another way, nature had ordained that age predecease youth, but civil war threw a hideous wrench into the natural order. And for Chesnut, this fact became a recurring theme. In the 1880s narrative, she recaptured her own sense that in 1862, she had not quite become inured to the blighting of the young she had already witnessed in the war's first year at military hospitals in Richmond and Columbia. For Chesnut, the meaning of the Civil War ironically hit closest to home in a context entirely extraneous to it; in that regard, Sally's Alabama plantation was so far removed from Chesnut's quotidian, early 1860s world that it might as well have existed on the moon. And yet, it was because young members of her own extended family had lost their lives to disease that the true horror of war in the divided nation penetrated her once robust defenses, putting an entry in the 1880s book from the time of First Manassas in interesting context: "July 1861; Burwell Boykin of Mt. Pleasant [Chesnut's maternal uncle], died of typhoid fever.... So many escape in spite of the dangers and perils of the battlefield. And they die in their peaceful homes" (127). This earlier death, painful, unanticipated, and mourned by the entire community (the beloved Boykin caught the typhoid as he nursed his slaves in the quarters) unfolded against the background of epidemic illness, a frequent reality in the nineteenth century, experienced by black and white, high and low, alike.

Sally Amelia Miller Boykin, Chesnut's younger sister, however, has no framework for understanding why half of her young family should be taken by disease. Indeed, so stricken with grief is Chesnut's sister that her hair has whitened overnight, aging her into unrecognizability. The sepulchral aura Chesnut reports having observed on her approach to the house proves an apt atmosphere for the phantom who awakens her in the dead of night several hours later. Sally has become a spectral shadow of Chesnut's once vibrant youngest sibling.[13] The 1880s narrative records that the following morning, Chesnut has a conversation with Sally's only remaining child and learns about the horrors of the previous several weeks. Mamie and Katie are dead, the girl reports: "Maum Hetty [Mrs. Miller's slave housekeeper] says they have gone to God, but I know that the people have saved a space between them in the ground for me" (464).

This little girl, who significantly goes unnamed by Chesnut, believes that "Katie died because she ate blackberries. I know that. And then Aunt Charlotte read Mamie a letter, and that made her die, too" (462). Told that her sisters have "gone to God," and forbidden by adults from mentioning the "departed," the little girl suspects that any one absent from the family circle necessarily must be on the way to heaven. According to her magical logic, blackberries have become poisonous and letters have assumed the power to kill. After all, three out of the six white people in the household have been stricken, and two have died. It is no wonder that the sole surviving child should notice that, though her sisters are said to be with God, there are two new graves in the cemetery, with one empty space in the ground between them.

Under normal circumstances, the fatalism underlying a four-year-old's analysis of the causes and effects of contagious illness would seem preposterous and be taken at face value as an index of the primitive mental functioning of children. Yet when in the 1880s narrative Chesnut (implicitly) juxtaposes such "logic" to the deadly folly of brother killing brother in the context of civil war, her representation of the child's resignation takes on a preternaturally portentous quality. Nothing could seem less imaginable, theoretically, than the intramural destruction of families at arms across the nation.[14] But untimely death never makes sense. Here, the report of a four-year-old's stoic resignation—indeed, her vivid expectation that death will claim them all—foreshadows the fatalism that will become a routine feature of domesticity in Richmond and Columbia and elsewhere along the lines of battle.

Having lost two of her three daughters, Sally lies in peril of being pulled into the grave herself. According to the 1880s narrative of her elder sister, the woman who emerges from the second family funeral seems neither dead nor fully alive: "She began at once in that same stony way, pale and cold as ice, to tell me of the death of her children. It had happened not two weeks before. Her eyes were utterly without life—no expression whatever. And in a composed and sad sort of way, she told the tale, as if it was something she had read and wanted me to hear" (463). Chesnut has noted a page earlier that Sally never has been prone to weeping. But the mechanical way in which her sister is said to tell the tale of loss, declaiming it as if it were a newspaper item or a paragraph from a book, gives pause to the writer's listening persona.[15]

More like an animated corpse than a grieving mother, Sally resembles the figures with whom Odysseus converses on his divinely ordained journey to Hades in book 11 of the *Odyssey*. There, he speaks to the shades of dead heroes from past generations into the present, from his former comrade Elpenor, to the prophet Tiresias, to his dead mother and the queens of history, to Agamemnon, Ajax, and Achilles. Odysseus (whom Chesnut refers to by his Virgilian name, Ulysses) hears prophecies and obtains instructions for how to proceed in his quest to return home; he gains insight about Ajax's unwillingness to forgive him for winning the competition for Achilles' armor; and he witnesses Achilles' assertion of regret for having chosen a short and glorious life, marked by *kleos*, instead of a long and unnoteworthy existence, unmentioned in the annals of heroic verse.[16]

Mary Chesnut the writer was less interested in seeking personal *kleos* than she was in commandeering the muse. And far from Olympian, her narrative point of view unfolded according to its own associative logic, which would have made little sense to Homer or Virgil.[17] Relatively early on in the 1880s manuscript, as already mentioned, she had begun referring to herself as Cassandra. It is important to note that her narrative persona reports leaving Alabama armed with no prophetic view of the future; equally lacking are any Tiresian guidelines for conducting those ritual acts that will ensure a good homecoming. What she has learned involves the nature of mortality itself, particularly in regard to its effects on those who survive, often in an emotional limbo from which there will be no return. The 1860s persona notes that on departing Sally's dismal home she has left the land of the dead for the "outside world" (465). This visit has imposed chastening lessons about what have heretofore been the more abstract horrors of war.

Recording an event that takes place two years later, the 1880s writer describes another epic passage from what she considers "life"—the excitement of wartime Richmond and Columbia—to "death," emotional exile on the plantation in Camden. Literally, of course, the younger Chesnuts were fleeing the Federal army's destruction of Columbia and environs for the safety of their rural home. That is, they were running from death toward life, at the rear guard of a retreat from near starvation at Lincolnton and Chester, South Carolina. It was late spring 1865, and the destitute, exhausted matron was homeward bound, finally reunited with her husband, now a brevet brigadier general, in the wake of Confederate defeat. Arriving at "Chesnut's Ferry" near Camden, the Chesnuts found that they could not pay the toll. More precisely, the couple reached the banks of the Wateree River, made the crossing as they had done without consideration or care for over twenty years, and were caught up short on the other side of the channel, unable to settle their debt to the boatman. Reflecting on this incident in her 1880s narrative, Chesnut notes, "when we crossed the river, coming home, the ferryman at Chesnut's Ferry asked for his fee. Among us all, we could not muster the small silver coin he demanded. There was poverty for you" (May 7, 1865, 805).

Several details deserve particular emphasis. Having given no conscious forethought to their lack of wherewithal for compensating the ferryman, the Chesnuts nevertheless had crossed over. Hailing from a long line of wealthy slaveholders whose "cause" for all time had been lost, they could not pay the toll and found themselves beholden to the poor white or newly freed black man whose job it was to manage the crossing.[18] That is, the economic structure of the life they had known for over forty years had been turned upside down. It was a scene both material and symbolic for a couple whose world was crumbling.

The 1880s writer represents this moment on the river's edge as the threshold of her second journey to the underworld. Grappling not with sacrificial blood and barley bearing the power to return her to the life of affluence she has known since girlhood, Chesnut's cup runs over with gall and woe. Awaiting her are a partially ruined plantation house, the setting for this penultimate sojourn, and her Lear-like, ninety-three-year-old father-in-law, Colonel James Chesnut Sr., who by her own account "is of a species that we will see no more. The last of the lordly planters who ruled this Southern world. He is a splendid wreck" (May 18, 1865, 815). A more ironic Stygian guide was unlikely to be found. Completely blind and almost equally deaf, the old Colonel utterly depends on his loyal black attendant, Scipio, whom Chesnut (in a relatively unprecedented echo of plantation romances) describes as having vowed never to leave his ancient master. Facing the prospect of rustication in abject poverty, neither Achilles nor Odysseus nor Aeneas she, there will be no deus ex machina to deliver the invalid, forty-two-year-old Mary Boykin Chesnut, represented twenty-odd years later by her sixty-something self.

But in lieu of a miraculous escape or recovery, there were local consolations. Though Chesnut writes in an 1880s entry for May 2, 1865, "I wept incessantly at first," she goes on to note Camden's bittersweet solaces: "'The roses of these gardens are already hiding the ruins,' said Mr. C. 'Nature is a wonderful renovator'" (800). It is true that the 1880s book depicts little beyond the physiological and aesthetic restoration afforded by abundant spring produce and exquisite flowers. The transformed narrative does, however, chart a great crossing over, for Chesnut and her class as well as for less-privileged white Southerners, for her own former slaves and the freedpersons of the South, and indeed for the fractured nation itself. In the 1880s epic, the story Chesnut tells of her culture's undoing twenty years earlier attempts to redress a toll that cannot be paid: the tragedy of African American bondage; the history of a murderous war, fought on one side to preserve and won on the other to abolish American slavery; and the hubris and folly of those whites who staked everything on upholding the institution and all that it enabled of privilege and injustice.

If Lee's surrender at Appomattox officially ended conflict in the major theater of the war, it did not obviate the travail of many Americans, Northern and Southern, black and white, poor and rich, who had suffered momentous casualties. More than 630,000 men had been killed; countless hundred thousands more were wounded, many of them permanently disabled. In the four years of the fray, the pastures and farmlands of Virginia, Maryland, Pennsylvania, the Carolinas, Georgia, Alabama, Kentucky, Missouri, Arkansas, Tennessee, and Mississippi had become de facto cemeteries. Many of those slain in battle or who died from untreated injuries had been buried in mass graves, their families denied local sites for remembrance. For the ancient Greeks, this would have been anathema. Homer's audience believed that the dead who were improperly buried—lacking silver coins under their tongues—would be denied passage across the river Acheron (or Styx) by Charon, ferryman of the underworld. Indeed, according to ancient Greek religion, individuals unsuitably interred were doomed to wander forever, eternally proscribed from repose.

But the Chesnuts and their unnamed companions waiting to cross the river had been spared the fate of neverending itinerancy; despite lacking the currency to pay their way, they had been granted passage. It is likely that the ferryman had recognized them and taken pity on their bedraggled state; or, perhaps, the Chesnuts had struck some sort of bargain for deferred payment of the toll. Unbeknownst to the boatman, and instead of valuable metal placed in her mouth like a dead Greek, or in her hand, like a wealthy Southern matron, Mary Chesnut carried home an unrecognized treasure that would provide her own passport to immortality: those remaining, unburned 1860s Civil War diary fragments she would reimagine and develop for the next twenty years. Her silver tongue—that precious gift for lyricism in the vast panoramic context of epic composition—constituted what became, if belatedly recognized, "repayment" beyond measure for much of the blood and treasure that she and her family had lost.

CHAPTER THREE

Seeds

FERTILITY, FLOWERS, AND FRATRICIDE

Despite the devastations of war, James Chesnut Jr. remained able to appreciate the perennial springtime beauty of South Carolina's gardens as hints of renewal to come. This unexpected horticultural imagery at the end of the 1880s narrative reprises Chesnut's earlier pages, which brim with representations of floral tributes paid the writer by exquisitely attentive middle-aged beaux. Such entries would seem explicable in psychological-biographical terms; the sixty-year-old writer was reflecting on the fading charms of her forty-something avatar, who had sought to remain at society's center during the Civil War. Accordingly, the writer recorded receipt of such offerings as paeans to the belle of yore; she was the woman, after all, who in the 1860s diary noted about her even *younger* self: "[M]en fell in love with me wherever I went . . . then" (*TPMC,* 21).

Those readers, however, who continue to puzzle over the significance of flowers depicted across the many pages of Chesnut's 1880s book may have discerned something beyond personal vanity in this recurring motif. Related to her list of proliferating bouquets are the scrupulously detailed instances of elaborate dinners of which she had partaken as an invited guest, as well as numerous edible gifts given by devoted friends: baskets of peaches, bowls of blackberries and apricots, a bottle of cherry brandy. After describing in the 1880s narrative how she had languished in and out of consciousness and without appetite during a two-week illness, she attributes the physical restoration of her then-forty-year-old self to the powers of a simple dish of tomatoes with homemade dressing concocted by a male admirer. That such humble food could play a leading role in Chesnut's imaginative repertoire exemplifies the way mundane objects take on profound meaning in the epic she built of miniatures.

Epics are replete with catalogues ordinary and exceptional, and Chesnut's edible inventories can be read fruitfully in this way, among others. Her lusty celebration of Southern produce—particularly the peaches over which she rhapsodizes after another spell of sickness—might also mark a nod to the local-color tradition gaining prominence among women writers in the years Chesnut undertook the transformation of her narrative. Less probable would be the notion that in such food imagery, Chesnut uncharacteristically deployed key conventions of the sentimental fiction she most loathed: the work of female domestic authors such as Susan Warner, Harriet Beecher Stowe, and Maria Cummins, who lavished narrative attention on scenes of both food preparation and communion in the kitchen.[1]

But as if to defy the sanctifying significance of *The Wide, Wide World*'s and *Uncle Tom's Cabin*'s gastronomic tableaux, the 1880s writer reports having consumed such fare in boardinghouse beds, alone, rather than at table or in company. Tellingly, she also had composed her 1860s private diary from a series of different four-posters, settees, and couches. Despite never having had the good fortune of "lying in" enjoyed by most nineteenth-century women, Chesnut nonetheless had produced imaginative fruit from various South Carolina and Virginia sleeping chambers, the seeds for later literary transformation, the first draft of what eventually would become Mary Chesnut's unfinished Civil War epic.

The literary significance of flowers and food in Chesnut's 1880s book, her versions of homey epic catalogue, local-color flourish, or domestic sentimental convention certainly are worth considering. But most significantly, the work's interest in "seeds" broadly conceived—and in fertility itself—links Chesnut's project to a central subject of epic literature from the *Odyssey* through *The Waste Land*. Chesnut's own unfruitfulness, other women's belated pregnancies, and particularly, what seemed to her the fecundity of Mulberry Plantation's slave women preoccupied her throughout her scribbling life, from the initial 1860s jottings through the reworkings undertaken in the years before her death in 1886. I argue in this and the following chapter that the relation of fruit and fertility offers a heretofore unavailable key to some of the deepest structures of the messy, marvelous book she left off completing in 1883. To begin, I turn to Chesnut's own experience of fruit, fertility, and its absence.

A Blighted Crop

Very early in the 1880s narrative, Chesnut makes reference to an event that C. Vann Woodward in an editorial footnote, echoed by Elisabeth Muhlenfeld in her biography, identifies as "an otherwise unmentioned miscarriage—in view of the sentence following."[2] It concerns an exchange Chesnut has with her father-in-law: "[H]ope told a flattering tale. We had no children. They were to carry on his line and inherit the estates he loves so well. Now he is under no delusion. He said . . . 'With your husband we die out. He is the last of my family'" (September 9, 1861, 190–91). This account of entailed estates and the extinction of family lines conjures the fiction of Jane Austen, though in a decidedly uncomic register. When in the fall of 1861, old Colonel Chesnut ostensibly uttered his pronouncement, he could not have known what ultimately was comprehended by the daughter-in-law who went on to record the bleak summation in her literary narrative of the 1880s.

In 1861, Mulberry's prospective male heir—the only of his grandsons loved and valued by the old man—was John Chesnut III, nicknamed the Cool Captain by the aunt who cherished him alone of all of her relations by marriage. Johnny, who enlisted as a private and rose to become a cavalry officer serving under Generals J. E. B. Stuart and Wade Hampton, would survive the war only to die unmarried and childless three years after Lee's surrender. Unlike the sycophantic Reverend Mister Collins of *Pride and Prejudice* who, Austen suggests, sensibly weds the ever-decent Charlotte Lucas (assuring the reader that his undeserved patrimony will be managed by capable hands), Mary Chesnut's surviving kin by marriage—Johnny's younger siblings—have no redeeming attachments and appear in the 1880s narrative as petty, greedy, and soulless.[3] This fact amplifies the pain the couple and their family feel over James and Mary Chesnut's inability to produce a child.

Concerning their failure to become parents, whether or not the Chesnuts consulted medical experts is unknown, though Muhlenfeld notes that the couple traveled to Saratoga and Newport and afterward, unexpectedly, to England, relatively early in their marriage, after Mary had fallen ill. James Buchanan, then secretary of state, had hurriedly dispatched an official note of introduction for James and Mary, in order to pave the way for letters of credit not yet secured. In it, Buchanan commented that James Chesnut Jr. was traveling to Europe seeking "medical advice."[4] We know that Mr. Chesnut was not ailing at this time, while Mary evidently was; and though his mother, Mary Cox Chesnut, wrote to James Jr., "I suspect that you needed the voyage as well as Mary," she added somewhat officiously, "don't let Mary walk too much — you know its one of the things the Dr objects particularly to." Muhlenfeld accordingly speculates, "This last admonition suggests the possibility that Mary's illness may have resulted from a miscarriage" (56).[5]

The Chesnuts might well have sought treatment in Saratoga, Newport, London, or in South Carolina, but this remains undocumented. Even if they had conferred with "experts," medical understanding of infertility at this epoch was inchoate.[6] Not until almost fifteen years later would surgery on the female reproductive organs be attempted to cure the condition. Such procedures aimed to correct uterine blockages and cervical deformities, although this second wave of "remedies" for childlessness also proved largely unsuccessful.

It is possible (though improbable) that when she was still in her twenties, Chesnut could have been cared for by doctors employing the only treatments then available: uterine injections of "weak silver nitrate solution, acetate of lead, diluted euphoric acid or carbonate of potash. Some of the braver practitioners even painted the uterine cavity with silver nitrate."[7] That patients did not develop cancers and perish in droves from the toxicity of such procedures is remarkable. But, of course, neither the 1860s diary nor the 1880s narrative ever alludes to Chesnut's undergoing any such therapy. And by the late 1850s, when more was being done for infertile women, Chesnut and her newly elected senator husband had left South Carolina for Washington. At this point, it would have been unlikely that the forty-something Mary Chesnut would have sought or subjected herself to the new surgical "cure," the prospects for which, historians of infertility agree, were dubious at best.[8]

By "borrowing" the children of her sister Kate and others, Chesnut had coped with childlessness for almost her entire adult life; nevertheless, a sense of purposelessness plagued her thoughts and continued to materialize as a recurring motif in her writing. Lists of barren women who numbered among her friends and acquaintances figured prominently in the many catalogues she included in her unfinished epic. The female cohort that the *Richmond Examiner* sneeringly called Mrs. Davis's "ladies" — indicting the imperial pretensions of the women attached to the Confederate cabinet — included many who were childless. As the 1880s writer notes: "Of the ladies here — Mrs. McLean, Mrs. Joe Johnston, Mrs. Bartow, myself, Mrs. Joe Davis the elder, and Mrs. Joe the younger — six without children" (July 16, 1861, 101–2). Only Varina Davis, first lady of the Confederacy, and Louisa McCord, the pro-Confederate writer and ideologue who moved with this circle, had offspring in number, though during the war the former would lose a male child and the latter her soldier son.[9]

Woodward, Muhlenfeld, O'Brien, and others have commented on Chesnut's obsession with childlessness in the 1880s narrative, quoting those passages she records on barrenness in her milieu. Perhaps the most familiar is this:

> I did Mrs. Browne a kindness. I told those women that she was childless now, but that she had lost three children. I hated to *leave her all alone.* Women have such contempt for a childless wife. Now they will be all sympathy and kindness. I took away "her reproach among women." (March 18, 1861, 28, my emphasis)

Peopling Mrs. Browne's domestic resume with children—a brood conjured and cancelled rather than never born—Chesnut obviates any potential aspersion that could be cast on that lady's womanly reputation. For reasons unexplained, she feels compelled to correct the mistaken impression that her friend is childless altogether: without such an intervention, Mrs. Browne would be denied credit for having attained what Chesnut—echoing Southern society—considered a woman's greatest triumph. Bringing her particular narrative gifts to bear on the problem ("I told those women"), Chesnut attempts to reestablish at the level of talk what has been taken away by life; in the collective imagination of the Confederate elite, at least, Mrs. Browne no longer will be left "all alone."

Chesnut's impulse to rescue from anticipated contempt and reproach a friend bereaved of her children is significant. The 1880s narrative offers no account of whether Mrs. Browne has complained about being mistaken for a barren wife. Perhaps Chesnut desires to establish Mrs. Browne's maternal *kleos,* a mark of her epic aspirations to record Confederate fame of all sorts. The scene also might telegraph displaced wishes about Chesnut's own unfruitfulness in a culture that judges female achievement exclusively in terms of maternity. The writer never states that she has suffered the pointed contempt of those with children belittling her own situation. Nevertheless, her in-laws waste no opportunity to thrust old Mrs. Chesnut's erstwhile fertility in their daughter-in-law's face.[10] In an 1880s passage for March 1861, Mary Boykin Chesnut records the old Colonel vaunting: "Wife, you must feel that you have not been useless in your day and generation. You have now twenty-seven great-grandchildren" (32). Significantly, in Chesnut's 1860s diary, in which candor goes unchecked by propriety, it is Mary Cox Chesnut herself whose words are reported as indirect discourse: "«Mrs. Chesnut was bragging *to me* with exquisite taste—me a childless wretch, of her twenty seven grandchildren, & Col. Chesnut, a man who rarely wounds me, said to her, '*You* have not been a *useless* woman in this world' because she had so many children. & what of me!»" (*TPMC,* 44–45;

Seeds: Fertility, Flowers, and Fratricide 53

MCCW, March 21, 1861, 32). It may be that the 1880s narrator felt that the old Colonel, whose love for her she never doubted, constituted a sturdier target than the mother-in-law about whom she was more ambivalent and under whose judgment she had suffered.

Whatever her reasons, the 1880s Chesnut's almost seismographic emotional receptivity to slights and affirmations alike is, of course, what makes her point of view so invaluable to literary history. Accordingly unappeased by the fact that the elder Mrs. Chesnut's words are deployed with an utmost gentility of tone, she is cut to the quick by the self-satisfied nature of their content. The private 1860s diary showcases Chesnut's interpretive acuity in the face of her family and greater community's lack of discernment; not for nothing is one of her favorite French expressions "Au royaume des aveugles, les borgnes sont rois," translated, "In the kingdom of the blind, the one-eyed man is king." As a Cyclops of sorts in insensible Camden, Chesnut alone registers the fact that the sentimental phrases uttered by the angel of Mulberry actually may be masking disappointment and possibly even disapproval.[11]

This elided quotation concludes with a remarkable comment: "«(He did not count his children!)»" (*TPMC,* March 21, 1861, 45; *MCCW,* March 19, 1861, 33), an aside that suggests that Mary Boykin Chesnut suspected the old Colonel of sexual impropriety that may have resulted in illegitimate offspring. Connecting this to her remark that "«Rachel and her brood make this place a [horrid] nightmare to me»" (*TPMC,* June 14–15, 1861, 82; *MCCW,* June 10, 1861, 72), also elided in the 1880s narrative, scholars writing in the wake of the Woodward edition have argued that Chesnut seems to be implying that her father-in-law has more than one biracial child as a result of his visits to the quarters. In a footnote annotating the "He did not count his children!" entry in *The Private Mary Chesnut,* editors Woodward and Muhlenfeld comment: "Presumably a reference to those MBC believed Col. Chesnut fathered on a slave woman" (45 n. 4). In *Mary Chesnut's Civil War,* Woodward glosses the proof text from Genesis to which Chesnut returned in order to allegorize a subject apparently too distressing to address directly: "In Genesis 29–30, Jacob, unhappy with his wife Leah, also marries her sister Rachel. He has children by both women and their handmaidens as well. M.B.C. apparently believed old Mr. Chesnut had children by a slave whom she calls 'Rachel.' She confesses no such suspicions of her husband" (*MCCW,* March 18, 1861, 32 n. 5).

Mary Boykin Chesnut's apparent distrust of her father-in-law has been the subject of an entire strand of criticism in the secondary literature on her 1880s narrative, though it is based on one passage, written in distress in the 1860s and elided from her reworked narrative, in concert with the two elided "Rachel" references. While the 1850s census for Camden, Kershaw County, South Carolina, identifies thirty-eight "mulatto" slaves between the ages of one and seventy owned by James Sr., the parentage of these persons, who are not even named, but only identified numerically, remains unspecified. Remarkably, the 1860s census lists not a single "mulatto"; all nonwhite persons are catalogued as "B," for black.

It would not appear that the Chesnut mulatto population had been decimated during this ten-year period. Instead, more plausibly, the recorder of the census data took an illegal clerical shortcut, which seems to have resulted in the lumping of all slaves into the color category "B," in direct violation of the 1860 census instructions: "Those who are in any degree of mixed blood are to be termed 'M.'" This official U.S. racial taxonomy mandates that someone identified as a "mulatto" is by no means necessarily the child of one black and one white parent. Rather, the label recognizes a nearly infinite number of possible genetic permutations and combinations at work, not only for the Chesnut quarters, but throughout the nation. Accordingly, there is no way to determine the genealogical origins of the Chesnut "mulatto" slaves classified in the 1850 census.

As this document shows, thirty-eight or more biracial people served as slaves of James Sr. during the many years in which Mary Boykin Chesnut was in and out of residence on his properties, when she was not living in her different homes in Camden, or in Washington, Montgomery, Richmond, or Columbia during various epochs of the Civil War. That is, there were mixed-race Chesnut slaves living on her husband's father's plantation during her years as a young bride and young and early-middle-aged matron, a presence that could have suggested white male sexual exploitation in the past as well as the present, and that might have inspired the "Rachel and her brood" rantings of the 1860s dairy. But the dearth of documented evidence has thus far rendered it impossible to trace the parentage of these enslaved men, women, and children. That such obscuring of genealogical ties would become a universal feature of the Southern archival record should come as no surprise: slaveholders went to great lengths to erect a legal and actuarial system that would enable them to conceal paternity out of wedlock and links to biracial offspring. Such connections remained the subject of plantation gossip across the South, but were very difficult to prove. Ultimately, Chesnut excised her suspicion of the old Colonel during her reworkings of the 1860s diary. She may have changed her mind about his potential relation to "Rachel"; she may have been unwilling to accuse her then-deceased father-in-law; or she may have been reluctant to tackle such issues directly in a text she intended for publication, in keeping with her commitment not to mirror the nasty Harriet Beecher Stowe. And some other, altogether unimaginable reconsideration may have influenced Chesnut's decision to refrain from familial accusations when it came to the Southern racial problem that most distressed her.

In a book that takes a literary approach to Chesnut's 1880s narrative achievement but that uses historical materials to flesh out claims about theme, character, and form, it seems crucial to address the received wisdom about the writer's elided accusation, articulated in one specific and two allegorical passages. It may be more productive to think about the larger implications of this particular bête noire, white men in the quarters, a subject that is pertinent to the practices of the entire slaveholding South. Put another way, whatever provoked the 1860s Chesnut to voice her suspicion on the domestic level and to raise a bevy of unanswered (and probably, unanswerable) questions, a critique of her 1880s elisions, coupled with general remarks she makes about white Southern patriarchs and the way in which the domestic and the social illuminate each other in the 1880s narrative, becomes most trenchant when it operates on the broader cultural level.

In light of Mary Chesnut's despair about her own childlessness, it is particularly ironic that the writer has become famous for two quotations involving her condemnation of slave masters whose "visits to the quarters" result in the births of biracial children. Consider what, however incongruously, might be the most well-known Chesnut quotation afloat among historians and Civil War enthusiasts alike, an 1860s diary entry for March 18, 1861:

> «Like the patriarchs of old our men live all in one house with their wives and their concubines and the mulattoes one sees in every family exactly resemble the white children—and every lady tells you who is the father of all the mulatto children in everybody's household, but those in her own she seems to think drop from the clouds, or pretends so to think.» (*TPMC,* 42; *MCCW,* 29)

Chesnut's observation rings a hauntingly accurate sociological note when paired, say, with recent DNA discoveries about descendants of Thomas Jefferson's slave Sally Hemings. Focusing on the Y chromosome, scientists have revealed that either Jefferson himself or one of his nephews was the father of Hemings's last child, Easton Hemings. Plantation daybook records show that, in fact, Jefferson was in residence at Monticello for a significant period of time at least nine and a half months prior to each one of Hemings's deliveries, making his paternity of all her children possible, if not probable.[12] In his will, Jefferson manumitted both Easton and his brother Madison; and he directed that Sally be "given her time," apparently an informal mode of emancipation, as well as permission to move to Charlottesville with her freed sons. (Had Jefferson freed her, Hemings would have been forced to leave her family by the 1806 Removal Law, which made it illegal to remain in Virginia for more than a year after manumission.) Additionally, a lineal descendant of Madison Hemings has gone on the record telling a family story about young Easton Hemings; not only did the child have red hair; apparently, his face struck all who met him on Monticello as a cameo-copy of Thomas Jefferson's visage. Or, to reprise what Chesnut wrote thirty-five years after Jefferson died, "the mulattos one sees in every family exactly resemble the white children," or in this case, the white father.

The other infamous Chesnut remark, cited above, about "Rachel and her brood" is obscure, coming as a sort of non sequitur: there seems to be no precise black female referent for "Rachel," and nothing in the extant Chesnut scholarship satisfactorily identifies the figure as a specific living person in the Mulberry community, black or white.[13] As we've seen, the writer of the 1880s has made an earlier allusion to "Rachel," also in the 1860s diary and also elided from the 1880s book; but the name functioned allegorically in that passage, as part of a biblical story Chesnut deployed to express her disapproval over the nonmonogamous practices, including visits to the quarters, of more than a few Southern white men.

One such figure, whom Mary Chesnut knew and with whom her husband briefly served in the U.S. Senate before he died in 1860, was James Henry Hammond, a rich South Carolina planter notorious not only for the sexual violation of at least two slaves, mother and daughter (with the former, Hammond had several biracial children whom he kept as slaves on his plantation), but also of his own nieces. Socially ruined (none of them ever married), these victims were the daughters of his wealthy brother-in-law Wade Hampton, who during the Civil War served as the commanding general of the Confederate cavalry after the death of J. E. B. Stuart, and in the decades following, was elected governor of South Carolina during Redemption. Hammond, who sexually assaulted Hampton's daughters over a period of many years before the war, comes to mind as the worst example of the class Chesnut abhorred.[14]

The anecdote about Rachel and her brood echoes Chesnut's virulent critique of white male exploitation of slave women in the passage on mulatto children dropping "from the clouds." No known Chesnut scholar or historian of South Carolina has published or claimed to have found any specific data that either could verify or disprove Mary Chesnut's intimation that mulatto children resembling particular white fathers could have lived at Mulberry or Sandy Hill (the family's summer plantation), or at Bloomsbury (their home

Seeds: Fertility, Flowers, and Fratricide 57

in Camden), any of the three Chesnut residences at which she lived during those epochs of the war in which she and James Jr. were not in Montgomery, Richmond, or Columbia with the Confederate government.[15]

There is a fascinating historical backstory, however, that may shed some light on Chesnut's cryptic references. Figuring in the 1816 will of the old Colonel's father, John Chesnut Sr., were two mulatto children. Both Edward Burke and Juliana are mentioned after a bequest to a favorite, particularly "faithful" and devoted slave woman called Sue. John Chesnut bequeaths Sue to his daughter, the old Colonel's sister, Margaret Deas, under the stipulation that Sue be given her own house, treated with "especial care," and awarded thirty dollars a year as a kind of pension. And, should Margaret Deas predecease Sue, the latter is to become free. The will further dictates that Edward Burke and Juliana should be manumitted at ages twenty-one and sixteen respectively, and trained for a trade in Charleston. John Chesnut particularly desires that Juliana be apprenticed to a "Mantua maker."[16]

The logical implication here (given the nature of these bequests and their contiguity) is that these two young people were John Chesnut Sr.'s mixed-race children, whom he could have fathered with Sue after the death of his wife, and who were to be lifted out of their mother's "condition" once they came of age. One can speculate that the mulatto children Chesnut blasts in her famous "drop[ping] from the clouds" quotation could be descendants of the biracial Edward Burke and Juliana, who may have been half-siblings of James Chesnut Sr. and, therefore, her own husband's biracial uncle and aunt. This assumes, however, that both Edward Burke and Juliana returned to Mulberry as free people to remain among their "family," a relatively unlikely prospect for which there exists no documentary confirmation.

Whatever the reality of past-generational racial crossing in the greater Chesnut family, the 1880s narrative makes it clear that having to witness the fertility and vitality of women and children of all sorts, black and white, slaves and planters, sandy-hillers and shopkeepers alike, gave Mary Chesnut great pain. And living with what she felt to be familial contempt and reproach, in addition to her own perpetual sorrow over the childlessness that had evoked it, Mary Chesnut was burdened doubly. Nor were these the only disabilities from which she suffered. But, paradoxically, her very afflictions made available to Chesnut unprecedented privacy and unstructured time, enabling her to write with commitment during the Civil War, into the 1870s, when she attempted to compose novels, and in the 1880s, when she transformed her diary jottings into an epic narrative. As Lennard Davis notes about the potentially productive dimension of female suffering:

It is possible that disability served some positive, adaptive function for eighteenth- and nineteenth-century women. As invalids or "sick" women, females could avoid the undesirable aspects of care giving and attain greater privacy, perhaps even a sickroom of one's own, which would permit concentrated and uninterrupted intellectual and creative work.[17]

Multiple modes of incapacity afforded Chesnut an exceptional perspective from which to witness and chronicle America's most tragic conflict. As what she called a "childless wife," she had mourned lost prospects for at least twenty years before the Civil War began. Such grief may have helped to prepare her to bear the cataclysmic slaughter she surveyed between 1861 and 1865. Enduring chronic physical pain for the final four decades of her life, Chesnut had became inured to a suffering body as well; with defiance of death as a métier, she had been poised to appreciate the magnitude of both the local hardships and the cultural enormity of the disaster she beheld, contemplated, and gave narrative form during the post-Reconstruction era; and, in addition, while her peers were overwhelmed with the totality of defeat by 1865, she was able to value as a positive achievement the fact of survival itself.

Across thousands of manuscript pages, Chesnut's 1880s Civil War epic catalogued terrible Southern fates: naming the dead and the wounded, recalling how surviving families collapsed under the burden of sorrow and sickness, illuminating in narrative form what in 1863 Timothy O'Sullivan's photographic study of Gettysburg revealed as "a harvest of death."[18]

Chesnut's roll call of the fallen can be divided into two primary categories, the first comprising what we might term the intimate catalogue of fatalities: the husbands, brothers, and sons of her family and friends. This list is inaugurated in the 1880s narrative for an entry in July of 1861 with the death at the first battle of Manassas of General Bartow, husband of another childless Chesnut companion. Meanwhile, the second, public register of heroic dead includes celebrated Confederate officers who have perished on the field or soon after, figures like Albert Sidney Johnston, Stonewall Jackson, and J. E. B. Stuart.

Scrupulous study of Woodward's index will afford Civil War aficionados a complete inventory of those in Chesnut's purview killed in the war and immortalized in her 1880s narrative, even when they appear only as names in a catalogue, unsituated by a contextualizing narrative. The 1880s writer sums up the first circle with the following comment:

> Of that group Mrs. McCord and Mrs. Goodwyn had lost each a son — Mrs. McCord her only one. Some had lost their husbands, brothers, sons. The thought that their lives had been given up in vain was very bitter to them. *The*

besom of destruction had swept over every family there. Miss Middleton's only brother, the brave little Oliver, only a child, after all—but he would go. (January 16, 1865, 702, my emphasis)

Woodward adds in a footnote to this passage, "Susan Matilda Middleton's brother, Oliver Hering Middleton, Jr., was eighteen when killed while on duty with the Charleston Light Dragoons in Virginia in May, 1864" (702 n. 9). It is a gruesome accounting.

One could write an entire book on the subject of the intimate dead in *Mary Chesnut's Civil War.* This study, however, focuses on the ways in which several of those who are killed at the front or who die of camp-borne infection have particular, life-transforming impact on the fates of their relations in Chesnut's community. In four cases depicted in the 1880s narrative, battlefield and home front collide in ways so tragic as to seem incredible—as if they were the stuff of second-rate romantic fiction rather than the mark of human experience at its nadir. These specific family catastrophes emblematize Chesnut's overall conclusion: civil war entails the fatal interrelation of martial theater and domestic arena. What happens on the battlefield produces a horrific ripple effect at home, and the resulting devastation inevitably blights the future of the entire South.

A Fatal Harvest

A woman Mem knows [Miriam Cohen, Chesnut's beloved Jewish friend] heard her son was killed—had hardly taken in the horror of it, when they came to say it was all a mistake—a mistake of name. She fell on her knees with a shout of joy.... The household were totally upset. The swing back of the pendulum from the scene of weeping and wailing of a few moments before was very exciting. In the midst of this hubbub, the hearse drove up with the poor boy in his metallic coffin.

Does anybody wonder so many women die? Grief and constant anxiety kill nearly as many women as men die on the battlefield. Miriam's friend is at the point of death with brain fever; the sudden changes from joy to grief were more than she could bear. (June 9, 1862, 371)

As one of the war's most gifted registrars of "grief and constant anxiety," Mary Chesnut remained committed to recording stories such as these twenty years after the fact. Chesnut's particular double consciousness—her interest in the relation of battlefield to home front—offers a unique perspective on the epoch rarely found in the work of soldier-memoirists. The civilian casualties that most intrigued her concern near or exact peers: middle-aged wives whose spouses and adult sons had gone to battle. Among Chesnut's numerous friends between 1861 and 1865, several families compelled particular interest: the Haskells, Singletons, and Barnwells, a set of married sisters linked by their mother, Mrs. Singleton; the Meanses, a husband, wife, and two grown children; and the Hamptons, child, wife, and husband. Alex Haskell's mother was the sister of Chesnut's admired friend and fellow writer Louisa McCord. Frank Hampton was Caroline Preston's nephew, her brother Wade's son. Chesnut had been a wedding guest at the nuptials of at least one of the young couples in this group.

What all these connections shared, and what proved nearly novelistic for the observing Chesnut, was a whirlwind passage through the cycles of human life. While marriage, childbirth, and ultimately, death, unfolded for most clans over many decades, Chesnut's unfortunate friends experienced all three major milestones in the course of little more than one year.

The Singleton-Haskell-Barnwell catastrophe marks the first installment in the interior drama of decimated families in the 1880s narrative. The writer records Rebecca Singleton's precipitous marriage to Alexander Haskell just before he must leave for the front—indeed Chesnut relinquishes her room in an overcrowded hotel to ensure that the couple enjoy a wedding night. She watches Alex depart and the unfolding pregnancy of "Decca," the new wife left behind. In an entry for June 16, 1862, Chesnut records that Decca Haskell has had a baby girl. Nine published pages later, under the heading June 27, 1862, she writes:

> Rebecca Haskell is dead—poor little darling! Immediately after her baby was born, she took it into her [head] that Alex was killed. He was wounded, but they had not told her of it.
> She surprised them by asking, "Does anyone know how the battle has gone since Alex was killed?"
> She could not read for a day or so before she died. Her head was so bewildered, but she would not let anyone else touch his letters, so she died with several unopened ones in her bosom. (397)

Chesnut emphasizes that narrative (Alex's letters) might have saved the day after withheld information ("they had not told her of" his wounding) has provoked Decca's misapprehensions. Reduced to an infantile state ("she could not read")—the ultimate horror for the bibliophilic Chesnut—Decca clutches the unopened letters at her breast rather than her newborn daughter, who goes unrepresented in the deathbed tableau. In her account of the scene, the author suggests by omission that the raving Decca is oblivious to her infant, who only appears at anecdote's end, as one of Mrs. Singleton's three unnamed orphans. That war produces widows and renders children fatherless is a universal fact.

Seeds: Fertility, Flowers, and Fratricide 61

But Chesnut's indictment concerns the horrific scope of martial destruction, its extensive power to reach the home front, blasting soldiers' wives and babies as well.[19]

The writer of the 1880s also portrays the ramifications of this calamity on the survivors, who express their loss in an uncannily similar manner:

> Mrs. Singleton fainted dead away, but she shed no tears. We went there. We saw Alex's mother, who is a daughter of Langdon Cheves [Mrs. McCord's sister]....
>
> One needs a hard heart now. Even old Mr. Shand [a Columbia minister] shed tears. Mary Barnwell [Decca's sister] sat as still as a statue—white and stony. (397)

A famously inveterate talker, Mary Chesnut is struck by the silent stoicism of her devastated friends.[20] Mrs. Singleton's swoon seems to reprise Rebecca's final collapse. Remaining nominally conscious, meanwhile, Mary Singleton Barnwell is figuratively ossified, as if she has gazed at the face of the Medusa and been turned to stone. Neither mother nor sister utters a sound. Decca's passing, literally, is unspeakable.

But despite death's blows to survivors, stunning them into unconsciousness or paralyzed silence, the demands of war prove even more relentless. Immediately after this description, we learn that Mary Barnwell's husband, serving as chaplain under General Wade Hampton in Lee's Army of Northern Virginia, has been called back to Columbia, presumably to officiate at his sister-in-law's funeral service.

> Then came a telegram from [General] Hampton
> "All well—so far we are successful." Robert Barnwell had been telegraphed for.
> His answer came: "Can't leave here—Gregg is fighting across the Chickahominy." (June 27, 1862, 397–98)

The conduct of the battle must go on, trumping even spiritual stewardship over the rituals of human life that mark its untimely passing for those who remain.

Within sixteen months at most, however, death will finally outdistance war for the Barnwell family: Mrs. Singleton will lose a son-in-law as well as another daughter in a drama that again involves the withholding of information concerning the fate of a soldier-husband from a parturient wife.[21] The 1880s writer records the following news in an undated entry, possibly for September of 1863: "Robert Barnwell is in desperate condition. Mary is expecting her confinement every day" (452). Mary Barnwell has been insistent: she *knows* that her husband's apparent mental aberration has been misdiagnosed as derangement. Dissenting from this view, she remains convinced that his mind has been addled by an unspecified "fever." Nevertheless, Robert Barnwell has himself asked to be removed to "the insane asylum at Staunton" in order to spare his wife in her own time of trial. Until the moment he is removed by ambulance, the pregnant Mary has "nursed him to the last," most probably infecting herself with her husband's disease.

Just before delivering her baby, she receives news that induces an ecstatic response, tragically revealing of how madness was viewed in Southern bellum culture. "'It was [typhoid] *fever* the matter with Robert, nothing more.' Mrs. Singleton says she will never forget that triumphant expression of Mary's eyes as she turned and looked at her." Mary gives birth, and as Chesnut's 1880s narrative immediately recounts, "Mrs. Singleton got a telegram, 'Robert is dead.' She did not tell Mary. She was . . . looking for Robert's body, which she knew might come at any moment. As for Mary's life being in danger—she had never thought of such a thing" (453). In the next sentence, we learn that Mary Barnwell, despite having successfully delivered two older children, has perished in childbed, and Chesnut offers her sad epitaph: "They were brought—husband, wife, and child—and buried at the same time in the same grave in Columbia. And now Mrs. Singleton has three orphans. What a woeful year it has been to her" (452).

Mrs. Singleton has endured twelve months from hell, although three orphaned grandchildren remain to impel her into the future. In that regard, the Haskell-Barnwell survivors are luckier than some, the Means family among them. Chesnut includes her friends' sad story in the 1880s narrative, in an entry probably for September 1862:

> Then came fatal Sharpsburg [the battle of Antietam, fought on September 17, 1862, the war's single bloodiest day]. My friend Colonel Means—killed on the battlefield, his only son [Stark Means] wounded and a prisoner. His wife had not recovered from the death of her other child, Emma, who had died of consumption early in the war. She was lying on a bed when they told her of her husband's death—and then they tried to keep Stark's condition from her. They think now that she misunderstood and believed him dead, too. She threw something over her face. She did not utter one word. She remained quiet so long, someone removed the light shawl which she had drawn over her head. She was dead. Miss Mary Stark [Mrs. Means's sister] said afterward: "No wonder! How was she to face life without her husband and children. That was all she had ever lived for." (426)

In each of these stories, Chesnut refrains from her typical disparaging judgment, offering no criticism over the way her friends join forces to "protect" their women from hearing bad news from the battlefield. In the first case, she simply reports that the Singleton-Haskell's have said nothing to the fragile Decca, still in her confinement, about her husband's combat injury (he has lost an eye); accordingly, we learn that in her fevered confusion, Decca misreads this silence as a sign that Alex has died. Soon after, she expires, perhaps believing herself released from any continuing obligation to fight against her own illness; reunion with her "dead" husband in heaven may seem more compelling to the young mother than the prospect of life without him on earth.

By the time her own bad news from the front arrives, Mrs. Means already numbers among the home front wounded—having suffered the blow of daughter Emma's death early in the war. An unspecified "they" announce to the anguished woman that her husband has perished on the field; simultaneously, they try to suppress reports of her son's condition—that he has been shot and taken prisoner. By autumn of 1862, with grief serving as the base line for her emotional state and freshly afflicted by the news of her husband's death, the shattered Mrs. Means misconstrues "their" mutterings and mistakenly believes that Stark, too, has been killed.

Seeming seconds later, according to the 1880s account, Mrs. Means is dead, either having suffocated herself with the "light shawl" she has thrown over her face—a gesture Chesnut herself has described performing when overwhelmed by war news—or having died of astonishment, perhaps following a sudden heart attack, as the harrowing result of learning that her entire family is no more. In representing these two home front fatalities, Chesnut has crafted an epic type scene with a twist. Rather than spotlighting the two male military casualties, she attends instead to the subsequent deaths of the female dependents of the soldiers, elucidating a rarely represented aspect of the Southern travail.[22]

The final account in Chesnut's heartrending home front anthology chronicles the demise of the Frank Hampton family, an appalling narrative, the details of which unfold in reverse order from the previous examples. Chesnut reports for February 1862 that "Mrs. Frank Hampton" has a "child in extremis" (287). In an entry for June of the same year, she notes: "And a child of Mrs. Frank Hampton was dying" (372). Chesnut never clarifies whether the youngster who is expiring in June is the same child who had a foot in the grave only four months earlier. Then, without any hint or explanation, she announces in an entry for July 1862, only weeks later, that Mrs. Hampton herself has passed away: "Mrs. Frank Hampton is dead. Her mother could not come south. The war killed Sally Baxter" (420).

Those readers lacking a Tolstoy-esque mastery of the maiden names of plantation mistresses in Chesnut's circle have to use Woodward's index to learn that Sally Baxter *is* Mrs. Frank Hampton. Chesnut identifies the subject of her anecdote in a defamiliarizing way. Somehow in death, Mrs. Frank Hampton loses her marital title and cultural place and reverts to the name of her girlhood. It is as if, by passing away, the woman whom Chesnut has called "Mrs. Frank Hampton" has yielded her status in the formal record; instead, an earlier incarnation, socially unconnected to the aristocratic Hamptons, materializes as their line begins its disappearance.[23]

A mere eleven months later, in the greatest cavalry battle of the Civil War, which ended in stalemate, the family of Frank Hampton comes to an end:

> Frank Hampton killed at Brandy Station . . . Willie Munford had shown me where the body—all that was left of Frank Hampton—was to be laid in the capitol. . . . How I wish I had not looked! I remember him so well in the pride of his magnificent manhood. He died of a saber cut across the face and head and was utterly disfigured. Mrs. Singleton seemed convulsed with grief. In all my life, I have never seen such bitter weeping. She had her own troubles, but I did not [yet] know [about the deaths of Robert and Mary Barnwell]. . . . We talked of it all. . . . I met Frank Hampton bringing his beautiful bride from the steamer.
>
> And now, it is only a few years, but nearly all that pleasant company are dead—and our world, the only world we cared for—literally kicked to pieces. (452)

In a phrase made famous by the literary theorist Elaine Scarry, the kinship ties of Chesnut's closest friends have been completely "unmade."[24]

Consider the profound agitation Chesnut records having suffered while viewing Frank Hampton's mangled corpse. A few pages after reporting his death in the 1880s book, she observes: "There must have been hard hitting, the day Frank Hampton was killed—hand to hand. That ghastly cut across his head has haunted me" (457). Her diction in the passage, emphasizing the dead horseman's disfigurement, is particularly evocative. In the entirety of the 1880s narrative, Chesnut describes going to view only one other fallen body—that of Stonewall Jackson—who also lies in state at the capitol after his death in 1863. Chesnut does not clarify whether Jackson's casket is open or closed, though a local newspaper reported that the corpse was embalmed and that the coffin included a glass window that allowed passing mourners to view the general's face. In the case of the great Stonewall Jackson, it is the reputation of the deceased rather than her own reaction to the physical condition of his remains that concerns the writer.[25]

But there is something about Frank Hampton's scarred features, described at nearly the midpoint of her epic, that speaks more deeply to Chesnut. Obviously, the fact that the slain Hampton is the nephew of Caroline Preston, Chesnut's closest confidante, makes viewing his mutilation particularly excruciating. Yet even more is at stake in this episode than witnessing visceral trauma and contemplating the agony of Mrs. Preston's loss. Chesnut's look at Hampton's wounded countenance constitutes a "facing scene," a direct confrontation with another in which identity is confirmed or denied. Across the breadth of the reworked narrative, Chesnut crafts a series of incidents in which she represents gazing into the countenance of another, or into a mirror, in an exchange that carries the metaphysical weight of a struggle with identity and difference.[26] In such moments, psychologically and philosophically, the very reality of selfhood seems to waver in the balance. Do I exist as I? Or has my identity dissolved under the obliterating power of the other's gaze?

Chesnut's 1860s persona confronts a series of actual others, including, as I will discuss at more length in chapter 11, a Confederate officer who incorrectly identifies her hotel room as that of his trysting partner, and an overrouged, bejeweled, railroad-inn hostess, who mistakes the ragged refugee Chesnut for a penniless imposter. In the first instance, the encounter provokes the matron's hysterical anxiety; in the second, Chesnut records feeling outrage and resentment. Neither scene, however, imports the effects of physical violence, much less mutilation, into the encounter. Put another way, what Chesnut discovers in these uncanny reflections disrupts her conception of herself as a unique member of an established social order. In neither interlude does she experience a threat to her own metaphysical integrity.

In viewing Frank Hampton's remains, however, Chesnut confronts an entirely different kind of "mirror." The sight of his disfigured visage emotionally catapults her into a deconstituted domain. If Stonewall's embalmed face has provoked her grief, awe, and apprehension for the fate of the Confederate army, Frank Hampton's countenance elicits something far more personal and disturbing, involving the operations of identification itself. The once dapper, saber-wielding Frank Hampton serves as a sort of doppelganger for the writer. Both Carolinians do their fateful work with implements intended for inscription. Chesnut's emphasis on the fact that Hampton suffered his wounding and death in "hand to hand" combat can hardly be an insignificant detail. It is as if the Union cavalryman who slashed his saber across Frank Hampton's head was etching the signature U.S.A. on the essential locus of the Rebel officer's identity. Chesnut's friend is literally defaced, and her account of that wound at the center of her project can been read as a figure for the ways in which autobiographical creation by definition cannot render images of its subject without also marring them.

To underscore what might otherwise seem a farfetched connection between the dead Hampton and the living writer, Chesnut, too, has described herself as disfigured in an entry of the 1880s narrative. Traveling to Flat Rock, North Carolina in the late summer of 1862, Chesnut hopes to repair her health at the home of her sister Kate. As Southern ladies do not undertake journeys without escort—a genteel custom, the writer will show, that becomes nearly untenable by 1865, when Southern male chaperones have become as scarce as hen's teeth—she makes her trip in the company of young George Cuthbert, a family acquaintance who will die within the year from wounds received at Chancellorsville.[27] At a rest stop, Cuthbert spies an unnamed "friend and crony." Alighting to chat with his chum, he abandons his veiled and exhausted companion in the carriage, at whom the friend cannot help glancing with interest:

> Suddenly I bethought me to raise my veil and satisfy [the man's] curiosity. Our eyes met, and I smiled. It was impossible to resist the comic disappointment of his face—a woman old enough to be George Cuthbert's mother, with the ravages of a year of gastric fever, almost fainting with fatigue then. (August 1862, 424)

The episode marks a humorous counterpart to the hysteria-inducing and pride-assaulting facing scenes mentioned above. Clearly, the writer's willingness to laugh at herself soothes any narcissistic wound she might have suffered as a result of upsetting the romantic expectations of Cuthbert's anonymous friend. Gastric fever, apparently, has wreaked havoc on Chesnut's countenance, rendering her unrecognizable, erasing the sparkling self of the years before the war.

But a final, even more unexpected conjunction than ravaged faces links the dead cavalry officer and the living writer; it is a notion so hubristic that Chesnut cannot allow it to stand in the 1880s book. Across the pages of the 1860s diary, and restored by Woodward in his edition of the 1880s text, Chesnut confesses repeatedly that she wishes she had been born a man; then, she maintains, she might have influenced the outcome of the war directly: "«If I had been a man in this great revolution—I should have either been killed at once or made a name and done some good for my country. Lord Nelson's motto would be mine—Victory or Westminster Abbey»" (*TPMC,* October 17, 1861, 180; *MCCW,* October 15, 1861, 217).

These ruminations erupt in the 1860s diary during a particularly frustrating epoch for Chesnut, rusticated in Camden. For October 15, 1861, she writes:

> Shocked to hear that dear friends of mine refused to take work for the soldiers because their sempstresses [*sic*] had their winter clothes to make. I told them true patriotesses would be willing to wear the same clothes until our siege was raised. They did not seem to care. . . . They know nothing of the horrors of war. One has to see to believe. They take it easy and are not yet willing to make personal sacrifices. Time is coming when they will not be given a choice in the matter. (217)

Chesnut turns to daydreams to relieve the aggravation she suffers over her neighbors' selfishness; she imagines herself as a warrior of heroic stature. That she should pick Admiral Horatio Nelson—the most celebrated officer in recent British naval history, tragically killed at Trafalgar, thus combining "victory" with "Westminster Abby"—is a mark of her ambition. Such fantastic identifications, hardly typical of the plantation mistress class, recur throughout the 1880s book; and they suggest why Chesnut's gaze at Frank Hampton's ruined face evokes particular horror. It is possible that in the sort of imaginative migration Adam Smith theorizes as the working of moral sympathy, Chesnut has come to identify herself with the slain cavalryman, even if only for a moment; no longer the childless wife of a local South Carolina politician, she is a Confederate officer, disfigured and slain at Sharpsburg, lying in state at the capitol.[28]

Identifications unfold across the 1880s epic: consider Chesnut's expression of fellow feeling for the most unlikely spiritual kin: Abraham Lincoln, whom she initially loathes, because she comes to appreciate the crudeness of his humor; rough-hewn Southern countrymen at a railroad station, because she shares their devotion to the Cause; British naval heroes from the Napoleonic wars, for their bravery and prowess in battle. Chesnut's elective affinity with the late Frank Hampton is, in this context, neither extraordinary nor bizarre. Rather, it reveals the remarkable complexity of the imagination of the woman who created the unfinished Civil War epic.

The Crop of Fame, All Underground in the Sod of Virginia

The soldiers—the army. They are the very flower of Southern life &c&c&c. (November 8, 1861, 229)

But these poor boys of between 18 and 20 years of age—Haynes, Trezevants, Taylors, Rhetts, &c&c&c—they are washed away, literally, on a tide of blood. There is nothing to show that they were ever on earth. (July 1862, 412)

Nine-tenths of our army are underground. Where is another one to come from? Will they wait until we grow one? (April 7, 1865, 783)

The soldiers of the South, the very flower of its life, nine out of every ten now underground, washed away on a tide of blood—so the 1880s writer describes the declining fortunes of the Confederate army in a series of entries spanning the autumn of 1861 through April 7, 1865, two days before Lee will surrender to Grant. The implications of the picture she paints extend beyond her intuition that the South cannot win the war; Chesnut's deepest fear, expressed

FIGURE 4. *"A Harvest of Death, Gettysburg, Pennsylvania"* (photograph, July 1863). *This iconic photograph created by Timothy O'Sullivan for Alexander Gardner's studio may be the best-known image of the war, illustrating the antipastoral quality of the desecrated Pennsylvania landscape. From Gardner's* Photographic Sketch Book of the War, *vol. 1 (Washington, D.C: Philip and Solomons, ca. 1866), no. 36. Courtesy of the Library of Congress (LC-DIG-ppmsca-12557; digital file from original photograph).*

for 1862 in the 1880s narrative, is that an entire rising generation is being annihilated. There will be "nothing to show that they were ever on earth," she agonizes—save, perhaps, her own narrative memorial. In an item for March 12, 1862, the writer remarks, quoting Columbia's *Daily South Carolinian*, "today's paper calls enlisting students exhausting 'seed corn'" (305–6). Such agricultural imagery was not limited to Chesnut or her fellow literati of the bellum and postbellum South. As she demonstrates in her own invocation of the daily newspaper, pastoral tropes had proliferated throughout Confederate culture from the beginning of the hostilities.

Ironically, given Rebel insistence that Southerners possessed a unique way of life, such bucolic conceits transcended region during the Civil War; in fact, they were employed frequently by Northern artists and writers as well their Confederate counterparts. Literary scholar Timothy Sweet raised "the question of pastoralism in relation to war photography" by citing a *New York Times* review of the first Civil War battlefield images that began to appear in July of 1862.[29] The *Times* writer appealed "to pastoralism . . . in an attempt to control the traces of war that appeared in photography in 1862. He begins by comparing the photographs of dead bodies 'fresh from the field,' suggesting a rustic conceit that [Alexander] Gardner and [Timothy] O'Sullivan would also adopt; 'a harvest of death.'" Sweet notes that "the corpses and the terrain harmonize to present a unified image of desolation. The inversion of the pastoral does not produce the antipastoral, but preserves the essential conventions of the mode, one of which is the pathetic fallacy. The landscape is in sympathy with man as mother earth sheds tears for her children."[30]

This astute reading of bucolic iconography in the photographic archive of the conflict, concentrating on Alexander Gardner's *Photographic Sketch Book of the War* (1866), has enriched my thinking about the significance of seeds, flowers, and fruit in Chesnut's 1880s narrative. Sweet argues that by creating an image in which Confederate soldiers' corpses scatter the landscape with the surrounding wheat, the Northern photographer naturalizes Union victory.[31] The achievement of the Federal army becomes an organic (rather than intrusively mechanical) phenomenon. Even the pattern assumed by the dead Rebels, strewn about the ground like bales of hay, echoes the harvest rhythms of rural life.

Northern exegetes may have read photographs like O'Sullivan's "A Harvest of Death" in pastoral fashion, but Southerners did not. According to the Northern interpretation, the landscape itself would redeem the war's losses through the natural cycle of the coming year; the changing seasons would transform death's decay into new growth and thus fertilize a restored Union.

But against the background of a losing war, the Southern use of figures such as "seed corn" and "fertile ground" unfolded in the context of an overturning and decimation of bucolic life. As the 1880s Chesnut suggests, the flowers of the Confederacy will be cut down; Southern seeds will sprout prematurely or be blighted in the ground; and the earth itself will continue to be soaked with the wasted blood of Rebel youth. For those Confederate readers who maintained some sort of access to Northern newspapers or *Harper's Weekly* despite the blockade (Chesnut herself received smuggled editions of English periodicals from friends in Columbia such as John R. Thompson, the editor of the *Southern Literary Messenger*), the last thing O'Sullivan's grim reaper imagery would have conjured was a fantasy of cultural renewal.

Certainly, Chesnut's obsession with infertility and the blighting of children and youth alike can be understood in the context of the defeated South as *ruined* garden, inverting the pastoral motif by which Sweet reads "A Harvest of Death," "Where General Reynolds Fell," and "A Sharpshooter's Final Sleep."[32] The writer's deployment of such conceits as "the good seed are in the army— only the chaff remains at home now" (427) and "we wait for the yearly crop of boys, as they grow to the requisite age" (360) operated in keeping with the *Daily South Carolinian*'s reverse-bucolic thematic.

Nevertheless, expressing anxiety about failing Confederate fortunes through inverted pastoral motifs marks only one of several ways in which Chesnut employs flowers and fruit in the 1880s narrative. Centuries before its landscape came to be symbolized as a once green world blackened by war in Gardner's photographic "sketchbook," the South had been mythologized as a cavalier Eden. This idyllic image stood in sharp contrast to the Puritan wilderness of the North, where grimness and toil obtained, rather than leisure and pleasure (enabled, of course, by the expropriated labor of slaves).

The 1880s narrative almost entirely avoids recapitulation of these careworn tableaux, the nineteenth-century literary genealogy of which can be traced to fellow South Carolinian William Gilmore Simms, whose romances of the Revolutionary era were famous for their bucolic landscape painting. Chesnut's literary investment is in manners and mores rather than meadows and marshes; accordingly, the majority of the narrative's most important anecdotes and dramatic episodes unfold indoors. But Chesnut does include two idyllic, if brief, South Carolina interludes that stand out precisely because they are exceptional: the first involves her visit to the old DeSaussure house in Columbia in 1862, a year before Lee's Army of Northern Virginia is defeated at Gettysburg; the other concerns her passing return to Mulberry House in the spring of 1864, one year before the end of the war, as Lee faces Grant in Virginia.

Both the shaded piazza of the DeSaussure mansion in Columbia and the expansive gardens of the Chesnut seat in Camden signify something beyond islands of isolated beauty adrift on a sea of political chaos. Describing the serenity of the first spot, the 1880s writer reports:

> Magnolias in full bloom—ivy, vines of I know not what. And roses in profusion closed us in. It was a living wall of every[thing] beautiful and sweet. I have been thinking of it ever since. In all this flower garden of a Columbia, this is the most delicious corner I have been in yet. (June 16, 1862, 390)

This lush flora—bountiful and embracing—testifies to the augustness of the property: living walls require decades of cultivation to achieve the verdant abundance of the DeSaussure piazza. But beyond the enticement of enchanting perfumes and the visual delight afforded by deep greens and brilliant pinks, this garden also tells a story about the home it adorns and the family it represents.

Victorianist Beverly Seaton offers a comprehensive key for decoding the "language of flowers" among au courant French, English, and American ladies; it enables us to "read" the floral décor of the DeSaussure piazza with a fluency that Chesnut and her cohort probably took for granted.[33] Magnolias signify dignity; ivy conjures friendship and reciprocal tenderness; roses suggest both beauty and its ephemerality.[34] Flanked by a walled garden, the old DeSaussure house offered an idealized miniature of the South in its golden age: set apart; majestic, embodying the abiding values of loyalty and connection. The exquisite tranquility of the place affords the 1880s writer a represented trace of Eden in the postlapsarian, war-torn present, conjuring something already long lost.

Equally elegiac is Chesnut's description of Mulberry's gardens in an entry for May 8, 1864; her 1860s persona visits Camden only three months after the death of the matriarch, Mary Cox Chesnut, in late winter:

> Sad enough at Mulberry without Mrs. Chesnut, who was the good genius of the place. It is so lovely here in spring—the giants of the forest, the primeval oaks, water oaks, live oaks, willow oaks, such as I have not seen since I left here. Popinacs, violets, roses, yellow jasmine—the air is laden with perfume. Araby the blest was never sweeter. (606)

Again, using Seaton's appendix to a "combined vocabulary" of floral symbolism, we can read this landscape's dynastic story: the blossom of the white Mulberry tree conveys wisdom, while that of the black communicates "I will not survive you," as if the "good genius of the place" is speaking to her daughter-in-law through the very name of the plantation itself. The "primeval" oaks connote hospitality, bravery, and love of country; violets suggest modesty and love; roses, again, signify beauty and its fleetingness; and yellow jasmine, the first languor of love, signaling, perhaps, the aura of dreamy unawareness Mary Cox Chesnut herself cultivated.[35] What better than perpetual lassitude to defend against the reality that, despite the mistress's ministrations, at the end of the day Mulberry's African Americans remain enslaved? As the 1880s writer describes her mother-in-law in an entry for October 1861, "[S]he hides her head in soft, comfortable wraps. She is blind to all but beautiful things, rose-tinted beliefs and pure imagining" (202).

Chesnut's final comment about the garden's delectable scents, which are as hypnotic as the "odours" of "Araby, the blest," features an allusion from book 6 of *Paradise Lost* (lines 162–63). The reference could not be more apt. In that section of the poem, Milton's epic narrator describes Satan's flight from Hell to Earth, where he hovers above the walled Garden of Eden. Possessed of a perfect view, and wracked with envy, the fallen angel conducts a reconnaissance on Adam and Eve, seeking a strategy for tempting the pair to disobey God so that they might be expelled from Paradise, just as he has been ejected from Heaven.

It has become a scholarly commonplace that Milton's martial referent for Satan is Oliver Cromwell, leader of the Puritan New Model Army during the English Civil War. The cosmic battle of the poem reprises dimensions of this conflict (1641–52), and its resolution echoes the restoration of the monarchy (1660). Though the allusion could appear to be nothing more than rustic scene painting, its literary context affords a disturbing cognate for Chesnut's own fratricidal subject matter. According to the extended metaphor, if Mulberry represents the paradisiacal South before its "fall," surely the American Civil War marks Satan's entrance to the garden. And by the war's penultimate year, the good genius of the place, the "angelic" Mary Cox Chesnut, has passed away.[36] Again, the writer's literary return to a green South Carolina world constitutes as much a journey backward in time as it does a movement in space.

The pastoral enables the literary Chesnut to retreat imaginatively to a once-peaceful world, as she does both at the DeSaussure house and at Mulberry. But flowers also play a reparative role as tokens of social exchange during wartime, something the 1880s writer amplifies into a theme. In fact, the bouquets and numerous edible gifts Chesnut receives between the attack on Fort Sumter and the fall of Richmond sustain her emotionally during illnesses in 1861 and 1862 and in the face of starvation in 1865, revealing the depth and strength of Chesnut's human attachments in an otherwise crumbling world. Such offerings shore up the failing matron at the very moments during which the boys and men she eulogizes as the "flower of the South" are themselves being cut down by the Federal army.

From hothouse bouquets to wild flowers picked on the perimeter of military parade grounds, horticultural references cluster: Mrs. McCord sends a "bouquet" (the composition of which remains unspecified) to adorn Chesnut's table on the occasion of a highly anticipated breakfast she hosts for Jefferson Davis when, in 1864, the Confederate president pauses for twenty-four hours in Columbia, en route to reviewing the western armies. At the McMahon's lodging house in that city, where the Chesnuts "stop" (her British parlance for stay at length), flowers are a constant (351). Meanwhile, in a list of offerings the ailing Chesnut receives during the same period, with the donors unspecified, Isabella Martin logs "bunches of flowers" (762). Throughout the 1880s narrative, roses and violets—the very blooms Chesnut admires at both the DeSaussure mansion and Mulberry House—are the varieties that most frequently appear in her accountings. White violets and roses are picked for Rose Freeland's wedding; and when Chesnut flees Columbia ahead of General Sherman, arriving in Chester, South Carolina, during the winter of 1865, the writer of the 1880s relates having received a spray of violets from Mrs. Pride (770). Roses and violets are perhaps ubiquitous in the narrative because they flourish during the long summers and in the damp climate of the coastal Southeast. Both plants also can be cultivated in hothouses, though Chesnut never alludes to visiting a florist; town-dwelling Columbians such as the Prestons and the Martins have their own gardens, and it is largely in Columbia that Chesnut represents her 1860s persona accepting bouquets.

But across the vastness of her narrative, one scene featuring the exchange of blossoms proves more haunting than any other, in Chesnut's account of the death of the six-year-old son of Jefferson and Varina Davis: "The morning I came away from Mrs. Davis, early as it was, I met a little child with a handful of snowdrops. 'Put these on little Joe,' she said. 'I knew him so well.' And then she turned and fled without another word. I did not know who she was, then or now" (May 8, 1864, 602). The episode is set in the earliest hours of the morning, following little Joe Davis's death from a fall from a "high north piazza" the day before (601). Chesnut reports going to the Confederate White House to sit in the drawing room with a few close friends. The stricken (and greatly pregnant) Varina Davis is in seclusion, and Jefferson Davis spends the night pacing across a third-floor space above them, unable to be still: "I could hear the tramp of Mr. Davis's step as he walked up and down the room above—not another sound. The whole house was silent as death" (602). Staggering home,

Chesnut encounters an unnamed child holding a bunch of snowdrops, and the little girl asks the strange lady to "put these on little Joe."

The presence of an unattended female child on a Richmond street in the early morning hours suggests that the *status quo ante bellum* has been turned upside down. Chesnut does not identify the child's race, though her impulse throughout the 1880s narrative is to denote black characters as slave or free, while this little girl goes unremarked. Nor does she speculate about the child's age, though the phrase "little" suggests a preadolescent, no older than twelve and possibly younger. Never explained is how this girl knew Joe "so well." Perhaps she is the older sister of one of the dead boy's playmates; less likely (because she is walking city streets alone) is the prospect that she has been a schoolmate.

The strangeness of the child's language—the girl's unusual choice of preposition in the request that the matron put her flowers "*on* little Joe"—is striking. Chesnut's prescient ear for and representation of such unidiomatic speech in her 1880s account telescopes the feeling of growing disorder that is set into motion by the first family's untimely tragedy.

The girl might want the bouquet to be buried in the coffin with her chum, resting in his lifeless arms as a token of her friendship that can be carried with him into the afterlife. Or, she could mean that she would like the blossoms to top little Joe's soon to be dug, filled, and covered grave. This second reading would suggest that she understands the rituals of burial; that is, she knows dead bodies are placed in caskets and interred in the earth. Accordingly, the awkward way she expresses the relation of the "little Joe" she knew "so well" to the material remains that will be put into the ground signifies linguistic rather than metaphysical confusion. But since she characterizes the dead boy as "little Joe," it is not clear that she actually fathoms what has befallen him, or if she realizes that "little Joe" is little Joe no more.

Of course, there is no way to determine her precise meaning if, in fact, she even intended one. But her odd syntax suggests at the very least that she is worried about how "little Joe" will be disposed. And, for Chesnut's narrative purposes, the child gives voice to a growing problem, for Yankee and Rebel alike: what, indeed, has happened to the dead sons of the nation? A Delphic figure emerging as if out of the ether, the little girl disappears almost as quickly, her phantom presence marking little Joe's fleeting life; both her otherworldliness and her anonymity haunt Chesnut across the years.

Whatever the unnamed child means or does or does not understand, she has registered the loss of her friend. Furthermore, she is aware that the flowers she carries flourish no more, although they too have been alive (as little Joe has lived and breathed). The snowdrops express her connection to and feelings about little Joe, whose death seems something out of a bad dream. The weirdness of the child's locution strikes Chesnut deeply. Accordingly, by the transitive property kindled by narrative sympathy, it disturbs us as readers as well. The scene unfolds the absolute horror and incomprehensibility of a child disappearing from the world of other young people; additionally, it speaks to how profoundly out of joint are the times, when offspring come to predecease parents.[37]

Though the girl Chesnut meets as she returns from the grieving household may be possessed of an idiosyncratic understanding of death, her floral offering could not be more conventional or appropriate; in Seaton's appendix, snowdrops evoke "consolation" and "hope," fitting blooms for a heartrending occasion.[38] Chesnut reports that even beyond the Confederate faithful who flock to the Davises' at what was surely one of the lowest points in their personal lives, crowds of children (apparently excluding the solitary little mourner) turn out for the funeral service, throwing unidentified flowers and also green boughs, for "everlasting remembrance," onto little Joe's grave.[39]

But what for the creator of *Uncle Tom's Cabin* might have been a sentimental tableau is transformed by Chesnut into a scene of chaos and disruption, for Richmond's "sympathetic" youth could not be less Stowe-like. Far from being spiritually exalted, or inspired by the potential illumination afforded by the death of the angelic child, we see them "shoving and pushing rudely." A reader brought up on the domestic fiction of the era would have expected a lachrymose, redemptive embrace between mourners; but the formally ambitious and forward-looking Chesnut gives us something very different: children thrusting and heaving in a crowd rather than patiently awaiting the inspiration of God's grace—the very sordid realism, that is, that her mother-in-law abhorred.

In the language of flowers, we find a remarkably apt footnote to Mary Chesnut's 1880s narrative. If the Mulberry flower connotes wisdom and the fleetingness of survival, the chestnut blossom, according to Beverly Seaton, means "render me justice."[40] This notion echoes the exact idiom the diarist of the 1860s invoked to talk about photographic representation. "Justice without mercy," she joked about the images her friends were purchasing of themselves.

Righteously honoring the validity of her particular memories of the war in all of their chaos and disruption becomes the writer's abiding commitment. When Chesnut again takes up her manuscript in the 1880s, it is against the background of post-Reconstruction bitterness, when memorializing movements such as the Daughters of the Confederacy begin their revisionist project to create the secular religion of the "Lost Cause." As a Southern woman in this milieu, Chesnut stands virtually alone. Unlike Jefferson Davis, Jubal Early, and other male war memoirists, she passionately refuses to sentimentalize the Confederacy; nor is she willing to deny the fact that slavery constituted one of the originating causes of the war, as Jefferson Davis would aver to his death.[41] Accordingly, "render me justice" can be thought of as Chesnut's motto for her project, her motivation for returning to the Civil War diary and transforming it into an epic, or in a phrase that she will delete from her revision, the attempt to "«look [the] defeat of my personal ambition in the face»" (August 13, 1861, 142).[42]

CHAPTER FOUR

Seeds

FRUITS AND FAMINE

The 1880s Chesnut adroitly deployed images of "seeds," in their various incarnations as buds, blossoms, and moldering dust, as conceits for her own infertility, as well as for the ways in which the violence of civil war had transformed a pastoral region into a blighted wasteland. Tracing the darkest phases of the cycle of Southern life, the writer telegraphed examples of blooming youth and romance (Frank Hampton courting Sally Baxter), but lingered over Hampton's fatal facial injury. She also gave expression to what contemporary Civil War photographers termed the "grim harvest" of death, the corpses of Confederate soldiers strewn across battlefields in Virginia, Pennsylvania, Maryland, and beyond. In this chapter, I again take up Chesnut's images of seeds in order to move from their floral to their fruitful significance as crucial motifs in the 1880s narrative. The seeds in question here have ripened into edible artifacts, and they preoccupy the 1860s Chesnut well before food actually grows scarce in Richmond and Columbia in the winter of 1864–65.[1] Through a series of scenes featuring the unexpected gifts of garden-fresh provisions, particularly seeded and stone fruits and delicate spring peas and asparagus, the 1880s writer reveals the way in which this rarified diet, enabled by the generosity of privileged friends, set her apart from even the most elite Confederates with whom she traveled. Similarly, the writer's ethnographic account of her Northern-born mother-in-law's gustatory habits, unchanged despite sixty years on a Southern plantation, constitute an incisive picture of the link between food ways and identity.

An important analogy exists between the particular flowers featured in chapter 3 and the wartime culinary preferences of Columbia aristocrats John and Caroline Preston central to this chapter: French haute cuisine represents a gastronomic version of Chesnut's South Carolina horticultural paradise lost. Just as she expresses nostalgia for a Southern pastoral that, by 1862, exists only as a trace, the Prestons' cuisine commemorates a cosmopolitan, Francophilic Southern tradition also en route to vanishing.[2] The most cultured and sophisticated of the writer's local friends, the Prestons had been living in Europe before the outbreak of the war. Among their other transatlantic activities, in Florence they had patronized expatriate American sculptor Hiram Powers, about whom Hawthorne wrote in *The Marble Faun* (1860).[3] Connoisseurship, collecting, and providing their children with an elite European education had been the Prestons' prewar avocations.

With the benefit of a highly accomplished slave retinue, John and Caroline Preston had been able to reproduce key dimensions of their Continental life when they returned to South Carolina on the eve of the secession crisis. Mr. Preston would work for the Confederate cause, initially as an aide to Beauregard, with James Chesnut Jr., during the first battle of Manassas; then as superintendent of Yankee prisoners in Columbia; and finally, as a general in the army, in which his two sons also would serve (and in which the younger would die). Basing family operations in their Columbia town home, the Preston boys joined the military while Caroline and John and their three lively young adult daughters took up the childless Chesnut, well-known for her quick wit and cultured intellect, as their most sought-after visitor.

In an 1880s entry for May 1862, Chesnut muses: "I do not know where Mrs. Preston's [slave cook] got his degree [took his culinary training], but he deserves a medal" (347). Though the 1880s writer records virtually every meal of note she consumed during the war, her culinary catalogues reveal that haute cuisine was the exclusive provenance of the Prestons. Somewhat earlier for the spring of 1862, she remarks: "Pate de foi[e] gras and dindon [turkey] aux truff[e]s exactly suit this invalid. We dined today at the Prestons with that bill of fare. Now, at McMahons, everything gives me a headache" (April 2, 1862, 323).[4] Throughout her narrative, Chesnut will complain about the revolting quality of boardinghouse cookery, bemoaning in an entry for March 19, 1861, "that den of dirt and horror, Montgomery Hall" (31), and in an excised passage from the diary for May 22 of the same year, describing herself as "«overcome with fatigue and the remains of indigestion brought from that den of horrors, Montgomery Hall»" (*MCCW*, 63).

The dyspepsia from which Chesnut suffered was not only a chronic medical condition, but also a protest inflected by class privilege. She never endured indigestion after consuming rich French food at the Prestons', but seemed perpetually vulnerable to digestive trouble when dining at Montgomery Hall in Alabama or the Spotswood Hotel in Richmond. As previously noted, Chesnut was afflicted with chronic gastric fever, a stomach illness related to typhoid, featuring abdominal pain, inflammation, and diarrhea; she also lived with angina pectoris, characterized by a sense of suffocating contraction or tightening of the lower part of the chest (and translated into twenty-first-century medical terminology as chest pain and hardening of the arteries).[5]

Bronchial and pulmonary infections also assaulted her permanently weakened immune system, particularly during the epoch in which she shared the Prestons' table in 1862. In an 1880s entry for April 21, 1862, she notes: "Have been ill. One day I dined at Mrs. Preston's—pate de foi[e] gras and partridges, as I like them prepared for me ... I did not know I was bodily ill" (326–27). Thus ensued the diagnosis of croup, which in the nineteenth century was the term for what we now either call pneumonia (inflammation of the lungs) or diphtheria (an acute infection of the air passages and the throat). The rich meal she had enjoyed obviously bore no relation to her chest infection, though her recovery could be attributed to Mrs. Preston's swift reaction in identifying Chesnut's discomfort as illness and immediately calling for the doctor.

Nevertheless, it was ironic in the extreme that the foods that "suit this invalid" were steeped in fat, the damaging effects of which, of course, were little understood in the nineteenth century, and which actually might have exacerbated her discomfort. Muhlenfeld notes, however, that whereas sea travel made her companions unwell, Chesnut never reported an instance of seasickness; on the contrary, her biographer suggests, the writer's health often improved when she got away from Camden, no matter the mode of conveyance.[6] So, too, her stomach affliction seemed unprovoked by the Preston's cuisine, even though such rich fare might have upset the digestion of many of her compatriots.

The Preston menus, unlike any others in the 1880s narrative, are recorded in French, marking their domestic practices as cosmopolitan, refined, exquisite. And Mr. Preston is a gourmet of the highest order:

> Before the war shut him in, Mr. Preston sent to the lakes for his salmon, to Mississippi for his venison, to England for his mutton and grouse. It is good enough—the best dish in the house what the Spanish call "the hearty welcome." (May 24, 1862, 349)

In contrast, Chesnut's father- and mother-in-law are known for the sort of hospitality and groaning board befitting planter grandees in their most local incarnation. Chesnut describes the way in which "the planters live 'within themselves,' as they call it. From the plantations come mutton, beef, poultry, cream, butter, eggs, fruits and vegetables. It is easy to live here" (May 23, 1862, 347). The senior Chesnuts' insularity is enabled by and reflected in the ingredients grown on Mulberry, from which their cook Romeo and the other kitchen slaves concoct the family's meals. It is hard to imagine the old Colonel sending to England for any comestible, save his treasured port and sherry; it is my sense that he would have scornfully dismissed such cosmopolitan aspirations as dandyish at best.

Chesnut commends other fine meals she eats outside the purview of the Prestons', including a fete at the Lyonses' (whose house will be burned by a slave incendiary in 1864), and a Mulberry Christmas dinner featuring vast quantities of game birds and oysters and numerous varieties of fine wine. But the diction with which the 1880s writer catalogues these bills of fare suggests that the potentially glamorous ingredients have been prepared in conventional fashion. Slave cooks seasoned their dishes with the spices of the Caribbean and West Africa, which gave what we now understand as "Southern" cuisine its most vibrantly imaginative tones.[7] But it also was the case that these bound chefs were cooking at the instruction of their mistresses, whose cultural sophistication varied according to the particularities of their education and the likelihood of their exposure to Continental tradition.[8]

While the Prestons' cook clearly underwent European culinary training, his counterpart at Mulberry learned his craft in far more colloquial circumstances. As the 1880s Chesnut explains in an entry for May 24, 1862: "Old Mr. Chesnut's Romeo was apprenticed at Jones's in town" (347). By "town," the writer means Camden rather than Charleston and beyond, and this would suggest that Romeo's mentors most likely would have been slaves themselves leased out from other owners: when the younger Chesnuts went to Washington in 1858 to begin James Jr.'s senatorial career, many of their bondspeople were "hired out to the Camden hotel" (March 25, 1861, 33). Accordingly, it is hard to imagine that Romeo's experience extended beyond mastery of local and regional delicacies; and though his training would have been informed by his teachers' African and African Caribbean culinary accents, instruction in French techniques by no means would have been guaranteed.

Chesnut is not unappreciative of the more conventional fine cooking practiced by Romeo and his counterparts serving her friends in the Confederate elite. As noted earlier, she praises these chefs whenever she partakes of their fare. Her critique is more subtle, raised against what she sees as the complacent mindlessness of her planter relatives, who seem to imagine that the rarified bubble of luxury in which they live is immune from the ravages of war. Describing in the 1880s narrative the holiday dinner at Mulberry for 1862 mentioned above, she writes:

> There was everything nice to eat at that table. Romeo is a capital cook—and the pastry looks as good, with his plum puddings and mince pies. There was everything there that a hundred years or more of unlimited wealth could accumulate as to silver, china, glass, damask—&c&c. But without Meta dull as ditch water! (270)

Chesnut clearly implies that quantity trumps quality at Mulberry and that the human society there—but for the fortuitous inclusion among the guests of Meta, a young woman with a lively wit who transforms the evening—is as moribund as the tableware is antique. In this observation we see Chesnut's compulsion to parse out what really was at stake in the so-called Southern way of life, both its visceral pleasures and its profound limitations.

Two years in Washington had given the ambitious Mary Chesnut a taste of life's social, intellectual, and cultural heights. In the 1880s narrative, she writes of the numerous thrilling and delectable dinners she enjoyed as a senator's wife. Even more striking is the following rumination, made originally in the 1860s diary for October 10, 1861, and excised by Chesnut in revision: "«Went to Mulberry and spent the day alone, arranging library and assorting boxes of letters and papers—got about half-through, a melancholy pleasure, reading my French cook Therese's bills for the delicious dinners Mary Stevens and I ate so ravenously in Washington, with the appetite our frantic exercise and fatigue in the pursuit of pleasure gave us»" (212). Stevens was a twenty-something protégée whom Chesnut had invited to the capital for company, and Chesnut's sorrowful satisfaction in the face of these written traces of pleasures shared only three years earlier suggests why the Prestons' French cuisine affords her such bliss. Like the trip to the DeSaussure piazza, Gallic food transports the matron, affording imaginative access to the delights she took for granted during the happiest era of her life.

If twenty-four months in Washington mark the apogee of Chesnut's social experience, rustication in Camden proves the nadir; particularly excruciating is sharing a roof with a family she finds, more often than not, intolerable. The 1860s diary provides the most brazen accounts of Chesnut's "family troubles," a phrase that the 1880s writer turns to haunting effect in characterizing the back story of Betsey Witherspoon's murder by her slaves. But Chesnut's dappled portrait in the narrative of complicated parents-in-law and monstrous nieces reveals in more measured fashion some of the edgier moments of contention and critique that constitute the affective heart of the uncensored war dairy.

With first-rate intellects, and widely read to the point of its being commented upon, the junior and senior Mary Chesnuts might have enjoyed a harmonious, even mutually enriching, rapport, based on common interests. Yet Mary Boykin Chesnut could not abide Mary Cox Chesnut's capacity for denial; she was critical, particularly, of the elder woman's apologist attitude toward unwed slave mothers and those whose children may have been fathered by white men. The younger Mary Chesnut believed that miscegenation represented all that was most evil about the institution, especially in its debasement of white mistresses and black bondswomen alike. In light of this apparently ubiquitous Southern problem, she felt that the elder Mrs. Chesnut willed her own blindness, despite her enormous intelligence. She herself, in contrast, refused to "hide her head" in the sand, preferring, as she comments in an entry for October 24, 1861, to look such realities "in the face" (202).

But while playing Pollyanna, the elderly mistress simultaneously exhibited a passive-aggressive streak that was novelistic in its effects upon her family's and slaves' behavior. She also controlled access to the plantation library, keeping risqué books locked away, though she had deputized her husband as gatekeeper in this instance, insisting that he carry the library keys in his own pocket. This sort of feigned female propriety is central to the way Mary Cox Chesnut disowned responsibility for the policing of sexuality that she mandated in every domain of plantation life save for the behavior of her slave women, a theme to which I will return.

Another scene in the 1880s narrative emphasizes a more subtle aspect of the elder Mrs. Chesnut's protest against the Southern racist culture that had made her an abettor of slavery. She refused to eat those staple foodstuffs at the heart of the Southern culinary repertoire: plain hominy or rice, without relish to disguise it, as well as cornbread in any form. The elderly mistress consumed buttered biscuits only with "discretion," a phrase suggesting that ingesting such fare required moral forethought on her part; and she rarely partook of watermelon and sweet potatoes, though Chesnut and the extended family frequently and heartily enjoyed the latter (in fact, throughout the war, watermelon restored the failing writer's energies when she traveled on torpid steamboats and overheated railway cars).

The connection that the elderly mistress drew between Southern slavery and such dishes—neither of which, it seemed, she could swallow with ease—

most likely was unconscious. But it was nurtured in a particular historical and cultural soil. Mary Cox Chesnut was born in Philadelphia to an elite family associated with George Washington—Colonel Cox, the writer tells us, "at one time had been on General Washington's staff" (September 24, 1861, 201). And the young Mary Cox had not been unfamiliar with chattel bondage. "Did you not know that my father owned slaves in Philadelphia?" she queries her assembled family in an 1880s entry for September 24, 1861, during the aftermath of the Witherspoon murder. "In his will he left me several of them. Also he left them to be freed after a certain time & c" (201). Although the gradual emancipation protocols passed in Pennsylvania in 1780 freed not a single one of the state's six thousand slaves, they did legislate the manumission of individuals at the age of twenty-eight years; and owners such as Colonel Cox could design their wills so that specific bondspeople could be liberated according to individual timetables, as Mary Cox Chesnut indicated her father, in fact, had done.[9] As the 1880s writer notes of her mother-in-law, "Mrs. Chesnut, ever since she came here sixty or seventy years ago as a bride from Philadelphia, has been trying to make it up to the negroes for being slaves" (201).

In incredulous tones, Chesnut reports that after more than half a century, the elder Mrs. Chesnut still resists acculturation to Southern ways. Her sentiments and judgments remain strictly Philadelphian:

> Mrs. Chesnut, my mother-in-law, has only been sixty years in this country—and has not changed in feeling or taste one iota. She cannot like hominy for breakfast and rice for dinner without some relish to give it some flavor. She cannot eat watermelon and sweet potatoes sans discretion, as we do. She will not eat hot cornbread avec discretion—and hot buttered biscuits without any. (September 24, 1861, 351)

The senior Mrs. Chesnut is not unwilling to eat unadorned rice and hominy, but *unable:* she "*cannot* like" them, and "*cannot* eat watermelon and sweet potatoes sans discretion." Chesnut here implies that her mother-in-law literally would choke on such foods, were the former two not masked by spicy condiments or sauces, which would alter not only their basic flavor, but also their pale coloration.[10] And, apparently, cornbread absolutely is off limits; avec or sans discretion, "she *will not* eat hot cornbread," while hot buttered biscuits remain on the "avec discretion" list.[11] The elder Mrs. Chesnut insists on dressing up—transforming the taste of—those particular grains cultivated on the plantation and eaten by black slave and white master alike. Plain white rice, a South Carolina staple, and corn, the edible mainstay grown on Mulberry,

Seeds: Fruits and Famine

ground into meal and then baked into cornbread, apparently proved offensive to the once-young bride, now in her nineties, with tastes unchanged by time or experience.

If, according to the senior Mrs. Chesnut's daughter-in-law, white masters across the slaveowning South have spread *their* seed with their own bondswomen, then senior Mrs. Chesnut has countered this disavowed reality with an unconscious enactment: she refuses to ingest, take in, or incorporate those kernelled foods (rice, corn) and seeded fruits (watermelon) she associates with slavery in its every manifestation—whether in the South Carolina Low Country (where rice is produced in the fields of her friends), or upcountry, on Mulberry itself, where slaves plant, hoe, and harvest the corn as well as perform the kitchen labor that transforms both grains into breakfast dishes and staple bread.[12] Mary Cox Chesnut's idiosyncratic aversions do not quite add up to a hunger strike. Nevertheless, to reject plain rice, hominy, and hot cornbread at an upcountry plantation table across sixty years certainly constitutes a long-fought form of resistance to food ways that bespeak themselves of slavery and that seem to be understood as such, if only by the daughter-in-law who so threatens her cocoon of denial.

If in the case of the elder Mrs. Chesnut to decline hot cornbread is to resist assimilating the fruits of black bondage, the connection between both corn theft and reduced corn production on the part of the Chesnut slaves during the war is also significant. Scholars of African American chattel servitude long have argued that though full-scale slave rebellions were rare in the antebellum South, everyday resistance—slow downs, sick outs, and the breaking of tools—was a commonplace. The prospect of such opposition seems to have reached Mulberry belatedly, only once the war had begun, although one can speculate that Chesnut may have been insensitive to such issues during her absentee years in Washington.

Nevertheless, some sort of black defiance seems to have materialized on the Chesnut plantations in 1862, 1863, and 1864. In 1880s entries for these years, Mary Chesnut records the grumblings of both her husband and his nephew Johnny regarding reduced production on both Mulberry, the Jameses Sr. and Jr.'s property, and the Hermitage, Johnny's patrimonial estate, inherited from his father John Chesnut II, who had died when he was a boy. Both men complain about smaller crops and missing corn supplies. James Jr.'s remark, recorded in the 1880s narrative for November 30, 1861, reveals his suspicions: "an immense income is consumed by the young and old unprofitable servants" (251).

Such a gripe would have been understood as normative among Mr. Chesnut's slaveholding peers, since the ideology of the planter class operated according to the logic of what sociologist of slavery Orlando Patterson has called human parasitism and ideological reversal.[13] Masters justified the basic inhumanity of holding black souls in bondage by reassuring themselves that without the benefits of white planters' paternalistic "care"—often barely adequate food, clothing, and medical attention and, typically, substandard housing—African Americans could not survive, much less provide for families, as freed people.

This characterization of the master-slave relationship, of course, inverted the identity of just who was reliant on whom. In fact, the security of the master class rested exclusively on collective denial of the fact that, without the unremunerated labor of slaves, owners never could have accrued the affluence and prestige enabling their very superiority *as* masters. In other words, all the while they were enriching themselves from the stolen labor of their bondspeople, the planter class depended on the myth that it was the slave who was the parasite, draining the economic life blood from the owner. Thus, James Chesnut Jr. reproved his slaves for consuming property (hogs, corn) that would not exist—much less provide vast profits—in the absence of their toil across many years of servitude.

Chesnut records her husband's amplified accusations in a narrative passage for one week later, December 8, 1861, where she represents his argument that he is the economic victim of his own slaves:

> [H]is negroes owed him about fifty thousand dollars now for food and clothes. "The lazy rascals! They steal all of my hogs and, I have to buy meat for them. They will not make cotton. If they don't choose to make cotton—spin it and weave it—they may go naked for me. Yes, naked as they went in Africa. There are plenty of sheep. Let them shear sheep and spin that too." (261)

What goes without comment, here, is the fact that generations of Chesnut masters have been appropriating the labor of generations of Chesnut slaves. Also obscured in the accounting are the hundreds of thousands, if not millions, of expropriated dollars this long history entails. In an 1880s entry for June 3, 1862, a mere six months later, James Jr. adds to the indictment:

> There was corn enough on the place for two years, they said in January. Now in June they write that it will not last until the new crop comes in. Somebody is having a good time on the plantation—if not my poor horses. (355)

Meanwhile, despite a reputation for showing a soft heart toward his slaves,[14] John Chesnut Jr. (Johnny) resents his bondspeople for what he calls "feathering their nests . . . at my expense" (November 5, 1863, 486). His remark suggests

Seeds: Fruits and Famine 87

not only that he suspects graft among his slaves but also that this dishonesty reduces them to the level of grasping creatures. A connection obtains between this "missing" corn and both the Chesnut men's distorted identifications of their chattel as parasites.

This moment in the history of black-white Chesnut relations is the second act of a three-part sociological production imagined as "the drama of the corn." In act 1, which begins in the late-eighteenth century, Chesnut masters have appropriated grain grown by Chesnut slaves, allotting them provisions from the crop that constitute only a small percentage of what could be sold for profit. In the second act of the ongoing performance, circa 1864–65, slaves on Mulberry have "reclaimed" the corn, expropriated (or, from the Chesnut masters' point of view, stolen) for their own use a certain amount of the crop. The denouement, act 3, is orchestrated by the vicissitudes of a decimated wartime food supply rather than any human agent of retribution. In a reworked entry for early spring of 1865, Chesnut writes:

> Columbia is but dust and ashes—burned to the ground. Men, women, and children left there, houseless, homeless, without one particle of food,—picking up the corn left by Sherman's horses in their picket ground and parching [it] to stay their hunger. (March 6, 1865, 744)

In a passage for several days later, the writer adds, "In Columbia, the munificent Childs tells me, our friends are following horses to pick up grains to parch" (755).

In keeping with the Dantesque logic Chesnut discovers in events and develops in her 1880s narrative, the connection between James' and Johnny's allegations that slaves have "stolen" Mulberry and Hermitage grain offers a final twist to the corn-related tale. Chesnut reports that her once privileged, white planter friends in Columbia have been reduced to a state of abjection: the threat of starvation has forced entire families to trail after departing Federal horses in order to recover leavings of corn, which, if roasted, convert animal provender into human fare. If institutional slavery has figured African Americans as parasites, and Johnny imagines his bondspeople as rapacious birds, the war has overturned the ideological reversal that supported such attributions. By 1865, quite literally, it is the former master class itself that has devolved into human scavengers.

These shifts of fortune bring to mind the analogy of another epic downfall. In his wanderings post-Troy, Homer's Odysseus has fallen from the heights of king to the depths of beggar; and when he lands on Ithaca and is found by

Emaeus, the goatherd does not recognize his former monarch. The gods have wrought this downward metamorphosis to teach the hero something about the fragility of status and the meaning of endurance. Chesnut's unfinished epic charts similar assaults on its heroine's social order, which the planter elite not only had believed was immutable, but nearly understood as divinely ordained. But with the drama of the corn, Chesnut embeds in her 1880s narrative a further lesson: she shows not only how the fortunes of war have reordered the Southern chain of being, but also that to confuse the maintenance of rank with the value of survival is to miss the central point that, by the time of the 1880s reworkings, the war has come to teach her.

Fantastic Food

To leave the epic for the quotidian, while two of Chesnut's Columbia friends have reported grubbing after fodder to parch into food, three other women send letters featuring more imaginative, if less sustaining, strategies for contending with diminished provisions. Chesnut, following the trail of her husband, has left Columbia and is retreating through North Carolina when she receives these communiqués; her goal is to avoid conjunction with Sherman's army as it plunders its way across rural South Carolina. It is the spring of 1865, less than a month before Lee's surrender at Appomattox.

Starvation for those in Columbia, now a potential reality, has been on the minds of Chesnut's Richmond cohort for the past two years. In an 1880s passage for December 2, 1863, Chesnut notes, "And now I am in fine condition for Hetty Cary's starvation party, where they will give thirty dollars for the music and not a cent for a morsel to eat" (497). In this earlier moment, going without refreshment functions as a humorous conceit by which Southern aristocrats play at sacrifice with no cost to their well-being. Only fifteen months later, Jack Middleton writes to Chesnut from Richmond: "The wolf is at the door here. We dread starvation more than we do Grant or Sherman. Famine—that is the word now" (March 8, 1865, 747).

By early winter of 1865, daily life for even the elites of Columbia has become a struggle for survival: there is no longer access to basic foodstuffs—flour, sugar, meat, coffee—all of which, when available, command exorbitant prices.[15] Chesnut hopes to carry away from Columbia several boxes of provisions ordered from Mulberry; but sensing the difficulty, if not the danger, of his wife's traveling so encumbered, General Chesnut cancels the requisition, and Mary Chesnut is left in precarious circumstances. Arriving in Lincolnton,

North Carolina, she befriends a Mrs. Glover, who is as preoccupied with hunger as Chesnut's Columbia friends. In the 1880s entry for March 8, 1865, the writer reports:

> Mrs. Glover, to prove to us that plenty had reigned here in peaceful times, described an "infair" she had attended here in the early years of the war. An "infair" means a table standing for days, against all comers. At this one they began to dine at two o'clock in the day and dined on continuously. As soon as one relay was glutted (forgive the vulgar phrase), another came, table — or tables — constantly replenished.
>
> There were two tables in separate rooms — one for beef, bacon, turkey, fowls, all meats, and vegetables, the other for sweets.... Mrs. Glover heard ravenous soldiers aver with delight that they had dined three times that day. And the last dinner was as good as the first. I record this because I have never known of an infair before. Perhaps you may be as ignorant. (751)

Suffering deprivation from a sharply diminished supply of food, along with her fellow Lincolnton residents, women like Mrs. Glover find that describing remarkable meals from the early years of the war constitutes a restorative diversion; such word of mouth accounts stand in lieu of consuming abundant fare with the very friends and companions who constitute the audience for such gastronomically themed conversations.

This phenomenon constituted a nineteenth-century version of what women who read gourmet magazines while undergoing weight loss regimes have called "dieter's pornography." A less anachronistic term for Mrs. Glover's practice might be something like culinary sensationalism: in times when food is scarce, speakers substitute narrative for gustatory pleasures by recounting feasts and fetes from fiction or former experience.[16] Reciting recipes aloud would seem to offer the most easily available form of such oral indulgence. In the 1880s book, Chesnut quotes a choice morsel from a letter penned by her friend Miss Middleton, who also has fled Columbia: "We keep a cookery book on the mantelpiece, and when our dinner is deficient we just read a pudding or a crème. It does not entirely satisfy the appetite, this dessert in imagination, but perhaps it is as good for the digestion" (778).

The 1880s writer well understood the power of such displacements, and the following example might stand in miniature for what she attempted to achieve in the larger narrative. Here, her own epistolary catalogue of the delectable foods "donated" by her new friends in Chester, South Carolina, is regurgitated, so to speak, in a letter replying to her own. Mrs. Munro, who has played the role of fairy godmother to the dispossessed, refugee Chesnut only a month earlier, reprises in her note to Chesnut the very menu that Chesnut has translated from actual meal to narrative representation. Mrs. Munro writes:

> The description you give of your present style of living—the wonderful donations you receive—have so astonished us here we fear that your fever has returned and that it [is] all the ravings of delirium. And these feasts are visions, merely wild phantasmagoria—bowls of white sugar, hams baked in biscuit dough, trays of innumerable delicacies! I can't bear to think of it! The other parts of your letter showing no trace of a "mind diseased"—I must relinquish my theory. (April 4, 1865, 780)

In the first movement of this culinary twice-told tale, Chesnut recounts how her newfound friends have bestowed dishes that echo the glory days of Southern cooking: sugar abounding (most likely grown by Louisiana bondspeople) and hams (from hogs grown, slaughtered, and cured by slaves like those on Mulberry) wrapped in pastry (one of her slave Molly's greatest specialties). Communicating her delight at these delicacies, Chesnut provides her famished friends with narrative grist for the mill; in turn, they echo back the glories of her marvelous refugee repasts. Like the entire 1880s narrative itself, the menu in miniature from the week before Lee's surrender reprises for posterity the ephemeral pleasures found as well as difficult struggles faced in Chesnut's Civil War experiences.

The Gift of Seeds

War has enabled the unexpected circulation of food among former Southern elites, not only as gastronomic narratives that enrich the imagination, but also as culinary offerings that nourish the flesh. In the 1880s narrative, edible bequests become the subject of Chesnut's most vivid catalogues; she records having received both delectable fruits and vegetables (early in the war) and also substantial main course dishes (in the winter of 1864–65) in Richmond, Columbia, Lincolnton, and Chester. The gratitude she expresses over the simple fruits sent by concerned friends during the early years of the hostilities is one of the more striking features of these pages. In spring of 1865, devoid of all resources, Chesnut and her maid Ellen survive the final month of the war solely by the grace of near strangers, who tender them staples at the most dire of moments: gifts of bread, biscuits, chicken, and spareribs constitute the deus ex machina of Chesnut's unfinished epic.

But most significant is Chesnut's focus on stoned and seeded fruits: in the first half of her narrative, peaches (102, 418–19), tomatoes (134, 153), apricots

(344, 369, 393), cherries (451), blackberries (464), and watermelon (466). Such fruits seem to be the only foodstuffs that tempt the invalid's jaded palette during the earliest epoch of the Confederacy, 1861–62. Chesnut is no vegetarian; nor does she ever report being abstemious when it comes to gustatory pleasures involving meat and seafood. In an 1880s entry for December 3 of 1863, she describes attending a party on a French frigate with assorted Richmond belles such as Mrs. Randolph and Mary Lee, the general's eldest daughter, both of whom she eats under the table:

> Captain Owen said with a sigh: "How Confederate women pitch into a good dinner. Where have I been? I saw them eat the last oyster." And I retired in dismay. (497)

Self-consciously appearing as the Rebel woman who devoured "the last oyster," Chesnut expresses a tongue-in-cheek shame. Nowhere in her narrative is she anything less than candid about her own robust tastes; across the remainder of her account, Chesnut depicts herself avidly consuming assorted fowls—pheasants, turkeys, chickens—as well fried oysters (Molly's other specialty) and both mock turtle and "soup a la Reine" which, she notes in an entry for January 24, 1862, "had everything nice in the world in it" (285).

Apropos of Chesnut's own account of her enthusiastic appetites, it remains perplexing that, in the early months of the conflict, she partakes of almost nothing beyond rice and milk prepared by the slave Laurence, a menu varied only by gifts of stoned and seeded fruits. Medical thinking of the period affords one set of answers, but the symbolic dimensions of this diet reveal the ultimate insights into Chesnut's imaginative investments for her unfinished epic.

Remember, first, that the writer has called the chronic stomach affliction from which she suffers "gastric fever," identified, as we've seen, as a form of typhoid involving successive weeks of high temperature, diarrhea, muscular debility, and prostration. Dr. Nathaniel Chapman, a leading physician in Philadelphia, wrote what is considered the definitive early-nineteenth-century paper on one of gastric fever's major symptoms, "Remarks on the Chronic Fluxes of the Bowels." In the 1880s narrative, Chesnut reports following a course of therapy very like the one Chapman outlines in the essay: she takes calomel, and "[Dover's] blue pills . . . given in minute doses with opium" (March 12, 1865, 762).[17] Chapman also recommends "the blandest nutriment, thus making it harmonize with the other parts of the treatment," "farinaceous matters" including "arrowroot, rice, and flour." In a final paragraph concerning suggested diets for sufferers of flux, he writes: "Fruit I have sometimes known to be appropriate, particularly peaches. The dew or blackberry has a large share of popular confidence in this respect. . . . These, and I may add oranges, habitually and almost exclusively used, have cured the disease."[18]

Highly fibrous fruits are precisely what sufferers of "flux" are today counseled to avoid. Accordingly, the remedies Chesnut describes in the 1880s narrative seem confounding, if not bizarre. But, in fact, they constitute standard best practice for combating diarrhea, according to mid-nineteenth-century medical thinking. Thus, in an entry for May 23, 1862, Chesnut tells us, "Anna Coffin—now Mrs. Guignard—sent me delicious arrowroot and apricots" (344). And for July 16, 1861, "A quiet moment—a knock—only a delicious basket of peaches. My misery took the form of no appetite at breakfast. It failed to quench my taste for peaches, so I enjoyed them thoroughly" (102).

In *The Confederate Housewife,* a twentieth-century compilation of recipes and remedies culled from Civil War–era newspapers and almanacs, editor John Hammond Moore presents the following advice, which appeared in the *Edgefield Adviser,* a South Carolina weekly, on September 25, 1861, under the headline "The Prevailing Disease":

> The following are said to be the most effectual remedies for the cure of diarrhea: 1. Rice, toasted till black, then to be cooked with milk or water, seasoned with salt or sugar and nutmeg, and eaten one teacup full at a time.[19]

And from no more proximate a paper than Chesnut's own local *Camden Confederate,* Moore includes the "Cure for Diarrhea," dated August 2, 1863:

> According to the *Rome (Georgia) Courier,* it seems not to be generally known that the free use of ripe peaches is a prompt and certain cure for diarrhea. This writer has known cases of several months standing, which had resisted all ordinary remedies, to yield in a few days under unrestrained use of this fruit. At this season, when the disease and the remedy are both so common, the knowledge of this fact, for the truth of which the writer vouches, may save much suffering. If hospital patients suffering from diarrhea were treated freely with ripe peaches, instead of opium, the result would be greatly to the advantage of all concerned.[20]

The power of peaches, it would seem, extends beyond the profound physiological pleasure they afford. In the mid-nineteenth century, Southerners were convinced that peaches cured the flux.

Whatever historians of medicine make of this oddity, scholars of Western painting agree that peaches carry a symbolic import that extends back to biblical representations of the ancient Near East. In medieval and gothic genre paintings of the Madonna in her enclosed garden, Netherlandish artists such as Jan van Eyck frequently include bowls of peaches or represent the fruit dangling from trees adjacent to Christ's pregnant mother. While the walled garden figures her chastity, art historians have interpreted Marian peach iconography as signifying the Virgin's essential qualities of faithfulness and fidelity.[21]

In contrast to her relish for the peaches offered by friends, the writer routinely rejects as "horrid" and "horrible" the boardinghouse dinners and suppers served at Montgomery Hall in Alabama, the Spotswood Hotel in Richmond, and the Congaree House in Columbia, all of which housed and fed the peripatetic members of the Confederate cabinet and their families. The 1880s Chesnut never details precisely what dishes in any of these establishments caused her such profound revulsion; she saves her creative powers to lavish on descriptions of the Prestons' French cuisine. The "horrid" meals, however, may have featured some version of Civil War–era "mystery meat," that ubiquitous staple of public resorts and hostelries from time immemorial. In this context, it is not surprising that fresh, local produce, suggestive of spring renewal and the return of young life, should supplant the heavy, greasy, and squalid offerings of wartime cooking on a massive scale, particularly for a woman suffering from chronic gastric distress.

Chesnut seems to have embarked on a specific regime (whether medically or self-prescribed) of seeded and stoned fruits to combat illness in 1861. Apparently, apricots, cousins of peaches, served according to the recipe used by the Prestons' cook (smashed, sugared, and dressed with fresh cream) also gave her great pleasure. A particularly intriguing moment occurs in the 1880s narrative when Chesnut records her ecstasy over Wilmot DeSaussure's tomato salad in two entries for 1861. For August 8, she reports: "Wilmot DeSaussure makes an admirable salad dressing for our tomatoes, and I am so hot, so tired, so feverish I care for nothing else" (134). Then, for August 18, she adds: "The heat and the excitement—and a sort of slow fever that subdues me quite and takes away all appetite, leaving me to live on tomatoes alone—and Wilmot DeSaussure's salad dressing" (153). While it may strike readers as strange that a male friend should concoct this particular delicacy, culinary historian Susan Williams explains that salad, "one of the most pervasive French influences during the early nineteenth century," surprisingly "was dressed usually by the gentlemen, not the ladies. The gentleman was to 'mix up the dressing on a separate plate, and then add it to the lettuce, and offer it around as he chose.'"[22]

A medical explanation for the otherwise mysterious therapeutic powers of tomatoes appears in another local newspaper cited in Moore's *The Confederate Housewife:* apparently like peaches, fruity tomatoes, Southerners believed, could heal flux of the bowels. In the case of the tomato cure, Chesnut obviously is not a teething child, though her weakened condition certainly saps her of all adult energies. Accordingly, the *Southern Federal Union* for August 18, 1861, reports under the headline "Tomatoes for Children":

> There is no better remedy for the derangement of the bowels in children while teething than stewed tomatoes, fed to them plentifully, care being taken to keep the child's extremities warm.... The tomato ought to be ripe and fresh.[23]

Clearly, there is something about the magic of tomatoes, recognized across the bellum-era South, that makes the ailing Chesnut's body sing with relief and delight.[24]

The fruit Chesnut reports receiving during the early years of the conflict marks the first wave of a new form of food circulation; the peaches and grapes she offers to hospitalized soldiers in Richmond inaugurate a second such movement; and the third and most radical phase is set into motion when bread and meat become scarce, in the latter months of 1864. To measure the extent to which conditions have deteriorated, contrast the heretofore unimaginable lack of the so-called staff of life with an extraordinarily comic bread-related episode the 1880s author records for sometime around April 23, 1861. Colonel Robert Anderson, U.S. commander at Fort Sumter, is firing at Confederate ships near Fort Moultrie in Charleston harbor:

> They had cotton-bag bombproofs at Fort Moultrie, and when Anderson's shot knocked them about, someone called out, "Cotton is falling." Down went the kitchen chimney, and loaves of bread flew out. They cheered gaily, "Breadstuffs are rising." (51)

Against this moment's absurdity (and what later would be seen as the unfortunate destruction of precious provisions), in which for the first time, a food supply is affected by the vicissitudes of war, it seems nearly unbelievable that Columbians could be desperate for bread only three years later.

But the story of Mrs. Benjamin Huger Rutledge provides a cautionary tale:

> Then household difficulties were the topic. "If I had been taught to make bread!" Here Mrs. Middleton [Mrs. Rutledge's mother] came in. "You are not looking—dear, anything the matter?"

> "But mamma, I have not eaten one mouthful today! The children can eat mush—but I can't...."
>
> She does not understand taking favors and, blushing violently, refused to let Ellen make her some biscuits. I went home and sent her the biscuits, all the same. And they were nice ones. A few minutes later, a negro woman came in who absolutely bakes bread. She brought not a half bad loaf in her basket. When she found out how delighted I was, she went for more, and I sent her with three good fresh well-baked loaves of bread to Mrs. Rutledge. I almost felt we had saved her life. (February 19, 1865, 723)

Culinary scholar Karen Hess has noted that while slaves directed all the cooking on plantations, baking constituted the one aspect of food production conventionally supervised by white mistresses.[25] Thus it is that the 1880s Chesnut makes such a to-do about Mrs. Rutledge's particular kitchen ignorance, which derives, it would seem, from improper maternal training. And Mrs. Middleton's obliviousness to her daughter's hunger, as well as to Mrs. Rutledge's lack of vital skills, seems to confirm Chesnut's indictment.

Any potential superiority the writer might have felt in the context of offering such undesired aid comes full circle for Chesnut only three weeks afterward:

> Ellen said I had a little piece of bread and a little molasses today for my dinner—and then Mrs. M sent to ask me to dine with her today. Providential! (March 5, 1865, 747)

Only hours later, she reaches the bottom of the barrel, as her entry one day later reveals: "Today—a godsend. For even the small piece of bread and the molasses were a thing of the past. My larder was empty." Suddenly appearing with a tray covered by a "huge white serviette," and bearing "fowls ready for roasting, sausages, butter, bread, eggs, preserves," the mulatto maid of an unknown benefactress named Mrs. McDonald plays the role of deus ex machina.[26] Though Chesnut's slave Ellen insists that her mistress restrain overzealous expressions of gratitude, the writer quotes her dry comment once Mrs. McDonald's bondswoman has exited: "F'all that—its well enough—for we was at our last mouthful" (March 6, 1865, 748).

That chicken, turkey, wild ducks, partridges, and other assorted domestic and wild birds should have constituted vital bequests to Chesnut, particularly in the last twelve months of the war, is in keeping with a poultry motif she has employed throughout her narrative. Two important anecdotes, one from very early in the first year of the conflict, and the other from the early spring of

1864, foreshadow what are, the 1880s matron implies, the redemptive qualities of chickens and cows in a disintegrating world.

The first story comes from an entry Chesnut provides for July 19, 1861, just prior to First Manassas. While driving in a carriage through Richmond, Mary Chesnut, Mrs. Preston, and Mrs. Stanard spot an elegant-looking military man, sitting "his horse gracefully." Mrs. Stanard recognizes the rider as the great Robert E. Lee, but Chesnut has never before seen the general. Ever gallant, the "unnamed" solider joins the ladies and shares a few gracious pleasantries, including a pastoral rumination in response to Mrs. Stanard's flirtatious accusations about his ambition. On the contrary, he demurs, his only desire is to possess "a Virginia farm—no end of cream and fresh butter—and fried chicken. Not one fried chicken or two—but unlimited fried chicken" (116). Chesnut elsewhere mentions several occasions on which her husband and President Davis have met to strategize with General Lee, and she has reported his warm nod at her from his pew at St. Paul's Episcopal Church in Richmond, where the Chesnuts worship with the Davises. But otherwise, Lee is a shadowy figure in the 1880s narrative, and it seems significant that Chesnut's portrait of him in their only face-to-face encounter concerns, not the looming war or his expectations of military glory, but his longing for unlimited access to the bounties of the South.

The second anecdote contrasts Lee's pastoral daydream—about which the writer would seem to be dubious—with beloved nephew Johnny Chesnut's quite practical postwar planning. In an 1880s entry for February 5, 1864, Chesnut reports:

> Johnny has no unreasonable estimate of his own merits. He says if he should chance to be ruined after the war, he means to establish a chicken farm—that when he was a boy he succeeded wonderfully with his own chickens in his mother's yard. (558)

Johnny will not survive long enough after the end of the war to launch himself successfully in farmerly fashion; his efforts to restore Mulberry's fields with David Williams, husband to Mary's sister Kate and also a grandson of the old Colonel, fail dismally; then, in 1868, Johnny unexpectedly dies of causes neither documented in any archive nor recalled through the oral tradition of the Williams family.

Nevertheless, it is no accident that after the war his devoted Aunt Mary takes up precisely his wished-for line of work in the ravages of South Carolina. In accord with the heroic sentiments expressed in the unpublished 1860s

Seeds: Fruits and Famine

diary—her staunch claiming of "Victory or Westminster Abbey"—raising chickens in the mode of both Lee's whimsy and Johnny's ambition takes on an entirely new resonance for her soldierly identifications. Poultry and dairy labor no longer are the exclusive provenance of slaves working provision grounds or poor whites undertaking scratch farming; nor is such toil relegated to the charmingly bucolic vocation of the fictional dairymaid heroine of the Rebel elite's favorite comic opera, *Bombastes Furioso*. Instead, this very rustic work enables the survival and endurance of Chesnut and her extended white family and the black freedmen remaining on Mulberry for nearly twenty years after Yankee destruction and the poverty guaranteed by defeat.

Considering this rural symbolism the other way round, if Chesnut is not the farmer of the scenario, but the chicken or the cow, she has neither produced viable eggs nor given milk. But this does not preclude her from the dairy (or the diary) business: metaphorically, the creative labor that is her writing, and materially, the butter-and-egg venture that she and Molly begin as early as 1862. In an 1880s entry for January 24 of that year, she reports that Molly brings her "butter and chicken money. We run the business on shares" (285). And in an additional reworked passage for two and a half years later, she notes, "And I sell my eggs and butter from home for two hundred dollars a month . . . in Confederate money . . . Helas!" (September 19, 1864, 643).

Most extraordinary of all, archival material from the postwar decades documents that Molly, obviously a freedwoman by the end of the war, remained Mary Boykin Chesnut's partner in the dairy business for at least six years after Southern surrender. In a small paperback daybook, which the aging matron used to record her now-meager accounts, she indicates payment of three dollars in wages for Molly, for February 1871. This may not seem significant until the final income for that month, from all such sales of butter, eggs, and milk is calculated, totaling twelve dollars. With this tiny sum, Chesnut is supporting herself, her husband, her sister Kate's "borrowed" child David, her aged mother, as well as paying assorted black laborers. Despite the reality that the writer has multiple mouths to feed, Molly remains a one-quarter partner in the "family" enterprise, suggesting that her relationship with the aging Chesnut is as substantial and as productive postslavery as it was during the war, despite her then-chattel status.

In a letter written seven months after the deaths of her husband and her mother, in what would prove to be the last year of her own life, Chesnut speaks of attachments that poignantly link the themes of fertility and fruit, and that bring this discussion full circle. She has moved to Sarsfield, the home James built for her from bricks fired at Mulberry. In the absence of children and

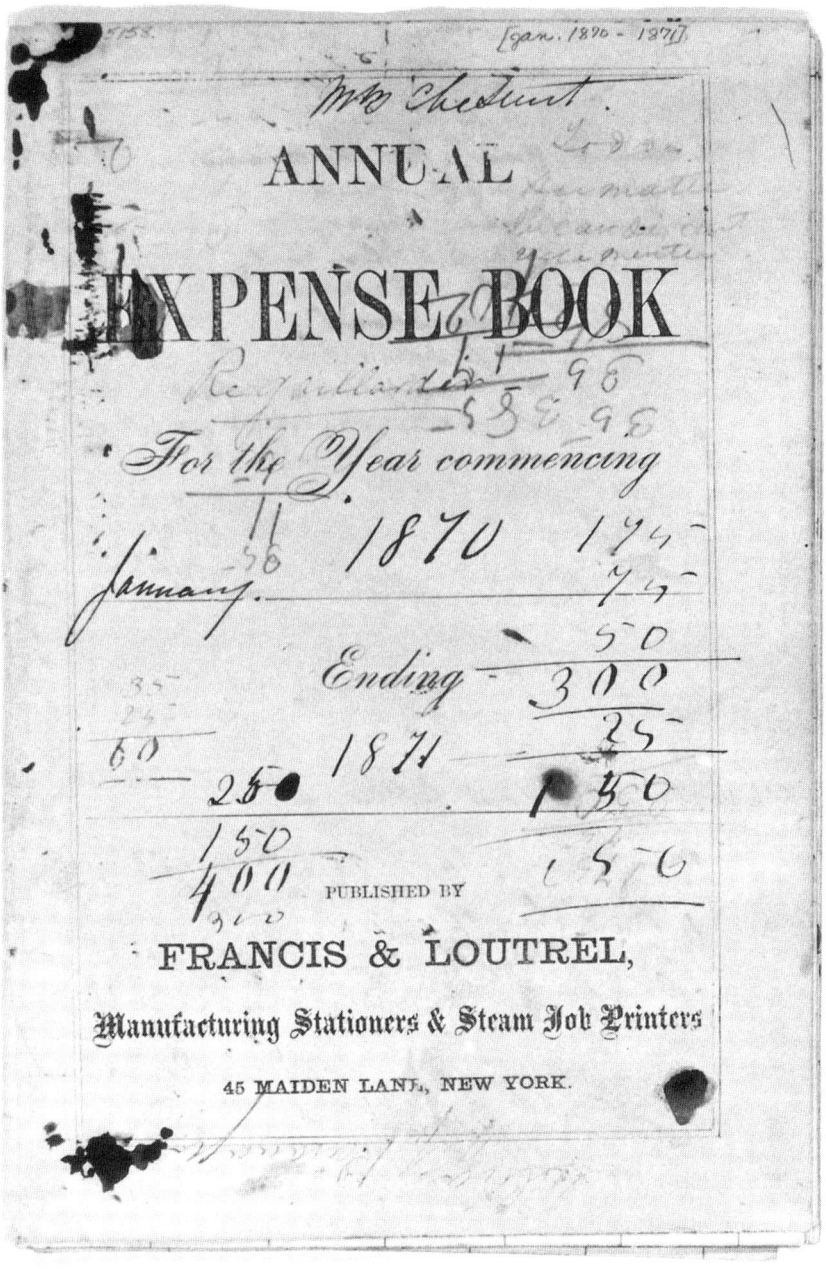

FIGURE 5. Mary Chesnut, "Annual Expense Book" (cover page, 1870–71). Courtesy of the South Caroliniana Library, University of South Carolina, Columbia.

Days.	Labor or Services.	Physician and Medicines.	Railroad Fare or Riding Exp's.	Charities.	Contingent Expenses.	Amount of Cash Received.
1					brought over	26 40
2						
3					Butter	1 00
4					Mutton	1 50
5					Came back to Mulberry.	
6						
7					Butter	2 00
8						
9						
10					Butter	1 00
11						
12					Butter	40
13						
14					Mutton	1 35
15						
16						
17					Butter	1 00
18						
19					Butter	75
20					Moses - 4 pounds meat	1 00
21						
22						
23						
24					Butter	1 00
25					Mutton	1 50
26						
27						
28					Butter & eggs	1 75
29						
30						
31						13 75
Total						

FIGURE 6. Mary Chesnut, "Annual Expense Book" (entry, February 1870). Chesnut's daybook entry reveals that her dairy business continued to operate well after the Confederate defeat. Courtesy of the South Caroliniana Library, University of South Carolina, Columbia.

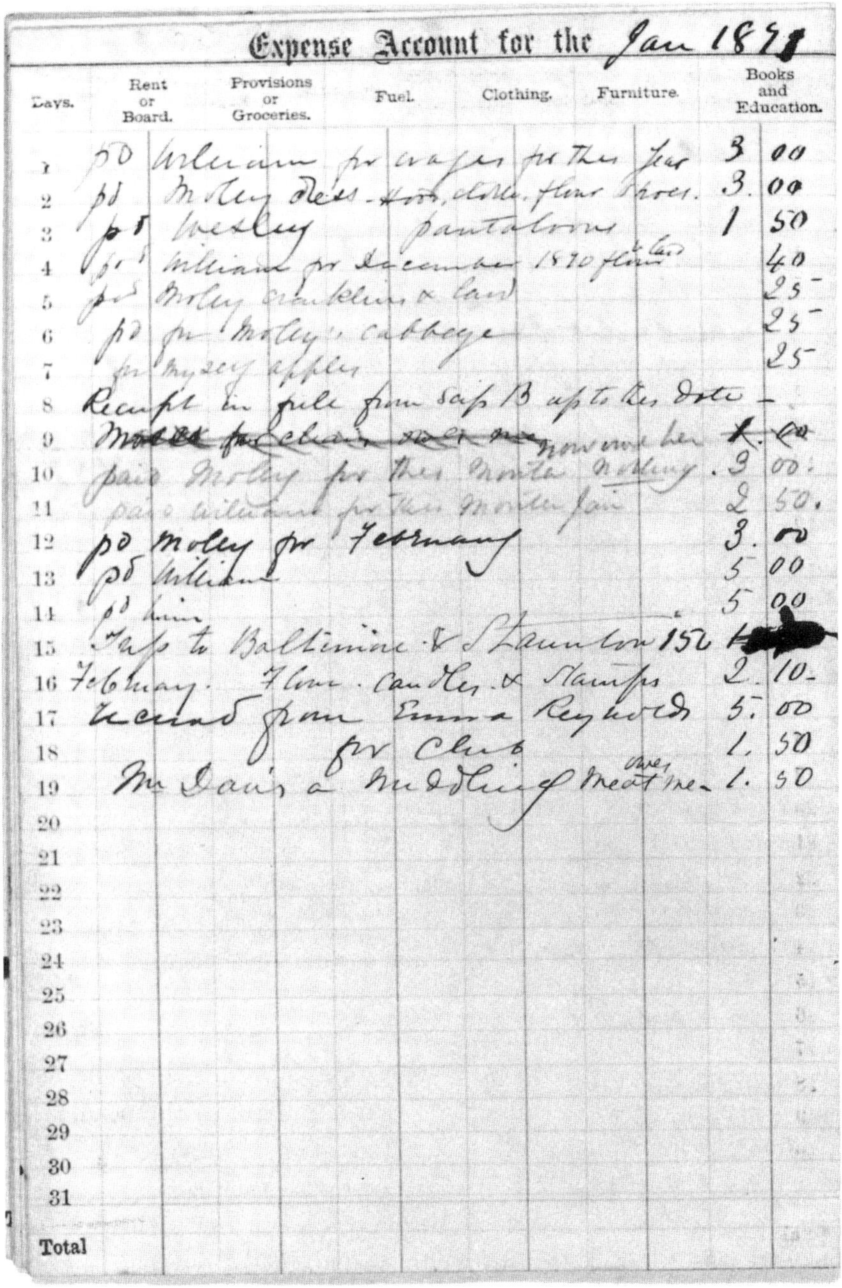

Days.	Rent or Board.	Provisions or Groceries.	Fuel.	Clothing.	Furniture.	Books and Education.
					Expense Account for the Jan 1871	

[Handwritten expense entries, partially legible:]

1. pd William for wages for this year — 3.00
2. pd Molly dress, hood, socks, flour, shoes — 3.00
3. pd Wesley pantaloons — 1.50
4. pd William for December 1870 flour — .40
5. pd Molly cracklins & lard — .25
6. pd for Molly's cabbage — .25
7. for Molly apples — .25
8. Receipt in full from Sep 13 up to this date —
9. Molly for [illegible] now owe her 4.00
10. paid Molly for this month [illegible] .9.00
11. paid William for this month Jan 2.50
12. pd Molly for February 3.00
13. pd William 5.00
14. pd him 5.00
15. Fare to Baltimore & Staunton 15 [illegible]
16. February — Flour, Candles & Stamps 2.10
17. Received from Emma Reynolds 5.00
18. for Club 1.50
19. Mr Davis a middling meat [over] me 1.50

FIGURE 7. Mary Chesnut, "Annual Expense Book" (entry, January 1871). Another entry from Chesnut's daybook shows that the maid Molly was still collaborating with her former mistress six years after emancipation. Molly's monthly income represents one-fourth the sum that would be brought in for February. Courtesy of the South Caroliniana Library, University of South Carolina, Columbia.

grandchildren, the writer nurtures her beloved livestock, which, in her imagination, have taken on a familial aura. Thus it is that Chesnut writes to Jane Pettigrew Williams, the wife of her nephew Miller:

> Do get Miller to send me the certificate of Serenola's register. . . . Also—a calf was dropped by Olly on the 14th of July and I want her registered too—as it adds to the value of this herd to be registered. Serenola is a perfect beauty. Rex died after a few days of fever—he was very fat—& had grown tremendously altogether pronounced the handsomest animal ever seen—Peter—Moses—and myself did all we could to save him. Now Olly's calf—being the last of Rex's progeny—(may be) I want this calf—of the 14th of July—named—Renee—Do I make it plain—Renee.
>
> Virginia Dare has fever & is very ill in point of fact she is under the oak tree [by] my back door—I dare say she will die too. About these animals not being insured—I blame myself hard and heavy. When I found it was not done for me as I begged so to have it—I ought to have taken matters in my own hands and written to friends in Columbia or Baltimore & had it done—. (August 16, 1885)[27]

Chesnut's description of Serenola's pedigree reprises, if in a reduced register, the writer's comments in the 1880s narrative about various first families of Virginia and South Carolina. In describing the marriages made between children of these elites during the war years and later, she rarely fails to comment on the merging of blue bloodlines. In her intimate correspondence at this moment two decades postbellum, however, it is distinguished bovine lineage, translating into the stock's elevated economic worth, that has become vital for the beset and struggling Chesnut; any notion of social preeminence has become irrelevant to her 1880s life.

Meanwhile, were the reader of Chesnut's lamentable words about Rex unaware that the regal name referred to the matron's prized bull, he or she might almost imagine that Chesnut is describing the demise of an old friend, for in addition to being deprived of her bull's financial value, the writer also suffers a stinging emotional loss. Waxing lyrical in the subsequent sentence about the animal's beauty, Chesnut mourns the passing of what now sounds like a favored child, cut off in the flower of early adulthood, rather than the well-fed member of a pedigreed herd. One could say that Chesnut's dashed hopes for children of her own have in a sense been projected onto her desire for healthy offspring from her dairy herd, but there too, her dreams do not always bear fruit.

Chesnut has come to believe, in the late summer of this last year, that Rex died not of fever, but from poison, the victim of neighbors frustrated by the animal's aggressive behavior toward cows on their property. This act of veterinary terrorism implies that formerly wealthy whites had started to turn on one another in acts of sabotage once associated with slave resistance.[28] Nevertheless, at the time of the writer's death in November of 1886, at least two of Rex's recent progeny still flourished on the forty acres adjacent to Chesnut's last and treasured home. Happily for the writer's notion of immortality, her remaining cows ultimately outlived her, which meant that nephew David R. Williams III, her sister Kate's youngest surviving son, could inherit them along with Sarsfield.[29]

Confectionary Coda

During several moments in the 1880s narrative, Chesnut is focused neither on agricultural endeavors, as she will be in the final years of her life, nor on biological sustenance, which clearly becomes an issue during her refugee days in winter 1865, but on pure gustatory pleasure. The writer reports several episodes of hot cocoa and taffy making during the war with visiting children, such as Kate's offspring, and the young ladies and gentlemen orbiting Buck Preston and her sisters, Chesnut's protégées in Richmond and Columbia. Pastry and candy making play the starring role here; far from fulfilling basic nutritional requirements, both cakes and confections constitute what I think of as a culture's felicitous culinary excess.

Macaroons, moonshines, and stickies, the three sweetmeats about which Chesnut writes at some length, are based primarily on sugar, *the* ingredient associated with slave labor in the Deep South: macaroons, concocted of sugar, egg whites, and almonds; "moonshines," meringue-like candies made from sugar and egg whites; and "stickies," taffy-esque cookies made of molasses or sugar, butter, eggs, and flour.[30] All three tempt the writer's appetite, though to various effect on her mood. The emotion-filled response to these confections the 1880s Chesnut records tells a revealing story about her notions concerning slavery, freedom, and the potential for coexistence across the color line after 1865.

The matron's encounter with macaroons involves overindulgence and its unfortunate consequences. In an 1880s entry for November 20, 1861, the narrated self of the 1860s shares the following confession of a venial transgression and its own automatic punishment: "All this war talk (or «from eating» macaroons unlimited)—nearly died of fright and horror in the night. «Waked J.C. screaming.» Nightmare in its worst shape" (*TPMC,* 206; *MCCW,* 241). Chesnut's late-night binge has been provoked by having heard her uncle Alexander

Hamilton Boykin regaling listeners with his experiences from First Manassas, where Colonel Boykin apparently took as prisoners Yankee soldiers hiding in an empty well.

The images of self-induced white captivity and "liberation" into a second state of nonfreedom affords no aid to a lady's slumber. In the wake of this horrific tale, the matron attempts to medicate her distress and anxiety with "unlimited" almond cakes. What results from Chesnut's intemperate pastry cure is the most traumatically disturbed sleep she reports enduring throughout the entire war. Fueled by an overdose of sugar, egg whites, and almonds, themselves products of slave agricultural labor—cane field plantation work; provision-ground poultry culture, and nut gathering—the 1860s persona cannot digest what she has ingested, both the distressing story about the taking of white prisoners and the edible fruit of enslaved black toil.[31]

The writer's ebullient account of the "moonshine and stickies" received during the depths of her refugee fortunes in Lincolnton offers a different kind of allegory: if macaroons, like black bondage, give the slavery-hating Chesnut nightmares, the white and brown candies foretell a future after emancipation that is both palatable and enduring. In the 1880s narrative for March 12, 1865, she records:

> Moonshine is a sort of paste—light and fairylike, white as snow, twisted and twining, shining, intangible, mystic, wonderful—crumbles under one's fingers when touched—a sort of magical "marvelles," and yet delicious. (763)

This is the 1880s writer's confectionary paean to whiteness, in all its fragility and ethereality. Indeed, like Southern white supremacy in the spring of 1865, "moonshines" are just that—offering "illumination" or pleasure that proves fleeting—and vulnerable to dissolution at the touch. Accordingly, Chesnut knows (both in the 1880s, but also even in 1865) that her erstwhile aristocratic culture is en route to extinction: first, under the weight of impending Northern victory, and soon after, under the economic ravages of Reconstruction.

Chesnut's description of "stickies" presents a very different picture: "Stickies are, as their names denote, cakes which are viscous with sugar—maybe molasses" (763). Unlike the pale sweetener used to make moonshines, the form of sucrose employed in stickies is of both uncertain origin and indeterminate coloration; the cakes either may be flavored with (white) sugar or (brown) molasses, or a combination of both. Substantial and adhesive, these delicacies signify a very different vision of the Southern future from that figured by moonshines: concocted of unidentifiable or even mixed component hues, stickies are long-lasting and tenacious. Like the disparate combinations of defeated white and newly free people of color whose qualities they suggest, Southern "stickies" cannot be brushed, flung, or shaken off, but remain solidly on the cultural menu. They are an essential ingredient in a nascent, yet to be developed Southern concoction, the ultimate taste and texture of which, at the time of Chesnut's 1880s reworkings, has not yet solidified enough to hold its new shape.

CHAPTER FIVE

Words

READING AND WRITING

Wartime provisions as elemental as peaches and as confected as "moonshines" all played a role in Chesnut's catalogue of the food ways of the Confederate elite. Beyond affording documentary detail of an aspect of bellum social history rarely included in the works of her memoir-writing contemporaries, food for the writer of the 1880s almost always bore social and political meaning. But Chesnut's compendium of convivial meals and edible gifts consumed over four years of strife constituted just one of several of the lists that contributed to the epic significance of the reworked 1880s narrative. Another of the writer's encyclopedic inventories can be summarized under the heading "words." In her 1880s narrative, Chesnut explored assorted practices of reading and writing, which for her transcended their basic, communicative function: witness her reaction to the pretensions of Southern "literary" ladies; her incredulity over misspelled Yankee letters found in deserted Federal army camps; and her responses to various English, French, and occasionally, American novels of the midcentury and bellum periods. In addition to judging contemporary and classical authors, the literary-minded writer meditated on the creative process itself. Such ruminations afforded access to her deeply felt beliefs about slavery's wrongs; her notion of the intractability of racial difference and class distinction; her opinions about female sexual morality (more judgmental than her mother-in-law's) and the question of spiritual sanctification; and her imperative that the artist be less like Milton and more like

Shakespeare: that she "take herself out" of her own literary creation, the better to open her imagination to the chaos, richness, and historical significance of war-torn times.

Speaking and Spelling

> In the drawing room a literary lady began a violent attack upon this mischief-making South Carolina. She told me she was a successful writer in the magazines of the day. But when I found she used "incredible" for "incredulous," I said not a word in defense of my native land. I left her "incredible." Another person came in while she was pouring upon me home truths and asked if she didn't know I was a Carolinian. Then she gracefully reversed her engine and took the other tack—sounded our praises. But I left her incredible—and I remained incredulous, too. (February 28, 1861, 11)

Early in the war, Chesnut learned that malapropisms were not, as she might have imagined, the exclusive provenance of vulgar, badly educated Yankees. In fact, the word-mangling Mrs. Malaprop of Sheridan's *The Rivals*—a play her Richmond cohort would perform in the winter of 1864—had nothing on the Southern periodical writer with whom Chesnut tangled in Alabama in the first year of the war. By vocation this figure might have been regarded as a sort of doppelganger for the narrated Chesnut, herself a scribbling woman, but in the 1880s narrative, their exchange borders on the surreal. It also prefigures by six months Chesnut's cynical conclusion that so-called literary people cultivate celebrity more than they do lyricism: "[W]riting people love notoriety" (August 27, 1861, 167).

This home-grown Malaprop has inaugurated her remarks to Chesnut with a verbal assault on the Palmetto State; apparently, she has failed to consider that the woman she's addressing could in fact be a native South Carolinian. Next, she boasts about the popularity and profitability of her magazine publications, a decidedly ungenteel remark to make to a stranger in the public rooms of a Montgomery hotel. With this unidentified author representing the distaff side of the profession of letters, it is no wonder that Chesnut's diary-keeping persona has expressed no wishes to write for publication.[1]

The lack of professional decorum and feminine modesty of this "literary lady" makes her confusion of "incredible" and "incredulous" particularly ironic and amusing. Unselfconsciously performing her own ignorance, she inadvertently enacts the meaning of her mistake: Chesnut's 1860s persona "[leaves] her incredible," as incredulous as Chesnut professes herself to be. Featuring wordplay so ludicrous that its distortions echo the opening patter of a mid-century minstrel show,[2] the anecdote constitutes one of the first satirical set pieces of the 1880s narrative, inaugurating an epic parade of genres that comes to include comedy, tragedy, farce, satire, romance, lyric, song, and epistle. It also reveals that Chesnut's 1860s persona does not take kindly to abuses of the writer's vocation: disregard for proper spelling and syntax, and flagrant misunderstanding and reckless misuse of relatively common words. Exposing the hubris of an author who seems to profit despite her absence of talent, the narrating self of the 1880s sets the stakes for her own claim to the laurel wreath.

"I am misserablle"

In an 1880s entry for Richmond, August 27, 1861, just after the Army of Northern Virginia's victory at First Manassas and its failure to pursue the Federal army to Washington, the narrating Chesnut records another astonishing misuse of language. A young Southern woman's orthographical errors in a letter of complaint prove so severe as to disqualify her, in the writer's mind, from the cultural mandate that a highborn woman must marry her social peer. The inability to communicate adequately, it would seem, is an index of significant debility in Chesnut's book:

> Today I saw a letter from a girl crossed in love. It was shown me and my advice asked. Her parents objected to the social position of her fiancé, in point of fact forbid the banns.
>
> She writes, "I am *misserablle*." Her sister she calls a "mean retch." For such a speller I said a man of any social status would do. They ought not to expect so much for her. If she wrote her "pah" a note, I am sure that such a "stern parient" would give in. I am miserable, too, today—with one *s* and one *l*. (166)

The epistle's author clearly hailed from a family elite or ambitious enough to forbid a marriage that apparently would lower the girl's social status.[3] Yet class elevation here does not correlate with educational achievement, as elsewhere in Chesnut's circle it does nearly without exception. Consider the intellectual accomplishments of the Preston daughters, who are fluent in multiple modern European languages; and of Isabella Martin, whose natural gifts and superior education win her a place among the foremost young ladies of Columbia, despite the fact that her father, a Methodist minister, is a man of little property. In the story of the girl "crossed in love," the 1880s narrator would recommend obviating the class prejudice of Southern society's upper reaches in favor of the young woman's making an egalitarian marriage of sorts: in this scenario, the groom's middling status would be equilibrated by the bride's relatively diminished abilities. The narrator's sardonic conclusion suggests that the young lady's snobbish parents take for granted the notion that she is marriageable at all. That this contretemps featuring a rebellious daughter seeking a problematic union unfolds against the background of Confederate disappointment in its army's "failure to pursue" is no coincidence. Across the totality of the work, the 1880s Chesnut brilliantly juxtaposes the political and the domestic, which mutually illuminate one another.

Compare the revelation that female education and class do not always go hand in hand with the writer's discovery that the professed preeminence of Northern free schools may be more myth than reality. In an 1880s entry for June 3, 1862, Chesnut notes:

> Comfort. Free schools are not everything. See this spelling. Yankee epistles found in camp show how illiterate they can be, with all their boasted schools. Fredericksburg is spelled "Freterxbug," medicine, "met-son," "to my sweat brother," &c&c. (358)

The lovesick girl who accuses her sister of being a "mean retch" well might have been paired with this Yankee writer's "sweat brother." In both cases, poor spelling conjures nothing more troubling than images of noisome bodily fluids (vomit and sweat). Perhaps such gibberish offers soothing "met-son" to the literary Chesnut, ever alert to regional advantage and troubled by the prospect that in cultural terms, Northern society may prove superior to her beloved South.

The example of the girl crossed in love may suggest that faulty educations are the exclusive failing of the South's female academies. But apparently, upper-class boys are equally vulnerable to the deficiencies of the schools attended by members-to-be of the Confederate ruling class. In the second year of the war, the Preston girls receive a missive from a male friend serving at the front. In an entry for June 25, 1862, Chesnut records the girls' amusement at her confusion upon reading it:

> Our girls showed me [a] letter from a gallant soldier boy—who talks well enough, too, but certainly his ideas of spelling are eccentric—"Oh, I am so glad to hear General Hampton's wound is a slit one."
> "Slit one"—what does he mean?
> "Stupid guesser that you are—a *slight* wound."
> "I was thinking the general's foot had been slit." (396)

In the case of the sister of the "mean retch," bad spelling does not obstruct semantic comprehension. But in the letter about Hampton's wound, orthographic confusion could lead to a misapprehension of the severity of the general's injury and consternation among his family and friends. The fact that its author "talks well enough," in this case, proves irrelevant, alas; when communication cannot occur face-to-face, but must be done in writing, confusing a slit for a slight can cause serious repercussions.

A final example of the literary Chesnut's interest in malapropisms and their significance involves a scene in which those experiences in parsing the relation of class, education, and region explored above enable her to confirm an instance of Yankee espionage about which her refugee community in Lincolnton, North Carolina, has been buzzing suspiciously. In an entry for February 27, 1865, Chesnut writes:

> Two very fine looking officers sat behind us at church. Said to be spies—Yankees—have been seen talking to negroes on the sly. Their papers examined—in pencil, badly spelled, every word beginning with a capital letter.
>
> "Papers very suspicious, but then all Yankees go to free schools and know how to spell."
>
> So we all thought until we began to pick up their letters on the battlefield, and that delusion was dispelled. (741)

Every sentence of this remarkable sequence diverts the forward trajectory of what would seem to be its logical flow: the handsomeness of the officers suggests that they must be Rebels; but their furtive conversations with local African Americans (legally emancipated, according to Federal decree, yet remaining in a state of suspended animation awaiting war's end) seem to belie that possibility. The men's misspelled papers suggest that they cannot be Federals in disguise, since Southerners have heard that Yankee free schools are acclaimed for excellence. Yet the 1880s Chesnut knows from her own experience that the missives of common Union soldiers tend to be riddled with spelling errors. Perhaps these men capitalize the first letter of every word in their papers to make the prose seem more "official." As the awkward telegraphing of class aspiration, such diacritical efforts would be touching, were the context not wartime, with its stakes of life and death. In a particularly witty concluding sentence, Chesnut ends the tableau with the word "dispelled." This pun on the orthographic vulnerabilities of the "fine looking officers" emphasizes how her own literary playfulness and agility in crafting her material trump the ingenuity of professional Northern spies.

"How much I owe the pleasure of my life to those much reviled writers of fiction"

The ambitious Chesnut of the 1880s includes unforgettable examples of the Yankee and Rebel correspondence that has come into her possession. Her scathing criticism of these inept young writers must be understood, however, against the context of Chesnut's love of books and admiration for literary artistry: inside her self-consciously crafted narrative, such commitment may be matched only by the bibliophilic zeal of the elder Mrs. Chesnut, whose taste is far less ecumenical than that of her daughter-in-law. An entry in the narrative for February 25, 1861, Chesnut's love-note to novelists of the English, French, and American nineteenth century might serve as her personal motto for a literary life: "How much I owe the pleasure of my life to those much reviled writers of fiction" (10). This literary life of hers is lived passionately when time allows, but, more often than not, interrupted by the crushing demands of family and nation. The pressing obligations of being, first, Mrs. Counsel-to-Governor-Pickens-Chesnut, and then Mrs. Confederate-Cabinet-Member-Chesnut, and later Mrs. Colonel, and finally Mrs. Brevet-Brigadier-General-Chesnut, not to mention Mrs. Butter-and-Egg-Farmer-Chesnut, and Mrs. Surrogate-Mother-Chesnut (for sister Kate's son David after the war), perpetually disrupted the writer's wish for what she called "peace—and a literary leisure for my old age, unbroken by care and anxiety!" (May 6, 1862, 335).[4]

Mary Chesnut's opportunities for composition may have been constrained during and after the Civil War, but her mania for reading remained unimpeded. Indeed, this trait immediately strikes almost every first-timer who picks up the 1880s narrative: nearly all remark on the thoroughgoingness of its account of Chesnut's voracious, quotidian, consumption of books; and they note, as well, the way that she weaves numerous details of a literary absorption, bordering on bibliomania, across nearly every one of its 835 (eventually published) pages. Sometimes the writer mentions titles without annotation; just as frequently, she provides critical commentary on the novel or history she just has completed. Threaded across what becomes the 1880s book is an extraordinary (and idiosyncratic) literary history of bellum, high cultural, Anglo-American reading practices.

In the original diary jottings of the 1860s, Chesnut lists far fewer novels and histories in her account of the daily round than she does in the 1880s narrative; there, reports of her fiction-reading are nearly ubiquitous. In the 1860s diary, stanzas of romantic and Victorian poetry (by Wordsworth, Byron, and Tennyson) and religious quotations (Jeremy Taylor's works on preparation, Thomas

More's injunctions to prayer) predominate. Despite the fact that she retains many of these passages in the 1880s narrative, their stark power, speaking to the desperation of the times, becomes diluted by avid discussion of Trollope, Dickens, and George Eliot. Chesnut's passionate engagement with character and theme thus displaces what had been the austere force of the prayers and hymns lacing the 1860s diary.

Most significantly, the 1880s diatribes against Harriet Beecher Stowe originate in a tiny 1860s diary remark, penned only weeks after Lee had surrendered at Appomattox. In an entry for June 1, 1865, Chesnut states that the family's "negroes" remain happier "than the readers of Stowe ever could conceive" (*TPMC*, 254).[5] If, as Chesnut claims in the 1880s, she in fact returned to *Uncle Tom's Cabin* five times during the war, those rereadings go unmentioned in the original diary. Of the prose writers catalogued there, Emerson, Trollope, Thackeray, and Dickens predominate. Chesnut apparently acquired the work of the latter three in 1850s book versions of the initially serialized novels; and she obtained Trollope's to-the-minute novelistic installments just off the English presses, in journals like *Blackwood's,* from like-minded literary friends who successfully had run the blockade, among them, John Thompson, editor of the *Southern Literary Messenger.*

The shortage of time informing the 1860s jottings also precluded the sort of critical meditations so central to the creative work of the 1880s. Chesnut may have kept a barebones list, no longer extant, of her wartime reading, with the intention of developing her literary commentary when she returned to transform the narrative in the years and decades following the end of the war. But as it stands, the 1860s diary is richer in religious references than it is in citations from the British or American fiction discussed in the 1880s narrative. In addition to devotional works, the diary is dappled with long quotations from Shakespeare's history plays, particularly the Henriad, as well as *Macbeth.*

Remarkably, the best-selling Southern author Augusta Jane Evans—whose second novel, *Beulah,* established her writing career before she'd reached the age of twenty—only appears in the 1860s diary as a kind of ghostly trace: Chesnut notes that friends sighted the Alabama author at a party that she herself also attended, though the two women did not meet. Later, Chesnut records a friend's praise of Evans's literary gifts, but the diarist remains taciturn on the subject herself. That the highly opinionated Chesnut would stay silent about this local luminary seems a particularly pointed omission. Evans goes completely unmentioned in the 1880s narrative, despite the fact that her 1864 novel *Macaria,* a paean to the Confederacy, not only broke sales records in the war-torn South, but was published in New York in a pirated edition and devoured by Yankee soldiers and civilians alike. So ubiquitous was the novel in the Union ranks that General Lorenzo Thomas actually ordered all copies found to be confiscated and burned.[6]

Evans's absence from Chesnut's 1880s manuscript is fascinating. *Macaria*'s creator was the region's most famous, best-selling, female author, while the Carolinian who excluded her never achieved recognition as a writer beyond her husband's former circle in the Confederate cabinet. And while this elite admired her for her superior intellect and trenchant wit, her diary jottings most likely remained unknown to many of them. According to Chesnut's extant correspondence, only Varina Davis and Isabella Martin were privy to her plans for the ambitious transformation of her wartime diary. Chesnut's prose saw print just once in her own lifetime, when she was paid ten dollars for a short sketch called "The Arrest of a Spy," which Woodward notes was "expanded from her current revision of the war diary for the Charleston *Weekly News and Courier* series entitled 'Our Women in the War'" (*MCCW,* xliii).

Given her literary ambition, Chesnut could have felt some resentment over and perhaps aesthetic disdain for Augusta Evans. Her standard of literary excellence derived from her favorite comic and realist authors, Thackeray and Eliot in England and Balzac in France. Bad feeling toward another author was something that the 1880s writer rarely, if ever, exhibited. She reserved her outrage for Harriet Beecher Stowe, an altogether more acceptable nemesis: she was a Northerner, abolitionist, propagandist, and deployed the sentimental form to do political work, all of which earned her universal revulsion below the Mason-Dixon Line.

In taking on the creator of *Uncle Tom's Cabin,* the 1880s Chesnut became one of a number of female Southern writers, most of the others ideologues (as she decidedly was not), affronted by that novel's *J'accuse* regarding the evils of slavery.[7] Louisa McCord herself had published a hostile, thirty-page review of the novel that remains canonical in the history of "anti-Tom" writing. Moreover, Chesnut's trenchant assault in the 1880s narrative on the sentimental tradition writ large was grounded in solid intellectual claims: among other things, it uncannily prefigured what would become the first phase of twenty-first-century literary historian Ann Douglas's evolving argument about the average sentimental novel of the nineteenth century embodying politics gone bad.[8] Chesnut clearly must have known of, yet could not countenance, the reality of Evans's acclaim; instead, she disavowed it. Such popular material did not deserve to be dignified as art.

Thus, in the 1880s narrative, she notes in an entry for March 11, 1864: "[T]oday read *Blithedale, Blithedale* leaves such an unpleasant impression. I like pleasant, kindly stories now. We are so harrowed by real life. Tragedy is for hours of ease" (581). Featuring a fictive coterie of midcentury radical reformers who join forces in a utopian community that ultimately fails, Hawthorne's 1852 satire on the self-absorption of philanthropists is a particularly fascinating choice on the part of Chesnut's 1860s persona at this moment in the war. Perhaps her swipe at Hawthorne's propensity to leave "such an unpleasant impression" affords what she also imagines might register as a slap at Stowe's authorial cohort; but if so, she certainly has misjudged Hawthorne's politics, as he was no abolitionist. More plausibly, the narrator is emphasizing that her task as an engaged citizen of the Confederate States of America is to study New England abolitionist culture to gain insight into what the enemy is thinking. Whatever her motivation for reading / conjuring *The Blithedale Romance* at this moment, the title and subject of *Macaria* remain unspoken and unmentionable; and Augusta Jane Evans is entirely absent from her narrative, nowhere to be found in the fifty-page index to Woodward's 1981 edition.

Macaria's fame cannot have rested on any ingenuity at the level of its plot: the novel's patriotic Confederate subject matter and its author's prior reputation from *Beulah,* rather than its quality or aesthetic complexity, were all that proved necessary to sweep the book to fame. Perhaps the 1880s Chesnut felt (though never conveyed in writing) there was something unjust about Evans's eminence: such celebrity must have been based on some fortuitous conjunction between *Macaria*'s patriotic, indeed, propagandistic subject matter and its timely appearance at the last moment of Confederate optimism in 1864, before the tide turned against Rebel armies, with Sherman's capture of Atlanta in September.

Chesnut expressed no envy of the very popular George Eliot or the well-known Elizabeth Barrett Browning, after all; only American women writers working in the sentimental vein and accruing wealth raised either her ire or her derision or, in the case of Evans, reduced her to silence.[9] As one of the more voracious readers represented in the pages of nineteenth-century American letters, Chesnut would have been out of character in actually shunning *Macaria*. She claimed to have hated Feydeau's *Fanny,* but finished it all the same. Perhaps she read Evans's novel, did not care for it, and kept her opinion to herself in the face of its mass popularity. Chesnut was not without the gift of tact, despite her reputation for occasionally excessive candor. The account of her otherwise voluminous reading is recorded scrupulously across the pages of the 1880s narrative.

How was it possible that a woman even of Mary Chesnut's obvious brilliance could go through the number of books she claimed to be consuming every day and still partake of the nearly frantic social regime that, despite her semi-invalid state, she also described enjoying? The 1880s narrative recounts that she often dined with three to four sets of friends daily, enjoyed leisurely walks and carriage rides, often attended multiple receptions, dinners, and parties on the same evening, and conducted late night confabs with her husband's colleagues, from whom she learned the latest news about the progress of the war. She also spent significant time confined to bed. And all the while, she read avidly. Learned and unschooled alike, nineteenth-century Americans were readers; yet the sheer volume of pages Chesnut claimed to have taken in every day stretches credulity.

It could be that her assertions about her reading practices were not indicative of her actual daily routine. The catalogues of books listed in the 1880s narrative may have been a literary stratagem by which Chesnut was able to conjure thematic resonances and telegraph central motifs, a kind of literary shorthand. So, for example, by invoking a celebrated English novel like George Eliot's *Silas Marner,* she could amplify the refrain of her own childlessness or reprise the theme of illicit, unwanted, or abandoned babies, in her case, African American infants and toddlers whose mothers had left them behind, decamping with the realization of emancipation in May of 1865. In this way, the two-year-old whom Silas Marner takes in, and who becomes his daughter Hepsy, could come to stand for those small black counterparts rescued on Mulberry.

The hypothesis that Chesnut's account of her reading was created for the 1880s narrative grows out of another, particularly charged, example: her treatment of Harriet Beecher Stowe. Chesnut mentions *Uncle Tom's Cabin* only obliquely in the 1860s diary, but in the 1880s narrative she continually claims to be rereading it throughout the war. Along with most literate Americans, Chesnut had read the novel on its publication (1852); and she very well might have carried it with her to Montgomery, Richmond, and Columbia and referred to it across the war years. Yet it remains a puzzle that Stowe is virtually absent from the 1860s diary jottings, especially as her great novel became essential to the imaginative fabric and social critique of Chesnut's 1880s literary narrative.

Perhaps the writer's reference to certain literary works functions as a kind of metacommentary on her central themes. Consider her numerous references to Thackeray's *Vanity Fair,* Chesnut's favorite novel, according to both her extant correspondence and the 1880s narrative. Numerous citations from Thackeray's book do not necessarily confirm that she repeatedly reread her old favorite (though perhaps she did). Instead, they might also signal that Chesnut had come to see the "council" that advised Governor Pickens in South Carolina (with the exception of her husband, a reluctant member), and the Confederate cabinet itself, as a collection of superannuated fools acting from impulses of egotism rather than patriotism. Accordingly, the elaborate list of books the

1880s writer said she had consumed between 1861 and 1865 in fact could have been studied or reperused in the years and decades following Confederate surrender; and the literary Chesnut could have claimed them as bellum reading experiences enriching her authorial enterprise, punctuating her vast book's thematic structure, and adding to its literary gravitas.[10] Such a tactic would be of a piece with what some scholars think of as Chesnut's "fictionalizing" efforts of the 1880s.[11]

In other words, it is possible that Chesnut may not have been consuming a five-hundred-page George Eliot novel per day in the early 1860s, despite what the 1880s narrative suggests. But such a prospect does not necessarily lend credence to the notion of scholars like Kenneth Lynn that Chesnut's book is some sort of historical hoax.[12] Woodward and Muhlenfeld have explained the ways in which Isabella Martin and Myrta Lockett Avary (1905) and Ben Ames Williams (1949) separately and carefully selected excerpts from the relatively uncontroversial portions of the 1880s narrative for their versions of the *Diary from Dixie* (though Williams added the Witherspoon murder to his edition, a significant supplement indeed).

Neither set of "editors" articulated the fact that the manuscripts from which their books drew represented an arduous transformation of the 1860s diary. Nor did they note that Chesnut's attempts at writing fiction in the late 1870s enabled her to reconceptualize the nature of her project twenty years after the Civil War, thus accounting for the substantial selection, elaboration, and reimagining of the 1880s narrative. Following the readings of Woodward and Muhlenfeld, this study accepts everything in the 1880s reworkings as "authentic," though certainly not "true to," much less "identical with," the jottings of the 1860s. The latter provide the epigrammatic scaffold for what, in the final decade of her life, she crafted into literary art. That is, Chesnut's editorial process allowed imaginative transformation of her original, telegraphic, jottings and accordingly was true to her 1880s vision of what the 1860s diary could become.

"How I miss that way of looking out into the world"

Last January I sent for all the English reviews. *Blackwood's,* &c&c—*Atlantic, Harper's, Cornhill,* &c. Threw away my subscription money. How I miss that way of looking out into the world. The war has cost me that. How much more? (November 20, 1861, 242)

Though ultimately the war would exact from Mary Chesnut and her family nearly everything but their lives and their heavily mortgaged plantation, the conflict's attendant deprivations started for her on the intellectual front. As soon as the Federal fleet captured Norfolk and inaugurated the blockade of Wilmington, Charleston, and Savannah, Chesnut's cosmopolitan, literary, and historical vision, what she called "that way of looking out into the world" was cut off abruptly. Thus, gifts of periodicals bestowed by blockade-running friends offered significant respite: the further installment of a Trollope novel or something new from Dickens. Her social set became a local circulating library, with various members sharing works that reflected their tastes. Like the Gallic cuisine that they provided her, the French novels, plays, and operas Chesnut devoured came courtesy of the Prestons:

> Today I read a French play—*Avant—pendant-apres*. But everything is flat after *Mariage de Figaro*—which was yesterday's bon bouche—and the day before *Barbier de Seville*. The Prestons have sent me Beaumarchais's works and a pile of Scribe to beguile the slow and steady hours when I do not leave my bed. (February 19, 1862, 292)

The implication is that French comedies and operas just may improve her health. Certain works of Gallic fiction, however, have a decidedly insalubrious effect:

> Got from the Prestons' French library *Fanny*, with a brilliant preface by Jules Janin [an eminent French literary critic with whose work Chesnut was acquainted]. Now, then, I have come to the worst. There can be no worse book than *Fanny*. . . . Of course it is clever to the last degree, or it would be kicked into the gutter. It is not nastier or coarser than Mrs. Stowe's, but then it was not written in the interest of philanthropy. (June 16, 1862, 390)

Apparently, Ernest-Amié Feydeau's 1858 novel makes no pretension of justifying the illicit sexuality it features; meanwhile, the author of the 1880s narrative finds utterly obscene the cross-racial sexual abuse implied in *Uncle Tom's Cabin*. It would seem that for Chesnut, impure books must be offered straight up, minus Stowe's heavy dose of moral reform. Or, perhaps, the fact that Feydeau's lovers are white and French, rather than biracial slave and white master, renders the Feydeau novel "clever to the last degree," while the overall effect of Stowe's book is execrable.

Ordinarily, Chesnut was enthusiastic about books she felt told the truth, what she termed in contrast to her mother-in-law's need for imaginative insulation, works "that tore off shams" (March 12, 1865, 762). The older Mrs. Chesnut could not abide what she considered brutalities represented in fiction; accordingly, the searing satires of Thackeray disturbed her, and she deemed their creator a "very uncomfortable, disagreeable creature" (761). One needs to know little more than this to understand the profound philosophical incompatibility of the two Mrs. Chesnuts. But such logic ran aground for Mary the younger when it came to Harriet Beecher Stowe's vision of the "seamy side" of Southern slavery (761). Despite what in nearly all other cases was Mary Boykin Chesnut's penchant for hard-hitting social critique in literary form, she completely rejected the notion that *Uncle Tom's Cabin* should be placed on such a list of "realist" works.[13]

In fact, Chesnut maintained that specific episodes Stowe related in her block-busting novel, featuring suicidal slave mothers or those who would euthanize their own infants to keep them from bondage, were based on grotesque exaggerations of slave experiences. Chesnut vigorously denounced these as worst-case scenarios; such criminal distortions were standing in for normative slaveholding. The realism of Balzac, in contrast, for all its sordidness, afforded Chesnut great pleasure. Perhaps absorption in scenes of the French class struggle provided a diverting escape from the ugliness of slavery and the horrors of Civil War. Thus, Chesnut happily received *Cousine Bette* from the Prestons (February 13, 1862, 288), and *La Peau de chagrin* from Mrs. Bartow (May 6, 1862, 336). Both constituted cornerstones of Balzac's *Comédie humaine*, an epic examination of human nature in nearly one hundred volumes. In company with the more overtly satirical *Vanity Fair,* these works profoundly influenced Chesnut's conception of the social commentary she wanted to offer in her 1880s narrative: "*Vanity Fair* once more. Can always reread Thackeray" (April 15, 1862, 326).

"*I am absorbed in it, up to the ears, . . .*"

After having declared eternal devotion to Thackeray, the 1880s narrator asserts a rival interest, in George Eliot and her sources, which suggests that she had outgrown her earlier delight in pointed British parody. Indeed, Chesnut's description of this change of taste in an entry for December 7, 1863, makes it sound as if she has joined some sort of holy order, where she speaks from a penitential cell: "I am absorbed in it, up to the ears, body and soul given up to Savonarola" (501). Far from having become a fanatic, however, the writer expresses *literary* devotion; she has joined the cult of George Eliot, her exact contemporary composing fiction in England. Perusal of comments from the 1880s narrative reveals numerous references to the great novelist (born Mary Anne Evans), whose works appeared roughly between the years 1858 and 1878, and detailed judgments about these novels abound. Chesnut had read two of the books written prior to the Civil War: *Adam Bede* (1859) and *The Mill on the Floss* (1860).[14] Both unfold in English country villages not unlike Chesnut's own semirural Camden, where the landed and wealthy, and their slaves, mingled with the middling and the poor, the tragic "sandy-hillers" she describes throughout her 1880s narrative.

Despite such familiar rural echoes, the Eliot novel that most occupied Chesnut in her reworkings of the 1880s is decidedly foreign and historical: *Romola* (1863) is set in late-fifteenth-century Florence, during the decade in which Savonarola, a radical Dominican monk, seeks to transform its citizenry by revolutionizing the workings of the Catholic Church. His antipapal movement flows into what has been percolating as a de facto Florentine civil war, with sides taken by the pope and his minions, who want to crush the common people and with them, Savonarola's proto-Reformation. This seemingly straightforward struggle between the Church and the populace is complicated by the involvement of the Medici family, which, in the opening pages of the book, having ruled Florence for decades, have lost power with the death of their patriarch, Prince Lorenzo the Magnificent. Medici factions call for the aid of the king of France and his army, which march into the city on their behalf. By the end of the novel, Savonarola has been tried for and convicted of heresy, executed, and his body burned at the stake in an astonishing spectacle of public martyrdom.

In animating a historical figure such as Savonarola, Eliot had made an abrupt departure from her earlier creative practice, where she peopled the landscapes of her novels with fictional figures exclusively. In *Romola* she wove actual Florentine luminaries, including Niccolò Machiavelli and prominent painters and poets of the period, into scenes with fictional characters such as Romola and Tito. Eliot's eponymous heroine, the exquisite, erudite, and independent Romola, against all expectations, slowly has come round to the party of Savonarola, despite her intellectual, aristocratic, and pagan heritage, and in defiance of her learned Greek husband, Tito, a "foreigner" who, by brilliance and cunning, has become one of the chief diplomatic agents of the divided city. At the climax of the novel, Tito attempts to broker a liaison between the aristocratic and papal factions; in fact, he is a traitor, with allegiance to no party but his own.

Well before this point, his marriage to Romola has faltered: just after her father dies, Tito coolly breaks his promise to keep the old man's treasured library intact; as a result, the couple live as strangers for the remainder of the story. In the final section of the novel, the crowd has been whipped to a fury after the spectacular public execution of Savonarola. Attempting to escape mob activity targeting him, among other suspected traitors, Tito plunges into the Arno, is swept downstream, and later that day, washes ashore, dead. Meanwhile, heartbroken over the murder of Savonarola, Romola flees the city in despair. She finds herself in a tiny village beset by plague and stays to nurse the afflicted, as she has learned to do from Savonarola's ministry. Eventually, however, she returns to Florence, determined to care for Tito's two illegitimate children and their mother, about whose existence she has learned during the chaos, and whom Tito has left penniless.

Romola became an intellectual focal point for Chesnut and her bookish community because at least one of her literary-minded friends (John Thompson, and perhaps also L. Q. Lamar) had had the good fortune to run the blockade just as Eliot's new novel had become available. The book surfaced in Richmond during one of the more trying phases of the war, the winter of 1864. Chesnut apparently had read it earlier, off-stage from the reported action of the 1880s narrative, for she is opinionated about it from the start. The narrating Chesnut of the 1880s obliquely mentions the book for the first time in an entry for December 7, 1863, after having received a biography of the revolutionary monk whom Eliot features as a central character: "John Thompson sent me [the] *[Life of] Savonarola*—no doubt to tune me up for *Romola*" (501). She tells us in an entry for January 18, 1864, that according to her friend Lamar, who also has just read the book, "across the water . . . it was the rage" (543). But Chesnut cannot agree: "I am sure it is not as good as *Adam Bede* or *Silas Marner*. It was not worthy of the woman who was rival to all but Shakespeare's name below" (543).

This dispute, in part, concerns not whether Eliot's new production is more intellectually ambitious, more learned, more exotic than any of her previous works of fiction. A Renaissance humanist setting, rife with religious controversy (involving a church and theology not Eliot's own), based on knowledge of abstruse doctrine, surely marks an impressive point of departure for the British novelist, who apparently did extensive research in Italian libraries and archives to prepare herself for the project. Instead, the 1880s Chesnut seems invested in *Adam Bede* and *Silas Marner*'s ethical dimensions: illicit sex begets pregnancy and infanticide, followed by extreme punishment; and goodness and charity are rewarded with filial love; while the abandoned child of an unacknowledged marriage, who has been fostered with devotion, cannot be remanded to the erring biological father, belatedly, whatever repentance he intends. In Eliot, childlessness is an affliction, though fortuitous adoptions can prove life-transforming. Such are the moral conclusions to be drawn from Chesnut's two favorite Eliot novels. Surely the celebrated British author has departed from her heretofore normative moral certainties in choosing to tell the story of a historical figure of enormous charisma who lived in pre-Protestant Italy four hundred years before her time.

Two aspects of *Romola*'s plot have particular resonance for the 1880s Chesnut: the setting is civil war, and the heroine is learned, bookish, childless. The narrator unfolds a sort of internal competition between Eliot's first four great works, parsing out those promulgating religious belief and morality and those in which such virtues take a back seat to ethical questions of a different sort. In that regard, *Adam Bede* always wins, and the humanism of *Romola* remains unsatisfying to the literary Chesnut.

In the 1880s narrative entry for January 4, 1864, she describes how with the impulses of a literary scholar she returns to the texts themselves in order to make her best case for the superiority of Eliot's earliest works over *Romola*: Chesnut prefers a night alone with George Eliot over a festive evening with friends:

> I stayed home and read *Silas Marner*. As good as *Adam Bede*. I understand her poor folk—the cobbler [Marner actually is a weaver] and the golden-haired treasure trove, God-given in the bitter moment. And the worthless gentleman and the prim [good] woman with her heart dried up within her for want of proper aliment, the childless wife! She, the writer, is not so orthodox pious as she was. Of course I took *Silas* at a draught—did not stop until I had swallowed the last word. (527)

Here, the narrator expresses a deep understanding of Eliot's portrait of bitterness in the face of isolation (Mary Boykin Chesnut, rusticated in an unforgiving Camden), and of outrage over having been robbed, materially and spiritually (Mary Boykin Chesnut, childless in the face of her mother-in-law's abundant fertility); and she also comprehends faith, the notion that the abandoned toddler has been sent from God to a shattered man whose belief still endures. Her interpretation of the childless wife offers insight into her own withered heart unfed by the nutriment of maternal devotion and filial love. It is no accident that Chesnut's metaphor for an extended reading session should be that of imbibing in one gulp an entire cup, given the poetics of starvation and thirst that run through the 1880s book.

In an 1880s entry for eleven days later, the narrating Chesnut makes a comment that indirectly explains why the recent advent of *Romola* has felt like such a blessing to her friends:

> And on Monday and all the week long, we went on as before, hearing of nothing but battle, murder, sudden death. Those are the daily events. Now a new

book—that is the un-looked for thing, the pleasing incident in this life of monotonous misery. We live in a large barrack. We are shut in, guarded from light from without. (January 15, 1864, 540)

Early in the war, Chesnut's 1860s persona had complained:

Now for the first time in my life, no book can interest me. But life is so real, so utterly earnest—fiction is so flat, comparatively. Nothing but what is going on in this distracted world of ours can arrest my attention for ten minutes at a time. (June 3, 1862, 359)

The 1880s narrator implies that she has undergone a psychological transformation: death has become normative, and a new book offers the only distraction of consequence. Perhaps for the literary circle in which Chesnut travels, imaginative absorption alone can combat the ennui of death's dreadful routine in the war's fourth year. The writer's world has turned upside down, and life and art have reversed positions.

Despite her seeming dismissal of *Romola* earlier in the winter, the narrator indicates that her 1860s persona is rereading the book, giving it the kind of second chance she almost never offers:

Mrs. Grundy [her landlady] lent me *Romola*. I had read it before, but I was hurried then. Now I will take time, consider my ways, and not presume to judge George Eliot rashly....

After they left I sat down to *Romola*—and I was absorbed in it. How hardened we grow to "war and war's alarms." The enemies canon or our own are thundering in my ears—and I was dreadfully afraid some infatuated and frightened friend would come in to cheer, to comfort, to interrupt me. Am I the same poor soul who fell on her knees and prayed and wept and fainted as the first guns boomed from Fort Sumter? (March 3, 1864, 577–78)

Most telling about this entry is the distance Chesnut shows herself traveling in response to the grim ambience of war: in 1861, in the face of the Confederate assault on Federal troops at Fort Sumter, she had trembled and supplicated God for deliverance from an engagement that turned out, in fact, to be nearly bloodless. Having endured four years of hostilities, she has become immune to the sounds of canons thundering only miles from her residence.

In a narrative entry for March 5, 1864, Chesnut's persona reveals that absorption in *Romola* has spared her anxiety over the Union cavalry threat to Richmond at the beginning of March 1864. The raid eventually was thwarted by the Confederate horse, whose counterattack resulted in significant Federal casualties and the hanging of Colonel Dahlgren, who led the Union charge.

Word had spread after the failed attack that Dahlgren had carried orders to seize and murder Chesnut's beloved Jefferson Davis; and though this rumor was untrue, presidential loyalists (fewer and further between by spring of 1864) were up in arms over the idea that a "national" leader would be targeted in such a way. The 1880s writer reports of this epoch: "And to think—here I sat reading *Romola* at my ease. And I might have been roused at any moment by fire and fury—rapine and murder—&c&c&c" (579). Again, Chesnut is emphasizing through her narrative strategies the fortuitously narcotic appeal of George Eliot's first major work of historical fiction, whatever its moral disappointments in comparison with *Adam Bede* and *Silas Marner*.

It might be said that the 1880s writer has staged a literary civil war, the front lines of which are George Eliot's pre-1864 oeuvre, in order to deepen her state of distraction. This preoccupation serves as an anodyne to the horror of battles in Virginia in the spring and summer of 1864—the Wilderness, Spotsylvania, and Cold Harbor, some of the bloodiest of the war. While the narrator serves as the commanding general of the *Adam Bede / Silas Marner* forces, her friends Thompson and Lamar fiercely oppose her as senior officers in the *Romola* army. Despite this schism, she seeks to be fair-minded to her opponents; thus she rereads *Adam Bede* "to measure the distance—up or down—to *Romola*" (579). Chesnut's was a magnificent obsession: she had created a contest between the accounts of hardworking, pious, English decency (against fornication, illegitimate birth, and infanticide) and Savonarolan conversion to a purposeful life of charity (countering illegitimate children and treachery). In the mind of an Anglophilic believer in the absolute distinction between right and wrong, the *Romola* camp, with its platform of paganism, Catholicism, and moral relativism (Romola forgives Tito for his "left-handed" wife and children) from the outset would have seemed doomed to defeat.

The battle of the novels also functions in Chesnut's narrative as an allegory for the apparently divided nature of George Eliot's soul. Chesnut had been troubled by ugly rumors that her fiction-writing idol might in fact be an atheistic wanton, living in sin with a married man. Literary history shows that Eliot had renounced the Protestantism of her childhood, coming to doubt the existence of God; additionally, she had lived and continued to live out of wedlock with intellectual George Henry Lewes until his death in the mid-1870s. Lewes's legal wife had committed adultery early in their marriage, bearing five children with her illicit partner. Because Lewes (somewhat like Silas Marner) had consented to acknowledge these offspring as his own, divorce was impossible; termination of the union on the grounds of adultery immediately would have delegitimated his wife's "left-handed" family. As if reprising the plot dynamic of an Eliot novel, Lewes acted to protect the children he loved, which cost him both the legitimation of his union with Mary Anne Evans and her subsequent reputation. The dilemma brings to mind the way in which Hepsy's biological father in *Silas Marner* realizes that he cannot reveal his paternal identity and take her from Silas without essentially destroying both father and daughter.

The Lewes-Eliot cohabitation unfolded as the result of impossible domestic entanglements rather than flagrant disregard for social convention and law, as in the case, say, of Byron: sexual profligate, possible perpetrator of incest, and another huge literary favorite of Mary Boykin Chesnut.[15] In her entry for March 11, 1864, immediately prior to her disparaging remark about Hawthorne's *Blithedale,* the narrator articulates her concern for Eliot's state:

> I do not believe Lamar. With *Adam Bede* fresh in my mind, I cannot believe the woman who wrote it "is a fallen woman"—"living in a happy state of high intellectual intercourse and happy, contented immorality." She could not be happy. Dinah and the retribution that overtook Hetty speak out that she knows good from evil. (581)

Across her book, the 1880s Chesnut shows her acuity in judging fellow citizens of Camden accused of various venial sins—drunkenness and philandering, for example. She compares rumor to direct evidence in order to draw thoughtful conclusions about the characters in question. But in assessing Eliot's case, Chesnut brings alleged scandal about the writer's private life to bear upon the behavior of her fictional creations, something that seems patently absurd in the twenty-first century, with our notions of the great divide between the personal life of the artist and the moral dimension of his or her work. Nineteenth-century intellectuals often saw the same distinctions, with the exception in this case of Mary Boykin Chesnut, who wants the ethical quality of the representation to vouch for the morality of the artist who has created it. It seems beyond her imagination that a truly depraved woman could have invented the character of preacher Dinah, with her Christian message of love and forgiveness. Equally dubious is the idea that a woman herself degraded ultimately would condemn Hetty, the unwed dairymaid who finds herself pregnant, alone, and after the birth of her baby, so insensible and indifferent as to expose it to the elements. In Chesnut's eyes, George Eliot clearly had mastered moral distinctions big and small; she simply could not be a "fallen" woman. Chesnut desires the paradoxes of life to be clarified by the certainties of art.

Compelling evidence against Eliot actually appears in the 1880s narrative entry for January 18, 1864, that anticipates her reading of *Romola,* but apparently the information fails to penetrate Chesnut's defenses against thinking ill of her idol. The following is the only passage concerning Eliot's reputation cast in dialogue form, suggesting that through the process of conversation, Chesnut (the leading speaker) may be able to synthesize a happy conclusion:

> Those heavenly-minded sermons preached at us by the authoress of *Adam Bede*. Bear them well in mind while I tell you. This writer who so well imagines and depicts female purity and piety. She was a governess or something of that sort, perhaps wrote for a livelihood. At any rate, she had an elective affinity, which he responded to, for Lewes. So she lives with Lewes. Lamar does not know if she caused the separation between Lewes and his legal wife. They were living in a villa on some Swiss lake, the Mrs. Lewes of the hour—a charitable, estimable, agreeable, sympathetic woman of genius. A fallen woman living in a contented—nay, happy—state of immorality. Such a terrible shock to our preconceived ideas of her. Lamar seemed without prejudice on the subject. At least, he expressed neither surprise nor disapprobation.
>
> He said something of "genius being above the law," but I was not very clear as to what he said at that point. As for me, I said nothing, for fear of saying too much.
>
> "My idol was shattered, my daystar fled."
>
> "You know that Lewes is a writer."
>
> "Some people say the man she lives with is a nobleman. Oh, we give it up. You know, they say she is kind and good, if—a fallen woman." And here the conversation ended. (543–44)

In response to the painful reports from Lamar about Eliot's private life, Chesnut poignantly strains to maintain her idealization of her artistic idol. Again, she seeks terms from the world of fiction to make her judgment. The narrator invokes "elective affinities," a nod to Goethe's famous 1809 novel of that name, which explores the so-called chemical attraction between men and women that, in defiance of obligations, can compel an extramarital connection. Eliot might be less wanton if her behavior echoes that of a Goethe character. Or perhaps the 1880s author is scoffing. Lamar closes his case with the argument that "genius is above the law," asserting the classic antinomian position in American thought. With Eliot's extraordinary goodness and kindness—despite the fact that she is unchaste and unwed—she really cannot be a fallen woman. One can hear the echo of the elder Mrs. Chesnut in such a rhetorical statement.

For much of 1864, the narrating Chesnut remains at work on her reconsideration both of *Romola* and of Eliot herself. Rereading from new quarters in Columbia, South Carolina, she reports in an entry for October 30:

Mr. Chesnut has *Joseph II. Romola* is in my hands. So without protest or fidgets we let it rain its worst.

Can this woman be a fallen woman—a creature Shakespeare would call a ——, Carlyle, an unmentionable woman? Dress it up as you will, smother the Seventh Commandment with [the example of Jacob and Leah and Rachel in] Genesis—here it stands. An unchaste woman must be immodest. We don't go into morals at all. You could as well imagine a man who was thief, liar, or coward to be good and decent the while. No, no. It is all Lamar's wrong hearing of English scandal. She writes such beautiful things of love and duty, faith, charity, and purity. They even say she is an atheist, that she believes in God as little as she cares for his commandments. (661)

After trying to work out the dilemma with unfavorable strictures from Exodus and favorable biblical precedent from Genesis, Chesnut's argument devolves into semantics: unchaste equals immodest; sex outside of marriage necessitates public shame in a culture where women's honor inheres in physical virtue. And then comes her cry of denial: "No, no." Lamar must have misheard the gossip. The moral rigor of Eliot's creative work immunizes the writer from aspersions about her personal life.

In the only instance in the 1880s text in which Mary Boykin could be mistaken for Mary Cox Chesnut, it is the younger Mary who—in words she once used to describe the elder—hides her "head like the ostrich," "blind to all but beautiful things, rose-tinted beliefs and pure imaginings" (September 24, 1861, 202). Chesnut cannot believe a writer can imagine innocence, let alone take clear moral and ethical stands, while living out of wedlock with a married man in a godless household. The elder Mary Chesnut must idealize and forgive unwed white mothers and slave women for their sexual vulnerability in order to endure the moral paradoxes of her own life. Here, her daughter-in-law refuses to draw negative conclusions about the purity of the greatest female writer of her century, all rumors to the contrary. Chesnut's faith in George Eliot is just that, a belief in a thing not seen; and her commitment to the "woman who was to rival all but Shakespeare's name below" endured for the remainder of her life.

In Chesnut's mind Eliot and Thackeray take a back seat to only one writer, William Shakespeare. Accordingly, her most devastating literary analogue for the "national" situation is his greatest tragedy, *King Lear*. In the 1880s narrative, Chesnut invokes the play for March of 1865, only a month from Lee's surrender. She has fled from Columbia to Lincolnton, North Carolina, in order to keep "ahead of Sherman," whose enormous army has annihilated Georgia and is now seeking to make South Carolina "howl."[16] Sherman of course means that he seeks to reduce the enemy to the state of wounded animals; but his diction uncannily echoes Lear's heartrending speech on learning that his beloved Cordelia has been hanged: "Howl, howl, howl, howl! O, you are men of stones" (5.3.256–60).[17] At this moment, the ruined king has lost everything save his now meaningless, fragile life. *Lear* is the Shakespearian tragedy that most closely portends the end of things. The 1880s Chesnut writes:

> Then they overhauled my library, which was on the floor because the only table in the room they had use[d] as a tea table. Shakespeare—Moliere—Sir Thomas Browne—*Arabian Nights* in French—Pascal's letter—folk songs.
> *Lear* I read last. The tragedy of the world—it entered my heart to understand it first—now.
> Spare us Regan and Goneril and the storm and eyeballs rolling around.
> And an old king, and I am every inch a king.
> That is not it. It is the laying bare of the seamy side—going behind the pretty curtain of propriety we hold up. Poor humanity stripped makes us shiver. Look at that judge—look at that thief. Presto—change sides—Which is the judge? Which is the thief? And more unmentionable horrors. He preceded Thackeray in tearing off shams. (March 12, 1865, 761)

Shakespeare may be first on Chesnut's list, but she reads *Lear* last because she knows it has the most to tell her about the unmaking of her universe. Indeed, she calls it "the tragedy of the world." If *Macbeth* and *Hamlet* link family to nation, the crucial distinction in both plays is that neither Macbeth nor Hamlet has a child to inherit a future. In *Lear,* the connection between family and nation is not an association, but an identity. Lear and his daughters are not simply a first family, like the Davises or the Lincolns. King Lear embodies pagan England, and his undoing by his depraved daughters instigates both civil war and the decimation of the nation that is the king's physical self.[18]

In the 1880s book, Chesnut proclaims that she has never understood the deepest meanings of the play before this particular reading, in the context of her shattering Confederate world. Imaginative sympathy with its characters finally has occurred because she has been able to embrace the story thoroughly for the first time. In that regard her experience echoes that of descriptions of religious conversion. But beyond being born a Presbyterian, and a believer, Chesnut's deepest faith has been in the power of literature to transform people's hearts.

The most astute of readers, she embraces the darkness of the play, taking away the horrific hanging of Cordelia, the madness, brief restoration, and heartbroken death of the king, the complete destruction of his immediate kin, and the devastation of the state. She does not dwell on Edgar's quasi-redemptive comment in act 4, in the disguise of Poor Tom, when he prevents his blind father's suicide: "The worst is not, so long as we can say, 'This is the worst'"; nor does she acknowledge that he is one of the few left alive at the end of act 5.

There are survivors in *Lear,* as in the years after the South's defeat. In her own family, her husband, James Chesnut Jr., will live until 1885, though tragically, nephew Johnny will have endured four years of war only to die in 1868 of an unspecified cause. This untimely loss so devastates the remaining Chesnuts and Williamses that they cannot bear to speak of it. In the extant family correspondence, the subject of Johnny's death arises only briefly, in several business letters addressed to James Jr. regarding an outstanding sum his late nephew owed to their cotton factor. Chesnut's sister Kate will survive the surrender and first decade of Reconstruction, but she will perish prematurely, in 1876, ten years before her older, invalid, sister; and Kate's beloved and beautiful daughter Serena, "Princess Bright Eyes" of the narrative, will die in the same year, unmarried and not yet thirty years old. By the time Chesnut makes her last great return to her manuscript in 1880, *Lear*'s reversals of fortune, its numerous horrors and losses, its vision of extremity, strike painfully close to home.

Taken as a whole, it is clear that this representation of a brief period in 1864 constitutes the literary narrative's treasure trove; no other span of entries in Chesnut's book is dedicated so entirely to works of fiction and drama, critical responses, thoughts about authors, and meditations on the mystery of artistic creation. The section culminates in an absolutely remarkable discussion of the comparative greatness of Shakespeare and Milton. It is the summa of the literary spring she describes in the 1880s narrative. After Chesnut's meditation on *Lear,* it seems only fitting that this ambitious writer consider the difference between tragedy and epic, particularly as both genres inform her narrative. Here is Chesnut on Shakespeare in an entry for March 12:

> He knew all the forms and phases of true love. Straight to one's heart he goes. Tragedy or comedy—he never misses fire. . . . And he effaced himself. He told no tales of his own life. Compare old sad, solemn, sublime, sneering, snarling, faultfinding Milton. A man whose family doubtless found his "absences delicieuses." (583)

Chesnut's celebration of Shakespeare's self-effacement conjures a remarkable rumination in the 1860s diary for March 11, 1861, a comment for which Mary Chesnut has become famous. Ironically, Chesnut elides it from the 1880s reimaginings, though Woodward restores it in his edition:

> «What nonsense I write here. However, this journal is intended to be entirely *objective*. My subjective days are over. No more *silent* eating into my own heart, making my own misery, when without these morbid fantasies I could be so happy....
>
> ... I think this journal could be disadvantageous for me, for I spend the time now like a spider, spinning my own entrails instead of reading, as my habit was at all spare moments.» (23)

Taking oneself out, apparently, is the Shakespearian virtue that newly minted author Mary Chesnut has chosen to cultivate, circa 1861. Perhaps she seeks to transform the silence of once self-devouring ways—observations of the world that had no outlet—into the greater "audibility" of writing. But she fears that her entrail-spinning may undermine what she has understood as the self-nurturing act of reading, in which the author can ingest the imaginative sustenance of books. In the literary narrative of the 1880s, however, Chesnut seems to have restored the balance between being reader and spider, as her unfinished book shows rich traces of both intellectual investment and imaginative flight.

Her view of Milton, in contrast to that of the Bard of Avon, would warm any literary feminist's heart:

> A domestic tyrant—guind[é], formal, awfully learned. A mere man—for he could not do without a woman. When he tired out the first poor thing—who did not fall down and worship him, obey him, and see God *in him,* and she ran away—immediately he arranges his creed to take another wife [and writes pamphlets advocating the moral righteousness of divorce]....
>
> ... The Deer Stealer never once thought of justifying theft because he loved venison and could not come by it lawfully. (March 12, 1864, 583)

In these assertions, the 1880s Chesnut combines trenchant literary criticism with a stunningly prescient reading of the sexual politics informing Milton's imaginative productions. Shakespeare's capaciousness—the richness of his fictional world and the generosity of judgment it reveals—trounces Milton's narcissistic self-absorption. The Bard of Avon has not translated his domestic politics into an entire system of divinity, including detailed portraits of both God and man. Chesnut hints at marital trouble only by cruelly objectifying wife Anne Hathaway as "the second best bedstead," the sole bequest to her in Shakespeare's famous will. Nevertheless, viewers and readers don't attempt to understand, say, Desdemona's marital problems in terms of William's provision for Anne. Life and art remain separate spheres. Meanwhile, that Eve gets the blame in book 9 of *Paradise Lost* would come as no surprise, Chesnut implies, to anyone who knows the early marital history of the Milton household; we have John Milton himself to thank for having aired his dirty linen in his divorce tracts.

Beyond offering dazzlingly sharp literary judgments that remain relevant in the twenty-first century, these passages, ultimately, tell us something profound about Chesnut's authorial vision. As a born Carolinian and the daughter and wife of slaveholders, Mary Chesnut could have been nothing other than a Confederate partisan. Despite this reality, her wish to efface herself as the author of the 1880s narrative suggests something crucial about the text she ultimately left transformed if unfinished at her death in 1886. In a moment composed for December 12, 1864, four months before the end of the war, Chesnut wrote: "[A] faithful watcher I have been from my youth upward—of men and manners. Society has been for me only an enlarged field for character study" (690). Her "book" was to be something more than yet another Confederate memoir; instead, its scope was to be panoramic, searching, and even attuned to "the seamy side," not unlike the fiction of William Thackeray or George Eliot. A little deer poaching by the playwright was not enough to deter the ever-moral, 1880s Chesnut from reveling in Shakespeare's dramatic works. Creating a cosmos and a pantheon in one's own image in order to rationalize domestic disorder, as did Milton, on the other hand, struck the literary Chesnut as grandiose and self-indulgent. The Miltonic argument for divorce is a haunting cognate to the Confederate convention's case justifying secession. And in making this analogy, Mary Boykin Chesnut tacitly deconstructs her region's credo.

The epic, tragic, and comic forms, her genres of choice, modeled by Homer, Shakespeare, George Eliot, and Thackeray, offered the 1880s Chesnut vital ammunition as she turned her sights on New England and the sentimental form. In this final literary agon, the writer took on Harriet Beecher Stowe directly. In her assault on domestic feminine literature of the midcentury, epic-minded Chesnut anticipated the analysis of contemporary feminist scholars of local color and early modernism, those thinking through what happened to the literature of sentiment. Indeed, Chesnut herself both prognosticated (as a literary critic) and participated in (as a writer contributing to a genre in formation) this turn in the tradition of American women's writing toward realism and tragedy. Anticipating both of these developments, but heretofore unacknowledged, Chesnut's 1880s narrative rightfully belongs in late-nineteenth-century American literary history.

CHAPTER SIX

Smells

THE STENCH OF SLAVERY AND SENTIMENT

Mary Chesnut firmly believed that from 1852 onward, the American campaign against slavery and the industry of sentimental fiction had been wedded inextricably by the work of Harriet Beecher Stowe. The creator of *Uncle Tom's Cabin* embodied for Chesnut all she believed the North had misunderstood about the "peculiar institution" and everything exploitive about a literary practice based on the affective manipulation of its audience. Yet whatever reasonably might be assumed about a midcentury, Southern, Stowe-hater, Chesnut never considered slavery itself a positive good. Nevertheless, her objections remained on the level of theory: as an economic and political institution with pernicious domestic consequences, the enslavement of blacks was a system that Chesnut detested in principle. As she claimed in her 1880s narrative: "Wherever there is a cry of pain, I am on the side of the one who cries" (May 13, 1862, 339).

But despite these genuine sympathies, Chesnut never transcended the racist attitudes of the elite Southern society in which she had been raised. She felt that the two centuries of abjection in which enslaved Africans in British North America and later the United States had been made to live had created a people plagued by ignorance and poverty; accordingly, she did not consider these men and women the equals of whites. What distinguished Chesnut from many of her compatriots, however, was her awareness that lack of learning and indigence were not "natural" or "African" traits, but had been produced in blacks by the brutal practices of slaveholders across centuries of forced emigration and interstate trade. Holding such views made Mary Chesnut a most unusual Confederate matron indeed. On a personal level, and not without guilty awareness, she acknowledged her pleasure in being pampered by house slaves at Mulberry; and she reveled in Molly's delectable cooking in rented quarters in Richmond and Columbia, while relying on Laurence's proficiency in running these households far from home. As for her objection to sentimental writing, Mary Chesnut was convinced that, as an aesthetic practice, the form mystified genuine emotion and fostered complacency rather than social action, as "feeling right" for *Uncle Tom*'s ideal reader became sufficient unto itself.

Nevertheless, Chesnut's agonistic engagement with the Stowe she had conjured in imagination (the two never met) had everything to do with an unarticulated but vital creative insight: to achieve epic status, the grand narrative she was designing from her Civil War diary had to contend with a literary forerunner that had affected American culture in profound ways. That is, in her struggle with Stowe, the 1880s Chesnut's loathing of abolitionist pieties and the burden of her own racial guilt ultimately proved secondary; most at issue were her enormous literary ambition joined to an uncanny knack for social analysis. In nineteenth-century America, such a masterful literary achievement had been accomplished, exclusively, by Harriet Beecher Stowe. Accordingly, *Uncle Tom's Cabin* became the precursor text that Mary Chesnut's 1880s book had to engage and surmount.[1]

The 1880s Chesnut recognized that despite her claim that characters like Eva "are mostly in the heaven of Mrs. Stowe's imagination" (March 13, 1862, 308), these figures offered a lens through which to perform important cultural inquiry. Archetypes from *Uncle Tom*—particularly the angelic Evangeline St. Clare—helped her to demystify the domestic dynamics of her husband's family, where both tyranny (old Colonel Chesnut as czar) and heavenly goodness (Mary Cox Chesnut as angel of Mulberry) vied to rule the day. Accordingly, Stowe's book "played" in a permanent loop in Chesnut's literary imagination after the war, serving as an internalized interlocutor on the subject of the Carolinian's own kin, and also shedding crucial light on the myths organizing Confederate culture writ large.

This chapter on Chesnut's scrutiny of slavery, sentiment, and Stowe unfolds in three parts. The first explores details of *Uncle Tom's Cabin* itself as they resonate in Chesnut's 1880s narrative. Particular characters—Tom, Eva, Topsy, and Legree—captivated and also inflamed the writer and her peers, particularly proslavery women such as Louisa McCord, who reviewed the novel in January 1853. Chesnut's own thesis was that Stowe knew nothing of slavery, plantation life, or "Negro" culture under bondage in America. Accordingly, her central grievance was offered on the grounds of Stowe's cultural ignorance.

Although she could not have known as she was writing her narrative, Chesnut seemed to intuit that in fact, her Northern nemesis had not visited the South before writing what became her famous book. Besides a short visit to border-state Kentucky in the 1830s, Stowe only actually began to travel below the Mason-Dixon Line in the late 1860s.[2] Her finest twentieth-century biographer, Joan Hedrick, notes that this paragon of so-called realist writing accrued much of her material for *Uncle Tom* at second and third hand.[3] In fact, the African American domestics whom she actually had employed in her Cincinnati household in the later 1840s—that is, the few black people she really "knew" and on whom she based characters such as Eliza—either were hired bondspeople still enslaved or fugitives pretending to be free. By paying these African American hirelings wages to do the household work she abhorred, Stowe indirectly participated in the very system she would come to condemn by 1852.[4]

To be sure, and equally unbeknownst to the 1880s Chesnut, Stowe had aided and abetted a fugitive slave who had been working as her domestic servant when it was revealed that the woman's master was searching for her. Swooped away by Stowe's husband, Calvin, and brother, Henry Ward Beecher, who was to become the most famous evangelical minister in midcentury America, the fugitive was safely delivered into the hands of a Quaker abolitionist, John Van Zandt, and then to the Underground Railroad, which expedited her escape.[5] But Stowe's personal involvement with the abolitionist movement largely came *after* the publication of *Uncle Tom's Cabin;* it was only then that she sought meetings with the nation's leading antislavery men in preparation for a trip to England (her first), where she was to be honored for her best-selling book and its enormous philanthropic impact. And, although Stowe had gotten along well with all parties in the internally divided abolitionist community, she never had aligned herself with any of its various factions; for example, she had refused to take up with the Garrisonians, although William Lloyd Garrison himself remained a fellow magazine contributor and friend for life.

Many of Chesnut's notions about Stowe, then, were not unfounded, but involved sharp intuitions rather than hard facts; and they were drawn from Chesnut's brilliance as a close reader of *Uncle Tom's Cabin* rather than from any actual knowledge of Stowe's life or biography. That Chesnut's critique of Stowe in the 1880s narrative was rendered across what would become over eight hundred pages in print also suggests a level of obsession with and, accordingly, a dimension of involuntary admiration for Stowe that cannot be denied.

After exploring Chesnut's "magnificent obsession" with *Uncle Tom's Cabin,*

I turn to the remarkable ways in which Chesnut inadvertently and unconsciously identified her mother-in-law, the profoundly Christian, charitable, and voraciously bookish Mary Cox Chesnut, with Stowe's heroine, little Eva. In fact, the 1880s writer ultimately used her own reading of *Uncle Tom's Cabin* as a guide for attempting to understand the paradox of the senior Mrs. Chesnut's enduring "philanthropy" on the one hand, and on the other, her razor-sharp intellect that well understood but did nothing to disturb (other than by ameliorating some of the hardships of) the sort of slavery practiced on Mulberry.

Unlike her daughter-in-law, the elder Mrs. Chesnut almost never acknowledged overtly the effects of black bondage: its sexual corruption of white men, who abused black women, and its production of biracial children whose paternity was denied, which made Mary Chesnut the younger apoplectic. Only once, in a 1860s diary passage for March 18, 1861, which Chesnut excised from the 1880s book but Woodward restored, do we see the elder Mrs. Chesnut offering a somewhat indirect but real critique of white Southern men's propensity to prey sexually on black slave women: "«My mother-in-law told me when I was first married not to send my female servants in the street on errands. They were then tempted, led astray—and then she said placidly, so they told *me* when I came here, and I was very particular, *but you see with what result*»" (*TPMC,* 43; *MCCW,* 31). Apparently, one or more of the elder Mrs. Chesnut's slave women had become involved with a white man or white men and may have had biracial children.

This reminiscence about the elder Mrs. Chesnut's sole critical reflection on the subject of miscegenation, made to her young daughter-in-law in the early 1840s and recalled during Chesnut's composition of her 1860s diary, only to be cut as she revised in the 1880s, constitutes the full extent of the elder woman's recorded thoughts on a subject that had became her daughter-in-law's *idée fixe.* Mary Cox Chesnut, it seems, had worked out whatever were her own attitudes through an adult lifetime of offering benevolent care to her bound black "people"; though she may have been motivated, her daughter-in-law cynically believed, from fear as much as from love. But in no way did she attempt to intervene with the old Colonel on the "problem" of slavery as it extended beyond her own purview as mistress.

Mary Chesnut the younger was obsessed with this unacknowledged contradiction in her mother-in-law, particularly because she felt Mary Cox Chesnut judged her harshly as a childless wife with bookish pretensions. It was true that in the absence of traditional maternal duties, Mary Boykin Chesnut sought to find other outlets for her critical intellect, but ironically, when it came to matters of mind, the elder Mrs. Chesnut was no less gifted than her brilliant daughter-in-law. The distinction between these two figures involved the elder's relatively rigid notion of women's proper sphere, which was thoroughly in keeping with her elite, eighteenth-century, Anglo-American upbringing. Mary the younger, on the other hand, born nearly fifty years after her mother-in-law, had been educated at the best French girls' school in Charleston and sent to live on the Mississippi frontier while her lawyer-father tried his hand and failed at cotton farming. She was extraordinarily independent and self-sufficient, and her experiences had expanded her mental horizons: few upper-class American women during the Civil War were reading naval histories, accounts of ancient Greek warfare, and details of Admiral Nelson's career along with the latest blockade-run installment of a Trollope novel. Mary Boykin Chesnut's seemingly effortless acceptance into the political world of men may have brought to culmination much of what had distressed Mary Cox Chesnut for many years about her daughter-in-law's interests.

The elder Mrs. Chesnut's involvements proved more local, rarely extending beyond the boundaries of Mulberry Plantation, except for her obvious interest in the military fates of her favorite grandson, Johnny, and her only surviving male child, James Jr. A close reading of a relatively famous and highly amusing tableau at the beginning of the war and involving the senior Mrs. Chesnut sheds important light on the complexities of her character: I speak here of the early moment in the 1880s narrative in which "mama smells a smell" at 2 a.m. and rouses sixty slaves and the entire white family to ferret out the purported smoke. Constituting only a few cryptic lines in the 1860s diary, Chesnut of the 1880s develops this scene into a comic masterpiece that reveals many of the unspoken anxieties and displaced compulsions plaguing the mistress of Mulberry.

Retaining focus on Mrs. Chesnut senior, I look in the final section of the chapter at her reminiscence about being invited, along with twelve other young ladies, to serenade president-elect George Washington at Trenton en route to New York for his inauguration in 1789. A Currier and Ives engraving captures for posterity an image of this "white-robed choir" (though the engravers take artistic license and tint the girls' dresses brilliant pink and blue). In her 1880s narrative, Chesnut remarks that Mulberry's numerous visitors routinely urged the elder Mrs. Chesnut to share the story of her shining hour at the dawn of the new republic. She would bring out the exquisite print and recount the momentous occasion, creating her own personal ritual from her memories. It is the evocative image of a girl in white that leads the writer of the 1880s to associate the young Mary Cox / elderly Mary Cox Chesnut with Stowe's angelic heroine.

This literary association also links Mary Cox Chesnut to the narrative's other Eva figure, a person whom she would never meet, little Joseph Davis, age five, the favorite son of Jefferson and Varina, president and first lady of the Confederacy. It is here that two different narrative domains, the domestic, guided by Mrs. Chesnut senior, the good spirit of Mulberry, and the national, sanctified by little Joe, the Confederacy's golden child, begin to interanimate one another. In the 1880s manuscript, Chesnut portrays Joe Davis as the most ethereal and devout of his family's three children. Famously dressed in his night clothes on a winter evening in the middle of the war when the Chesnuts come to call on the Davises, he rushes into the parlor so as not to miss saying prayers with his papa; the visiting couple are touched deeply, and Mary transforms her memory of this tableau of filial piety into a brilliant 1880s passage for December 14, 1863 (504). This moment offers the only glimpse of a little boy who came to take on a public significance in death that could not have been imagined by those who loved him while he lived.

Chesnut's two "Eva" figures perished in the spring and early summer of 1864, just before and during the horrible hundred days of relentless fighting in Virginia between Lee's Army of Northern Virginia and Grant's Army of the Potomac. Mrs. Chesnut succumbed to old age at ninety-two, on March 15, 1864, in Camden, South Carolina. Four months later, little Joe Davis fell from a second-story piazza of the Confederate White House in Richmond, dying instantly. In an oddly disorienting narrative maneuver, the 1880s writer describes the Richmond funeral of Joe Davis in ways that could stand as well for the burial of the well-loved Mrs. Chesnut. Despite great differences, in the imaginations of their respective communities, both Mary Cox Chesnut and Joe Davis functioned as little Evas: one, the matriarch of Mulberry, renowned for her goodness to her slaves; the other, the angel child of the Confederacy, known by Southerners for his religious faith. Accordingly, the writer's narrative superimposition of their final stories in the 1880s narrative offers just one example of the way Chesnut's epic vision identifies profound, if seemingly obscure, commonalities, ties between the domestic and political realms.

Becoming "beStowed"

If the 1880s writer clearly fixated on Harriet Beecher Stowe in a diagnosable fashion, she was not alone.[6] In fact, it was a commonplace among antebellum Southern writers to excoriate Stowe's novel in hostile book reviews, such as Louisa McCord's extended essay on the topic in the widely read *Southern Quarterly Review*.[7] Meanwhile, parodic plantation novels featuring contravening characters, plots, and denouements became a brief fad; the most famous of these was Mary Henderson Eastman's *Aunt Phyllis's Cabin* (1853).

Still, Stowe's role in Mary Chesnut's imagination went above and beyond the abolitionist author's place of opprobrium in either Southern intellectual circles or proslavery elements in American culture generally. Louisa McCord, busy running her own hospital in Columbia, South Carolina, after the tragic battle-related death of her only son in 1862, was not rereading *Uncle Tom's Cabin* twice yearly from 1861 to 1865 as her comrade in home-front activism purported to be doing. McCord's thesis in her 1853 book review had everything to do with what she felt was Stowe's failed analysis of the practices of upper-class slaveholders. Real ladies and gentlemen never would have treated their human chattel with the carelessness of a St. Clare or the brutality of a Legree: such handling would be both irrational and, perhaps even more noteworthy, bad for business. Nearly every Southern intellectual and novelist who responded with outrage to Stowe's book argued that she knew nothing of the South, real slaves, or the class-inflected behaviors of actual masters and mistresses; accordingly, in their creative and essayistic responses, they inverted Stowe's stereotypes without transforming them. Chesnut seemed to be the only writer in this cohort who felt that *Uncle Tom*'s scenarios were exaggerated but who could not cast Stowe's story or characters out of her mind.

Chesnut's obsessive rereading of and endless commentary on *Uncle Tom's Cabin* in the 1880s narrative is breathtaking: her wartime persona mentions the novel seven times, claims to have reread it four times, and even more significantly, cannot reread it—throws it aside on her fifth attempt—midwar. Ever at the edge of her imagination and tip of her pen, *Uncle Tom's Cabin* evokes scenic analogues from Chesnut's own experience, living parallels between characters in the novel and actual slaves, masters, and mistresses she has known across the antebellum South.

Nonetheless, it remains impossible to determine whether the historical Chesnut really had reread Stowe's book from cover to cover at charged moments during the Civil War, much less on multiple occasions. The 1860s diary contains only one reference to *Uncle Tom's Cabin,* penned in June of 1865. Still, whether the Chesnut who composed the diary fragments in real time actually steeped herself in Stowe's novel again and again, or whether the Chesnut reworking in the 1880s concocted her narrated self's repeated citations of the book for formal or polemical purposes, is not important. What matters is that Chesnut saw the famous novel in profound relation to her own work in progress. Stowe's great creative achievement had enduring power in Mary Chesnut's imagination, however many times she actually reread it.

Witness the ways in which Chesnut used Stowe's characters to help her transform real figures from her own life into literary portraits for her 1880s book. Augustine St. Clare's slave valet Adolph seems to be the doppelganger of Mr. Chesnut's "gentleman's gentleman," Laurence. This connection, however, sheds no favorable light on Laurence, as the fictive Adolph has a reputation with both his master and his enslaved peers of being a dandy and a fop; and certainly Laurence's fate toward the end of Chesnut's 1880s narrative suggests that a slave's overattention to grooming and haberdashery may have negative consequences when he is far from home.

Opining that she has known no Topsies, the 1880s writer goes on to discuss at length the figure of Simon Legree, calling him "Legare" (the surname of an aristocratic Charleston planting family). Chesnut laments the fact that Stowe has painted him as a bachelor; this strategy thus sanitized what otherwise might be a scathing portrait of the tendency of certain married masters to exploit their slave women sexually, producing mulatto offspring who look just like their fathers' other children, but who are doomed to serve as these men's slaves. This critique evokes the remark historians and literary scholars most often associate with the name of Mary Boykin Chesnut, the famous comment from the 1860s diary, deleted from the 1880s revision, that white mistresses are able to identify from the master class the paternity of all local mulatto children, except those in their own families.

The 1880s writer includes in her narrative a discussion with James Team, overseer of Mulberry, about the possibility that living Uncle Toms might be afoot in the South. In answer to her query in an entry for December 6, 1861, Team replies that the Chesnuts' own slave patriarch, "Grandfather Abram," was nearly a saint—and was revered as such—but that he never suffered the brutal treatment of Stowe's martyred hero. Additionally, Grandfather Abram from time to time helped himself to "refreshment" from Colonel Chesnut's wine cellar for "medicinal" reasons, in order to "soothe his stomach" (255). Team, whom Chesnut notes believed that slavery had run its course and needed to be abolished, might have been suggesting that even the far better-than-average conditions under which blacks lived as slaves on Mulberry occasionally required alcoholic self-medication.[8]

Moving from Stowe's characters to her narrative form, it is true that Mary Chesnut's hackles shot up over the slightest invocation of the sentimental, whether the provocation was a less-than-favorite relative's pious expression or the celebration of a new work of domestic women's fiction. One hilarious passage in her narrative involves Chesnut's tongue-in-cheek commentary on the novel *Say and Seal* by Susan Warner, an author immortalized in the female imagination of mid-nineteenth-century America for her best-selling, tear-inducing *The Wide, Wide World* (1850). Would-be book reviewer Chesnut pithily characterizes *Say and Seal* as all "piety and pie-making—equally so," ruminating on the number of Christian platitudes spewed per page by the hero, and philosophizing about why it should be that the heroine, a serving maid, seems to embrace with abundant energy tasks of cooking and housework, but refuses (on some unspoken grounds) when it comes to the burden of dressmaking (May 27, 1861, 65).

Despite the 1880s writer's animus against the genre for which Warner was best known, her disgust over its excessive exhibition of feeling, piety and pie-making evoked uncanny personal associations to her husband's mother. Mary the younger knew that the elder woman sentimentally spoke volumes. But the behavior she associated with her mother-in-law's emotional talk drove her to distraction. In an entry from the early days of the 1860s diary about which she apparently thought better and excised as she transformed her narrative in the 1880s, the younger Chesnut describes the events of her husband's homecoming on a brief furlough in the spring of 1861:

> «This is the end of the farce and sentimental talk of Mr. Chesnut's family— "They never could bear him out of sight." "He must never leave them." "Just recovering from the shock of his joining Beauregard." And *now*, three days after his return for so short a rest at home, [his parents] go to spend a week with Mrs. Reynolds—who is always here and who never since she was *made* sacrificed one instant or wish to their pleasure—and leave us *alone* at Sandy Hill. I am far happier without *them* but for the life of me cannot help wondering at such bare-face *cant*, &c.» (May 30 and 31, 1861, 66)

Here we see Mary Cox Chesnut, known for her effusions of familial dedication, declining to maximize her son's prospective companionship during his first (and for all she knows, his only) furlough of the war. Even more incredible to her daughter-in-law, James's mother seems oblivious to how she has snubbed him. Given her purported concern for her only surviving male child, the elder Mrs. Chesnut behaves in a manner that is perplexing in the extreme. Leaving James Jr. and Mary the younger entirely alone after spending only three days with them, the seemingly insensible mother—Mulberry's angel—decamps to the home of the daughter, Mary Cox Chesnut Reynolds, whom she has hosted and visited regularly. Even if unwittingly, the elder Mrs. Chesnut has sent a message, and one of its recipients, at least, is capable of interpreting its meaning. Thus, Mary the younger concludes that the episode marks "the end of the farce" that is the elder Mary's claim of devotion to James Jr. and the revelation of the "bare-face cant" that has marked her assertions of maternal attachment over many years. Her mother-in-law's emotional talk has revealed itself as empty; Chesnut has read through the false pieties, having learned through years of disappointment the way that sympathetic words sometimes mask hard-hearted actions.

Experiences like this guided the younger Chesnut to connect what she saw as the maudlin thinking of her mother-in-law with an accommodationist position regarding slavery's depravities, and to generalize about the link between sentiment and false feeling. She saw Stowe's novel as the other side of the coin of such sentimentality. While *Uncle Tom's Cabin,* with its harsh evaluation of figures like Legree, was crafted to convince readers to change their minds about the peculiar institution, it stopped well short of inciting its audience to rise up and put an end to slavery. Chesnut proved the rare Southern intellectual who not only could criticize the novel for the extremes to which it took its arguments via stereotyped characters that cast aspersion on Southern culture, but could recognize as well the ways in which the book's ethos of sympathy offered a seductive mask for political inaction.

Across the pages of her 1880s narrative, Chesnut offered this trenchant political critique of mid-nineteenth-century sentimentalism. Her view did not accord with the majority of American women readers of the genre, who were inspired by what they saw as this literature's "cultural work," to borrow a phrase from Jane Tompkins,[9] and whose historical position has been recovered by the labors of late-twentieth-century feminist literary critics. But Chesnut's implication that Stowe's appeal to her reader did not enjoin any response more than right feeling can be seen as cognate with the arguments of a most unlikely cohort of twentieth- and twenty-first-century scholars of African American literature, in the school of James Baldwin, who believed that *Uncle Tom's Cabin* did not go far enough by half.[10]

In that regard, the writer's literary insights were aligned to her political beliefs: she wished that novelists would abandon sentimentality and employ realism or satire to "tell the truth"; thus George Eliot was her great favorite, and Susan Warner was not. And when reflecting on the Civil War as a Carolinian, she thought it equally important to be honest about the realities of slavery and its injurious effects on Southern culture both before and during the war. Mary Chesnut remains unprecedented in the canon of post–Civil War Southern writers, standing virtually alone in explicitly *not* eliding the significance of slavery to the war's causes and in rejecting sentimental explanations for the demise of her culture.

Consider a startling contrast of postwar "historiography" Southern style. In 1881, Jefferson Davis, former president of the Confederate States of America, published his twelve-hundred-page memoir *The Rise and Fall of the Confederate Government,* in which he argued that slavery "was in no wise the cause of the conflict," that is, the Civil War, "but only an incident."[11] Writing the foreword to a 1990 reprint of the book, historian James M. McPherson characterized Davis's claim that slavery bore an only "incidental" relation to the origin of the crisis as "the virgin-birth theory of secession: the Confederacy was not conceived by any worldly cause, but by divine principle."[12]

Davis's strikingly ahistorical analysis, centering on Southern disavowal of racial guilt, afforded a balm to the cultural memory of a wounded region, the white population of which slowly was regaining its political autonomy in the wake of Reconstruction's failure. Generations of Southern memorializers took up Davis's slavery-free rationale for secession in order to forge what, in their studies of race and Civil War memory, twentieth- and twenty-first-century scholars, taking the lead from nineteenth-century Southern historian Edward Pollard, call the ideology of the "Lost Cause."[13] Far from just a nineteenth-century phenomenon, "Lost Cause" doctrine endured from the era of surrender at Appomattox Courthouse through the fiftieth reunion of Gettysburg and beyond; indeed, as we've seen, in works like *Confederates in the Attic,* Tony Horwitz identifies this dogma as alive and well as late as 1998.

David Blight argues in *Race and Reunion: The Civil War in American Memory* that the "Lost Cause" doctrine was predicated on "control of the *history* of the war and its aftermath; its use of *white supremacy* as both means and ends; and the place of *women* in its development."[14] It is thus not surprising that it spawned such spuriously powerful historical revisions as Margaret Mitchell's *Gone With the Wind* (1936). But as Blight has shown, belief in the righteousness of the "Lost Cause" offered Southerners far more than a "moonlight and magnolias" manner of remembering: in fact, "Lost Cause" ideology became a civil religion for the postwar South, not merely inflecting, but affectively dominating the political and social reunion of the formerly warring sections. According to Blight, the healing of the nation came to depend in equal measures on the very dialectic of remembering and forgetting that enabled "Lost Cause" ideologues to disavow the centrality of slavery to the Civil War.

As Davis was completing his magnum opus, his intimate wartime friend Mary Boykin Chesnut was laboring over her own monumental literary narrative of the years 1861–65. Roundly avoiding Davis's revisionism, however, Chesnut had become obsessed in the 1880s with the crucial connection between slavery, secession, and sentimental thinking, subjects to which she returned over and over again. Her narrative thus offers an idiosyncratic and vital exception to Blight's thesis in ways that significantly complicate an otherwise starkly amnesiac archive of Southern cultural memory. Rabidly antisentimental and flush with representations of slavery's pernicious effects on her disintegrating culture, Chesnut's narrative proves a fascinating antidote to the literature of the "Lost Cause," an epic instance of what cultural historians, post-Foucault, have come to call "countermemory."

If Chesnut's 1880s narrative counts as such a work, however, it is in no way because she sought to represent a contentious or dissenting view of the Confederate wartime society in which she had lived. Chesnut's oppositional vision had everything to do with the most basic aspects of her character, which impelled her to tell the truth as she saw it, rather than submit to Lost Cause or any other fashionable pieties in her Reconstruction and post-Reconstruction culture. The fifteen-year-old Mary Boykin Miller who had believed that slavery was wrong was the same person who, forty-five years later would not deny the centrality of African American bondage to the Civil War. This is not to suggest that there were no topics that were off limits or not painful for the 1880s writer: we have only to consider those scathing and accusatory passages penned about her in-laws in the 1860s diary but omitted from her 1880s reworkings. Nevertheless, scenes such as the one in which "mama smells a smell" offer an extraordinary critique, some of the most astute character portraits Chesnut ever drew.

Mrs. Chesnut "Smells a Smell"

The subtitle of this chapter, the stench of slavery and sentiment, raises the conundrum of what sentiment might *smell* like. When literary historian Ann Douglas took up the topic in her field-creating first book, *The Feminization of American Culture* (1977), she called such heightened nineteenth-century representations of feeling "political sense obfuscated or gone rancid." "Sentimentalism," she continued, "unlike the modes of genuine sensibility, never exists except in tandem with failed political consciousness."[15] In 1985, Jane Tompkins challenged this critical interpretation with the counterassertion that sentimental novels like *Uncle Tom's Cabin* did crucial "cultural work," and that a literature of feeling offered power to theretofore disenfranchised white, middle-class American women, enabling them to enter the public sphere collectively and make social reform possible.

Douglas nuanced her position in the early 1980s, acknowledging in two important essays, which became Penguin edition introductions to each novel, respectively, that at least in the cases of Susanna Rowson's *Charlotte Temple* (1794) and Harriet Beecher Stowe's *Uncle Tom's Cabin* (1852), literary history revealed that novels *could* inspire action or change in the culture in which they had been created. Douglas's revised argument best accounts for the actual dynamics at work in the finest examples of the sentimental genre (*Uncle Tom's Cabin; The Wide, Wide World; Incidents in the Life of a Slave Girl; Little Women*). But her initial observation in *Feminization,* that sentiment was what remained when politics had decayed, offered a fairly accurate account of the effects on their reading audience of second-rate emotion-charged domestic works. In certain proslavery novels, for example, we see it used to rationalize the "peculiar" institution as a positive good.[16]

A century prior to the advent of scholars such as Douglas, Mary Chesnut understood that second-rate emotion conveys a horrid stench. Accordingly, when the writer of the 1880s fancies Stowe and her New England abolitionist cohort at home, she depicts them flush with wealth, thriving in the midst of envy-inducing working and living conditions, and completely unaware of the realities of life for those they condemn:

> On one side Mrs. Stowe, Greel[e]y, Thoreau, Emerson, Sumner, in nice New England homes—clean, clear, and *sweet-smelling*—shut up in libraries, writing books which ease their hearts of their bitterness toward us, or editing newspapers—all [of] which pays better than anything else in the world. . . .
> . . . Now what I have seen of my mother's life, my grandmother's, my mother-in-law's: These people were educated at Northern schools mostly—read the same books as their northern contemnors, the same daily newspapers, the same Bible—have the same ideas of right and wrong—are highbred, lovely, good, pious—doing their duty as they conceive it. They live in Negro villages. . . . they strive to ameliorate the condition of these Africans in every particular . . . Think of these holy New Englanders, forced to have a negro village walk through their houses whenever they saw fit—dirty, slatternly, idle, *ill-smelling* by nature (when otherwise, it is the exception). (November 27, 1861, 245, my emphasis)

This sharp and unpleasant figurative smell is also what she identifies with her mother-in-law, a Northern-born woman who speaks in the sweet and low tones of the most genteel Southern ladies, but whose always benevolent language masks a will of iron that can be breached by no one. In counterpoint to this steely inner strength is the peculiar fact that the elder Mrs. Chesnut suffers from a hypersensitivity to scents that others consider pleasant, particularly the fragrances of certain flowers. Accordingly, she has to limit which, if any, blossoms surround her: of all the varieties of roses in Mulberry's gardens, only one particular species is tolerable. Candles and lamps have to be snuffed outdoors. And when it comes to bad odors, no one is more vigilant: she requires that the source of such smells be detected and eliminated immediately.

The elder Mrs. Chesnut's olfactory affliction is just the sort of problem that literary scholar Janice Carlisle explores among fictional characters in her *Common Scents: Comparative Encounters in High-Victorian Fiction.* In the "hierarchy of the senses," Carlisle writes, "smell . . . has been placed at the bottom." "Smell is inveterately low: corporeal, animalistic, primitive, and therefore degraded." Later Carlisle asserts that "according to Victorian psychophysiology, smell is the sense of difference." "Olfaction is the least intellectual and most purely emotional" of all the senses. "Unlike taste, the other sense dependent on incorporation, smell involves invasions of one's bodily cavities that are largely involuntary."[17]

Carlisle's reading of the way a smell invades the body of its partaker, regardless of his or her consent, sheds light on the problem of the elder Mrs. Chesnut's olfactory disturbances on her husband's plantation. This elderly gentlewoman generously has given of herself to her slaves, while simultaneously holding herself at a distance from them. For more than fifty years, she has never become involved in the slaves' political affairs or the conditions of their labor; instead, when necessary, she has turned to overseer James Team as the proper intermediary. Additionally, she has never strayed from the female sphere, beyond serving as devoted amateur physician to Mulberry's blacks, as well as quartermistress of the slave wardrobe, supervising the sewing of tiny outfits for babies and the cutting of material for the adults' seasonal changes of clothes.

Put another way, the elder Mrs. Chesnut has always rigorously controlled the degree to which she has been willing to get her hands dirty when it comes to her slaves, despite her benevolent involvement in their lives. In Carlisle's clinical terms, she has never incorporated with them, which might indicate a level of intimacy or familiarity with a servant that had become more normative, culturally, by the time of her daughter-in-law's generation. In the 1880s narrative, the younger Mary Chesnut portrays many such exchanges between herself and her husband's former nurse, old Betsey, as well as with younger house servants such as Mulberry's Maria Whitaker and her own Molly and Ellen, and between Buck Preston, her closest protégée, and the various slave women who have attended "Buckie" since birth.

The writer dramatizes no such relations between Mrs. Chesnut senior and her own female slaves who, tellingly, are never given proper names in the 1880s book, though it is also crucial to add that the elderly mistress virtually was on twenty-four-hour call to the quarters when it came to tending sick and dying Chesnut blacks. That is, while she kept a genteel social distance from her healthy bondspeople, ailing Chesnut slaves enjoyed her devoted attention. The 1880s writer records that bad smells alone had the capacity to disturb the elderly Mrs. Chesnut, suggesting that it is precisely because, without invitation, they could invade the sanctum of herself.

Only two months into the first year of the war, in the 1860s diary entry for June 21–23, 1861, Mary Chesnut records the following lines from Camden: "I woke in the night, heard such a commotion, such loud talking of a crowd—I rushed out, thinking what could they have heard from Virginia, but found only Mrs. Chesnut had smelled a *Smell*—and roused the whole *yard*. One of Colonel Chesnut's Negroes was taken yesterday with a pistol" (*TPMC*, 84). This gnomic passage, telegraphing Chesnut's semi-somnambulant conflation of hoped-for war news, an incendiary threat, and its relation to the daytime reality of a potential slave uprising, about which she knows nothing, but memories of which may have motivated the elderly mistress's terror, form colorful threads for what in the 1880s manuscript she transforms into a literary tableau:

> Down at Sandy Hill again—making ready for Richmond. Last night I was awakened by loud talking and candles flashing everywhere—tramping of feet—growls dying away in the distance, loud calls from point to point in the yard.
>
> Up I started—my heart in my mouth. Some dreadful thing had happened—a battle—a death—a horrible accident. Miss Sally Chesnut was screaming aloft—that is, from the top of the stairway—hoarsely, like a boatswain in a storm.
>
> Colonel C. was storming at the sleepy negroes looking for fire with lighted candles in closets—&c. &c.
>
> I dressed and came upon the scene of action.
>
> "What is it? Any news?"
>
> "No, no—only, mama smells a smell. She thinks something is burning somewhere."
>
> The whole yard was alive—literally swarming. There are sixty or seventy people here kept to wait upon this household—two-thirds of them too old or too young to be of any use. But families remain intact. Mr. C. has a magnificent voice. I am sure it can be heard for miles. Literally he was roaring from the piazza—giving orders to the busy crowd who were hunting the smell of fire.
>
> Mrs. C. is deaf, so she did not know what a commotion she was creating. She is very sensitive on the subject of bad odors. Candles have to be taken out of the room to be snuffed. Lamps are extinguished only in the porticoes—or further afield. She finds violets oppressive. Can only tolerate a single kind of rose. Tea rose she will not have in her room.
>
> She was totally innocent of the storm she had raised and in a mild sweet voice was suggesting places to be searched.
>
> I was weak enough to laugh hysterically. The bombardment of Fort Sumter was nothing to this. (Between June 16 and 26, 1861, 77–78)

Concluding the subject of the original 1861 entry, the 1880s Chesnut pens two brief passages and then closes: "Yesterday some of the Negro men on the plantation were found with pistols. I have never seen aught about any negro to show they knew we had a war on hand in which they have any interest" (78).

Sandy Hill Plantation, the Chesnut family summer retreat, was a place the writer loathed. Only twelve pages before this description of nighttime chaos, she remarks that it was at Sandy Hill that "everything good first emptied out of me" (66)—the only possible reference in the entire 1880s narrative to a miscarriage that may have occurred in the early days of her marriage. Chesnut and her husband, at this point an aide-de-camp to General Beauregard, were making preparations to reenter the hub of Confederate political life at Richmond. The Sandy Hill visit marked a pause in their forward movement.

Awakened by the "tramping of feet" (portending soldiers on the march?) and "loud talking" (the sound of orders being barked?), Chesnut's 1860s persona expresses visceral confusion over the way in which the stultifying, isolated summer plantation has metamorphosed suddenly into a battleground, marked by bestial sounds ("growls" and "loud calls"), the origins of which cannot be determined. Finding her "heart in [her] mouth," a trope that recurs throughout the 1880s narrative, Chesnut voices both her emotional horror and the physical discomfort attending such shocks. Ever conscious of the world-historical significance of the events of the summer of 1861, she cannot conceive that the sleep-shattering upheaval in late June of that year might have nothing to do with the unfolding Civil War.

In that regard, although the Sandy Hill concussion would prove to be a strictly "domestic" affair, in Chesnut's imagination, her husband's family—whom she represents throughout the 1880s book as pronouncing disparaging judgments on her political engagement, writerly practice, and constant comings and goings—serves as a telling microcosm for the national house divided. Indeed, sister-in-law Miss Sally Chesnut and orphaned niece Harriet Grant function for Chesnut as "the enemy within," whose despotism blights life on the home front. Thus, in a brutal if highly amusing description, she sketches this portrait of her comically exasperating sister-in-law, caught comporting herself in a decidedly ungenteel fashion, hoarsely screaming "like a boatswain in a storm." Under the withering gaze of the 1880s writer, the lace-festooned forty-eight-year-old spinster is fixed forever as a rude maritime mechanical struggling to keep afloat in stormy seas.

Meanwhile, the old Colonel, assuming his recurring role of tyrant in the narrative—whether as a czar, a general, or Napoleon—is in the process of mustering his sleepy slave troops when Chesnut appears on the "scene of the action." The martial language here is not untypical of the narrating Chesnut's diction: characteristically collapsing home front and battleground, she points up the irrelevance of the notion of "separate spheres" during a time of political crisis in which no American, male or female, remained unimplicated. The question "What is it? Any news?" immediately reveals the nondomestic orientation of her own allegiances: surely such commotion must signify a marshaling of a regiment or some disastrous consequence at the front lines. But her father-in-law's response snaps Chesnut's 1860s persona back to the depressing reality of Sandy Hill existence. It is neither Lee nor Longstreet but "mama" whose assessment of conditions—her smelling "a smell"—has determined marching orders for Mulberry's blacks.

Consider the symbolic and political significance of Mrs. Chesnut's keen nose as it relates to the notion that in her 1880s epic, Mary Boykin Chesnut has no interest in disavowing the centrality of slavery to the Civil War. It is crucial to know that the writer's mother-in-law had been born in Philadelphia around 1772 to a family of property, a father who had served in the Revolution with Washington and a mother whose closest friends had been the Custises, Martha Washington's family. Though the Philadelphia Coxes owned slaves themselves, and though by 1861 Mrs. Chesnut senior had lived in the South for nearly sixty years, it was well known that as a girl she had been terrified by the St. Domingo slave revolution, understood its implications for American slaveowners, and was ambivalent about the "peculiar institution." Furthermore, toward the beginning of the elder Mrs. Chesnut's married life, a slave rebellion had been thwarted in Camden. Mary Cox Chesnut and the old Colonel had lived through this convulsion in early July 1816, which was averted by the efforts of their slave Scipio, a brick mason, at that time in his teens or early twenties. The senior Mrs. Chesnut herself had been in her forties at the moment of the threatened rising, which the thwarted rebels had planned to inaugurate by burning down the town's most important homes. This history adds context to the meaning of smoke for old Mrs. Chesnut, who by the 1860s had compensated for her deafness by keenly developing her other senses, particularly that of smell.

If it makes sense that the elder Mrs. Chesnut associates the smell of fire with the danger of black uprising, there is another "smell" at Mulberry that the younger Mary Chesnut has identified—a metaphoric stench with no detectable odor. This particular miasma has the power, she wrote in the 1860s diary, to "haunt" her by "day and night" (*TPMC*, 29, 31, 72). Her spectral language of horror and nightmare, a stench without a smell, relates to Chesnut's continued disturbance by the possibility of cross-racial sexual activity in Mulberry's past.

As mentioned earlier, Chesnut excised all trace of this material from her 1880s book. But the writer's particular "horror" over sexual activity between white masters and black slave women in fact may have been connected to the trauma of her own infertility. Slave women seemed to be producing babies black, brown, and "yeller" at a prodigious rate, while Mary Boykin Chesnut, married for over twenty years at the time of the Civil War, had none. If a plethora of enslaved infants raised the census rolls for the quarters, that was one thing; such a population boom theoretically enriched her father-in-law. But there was no justice when "black" offspring were born to slave mothers and white master-fathers, infants whose personhood could not count in the public sphere of a slave state like South Carolina. The production of socially unclassifiable babies, whose lives could not be made meaningful in the eyes of whites unless they were manumitted by their fathers, was a crying shame in the face of the fact that Chesnut had no child of her own.

As we have discussed, it is impossible to untangle the genealogies of any biracial slaves on the Chesnut estate. But knowing that the 1850 census listed thirty-eight "mulatto" slaves on Mulberry, Chesnut's comment in the long "mama smells a smell" passage that despite there being many slaves "too old or too young to be of any use . . . families remain intact" is particularly pointed. Given the sociological practices of plantation life and the Chesnuts' own definitions of "family," the remark suggests that as slave masters go, male Chesnuts who might have "visited the quarters" consequently acted with relative benevolence in comparison to those owners who put the making of profit, not to mention the concealing of sexual guilt, well ahead of any respect for the emotional connections of bondspeople.

Immediately after making the observation about the Chesnuts' commitment to maintaining the integrity of Mulberry's slave families, Mary Chesnut notes that "mama" is completely deaf and thus unaware of the utter chaos she has set into motion with her smelling "a smell" on the night in question. One might discount the relation between these two statements as a non sequitur, but the trajectory of Chesnut's narrative unconscious in their juxtaposition is far too revealing to be dismissed. Chesnut's claim regarding slave family preservation and the observation about her mother-in-law's deafness can be linked to the elder Mrs. Chesnut's improbable ignorance of her own late father-in-law's possible conduct across the color line. Of all the remarks made by nineteenth-century Southern women on the subject of "miscegenation," the early and, again, excised entry from the younger Chesnut's original diary may be the most oft-invoked. Painfully apropos of the subtext of my central passage, it is worth quoting once more:

> «Like the patriarchs of old our men live all in one house with their wives and their concubines and the mulattos one sees in every family exactly resemble the white children—and every lady tells you who is the father of all the mulatto children in everybody's household, but those in her own she seems to think drop from the clouds, or pretends so to think.»

In light of this, the elder Mrs. Chesnut's deafness, a physiological reality as well as a figurative state of being, can be understood in connection with her moralistic refusal to tolerate ill words spoken about anyone in her vicinity. From the local "Charlotte Temple" (literary code for Camden's most notorious seduced and abandoned white woman, whom she defended bravely), to the numerous slaves pregnant out of wedlock who were a fact of life on many plantations, Mrs. Chesnut senior deigned it neither proper nor seemly to speak severely of those of her sex less fortunate than she. Degraded black femininity had no stauncher defender in Camden than the elder Mrs. Chesnut, though the possibility that the fathers of such women's illegitimate children might prove to be members of white women's families was, of course, the great unmentionable rejoinder to all such declarations of charity and forgiveness.

But not quite the Pollyanna her sentimental, pious persona might suggest, Mrs. Chesnut Sr. was known as much for her steely intelligence, exercised through a lifetime of unremitting reading, as she was for her angelic attitude toward fallen women, black and white. Two hundred pages into the 1880s narrative, her daughter-in-law notes:

> Mrs. C has a greediness of books such as I never saw in anyone else. Reading is the real occupation and solace of her life. In the soft, luxurious life she leads, she denies herself nothing that she wants. In her well-regulated character she could not want anything that she ought not to have. Economy is one of her cherished virtues. And strange to say, she never buys a book or has been known to take a magazine or periodical. But she has them all. They gravitate toward her. They flow into her room. Everybody is proud to send or lend any book they have compassed by any means, fair or foul. Other members of the family who care nothing whatever for them buy the books and she reads them. (September 24, 1861, 202)

In an earlier entry, Chesnut has recorded:

> Among the glaring inconsistencies of life. Our chatelaine locked up Eugene Sue and returned even Washington Allston's novel, with thanks and a decided hint that it should be burned. At least it should not remain in her house. Bad books are not allowed house room except in the library and under lock and key, key in the master's pocket. But bad women, if they are not white or only in a

menial capacity, may warm the house unmolested. The ostrich game is thought a Christian act. (April 23, 1861, 54)

Thus the writer of the 1880s sketches a woman who managed the ethical and emotional contradictions of her life through a complicated calculus of psychological displacement: devouring and then dismissing—or quarantining and thus controlling as contraband—sexually provocative literary work. Not merely denying the reality of female waywardness or, even more significantly, that of interracial sexual exploitation potentially having operated in her own lifetime, possibly under her younger, sharper, nose, she turned a blind or "ostrich" eye, one that aptly complemented her real deafness. And, simultaneously, the elderly mistress developed so keen a sense of smell that she could sniff from inside the walls of her plantation the scent of ash smoldering outdoors at a distance of two hundred yards.

A male Chesnut of generations past may have "invaded" his slave women—or at least one slave woman, "Sue." Mary Cox Chesnut clearly had no commensurate experience with any bound black person. She was ambivalent about slavery, emancipating according to his will only the black bondspeople her father had bequeathed her. What she had undergone in terms of "invasion" in South Carolina was really not comparable and operated in reverse: it involved occasionally suffering unwelcome "smells" emanating from the quarters, such as the smoke of July 1861 that assaulted her serenity in the small hours of the morning, rousing her to pandemonium.

Through her portrait of her mother-in-law, the sentimental slave mistress who could not abide the reality of the abuses that riddled the "paternal" system, but who did not speak out against the institution, the 1880s Chesnut communicated her own sense of slavery's lethal stench. She also highlighted the institution's relation to South Carolina's and the Confederacy's involvement in the Civil War. But in the midst of what otherwise might be seen as an antislavery narrative, however imperfect and biased against African American culture it may sometimes be, what do we make of the writer's rationalizations about her family's slave population's "uselessness"? Consider, below, Chesnut's invocation of taxes and doctor's bills paid for the slave community on Mulberry, as well as her fixation on black fertility and, implicitly, her own barrenness. In keeping with these assertions, contemplate the claim that the Chesnut bondspeople are "unproductive" in proportion to their vast (reproducing) numbers, a phenomenon that the writer of the 1880s never analyzes as a sign of potential black resistance to the system of slavery itself. Chesnut's blind spot to certain forms of black defiance, her inability to decode the meaning, say, of purported laziness, surely is notable. But of course, had slave challenges been legible to the master class, they could not have been effective as acts of opposition.

It is not certain that these contradictions can be clarified either by material from Chesnut's 1880s narrative or historical documents from the archives. Perhaps such ruminations reflect the writer's post-Reconstruction bitterness about her family's comparative poverty and the black community's relative elevation, itself more white fantasy than black reality, according to scholars of African American life in South Carolina.[18] Reminiscing about the early days of the war, the 1880s writer points out how well cared for the blacks were (the same doctor treated Chesnuts and Chesnut slaves alike) and how well oiled were the workings of the plantation (the taxes regularly paid). This may simply represent a strain of white antebellum nostalgia that, in general, is untypical of Mary Chesnut's 1880s narrative.

But surely it is not a coincidence that the 1880s narrator reports that slaves were found on Mulberry with pistols soon after the episode of the smelled smell. Tellingly, Chesnut does not report the fate suffered by these men upon their discovery with weapons. One only can imagine that they were arrested and possibly even hanged on charges of threatened insurrection. The 1860s version asserts simply that they were "taken." It is fascinating, however, to consider the 1880s writer's uncanny placement of the smelled smell just before her remarks about Chesnut blacks being found with guns, as if she understood the deeper meaning of old Mrs. Chesnut's smoke-anxiety, if not its link to an actual thwarted uprising. Reprising the elder Mrs. Chesnut's characteristic ostrichlike behavior, the 1880s narrator then comments on the ways in which her slaves never "showed" that "we had a war on hand in which they have any interest." Here, Chesnut's use of the rhetoric of acting is precisely her point: the 1880s book everywhere interrogates the issue of racial performance, particularly the ways in which the writer's own servants do or do not manifest their awareness of the political and social implications of the relationship between the inevitable end of slavery and the origins of the Civil War.

The Death of Little Eva

For Mary Cox Chesnut, the most significant martial struggle of her lifetime may not have been the Civil War unfolding from the coast of South Carolina, not the conflict involving her son (in the political sphere until 1864, then a brevet brigadier cavalry general of the South Carolina Reserves) and her grandson (a captain in General Wade Hampton's South Carolina Cavalry). The senior Mrs. Chesnut's real war, instead, may have been the American Revolution and its glorious aftermath, which constituted the centerpiece of her aristocratic upbringing in Philadelphia and New Jersey, a rich early life in a society that included Martha Washington's Custis relatives. Mary Cox's father, after all, had been quartermaster general of Washington's Continental Army. Indeed, even more than any Chesnut ancestors, Mary Cox grew up on the Revolution, foremost as what historians have come to call a "republican daughter."[19]

But by no means were the senior Chesnuts the only family in the Confederacy with a history of military service extending back to the Revolution. In fact, the younger Mary Chesnut recalled a conversation in Richmond with Mrs. Robert E. Lee around the time of the most significant cavalry battle of the conflict at Brandy Station, Virginia, on June 9, 1863, which she recorded in the undated 1862–63 "Memoirs" section of her narrative. In Chesnut's entry the fighting evokes familial associations to wars of the past, remembered in the words of Mary Custis Lee:

> She said Mrs. Chesnut and her Aunt Nelly Custis (Mrs. Lewis) were very intimate in the old Washington administration, Philadelphia days. I told her Mrs. Chesnut was the historical member of our family. She had so much to tell of the old Revolutionary times. And then she was one of the "white-robed choir" at Trenton Bridge—which everybody who writes a life of Washington asks her to give an account of. (450)

It is imaginable that the bright, teenaged Mary Cox experienced the events of April 21, 1789, when she was part of the welcoming celebrations for the president-elect, as the apotheosis of girlish dreams laid down by years of reading Spenser's *Faerie Queene,* Shakespeare's green world comedies, *A Midsummer Night's Dream* and *As You Like It,* and assorted tales of dashing heroes riding white chargers (as Washington certainly did), bedecked by flower petals, cascading from the baskets of white-robed young girls. Mary Cox was living out the early national version of this fairy tale: handsome General Washington, soon to become chief executive, gloriously dressed in blue uniform, on the requisite white steed, was expressing gratitude to her and the twelve other girls and their mothers for the beauty of their floral tribute and serenade. It was a *tableau vivant* of the republican family: the father of his country surrounded by warbling republican mothers and daughters alike.

So pleased was Washington by this extraordinary tribute that he composed a "Card" that was handed to the white-robed choir in response to their musical

"Sonata" in his honor. Below are selected passages from newspaper accounts of the event and the text of both of the Sonata and the Card. The *Gazette of the United States,* published out of New York, noted:

> Many persons who were in the crowd, on Thursday, were heard to say, that they should now die contented—nothing being wanted to complete their happiness, previous to this auspicious period, but the sight of the saviour of his Country.[20]

Again, from the *Gazette of the United States,* several days later, we get a narrative description of young Mary Cox's experience:

> When the Procession arrived on the bridge, which lies south of the Town, they were surprised with a scene to which no description can do Justice.
>
> As *Trenton* had been made twice memorable during the war, once by the capture of the Hessians, and again by the repulse of the whole British army, in their attempt to cross this bridge, the Evening before the battle of *Princeton,* a design was formed by the ladies of this place, and carried into execution solely under their direction, to testify to his Excellency, by the celebration of these actions, the grateful sense they retained of the safety and protection afforded by him to the daughters of New Jersey.
>
> A triumphal arch was raised on the bridge, 20 feet wide, supported by thirteen pillars. The center of the arch, from the ground, was about 20 feet. Each pillar was intertwined with wreaths of evergreen. The arch, which extended about 12 feet along the bridge, was covered with laurel, and decorated on the inside with evergreens and flowers. On the front of the arch, or that side to which His Excellency approached, was the following Inscription, in large gilt letters:
>
> > "THE DEFENDER OF THE MOTHERS,
> > WILL BE THE PROTECTOR OF THE DAUGHTERS"
>
> The upper and lower sides of this Inscription were ornamented with wreaths of evergreens, and artificial flowers, of all kinds, made for the purpose, beautifully interspersed. On the center of the arch, above the inscription, was a Dome, or Cupola, of flowers and evergreens, encircling the dates of the glorious actions, inscribed in large gilt letters. The summit of the Dome displayed a large *Sun-Flower,* which pointed to the Sun, was designed to express this sentiment or motto:
>
> > "TO YOU ALONE."
>
> As emblematic of the unparalleled unanimity of sentiment, in the millions of the United States.
>
> A numerous train of ladies, leading their daughters in their hands, assembled at the arch, thus to thank their Defender and Protector.

Just as His Excellency passed under the arch, he was Addressed in the following SONATA, composed and set to Musick for the occasion, and sung by a number of young Misses, dressed in white, and crowned with wreaths and chaplets of flowers.

SONATA

WELCOME, mighty Chief! once more,
Welcome to this grateful shore:
Now no mercenary foe
Aims again the fatal blow—
Aims at thee the fatal blow.

Virgins fair, and Matrons grave,
Those thy conquering arm did save
Build for thee triumphal bowers
Strew, ye fair, his way with flowers—
Strew ye Hero's way with flowers.

Each of the Singers held a basket in their hands, filled with flowers, which, when they sung, "Strew your Hero's way with flowers," they scattered before him.

When his Excellency came opposite to the little female band, he honoured the ladies, by halting until the Sonata was finished.

The Scene was truly grand; and the mingled sentiments which crowded into the mind, in the few moments of solemn stillness, bathed many cheeks with tears. The General most politely thanked the Ladies for their attention, and the Procession moved on to his lodgings.

The Ladies of Trenton have displayed a degree of taste, elegance, and patriotism on this occasion, which does them the highest honor, and I believe stands unexampled; but what particularly merits observation, all expence was most carefully avoided: The materials of the Structure were the most plain and unpolished, until so superbly decorated, which cost the Ladies but the labour of a few Evenings in preparing flowers.

The General being presented with a copy of the *Sonata,* was pleased to address the following CARD to the Ladies.

To the *Ladies* of Trenton, who were assembled on the 21st Day of April, 1789; at the Triumphal Arch, erected by them on the Bridge, which extends across the Assanpinck Creek.

CARD

General Washington cannot leave this place, without expressing his Acknowledgments to the Matrons and Young Ladies, who received him in

FIGURE 8. Currier and Ives, "Washington's reception by the ladies..." (lithograph, ca. 1845). This reproduction of the Currier and Ives print marks George Washington's triumphal return to Trenton en route to his inauguration in April 1789. It depicts thirteen girls, including the young Mary Cox, serenading the president-elect. Mary Cox Chesnut would routinely show it to visitors. From Currier and Ives's catalogue raisonné (New York: N. Currier, ca. 1845). Courtesy of the Library of Congress (LC-DIG-ppmsca-07649; digital file from original print).

> so novel and grateful a manner, at the triumphal Arch at Trenton, for the exquisite Sensations he experienced in that Affecting moment.— The astonishing contrast between his former and Actual situation at the same spot—the elegant Taste with which it [was] adorned for the present occasion—and the innocent appearance of the white-robed Choir, who met him with gratulatory Song, have made such an impression on his remembrance, as, he assures them, will never be effaced.
>
> *Trenton,* April 21, 1789[21]

In portraying her mother-in-law's moment singing and scattering petals at General Washington's feet—immortalized in the Currier and Ives print and reimagined by N. C. Wyeth in his 1930 engraving "Washington's Procession into Trenton"[22]—Mary Boykin Chesnut crystallized what may have been the public apogee of Mary Cox's life. Soon after she accepted the hand of wealthy and dashing Colonel James Chesnut, who had been nicknamed at Princeton the "Black Prince," the new Mrs. Chesnut decamped from the North in a coach and four to take up life as the mistress of a great South Carolina plantation. This sparkling alumna of the white-robed choir would have seemed to have done very well for herself indeed. Nevertheless, it was not clear that even such a splendid match could come up in her own mind's eye to that moment on the bridge under the arch with General Washington, where she was dressed as an angel and the setting came as close to situating her in the majesty of heaven as she ever would find herself placed on earth.

This extraordinary blending of a real American hero with significant situational magic, immortalized throughout the press and in works of art alike, left little for a young lady to dream of. Mrs. Chesnut went on to give birth to fourteen infants, though only four survived to middle age, and just three outlived her: James Jr., Sarah (Miss Sally), and Mary Cox Chesnut Reynolds. She nursed countless hundreds of slaves, dressed and tended to their ailing infants; made numerous visits of comfort, as well as early trips home to New Jersey for the summer with a rich assemblage of coaches and wagons; hosted the weddings of offspring, raised orphaned grandchildren, and devoured thousands of books and periodicals. These were the many accomplishments and responsibilities that marked Mary Cox Chesnut's very long life. That the elder Mrs. Chesnut and her husband lived on well past the mid-nineteenth century, and remained fairly vital (despite their deafness and his failing sight) well into the 1860s, made them virtually unique among their own set: at this moment in the United States, reaching the age of sixty was considered an achievement. Both senior Chesnuts were well over ninety when they died.

All of the facts of this rich and lengthy life must be juxtaposed to the extraordinary starkness of the announcement Chesnut makes in the 1880s book for March 15, 1864: "Mrs. Chesnut is dead" (586). The family matriarch had passed away just as the Civil War was taking its last fatal turn toward Union victory. Though Mary Cox Chesnut was Northern born and exhibited continued ambivalence to Carolinian ways, her fortunes had become completely linked to the fate of the Old South. In the face of her death, the reticence of her daughter-in-law—about whom she was also ambivalent and whose view of slavery was more associated with the North of Mary Cox's girlhood than the South she was tied to—represents a significant lapse. Chesnut's 1880s notation on the death of her mother-in-law offers us absolutely no access to her world of feeling, no suggestion of how her husband had responded to the news, nor how she felt herself about the loss of a woman who was loved by so many, but who conjured in her so much heartache and frustration. Instead of emotion, we get a list, the itemized bill for mourning clothes:

> Gave 375 dollars for my mourning. Which consists of a black alpaca dress and a crape veil. Bonnet, gloves, and all, it came to ($500.00) five hundred. Before the blockade these things would not have been thought fit for a chamber maid. (586)

Then, four days later, she notes:

> New experience. Molly and Laurence both gone home, and I am to be left, for the first time in my life, wholly at the mercy of hired servants.
> Mr. Chesnut being in such deep mourning for his mother, we see no company. I have a maid of all work. (March 19, 1864, 589)

And finally she comments on Johnny Chesnut's grief:

> He is here in deep mourning. Heard of the death of his grandmother. (March 24, 1864, 592)

These extraordinarily terse 1880s passages constitute the entirety of Mary Boykin Chesnut's written reflections on the loss of her mother-in-law, whom in a later entry she calls "the genius of the place" (May 8, 1864, 606). In the diary of the 1860s, *The Private Mary Chesnut,* there are no entries at all for the year 1864 against which we might compare these scant offerings. The above quotations constitute the sole remainder of the writer's meditations on a subject clearly worthy of more words.

Nevertheless, one remarkable document, a letter from her niece Harriet Grant, dated April 3, 1864, survives in the Mulberry Plantation archives from this period, shedding light on what otherwise remains a nonsubject in the 1880s book: the old Colonel's response to losing his wife of more than sixty years. Harriet initially requests help securing a decent black dress, presumably for her mourning wardrobe. Writing to her aunt at Richmond, she asks her to get a "bombazine, cashmere, de chine, or merino dress—black of course." She then goes on to worry aloud about her deeply bereaved, increasingly fragile grandfather, now ninety-four years old:

> I wish Uncle James and yourself could come home, Grandpa looks very badly and says every day that he is growing weaker, tho we do not perceive the change from day to day.
>
> He seems to want nothing but Uncle Jimmie and haunts the post-office for letters from him, which he makes us read until he can remember them.
>
> When Laurence told him you were coming the middle of May he answered, "I shall not see them" but he has brightened a little since Uncle Jimmie's letter appointing the middle of the month for your return.[23]

From this tender communiqué several things are clear: the old Colonel is declining swiftly, as many elderly people do when they lose beloved spouses of many years. It would seem that James and Mary Chesnut have not yet left Richmond for Mulberry. Apparently, their return to South Carolina is slated for mid-May, in adherence to a prior plan that the death of James's mother has not disturbed. Additionally, the old Colonel's world view, always pragmatic "au fond" according to Mary Boykin Chesnut, has become increasingly fatalistic in the absence of his wife's eternal optimism: he has become convinced that he will not have the strength to endure for another six weeks, long enough to see at Mulberry once more the son "he seems to want nothing but."

Most poignant is the fact that the old gentleman insists that Harriet and Miss Sally read and reread James Jr.'s letters so that he can memorize them, as by this point he has lost not only most of his hearing, but also his sight. Overwhelmed by his grief and the lonely days stretching out ahead of him, his impulse to internalize his son's words can be seen as a desperate attempt at reincorporation. The old gentleman is trying to take in, completely, the absent dear one, the fantasized reconnection with whom may negate his loss and restore him to wholeness, despite his physical diminishments. In this phantasmatic equation, son James stands in for his beloved wife.

The elderly matron's death most likely had been expected, but its unspeakability for Chesnut nevertheless offers an apt moment for consulting Freud's "Mourning and Melancholia" in order to make sense of the symptomatic quality of her writerly silence. Freud would say that disturbed mourning has jammed the works for the 1860s persona: accordingly, the 1880s narrator can write about high prices, shoddy fabrics, and male relatives' depths of grief as if she were describing the details of knitting socks versus sewing blankets at a Camden Ladies Aid Society meeting. What she cannot seem to tell us is how this loss has registered on her heart. In the final days of the war, she will note that she finds herself without words: "Richmond has fallen and I haven't the heart to write about it" (April 7, 1865, 782). It is thus equally plausible that she has been stricken by a "mal du guerre" for her personal loss in 1864, a war-induced emotional exhaustion.

In Chesnut's narrative, James Jr. and Johnny seem to have been transformed by grief into veritable zombies. The 1880s writer refers to their "deep mourning." This may allude either to a point of etiquette—in which deep mourning dictates the wearing of exclusively black clothes versus the subdued colors assumed in the later stage of half mourning—or to their psychic states, the level to which their spirits have sunk in the wake of losing Mary Cox Chesnut. Whatever the meaning of "deep mourning," grief has transported both men to an altogether other "front," so far away that they are beyond Mary Chesnut's reach. This intradomestic isolation, coupled with the interdiction on visiting during the official mourning period, must have been a disaster for the emotionally vulnerable writer, who was energized by tending to her friendships and plunged into despair when cut off from those beloved associations. Of her husband, she notes, "J.C. as depressed as I ever knew him to be. He has felt the death of that angel mother of his keenly, and now he takes his country's woes to heart" (April 1, 1864, 594). But she reduces her own state to a description of a cheaply made, bad-clothes-sporting automaton, draped in shoddy black alpaca, capped by a rough black bonnet, and stricken speechless. In the aftermath of Mrs. Chesnut's death and with the South's defeat looming, it is as if the hub has flown off from the wheel, and the carriage that is the Chesnut family is careening out of control down a bad road.

Penned in the 1880s as an entry for May 27, 1864, when she has finally arrived at Mulberry to visit her grief-stricken father-in-law, the passage below confirms Harriet Grant's diagnosis that "Grandpa" is "poorly":

> I have always been an early riser. Formerly I often saw him, sauntering slowly down the broad passage from his room to hers, in a flowing flannel dressing gown when it was winter. In the spring he was apt to be in shirt sleeves, with suspenders hanging down his back. He always had a large hairbrush in his hand.
>
> He would take his stand on the rug before the fire in her room, brushing scant locks which were shining fleecy white. Her maid would be doing hers, which were dead-leaf brown, not a white hair in her head. He had the voice of a stentor. And there he stood, roaring his morning compliments. The people

who occupied the rooms above said he fairly shook the window glasses. This pleasant morning greeting and ceremony was never omitted. . . .

This morning, as I passed Mrs. C's room, the door stood wide open. And I heard a pitiful sound. The old man was kneeling by her empty bedside, sobbing bitterly.

I fled down the middle walk—anywhere out of the reach of what was never meant for me to hear. (610)

If the significance of an individual life can be measured by the power that one has to touch the hearts of others, then by the lights of the old Colonel, Mary Cox Chesnut was the single most important person in his world. The scene above in which Chesnut inadvertently overhears the weeping widower, and then catches a glimpse of the elderly gentleman in supplication by the empty bedside, would break any feeling person's heart. Equally poignant is the narrator's respect for her father-in-law's grief, and her internal chastising of herself for having witnessed a scene that she would have done anything to avoid. Two fiercely dignified figures contend with loss. One unknowingly reveals the full depth of his vulnerability to the other; and with exquisite respect, his silent witness captures in prose the depth of his sorrow, the profundity of his love for his departed wife, and the breadth of her own compassion.

Given how few words the 1880s narrator has had to spare for her own feelings about her mother-in-law's passing, consider the numerous entries devoted to the tragic, accidental death of little Joe Davis. Chesnut records being with Maggie Howell, Varina Howell Davis's younger sister, at a prisoner exchange in Richmond, when Maggie learns a garbled version of the horrible news. In earlier passages, the writer has described these events as promenades of the living dead: the rituals of return for paroled Southern soldiers have struck her less as joyous reunions than haunting spectacles of pain and privation. Chesnut's description of this particular prisoner exchange, which takes place just before she is to leave Richmond for Camden, always a difficult shift in her life, is shaded with foreboding and authorial dread:

> Those last few weeks were so pleasant before the crash came. Poor little Joe. No battle, no murder, no sudden death. All went merry as a marriage bell. Clever, kind, cordial brave friends [had] rallied round me.
>
> But I must come to it.
>
> Maggie and I went down the river to see an exchange of prisoners. (May 8, 1864, 599)

After a page and a half of reporting on the scene, the narrating Chesnut continues with the horror she knows is coming, as her wartime self had not:

The band was playing "Home Sweet Home.". . . .

And someone slipped back in the dark and said in a whisper, "Little Joe! He has killed himself!" I felt reeling—faint—bewildered. The chattering woman clutched my arm. "Mrs. Davis's son? Now, was he? Impossible? Who did you say? Was he an interesting child? How old was he?" The shock was terrible, and enervated as I was, I cried, "For God sake, take her away." Then Maggie and I drove silently two long miles, broken only by Maggie's hysterical sobs. She was wild with terror, broken to her in that abrupt way at the carriage door. At first she thought it had all happened there and that the poor little Joe was in the carriage. . . .

We went in. As I sat in the drawing room, I could hear the tramp of Mr. Davis's step as he walked up and down the room above—not another sound. The whole house was still as death. . . .

Mrs. Semmes [wife of a cabinet aid to Davis] said when she got there, little Jeff was kneeling down by his brother. And he called out to her in great distress, "Mrs. Semmes, I have said all the prayers I know how, but God will not wake Joe."

Poor little Joe, the good child of the family, so gentle and affectionate, he used to run in to say his prayers at his father's knee. Now he was laid out somewhere above us—crushed—killed. Mrs. Semmes said he fell from that high north piazza, upon a brick pavement.

Before I left the house I saw him lying there, white and beautiful as an angel—covered with flowers. (May 8, 1864, 601)

It seems that only the abrupt horror of a small child's unexpected death would have the force to paralyze Richmond at war in the spring of 1864, with Gettysburg and Vicksburg long lost and the bloodbath of Virginia's Hundred Days still ahead. This was a period in which the 1860s Chesnut mistakenly supposed that the biggest trouble on her horizon was an extended return to Mulberry in the wake of her mother-in-law's death.

Little could she have imagined what was to confront one of her dearest friends, the first lady of the Confederacy. Varina Davis had had several miscarriages, and had lost a two-year-old to mumps, before giving birth to the relatively hardy brood who lived and played in the Confederate White House: little Maggie (named for Varina's sister), little Jeff (named for his father), and little Joe (named for the president's brother, who had raised him once they had been orphaned). Varina was nearly nine months pregnant with the baby who was to be her last and closest (a daughter named for her mother but known as Winnie) when she lost the boy Chesnut would later describe as the angel of the South.

The "immense crowd at the funeral" that the 1880s writer portrays could not evoke less the angelic, white-robed choir that assembled so decorously to serenade General Washington on the Trenton Bridge in 1789. Instead, they were "sympathetic but pushing and shoving rudely, thousands of children" (May 8, 1864, 602). The writer pictures these little mourners as an unruly mob, the very opposite of the chorus of believers, slave and free, in Stowe's fictional account of the glorious golden aftermath of little Eva's death. The angel of the Confederacy had no such supernatural powers to transform the lives of those he had left behind.

Chesnut continues with a description of the funeral, and her account carries unsettling echoes of another great loss:

> Here I see that funeral procession as it wound among those tall white monuments up that hillside. The James River tumbling about below, over rocks and around islands.
>
> The dominant figure, that poor old gray-haired man. Standing bareheaded, straight as an arrow, clear against the sky by the open grave of his son. She stood back in her heavy black wrappings, and her tall figure drooped. The flowers, the children, the procession as it moved, comes and goes. But these two dark, sorrow-stricken figures stand—they rise before me now. . . .
>
> Who will they kill next, of that devoted household? (May 27, 1864, 609)

The winding procession, the dominant figure a "poor old gray-haired man": it is easy to read into the scene the elder Mrs. Chesnut's burial, though that interment has taken place, undescribed, several months earlier. The details that tie the scene to Richmond are no deterrent to the thoughts readers cast back to that earlier death. Although it is little Joe Davis who is being mourned and buried here by his father, it could also be old Colonel Chesnut who stands exposed in the springtime cold.

This impulse to transform one burial procession into a composite rite is not the effect of careless writing. Instead, the Chesnut of the 1880s seems to have crafted an extraordinarily effective funeral montage for these two very different but dearly beloved figures. Her artistry here may have been unconscious, the displaced working through of a grief she otherwise does not express. In her narrative, two genuine Eva figures emerge from both America's North and its South. From her participation in the white-robed choir, an experience that cemented her connection to angelic ministrations throughout her days, Mary Cox Chesnut embodied the idea of a living blessing in her own lifetime. And in his all-too-brief existence, so too did little Joe Davis, who eased his father's heart during times of terrible trial and became a symbol of goodness and faith to the larger Confederate public who looked to the first family for inspiration and succor.[24]

Neither the woman nor the child described by Chesnut had Eva's Christic powers. Mary Chesnut's world view, perhaps more cosmopolitan and skeptical than Stowe's, did not offer the Incarnation as a reality accessible through her narrative. In Stowe's imaginative domain, as in the realm of her intensely Calvinist upbringing, Jesus' life story and message of transformation were now and eternally present. Accordingly, the little Eva created by Stowe the believer had transubstantiating power to change lives forever. Despite the death of the small fictional evangelist, her friend Topsy becomes a true Christian, transforming herself into a "good" girl, and her Aunt Ophelia becomes truly capable of loving a black child.

In Mary Boykin Chesnut's world, such Evas only seemed to appear every ninety years or so: accordingly, in the course of a century, one might get a Mary Cox Chesnut or a little Joe Davis. But when such angels on earth were taken by death, the horrors of this world remained, undiminished: slavery continued to brutalize African Americans; boys and men, North and South, continued to be slaughtered, falling to the violence and disease of war. In the absence of some sort of "real presence," the stench of sentiment and slavery remained no more than that: a very, very bad smell.

CHAPTER SEVEN

Masks

THEATRICALS IN BLACK

Mary Chesnut revealed the drama at work in episodes as seemingly innocuous as the "mama smells a smell" affair and in systems as clearly pernicious as slavery itself. She understood theater as a protean cultural form, and she recognized that it afforded unusual entrée into the Southern wartime consciousness: both black bondspeople and their white owners engaged in modes of performance that expressed otherwise unspeakable realities about cross-racial engagement in the years 1861–65. In the early sections of her 1880s book, the narrating Chesnut repeatedly commented on the seeming indifference of Charleston house slaves to the bombardment of Fort Sumter in April of 1861—their apparent failure to register the war's probable political ramifications for their status. As late as the 1880s entries for the winter of 1864, Chesnut rationalized her own social circle's obsession with the staging of charades and amateur theatricals against the disapproval of her husband. James Chesnut Jr. was appalled by this female frivolity during a low point in Southern fortunes. Foregrounding two very different modes of performance throughout her narrative, Chesnut explored the politically strategic dissimulation of slaves in the elite homes of herself and her peers; and she took up the tonic distraction of recreational drama put on by members of her white planter circle, calculated to elevate the sagging spirits of the Confederate generals and their officers and ladies posted in Richmond. By juxtaposing what might be called theatricals in black and theatricals in white, in this chapter and the following one I attempt to gain access to dimensions of slave consciousness and planter anxiety obscured at the manifest level of Chesnut's 1880s narrative.

The writer was acutely aware of the various theaters bisecting Southern political life: the home front versus the battlefield, the political arena versus the domestic realm, the world of elite white privilege versus that of slave servility. These domains not only overlapped but actually changed places before Chesnut's eyes during the Civil War years. So, for example, in her accounts of the beginning of the war, she reported that congressmen and their wives drove out to northern Virginia to observe the battle of First Manassas. Traveling in landaus with well-stocked picnic hampers, these champagne-drinking spectators anticipated a garden party to the tune of martial music, but fled in terror once blood began to be shed. Later in her 1880s book, Chesnut wrote about how Southern cities largely inhabited by women, children, the elderly, and remaining slave populations were invaded by Sherman's western armies: civilians became victims of martial conflict in ways previously unknown in America, as distinctions between public and private, political and personal collapsed under the weight of civil war.

Of all these theaters, the arenas most compelling to the 1880s writer were phenomenological rather than geographical, involving two radically different modes of performance: slave dissimulation before the master class, deployed as a tactic of survival, if not also resistance; and white playacting as antic diversion against Confederate despair.[1] Thus, African Americans held in bondage in South Carolina orchestrated the appearance of inattentiveness for distinctly political ends, while the white privileged classes seemed to be engaged in senselessly ludic behavior, apparently inappropriate modes of recreation during time of "national" trial.[2] The writer of the 1880s recognized that the amateur theatricals constituted a medicating balm for the military presence in the community. In that regard, such play also functioned importantly as work. How might both versions of performance unfold in tandem? Sociologically, what did exaggerated slave docility and mindlessness and, simultaneously, white "hospitality run mad" (517)—Mr. Chesnut's characterization of the Richmond theatricals put on by his wife and her friends—have to do with or say to each other?

"Theatricals in Black"

Intensely aware that she had lived through a historical crisis that forever would transform the relations between American whites and blacks, the writer of the 1880s reported how she vigilantly studied the racial ecology of her own household. In fact, Chesnut's fascination with the subject of cross-racial experience flowered during the twenty years that passed between the Civil War and the end of Reconstruction, that is, between her original diary jottings and her massive transformation of that material. In an entry in her narrative for April 13, 1861, the immediate wake of the battle for Fort Sumter, she writes:

> Not by one word or look can we detect any change in the demeanor of these negro servants. Laurence sits at our door, as sleepy, and as respectful, and as profoundly indifferent. So are they all. They carry it too far. You could not tell that they hear even the awful row that is going on in the bay, though it is dinning in their ears day and night. And people talk to them as if they were chairs and tables. And they make no sign. Are they stolidly stupid or wiser than we are, silent and biding their time. (48)

The narrating Chesnut's notion that in their displays of apathy, the bondspeople are "carrying it too far" raises intriguing philosophical questions. Perhaps African American slavery itself is an ongoing collective performance, directed by the white master class but subject to the improvisation of nonconsenting slave "actors." If so, then the condition of bondage mandates the staging of submissiveness, contentment, and affability in order to make the race-based sentence of lifetime servitude appear natural to any potential audience, black or white. Accordingly, Laurence and company's accenting of the very elements that dramatize the ur-condition of the slave ("sleepiness," "respectfulness," "profound indifference") functions theatrically, amplifying in fictive quotation marks what always already was a staged performance.[3]

The "loyal slave" constitutes one role in a rich Southern social repertory, in the totality of which the narrating Chesnut has been fluent since childhood. Her 1880s book is populated by gracious plantation mistresses (Mrs. Caroline Hampton Preston, her cousin Betsey Witherspoon, and above all, her mother-in-law, Mrs. Mary Cox Chesnut), courtly cavaliers (General John Preston, Governor John Manning), white-haired patriarchs (particularly her father-in-law, Colonel James Chesnut Sr.), and stoic generals (General Robert E. Lee). In light of this fact, the writer's use of the phrase "carrying it too far" suggests her own subtle acknowledgment of self-conscious slave theatricality. That is, Chesnut interprets Laurence's sleepiness before the booming canons of Fort Sumter as some sort of mannered performance, and this reading implies something important about her understanding of the factitiousness of the slave condition itself.[4]

The "ur" or "degree-zero" of slave performance would be that dramatic work, done day in and day out, in which African Americans enacted the parts of devoted bondspeople. Ironically enough, in the 1880s narrative, this degree-zero of slave behavior is most visible in representations of the black performance of unconsciousness, or slave expression of seeming political unawareness, which in many instances Chesnut may have recognized qua dramatic production. What follows is an explication of those places in which this ur-performance becomes self-consciously theatrical: that is, when playing the part of the devoted slave turns into a kind of parody of its own dramatic dimension, just long enough to reveal something unexpected about bondspeople's experience behind the mask.

Such figurative cracks in African American theatrical armor rarely exposed themselves in the surface narrative of Chesnut's 1880s book; in fact, she identifies her mother's butler Dick as the only slave whose performance of nonawareness fails to do its intended dissimulating work: "He is the first negro that I have *felt* a change in," she remarks in an undated entry from the "Memoirs" section, which spans the period from August 1862 to September 1863 (464, my emphasis). Chesnut's intuition about Dick's heightened attentiveness to the progress of the war registers only at the level of the writer's instinct; several sentences later, she notes that he is "inscrutably silent" on all subjects, not simply that of current events.

Yet it is no mystery that of all the slaves in Chesnut's purview, Dick should have registered the shift in political winds, particularly on the issue of emancipation. As the narrating voice explains, giving a virtual curriculum vitae of Dick's career, by dint of his status in the Stephen Decatur Miller household, this butler has been afforded opportunities for edification that other, less fortunate Miller/Chesnut slaves have not:

> I taught him to read as soon as I could read myself—perched on his knife board. He won't look at me now. He looks over my head—he scents his freedom in the air. He was always very ambitious. I do not think he ever troubled with books much. But then as my father said, Dick, standing in front of his sideboard, had heard all the subjects of earth and heaven discussed—and by the best heads in our world. (464)[5]

That Dick alone no longer can face Chesnut in 1864, one year after the Emancipation Proclamation has unfettered him legally (whether or not he knows it) but in which he has remained a Miller slave, not having "run to the Yankees," both profoundly disturbs the writer and makes perfect sense.[6]

Chesnut is disturbed over Dick's avoidance of her eye because the dynamic of looking the other in the face embodies a classic Hegelian moment of truth between slaveholder and bondsperson: the master gains power from the acknowledgment sought and found in the face of the slave, who registers the former's superiority and domination; the bondsperson perceives in the face of the master (in Hegel, the "lord") both the assumption of authority and, simultaneously, an absolute dependence on the slave's recognition of said preeminence and control.[7]

By 1864, Dick is a slave only by virtue of Confederate disavowal of Lincoln's Proclamation and geographical circumstance: Northern armies have not yet invaded the border region of Alabama and Florida where Mrs. Miller resides. Habituation and, perhaps, "loyalty" probably also play a part. Such alleged devotion is a quality, however, that the 1880s Chesnut scornfully if astutely understands as turning on Dick's knowledge of the inevitability of freedom while he bides his time in relative security and comfort. "Fidelity" is something he can afford. Dick cannot face Chesnut because the essential Hegelian dynamic that bound them as mistress and slave no longer pertains, though it remains in Dick's interest to pretend—to act—as if it does. In contrast to Dick, Chesnut writes, his fellow slaves "go about in their black masks, not a ripple or an emotion showing—and yet on all other subjects except the war they are the most excitable of races. Now, Dick might make a very respectable Egyptian sphinx, so inscrutably silent is he" (464).

Emphasizing masking, affective expression and its absence, and the drama of silence itself, this passage typifies the trenchant observation by the 1880s writer of her slaves' demeanor as it strategically unfolds or fails to be displayed over against the background of the war. Unlike the riddle of the Sphinx, the conundrum of Dick ultimately will prove indecipherable for Chesnut; though she will perseverate on the problem until the end of the narrative, such silence does not tell. What do Dick's mask and withholding of language mean? And why is she so haunted by both?

A clue may abide in the metaphorical field from which the 1880s writer draws to describe her frustration: in figuring her slaves as sphinxes, the writer evokes Sophoclean, tragic, associations. The first connection is to monstrosity: consider the Sphinx crouching outside Thebes, devouring men who cannot answer her riddle. The next link is to hybrid identity: the Sphinx is half woman, half winged lion. And the final connection involves a primal enigma about the meaning of human mortality. The Sphinx queries: What goes on four legs at dawn, two legs at noon, and three legs at night? As Chesnut's book of the 1880s implies, the answer might apply to the Confederacy itself.

Black dissimulation and silence become appalling for the 1880s writer because they signal a liminal epoch between bondage and freedom for the slaves, and between supremacy and defeat for the master class. Attempting to understand her servants' actions and lack of action as a means to calibrate bodily security in turbulent times, the narrating Chesnut is blocked by the impenetrability of the slave mask.[8] And in the interstices of speech, that is, in Dick's silence, she cannot decipher slave intentionality. Such impediments to white interpretation of black behavior strike terror in the heart of this watchful mistress and others of her ilk, for they are ever mindful of the history of slave rebellions, particularly those that crossed the color line (as did John Brown's raid on Harpers Ferry in 1859).

Even more impossible for the writer to ignore is the global significance of St. Domingo's slave revolution (1793–1803), which, as we have seen, is a recurrent historical reference in the narrative. Indeed, Chesnut does not simply allude to the initial decade of insurgent violence and liberation from French colonial rule in Haiti; she actually follows the history of the first black republic into her own era, citing a biography of black palace servant Faustin Soulouque, who assumed the Haitian presidency in 1847 as the supposed puppet of the mulatto elite, rump members of the prior Riche regime. Surreptitiously building his own base of power among influential figures in the black military, this so-called pawn of the former administration soon eliminated his enemies and crowned himself emperor.[9]

In Soulouque's story lies a parable about the ways in which the black performance of servility could mask a capacity for murderous political violence. It is telling that the narrating Chesnut of the 1880s finds herself drawn to this particular chapter in Haiti's ongoing saga, which she continues to refer to as the "fate" of St. Domingo, as if erasing the reality of slave revolution and black supremacy. Later in the book, Chesnut alludes to eighteenth-century St. Domingo in discussing her mother-in-law, who as a young girl in an elite Philadelphia slaveholding family was traumatized by contemporary stories of rebellious Domingian slaves slaughtering white masters. And as Muhlenfeld notes, Madame Talvande, the French headmistress of Chesnut's Charleston boarding school, had fled the island during the revolution, along with several mulatto teachers. Such haunting historical associations unfolded for the 1880s Chesnut against the familial import of her elderly cousin Betsey Witherspoon's slaying at the hands of her household servants. Slave silence, even among the most purportedly "loyal" slaves, as Mrs. Witherspoon's were thought to have been, bodes no good.

In the "Memoirs" entries for the winter of 1864, the eventual loss of the war constitutes a near inevitability hanging over Southern society. Chesnut uses the phrase "sword of Damocles" so often for the period between 1864 and 1865 that it becomes a leitmotif in the last portion of her narrative. Slaveowners begin to sense that once-normative social repertoires soon will be shattered, though whites and blacks remain suspended tenuously in status quo. Meanwhile, Chesnut's images of monstrosity, hybridity, and mortality all point to a degenerating state of affairs created by the masters and mistresses themselves. Demonizing blacks as hopelessly beastlike and socially dead, the white master class has been the architect of its own morally indefensible economic lot, a fact that Chesnut of the 1880s appreciates. Indeed, many passages of the narrative reiterate the writer's lamentation over the South's financial ruin, which she blames on slavery itself, though she implicates black bondspeople as culpable agents of this fate—as recipients of the "benefits" of the peculiar institution. Thus, at the end of the war, when she and her husband have been made destitute by the debt incurred for unsuccessful agricultural practices, James Chesnut Jr. rationalizes their economically devastated lot as the result of the care and feeding of his nearly five hundred slaves, whose lifetime's worth of stolen labor somehow never figures in his equation.[10]

Such white mystifications obscure the reality of black productivity and point to the larger issue of slave agency itself, a subject the 1880s Chesnut takes up in the passage quoted above, in which she likens her friends' treatment of their slaves to interactions with household items: "And people talk to them as if they were chairs and tables. And they make no sign. Are they stolidly stupid or wiser than we are, silent and biding their time." That she inserts no question mark at the end of her final sentence—that her query is at best rhetorical, and more likely a declarative statement—is a telling index of the astuteness of her observations about racial difference. Even more revealing are the writer's similes. Expressing the sense that masters talk to their slaves *as if* they were tables and chairs reflects an unusual awareness for a slave mistress of the tenuous ideological fiction undergirding Southern slaveholding: the cultural fantasy that bondspeople have neither independent minds and wills nor emotional attachments. Instead, slaves exist simply as chattel, property, so much furniture to be circulated from auction block to plantation house and cotton field.[11] What is suppressed in this characterization, of course, is the humanity of the slave, which has gone unrecognized precisely because to acknowledge black personhood would be to deconstruct the entire ideological fiction that has enabled the peculiar institution's existence.

In identifying the dangerous presumption of her class through the trope of white treatment of bondspeople as domestic things,[12] Chesnut uncannily prefigures the very example through which Marx will explore the commodity as fetish in volume 1 of *Capital* (1867):

> A commodity appears at first sight an extremely obvious, trivial thing. But its analysis brings out that it is a very strange thing, abounding in metaphysical subtleties and theological niceties. So far as its use-value, there is nothing mysterious about it, whether we consider it from the point of view that by its properties it satisfies human needs, or that it first takes on these properties as the product of human labour. It is absolutely clear to me that, by his activity, man changes the forms of the materials of nature in such a way as to make them useful to him. The form of wood, for instance, is altered if a table is made out of it. Nevertheless, the table continues to be wood, an ordinary, sensuous thing. But as soon as it emerges as a commodity, it changes into a thing which transcends sensuousness. It not only stands with its feet on the ground, but, in relation to all other commodities, it stands on its head, and evolves out of its wooden brain grotesque ideas, far more wonderful than if it were to begin dancing of its own free will.[13]

Marx's meditation offers a provocative backlight for thinking about Chesnut's understanding of the shrouding of material relations and ideological reversals on which, as a cultural practice, slavery depends. Her awareness of the fact that said tables and chairs are capable of dissimulation, or to borrow and redeploy Marx's terms, that they are able to stand on their heads and evolve out of their "wooden" brains "grotesque ideas," marks the 1880s writer's account of slave "words" and "looks," what she herself calls the "bronze mask," as particularly illuminating for our understanding of bellum racial phenomenologies. To combat the suppression of slave humanity, figures such as Dick and Laurence adopt the bronze mask, which obscures the eye contact Chesnut craves and communicates the uncanniness of slave consciousness. Wartime seems to have afforded this opening for resistance. If, according to the legal taxonomies of antebellum Southern culture, Dick's status is tantamount to that of an item of furniture, is he not Marx's table able to stand on its head, dancing "of its own free will"?[14]

Both slave narratives and works like Chesnut's raise questions about whether members of the master class contemplated, much less troubled themselves over, what their slaves might be thinking. Clearly, post-1831, white fear of slave insurrection was *the* topic—either sub rosa or sotto voce—haunting plantation owners in Virginia and the lower South. But the problem of imagining the consciousness of one's slaves, be it unified, double, or false, or of considering the phenomenology of the experience of bondage on a quotidian level beyond the issue of rebellion, is one that falls out of most historical accounts and even literary readings of narratives representing slavery, although it clearly animates Chesnut's reworking of her diary.

Keeping these questions in mind, consider the dilemma of scholarly access to slave consciousness. It is here that literary close reading of Chesnut's 1880s narrative, as much as historical analysis, might recuperate phenomenological traces as effects of black performance across the color line.[15] In the long quotation that follows, the narrating Chesnut provides an astonishing series of examples of black theatricality, both across the color line and within its bounds, that will set the terms of the argument:

> When Dick [who then served the Anderson family] married Hetty [a slave in the Miller household], the Anderson house was next door. The two families agreed to sell either Dick or Hetty, whichever consented to be sold. Hetty refused outright, and the Andersons sold Dick, that he might be with his wife. Magnanimous on the Anderson's part, for Hetty was only a lady's maid, and Dick was a trained butler on whom Mrs. Anderson had spent no end of pains in his dining room education. And of course if they had refused to sell Dick, Hetty had to go to them. Mrs. Anderson was very much disgusted with Dick's ingratitude when she found he was willing to leave them. As a butler, he was a treasure. He is overwhelmed with dignity, but that does not interfere with his work at all. My father had a body servant who could imitate his master's voice perfectly. And he would call out from the yard after my father had mounted his horse.
>
> "Dick, bring me my overcoat. I see you over there sir—hurry up." And when Dick hastened out, overcoat in hand—and only Simon! Particularly after several obsequious, "Yes, Marster—just as Marster pleases," my mother had always to step out and prevent a fight. And Dick never forgave her for laughing. ("Memoirs," September 1863, 464–65)

It is notable that the conditions under which bondspeople were living in the Miller and Anderson families were untypical: Miller and Anderson slaves were permitted to marry, a right that was denied to them under antebellum Southern law; or rather, Hetty and Dick's "marriage" was recognized by both sets of owners, hardly a norm in South Carolina. Additionally, Hetty and Dick were allowed to exercise consent over their place of (bonded) labor, a very unusual privilege for slaves who, by statute and definition, were persons explicitly divested of such entitlements.

Mrs. Anderson's characterization of Dick's "ingratitude" seems far more representative of elite white attitudes toward African American bondspeople than her relatively liberal policies on marriage and consent over habitation would suggest. As Philip Morgan notes, far from being organic to the institution of slavery since its seventeenth-century origins in North America, white masterly "beneficence" and its opposite number, black slave "gratitude," did not develop into central values until the nineteenth century. It was only with the growing hegemony of white paternalism, the ultimate romantic rationale for slavery, that the moralistic language of benevolence and thankfulness became key features of the cultural discourse on master-slave relations.[16] That Mrs. Anderson was piqued, disappointed, even irate over the loss of a prized slave should be conceivable to an audience of literary scholars and historians. But the "disgust" she felt, as if the labor that she had consumed unrighteously had, in "its" show of self-determination, repulsed her appetites—coupled with the bitter sting of "ingratitude" she suffered from a heretofore "loyal" bondsman—speaks volumes about the paternalistic attitudes at work in her family and her culture.

What made Dick "a treasure" was neither his hauteur nor his independent mind, but his "dining room education." Such skilled training apparently had cost his mistress "no end of pains"; simultaneously, it had elevated Dick's position on the hierarchical ladder of color and class dictating status in nineteenth-century America. Dick's importance in the Miller household was unquestionable. His duties were managerial rather than physical, involving the assessment of household requirements and the delegation of labor to lower-ranking house slaves. Dick enjoyed the privileges afforded to a majordomo: in that regard, the butler functioned as the domestic version of the field laborer's driver when it came to the managing of Stephen Decatur Miller's house servants.

Simon, on the other hand, shared an intimacy with Mr. Miller that was unique to his position as valet. His literally was a hands-on connection. It hardly is an accident, then, that Simon, rather than Dick, was the one who could "imitate his master's voice perfectly." Accordingly invested in the structures of power that obtained under slavery at the Miller's, Dick could play in his sleep the role of the loyal slave. Simon, ranking lower on the chain under the Miller's slave regime, undoubtedly resented Dick's pride and hauteur, as well as his authority to command Simon's labor. Thus the body servant employed his imitative skills, another version of "black theatricals," to teach Dick a lesson about slave pride: feigning the voice of Mr. Miller, Simon sent the butler scurrying for his master's overcoat, provoking in Dick a flood of obsequious language and a wasteful expense of "devoted" labor.

Slave ventriloquism took its most powerful form, however, in the episode of Simon at Sumter:

Once in Sumter, when my father was very busy preparing a law case, the mob in the street annoyed him, and he grumbled about as Simon made up his fire. Then he said in all his life he had never laughed so heartily. Suddenly he heard the Hon. S. D. Miller—Lawyer Miller, as the gentleman announced himself in the dark—appeal to the gentlemen to go away and leave a lawyer in peace to prepare his case for the next day—&c.&c. My father said he could have sworn to his own voice. The crowd dispersed, and some noisy negroes came along. Upon them Simon rushed with the sulky whip, slashing around in the dark, calling himself Lawyer-Miller-who-was-determined-to-have-peace.

My father heard him come back, complaining, "Them niggers run so he never got in a hundred yards of one of them." [Remainder of page torn out.] Simon was not aware that his master knew of his tricks or his personification of him. ("Memoirs," September 1863, 465)

In the case of Dick, Simon, and the overcoat, a slightly inferior domestic slave co-opts his master's voice to raise questions in the mind of his bound superior about the locus of power and authority on the Miller plantation, as well as to demonstrate the perils of slave hubris. In the second instance, "black theatricals" suggest a far more dangerous reality for the endurance of white supremacy. Under cloak of darkness, Simon so effectively assumes "Lawyer" Miller's vocal tones, patterns of speech, and even diction—save, perhaps, his use of the honorific, though such a class-marked gaffe would not have necessarily registered with the noisy rabble—that he is able to disperse a crowd of boisterous white men from outside the lawyer's window. The episode suggests that when race visually is illegible in the context of a struggle for power, white, black, or any shade in between, the craftiest speaker will win the day: woe to those who would argue a case for inferiority based on skin color.

But when Simon raises the sulky whip against his own black brethren, "some noisy negroes" disturbing the peace of "Lawyer Miller," the politics of parody in Chesnut's narrative takes a decidedly more menacing turn. It is one thing if a slave valet can fool a throng of "poor white trash" for the sake of the master's comfort; S. D. Miller is not threatened by Simon's cross-racial identifications when they keep intact the hierarchy of class.[17] It is another thing altogether if the said slave's performance of mastery is so convincing that it can rouse the attention and fear of other slaves or even of free blacks; that is, if Simon's vocal disguise carries the authority of the master class, elite slaveowners cannot feel safe in their own positions of power.[18] Just as no one in the abolitionist audience could believe that a man as eloquent as Frederick Douglass really could have been a slave, so no one in the dark at Sumter can imagine that Simon's voice emanates from a bondsman.

Given the evidence of these passages, literary scholars must attempt to decode what might be thought of as the symptomatic meanings expressed through the "bronze mask" of the 1880s narrative. In the case of Chesnut's slaves, such performances of impassiveness are complicated indeed: for the literary Chesnut has been mindful that her own blacks well comprehended the fact that their mistress was recording all that she heard and saw in the war years. Indeed, Chesnut significantly reports in the 1880s narrative that it was her bondsmaid Molly who had advised her to burn the 1860s diary in fear that it would fall into the hands of the Yankees: "In Stoneman's raid I burned my journal proper. It was Molly who constantly told me: 'Missis, listen to the guns. Burn up everything. Mrs. Lyons says they are sure to come, and they'll put in the newspapers whatever you write here everyday'" ("Memoirs," September 1863, 453).

Chesnut represents Molly, not only hearing "the awful row" of Yankee guns (48), but actually extrapolating from the audible menace that her mistress—and her mistress's prose!—are in danger from the approaching Union army. That is, far from feigning ignorance, at least one slave in the 1880s book seems to recognize the fact that it is Mrs. Chesnut who is at risk, not her black servants. And most significant, the said bondswoman articulates to the mistress without reserve her awareness of changes in political reality. Put another way, according to Chesnut's literary development of Molly as a featured character of the 1880s narrative, Yankee canons are speaking directly to Mrs. Chesnut's vocation; and ever the loyal slave, Molly has the insight to advise the mistress to spare herself further exposure by urging her to burn her diary.

This episode opens with the writer using slave dialect ("missis") to represent Molly's own perception of unfolding events. Then, suddenly, the narrative takes a sharp and potentially suspicion-inducing turn, with unexpected implications for the relation of mistress and slave: Chesnut records Molly's ostensible mimicry of sentiments spoken by Mrs. Lyons, a white woman possessed of a seemingly world-historical awareness of the future value of Chesnut's diary. Read most cynically, we see the footprints of the 1880s reworkings, a metanarrative gesture in which the narrating Chesnut inserts a self-promoting endorsement of her own writing into the mouth of her then slave. In this context, Molly's ventriloquized words constitute a kind of approving blurb from the black side of the color line about the importance of Chesnut's diary writing. This is a fascinating strategy for a white Southern woman to have used to assure a place for her narrative in the pantheon, suggesting as it does that even the lowliest figure in Southern culture, the female slave, appreciates the power of her prose. But perhaps more important, and indeed more troubling from the point of view of antebellum slave law, the anecdote implies not only that Molly can read, but that she *has* read Chesnut's words—that she has access to her mistress's writing and has illicitly availed herself of the diary. Such are the complicated subtextual residues of Chesnut's use of Molly here.

Simultaneously, and phantasmagorically, the writer has crafted a representation of her bondswoman's omniscience, in which Molly fathoms all the ways that her mistress's writings will afford historical readers a lasting testament to Southern struggle. Such a picture of intimate slave discernment of Chesnut's talent as chronicler of the war, coupled with evidence of Molly's utter devotion, represent a fulfillment of the writer's wishes to possess a slave so ideally attuned to her mistress that they virtually are merged. In this formulation, the narrating Chesnut of the 1880s discloses her longing for Molly's understanding, the fantasy that her maid can read her mind.[19] Thus, in the writer's imagination, Molly fully comprehends the crucial role composition plays in her mistress's ongoing quest for emotional self-regulation. And this wished-for Molly thinks, My mistress's diary is so vital to the Southern cause that publication by the enemy's press will be ruinous. Utterly absent from the portrait of supposed slave perception is any flicker of consciousness on Molly's part regarding the potential advantage of seeing her mistress's words bared in the newspaper. That is, no desire for the exposure of the machinations of the master class remotely taints Molly's assessment of the diary's significance or her loyalty to the white "family."

Understood less cynically and more radically, in an alternative reading, the Molly created by the writer of the 1880s is a literary character capable of growth, in the tradition of Chesnut's writer-idol, George Eliot, whose own fictive figures develop insight in the wake of trial and disappointment. Accordingly, Molly's consciousness blooms in the soil of Civil War culture, through which she has come to understand the importance of her mistress's diary-writing and later, her efforts to reshape and transform the work, as well as to appreciate the power of the press in influencing public opinion and, accordingly, creating political reality. In either reading, the passage dialectically charts a complex circuit of cross-racial consciousness, in which the 1880s Chesnut demonstrates her paternalistic relation to her bondswoman, as well as her need to reassure herself that with Molly as ever-vigilant guardian, all remains agreeable between them. Alternatively, she grants her slave's intelligence and acuity about the significance of writing, politics, and the power of print culture.[20]

Two important considerations temper this reading: First, Molly's elaboration as a character is only unfolded in the 1880s revisions. In fact, Chesnut only develops her African American cast in the rewriting and expansion of the narrative she undertook twenty or so years after Confederate surrender. For almost two decades, she pondered the issue of racial difference before making it a central theme of her epic narrative. Remarkably, and here it is not clear whether or not the Chesnut of the 1880s herself is aware of the psychic and political significance of what she is registering, Molly does not retreat behind a bronze mask into a show of silence or docility. Perhaps the bravado with which Chesnut paints Molly can be understood as the felicitous effect of the respect that she had developed for the black woman, her dairy business partner for at least twelve years.

Accordingly, if Chesnut's maid is not simply serving as a mouthpiece for the writer's own self-promotion, she is actively assuming the voice of Mrs. Lyons, a member of the master class, thus "signifyin' on" her own previously silent behavior. Two years before the episode Chesnut describes, Fort Sumter had fallen to Rebel troops, led in part by Chesnut's husband. Recall Chesnut's observation in her narrative that none of her slaves displays the slightest awareness that the guns booming outside have any bearing on their future freedom. In her 1880s entry for September 1863—having seen emancipation, black army regiments in the Sea Islands–Port Royale region of South Carolina, and Confederate defeat at Gettysburg—African American political savvy is expressed in a different mode. The silent performance behind the sphinx-like mask seems to have given way to a newer, more eloquent staging of opposition: the slave's mimicry of white speech.[21] Under this reading, strategically employing Mrs. Lyons's language, Molly communicates her comprehension of the politically damaging potential of her mistress's prose and the birth of her own, trenchant, political consciousness as well.

The political valences of slave silence over against the significance of the black mask or African American imitation of white speech are difficult to assess. But given that these tableaux are recorded by a once-elite, white Southern woman looking back from a vantage point twenty years after the Civil War, it would be naïve to opine that the second, radical way of reading Molly's mimicry is definitive. Yet even if we conclude that Chesnut's Molly of Stoneman's raid is a phantasmagoric figure, deployed to fulfill the author's postbellum wishes for a kind of slave loyalty most often seen in the plantation romance genre, there is an edge to this representation that must be acknowledged, a way in which the writer's image of her former maid resists totalizing authorial intention and control.[22]

If the significances of Molly's mimicry are multiple, even overdetermined, slave silence, the riddle of Dick, is unreadable; and it is this very obliqueness that drives the ever-interpreting, narrating Chesnut mad. The expression of impenetrability that the writer figures in specifically Greek theatrical terms may prove more amenable to explication than does the absence of slave speech. Analysis here may yield insight into retrospective white fantasies about black culture under bondage, if not unfettered access to "the real" of slave perception itself.

As a member of the educated class, Chesnut probably would have been familiar with the fact that actors in fifth-century Greek tragedies never performed without facial coverings. Chesnut journeyed to London in the 1840s, where she could have seen evidence of dramatic masking on those classical vases most often viewed by nineteenth-century Anglo-American travelers. As a young teenager, Chesnut had studied rhetoric at Madame Talvande's boarding school in Charleston, where she would have read Cicero, who discusses the employment of masks in Greek drama in *De oratore* and in *De officiis*. Fluent in German, which she also studied at Madame Talvande's, Chesnut could have found treatment of theatrical principles in Hegel's and Schlegel's writings on classical drama.[23]

None of these speculations over what the 1880s writer knew about the conventions of ancient Greek theater constitutes evidence. Nevertheless, it is likely that the narrating Chesnut's use of the figure of the mask is freighted with literary meaning beyond what one might call, anachronistically, its potentially Fanonesque import.[24] That is, far from seeing the behavior of her slaves through the minstrel lens of contemporary Southern writers, let alone Stowe's portraits of comic tricksters, the literary Chesnut accords slave consciousness—ever inscrutable, recoverable only as one effect of a masked performance—the status of tragic drama.[25]

In that regard, the action of slave rebels masquerading as docile Africans in Melville's *Benito Cereno,* published in 1855 in *Putnam's Monthly Magazine,* comes to mind.[26] There is, of course, no evidence that Chesnut read the novella, but its themes of disguise and struggle strike chords in her own work. Like the two carved satyrs struggling to the death that adorn the stern of Benito Cereno's slave ship, the San Dominick, Chesnut's slaves are masked, wearing inscrutable faces of "bronze." She also describes them as sphinxes, bringing resonances from Sophoclean drama to bear on their "performance."

She might also have had in mind the Egyptian sphinxes, those monolithic sculptures sporting women's heads and lions' bodies, rising up before the pyramids to guard the tombs of Egypt's ancient pharaohs. These dynastic aristocrats had ruled for millennia, commanding great wealth garnered through the toil of an enormous slave culture. So-called scientists of race as early as Count Constantin Volney, Jefferson's interlocutor on the subject of climate and degeneration in *Notes on the State of Virginia,* had argued for the Egyptian origins of the people who forcibly had been taken into slavery from the western coast of Africa starting in the sixteenth and seventeenth centuries. In this light, by taking up a sphinx-like demeanor, Laurence and Dick were not adopting a tragic façade but simply reclaiming the regal if mysterious identities of their origins.[27]

In her 1880s entries for 1861, Chesnut describes a notorious "abolitionist" letter she had written to her husband in 1842, railing against the evils of slavery. She refers to this epistle several times, though apparently, the famous letter is lost.[28] The 1880s associations to masks and sphinxes in entries for 1864 point symbolically to the truth her communiqué apparently addressed directly: that African American bondage was pernicious, that Southern culture was doomed by its own hubris and misjudgment, and that the consequences would prove tragic for elite whites such as themselves.

She was indeed the Cassandra she painted herself: offering not only the warnings of her hindsight vision from the decades in which she had reshaped her Civil War–era diary, but her prediction of the demise of black bondage long before that diary was begun.[29] Reflecting in the 1880s on the war years, but maintaining fidelity to her 1860s experience, Chesnut imagines a Sophoclean or pharaonic—a disastrous—denouement awaiting slaveholders.

But she provides the African American victims of slavery with an altogether different form of narrative closure, what critics like Northrop Frye would call the comic unfolding of Christianity.[30] Comedy in this context connotes a movement of plot from death to rebirth, and this was in fact the very structure of the black Methodist conversion experience. The wartime Chesnut regularly witnessed testimony to this turning around of the heart on her father-in-law's plantation when the white family joined its bondspeople in worship. In the wake of restrictions on slave religious assembly following Nat Turner's rebellion in 1831, mixed-race brotherly fellowship became the manifest argument for a latent form of white social discipline.

In Chesnut's 1880s representations of Mulberry's slaves, Christian piety constitutes the form of black "theatricality" most knowingly performed and, paradoxically, most earnestly and unselfconsciously felt. Twenty years earlier, in her 1860s diary, Chesnut made brief note of the autumn 1861 service, but showed little interest in exploring the scene of slave piety unfolding there. The 1880s reworkings reveal that in the postwar decades, Chesnut had developed a fascination for the richness of black folks' spirituality. Ecstatic in its physical expressiveness, the origins of which scholars trace to African spiritual practice, slave worship in *Mary Chesnut's Civil War* marks a world apart, a physical space and an affective arena absolutely distinct from the regime of bondage and also separate from segregated, white, religious experience. An orchestrated panoply of oratory, music, movement, and stage directions, black spiritual practice unfolds both before the gaze of the white family and for the benefit of the slaves themselves. That is, African American religious experience in *Mary Chesnut's Civil War* involves the very forms of restored behavior theorized by Joseph Roach as performance per se; the presentation resonates with multiple implications, depending on whether or not one views the spectacle from inside or outside the circle of the faithful.[31]

Like many large plantations in the nineteenth century, Mulberry included a physical structure for the organized religious worship of its slaves; an itinerant, white Methodist minister appeared twice a month to lead the service.[32] Denominational distribution in antebellum South Carolina could be mapped largely, though not exclusively, onto disparities of race and class: thus, though white Methodists abounded, they often came from the middling and lower ranks, while planter elites like Colonel Chesnut and his family or the Jefferson Davises belonged to the local Presbyterian or Episcopal Church, respectively.

Stirred by the variety of spiritual expressions on view across denominations, Chesnut considered the Southern religious scene an evocative social arena, indeed, a form of theater. A more ecumenical, tolerant Protestant would have been difficult to find in this community. Thus, far from being the antipapist of many from her class, the schoolgirl Mary Boykin Miller had enjoyed weekly lunches seated next to the Catholic bishop of Charleston, John England, every Wednesday at Madame Talvande's; there, she carried on conversations about all matters of doctrine and practice with a man Muhlenfeld calls one of the "foremost Catholic divines of his generation."[33] She was equally captivated by the cultural practices of her beloved Jewish friend, Miriam "Mem" Cohen. Not one to worship exclusively at Bethesda Presbyterian of Camden, where her own parents and grandparents, the Millers and the Boykins, enjoyed membership with the senior Chesnuts, she also attended Episcopal services with the Davises in Montgomery and Richmond, shared black Methodist devotions with her slaves on Mulberry, and observed the Sabbath with her friend Isabella Martin, whose father was a Methodist rector in Columbia.

That the writer of the 1880s dedicated to her experience at the Mulberry Negro church what, in their published form, constituted over two long pages, more than the space allotted to the battle of Shiloh, the death of Stonewall Jackson, or even Lee's surrender, underscores its significance. This elaborate scene painting, not found in the 1860s diary, suggests that the issue of slave spirituality was a topic to which she devoted searching meditation over the course of twenty postwar years. Worship on the plantation afforded less a gothic opportunity to scrutinize the behavior of the family slaves at rest than an occasion to understand better what Chesnut saw as inscrutable black ways. Because African

American Methodist practice magnetized her observation, she developed in the 1880s what had been a tiny 1860s diary entry into one of the richest and most memorable scenes in her book. In an entry for October 13, 1861, she writes:

> At Mulberry we went in the afternoon to the negro church on the plantation. Manning Brown, Methodist minister, preached to a very large black congregation. Though glossy black, they were well dressed—some very stylishly gotten up. They were stout, comfortable looking Christians. The house women in white aprons and white turbans were the nicest looking. How snow-white the turbans on their heads appeared. But the youthful sisters flaunted in pink and sky blue bonnets which tried their complexions. For *the family* they had a cushioned seat near the pulpit, neatly covered with calico. (213)

Here the slave "cast" all appear in costume: house women wear white, of which Chesnut clearly approves, contrasting it with the choices of the congregation's younger members (possibly female agricultural workers), who are adorned in vulgar pink and blue. In Chesnut's notion of slave caste, domestics prevail over field hands in their superior taste, not to mention their propensity for maintaining the clothing protocol of house service (white linen on black dresses), even on Sundays. Meanwhile, their less elevated sisters, aspiring to be fashionable, appropriate the color palette of bonnets worn by white women. It is not clear whether what seems a telling instance of slave ambition to higher status is lost on the narrator or not. But in her hauteur, the narrating Chesnut dismisses the blue and pink bonnets as evidence of buffoonery.

Shifting from her sartorial inventory of slave attire, Chesnut turns to a theological précis featuring her own spiritual self-examination. Deployed in the characteristically ironic mode that makes her prose seem contemporaneous with our own, she records:

> Manning Brown preached hell fire—so hot I felt singed, if not parboiled, though I could not remember any of my many sins worthy of an eternity in torment. But if all the world's misery, sin, and suffering came from so small a sin as eating that apple, what mighty proportions mine take. (213)

After opining that her numerous if venial transgressions are inaccessible to memory, paradoxically, the narrator reflects that her spiritual culpability must be great, indeed, if one credits Manning Brown's and the Methodist Church's interpretation of the story of the Fall.

Far from a casual or simply sardonic reflection, of which the writer fully is capable, the narrating Chesnut's commentary on original sin resonates in important theological ways: scholars of African American religion assert that though white evangelical preachers showered fire and brimstone on their black congregations, original sin itself never registered as a relevant moral category for slave believers. Bondspeople, struggling to survive and endure, viewed the Fall of Man as a spiritual predicament pertinent only to white folk. Donald Mathews writes that

> black Christians, on the other hand, did not have that sense of original sin which so confused and burdened white Evangelicals. Like latter-day Methodism and liberal Christianity, the taint was not imbedded into their very souls; but unlike members of those two forms of "white Christianity," blacks did not lapse into optimistic sentimentalism. Their social condition made that change impossible.... [B]lack Christians did not dwell on the taint of their bondage; they celebrated their release from it. While whites might rightfully be said to have "broken down" under preaching, blacks were lifted up, enabled to celebrate themselves as persons because of their direct and awful contact with divinity which healed their battered self-esteem with the promise of deliverance, the earnest of which was the vision itself.[34]

Mathews's assessment puts the 1880s rumination on apple-eating and Chesnut's own wickedness in important cultural context. The narrator's description of the varieties of religious experience she had undergone during her visit to Mulberry's black church at the beginning of the war becomes a central moment in her literary narrative. These expanded 1880s passages constitute a primal scene for the writer, a symptomatic expression of the ways in which, as she transformed the wartime diary into a work of art, she had come to understand that her own and her region's original sin inhered in slave holding itself.[35]

This epiphany manqué in the 1880s, a revelation of the heart at the expense of the intellect, comes as the narrating self contemplates the spiritual exercises of Jim Nelson, slave class leader on Mulberry. She remarks: "Jim Nelson, the driver—the stateliest darky I ever saw. He is tall and straight as a pine tree, with a fair face—not so very black, but full-blooded African. His forefathers must have been of royal blood over there" (213). Such an articulation of romantic racialism may have remained the norm for the 1880s writer's class and culture. Indeed, Nelson's noble savagery is fully congruent with that of Melville's fictive Atufal, once an African prince as well as slaveholder before he himself is kidnapped into bondage in *Benito Cereno*. But the 1880s writer also is praising the African purity of Nelson's background. Put another and more pointed way, there is no trace of white South Carolina lineage about Jim Nelson: his family remains untainted by the potential predation of white men "in the quarters." Chesnut continues: "This distinguished gentleman was asked to 'lead in prayer.' He became wildly excited. Though on his knees, facing us, with his eyes shut, he clapped his hands at the end of every sentence, and his voice rose to the pitch of a shrill shriek" (214).

Representing his altered intonations and percussive hands, the writer depicts Nelson engaged in what is called Methodist "shouting": a vocal and kinesthetic expression of African origin that remained as a syncretic form in what Mechal Sobel terms Afro Christianity. The shouting tradition took what Sobel describes as "the African Sacred Cosmos" and merged it with the emotional evangelical practices of the First Great Awakening, ritual behaviors that remained in African American Methodism well past the eighteenth century. (White converts during the Awakening "shouted" as well, though this embodied repertoire began to die out of white evangelical practice by the early nineteenth century.)[36] "Still," Chesnut continues, "his voice was strangely clear and musical, occasionally in a plaintive minor key that went to your heart. Sometimes it rung out like a trumpet. I wept bitterly" (214).

Immediately after acknowledging that Nelson's music has rent her heart, the writer disavows its significance:

> It was all sound, however, and emotional pathos. There was literally nothing in what he said. The words had no meaning at all. It was the devotional passion of voice and manner which was so magnetic. The negroes sobbed and shouted and swayed backward and forward, some with aprons to their eyes, most clapping their hands and responding in shrill tones, "Yes, my God! Jesus!" "Aeih! Savior! Bless de Lord, amen—&c." (214)

That Chesnut reports shedding disagreeable tears and then dismisses the notion that Nelson's singing has provoked them immediately raises questions about her narrative strategy.

As her epic clearly reveals, Chesnut feels nothing but hostility toward sentimental expression. She has linked her in-laws' articulation of conventional (clichéd, false) feeling with Harriet Beecher Stowe's mode of appeal in *Uncle Tom's Cabin* and that novel's overheated, "fanatical" analysis of slavery. Loathing what she deigns the maudlin pieties of white evangelical religion and popular sentimental fiction alike, the writer remains suspicious about the manipulation of mass emotion in any context. But as Mathews notes, sentimentalism is a luxury enjoyed only by white Methodists, Baptists, and other evangelicals: to repeat, the "social condition" of slave believers "made that change impossible." Whatever the literary Chesnut recalls having witnessed at the Negro church in 1861 transcends the white sentimental verities of which she has been so critical, for on hearing Jim Nelson's plaintive voice in prayer, the writer reports weeping, noting:

> It was a little too exciting for me. I would very much have liked to shout, too. Jim Nelson, when he rose from his knees, trembled and shook as one in a palsy. And from his eyes you could see the ecstasy had not left him yet. He could not stand at all—sunk back on his bench. Now, all this leaves not a trace behind. Jim Nelson is a good man—honest and true. And so he continues. Those who stole before steal on, in spite of sobs and shouts on Sunday. Those who drink continue to drink when they can get it. . . .
>
> Suddenly, as I sat wondering what next, they broke out into one of those soul-stirring negro camp-meeting hymns. To me this is the saddest of all earthly music—weird and depressing beyond my powers to describe. (214)

Across this passage, the writer describes crying bitterly at the sound of Nelson's sorrowful music, becoming overly excited, wishing to call out, suppressing this impulse, disavowing the lasting significance of Nelson's performance in a dismissive series of sentences (perhaps attempting to regain her emotional equilibrium), and plunging into depression over the sorrowfulness of the hymn she has heard.

In response to witnessing and remembering such performance, what is it about slave religious ecstasy that Chesnut finds threatening enough to assert that it "leaves no trace"? Mathews notes:

> Every white observer or participant who commented on it agreed with black people that black worship was radically different from that of most whites, even when those whites were in the same church at the same time. Autonomous black congregations and those associated with and meeting separately from white churches were best able to express themselves as they wished. By the 1830s, emotional breakdowns of white people under Evangelical preaching became much less common than it had been, limited for the most part to special revival seasons or camp meetings. Moreover—and this may be the crux of the matter—impressions of whites' conversion experiences differ markedly from those left by blacks' religious exercises. Blacks shared with whites, especially *sentimental* white Methodists, the initial emotional explosion of conversion as well as a persistent emotionalism afterwards, but blacks' "possession" and visions appear to have been qualitatively different from whites' experiences. For whites, the emotional fireworks resulted from relief at being saved from God's wrath, the release of tension brought to a breaking point by contrast between God's expectation of perfection and man's inability to achieve it.[37]

The writer's initial, uncertain conviction of her offenses, about which she jokes in the opening of this episode, undergoes a profound shift as she meditates on spiritual matters against the background of Jim Nelson's haunting "music." In this regard, she recalls Hawthorne's heroine Hester Prynne in *The Scarlet Letter,* who, because of overcrowding in the Congregational church, must audit the

Reverend Arthur Dimmesdale's election-day sermon from outside its walls, beyond the circle of the faithful. Unable to hear or understand the minister's words, Hester nevertheless finds herself transfigured by the emotion communicated in the musicality of his voice; in this way, she experiences a kind of transcendentalist transvaluation of Puritan theology in the form of a romantic epiphany.

Chesnut cannot deny the power of Jim Nelson's "music" to stir her soul. But she must reject any acknowledgment of its spiritual efficacy in order to disavow its inherently revolutionary dimension. In this regard, the driver is a slave radical more in the mode of Jesus Christ than of Nat Turner. Put a different way, the 1880s writer asserts that the value of Nelson's shouting is transient because the inebriates among the fold are as moved as she is, only to return to their tippling when the service ends—circumstantial evidence that the driver's message does not have a lasting grip on Mulberry's bondspeople. But in arguing this point, the writer misses the deepest dimension of Jim Nelson's sonorous expression: his fellow congregants must die to sin in order to be born again through the beneficent work of Christ's atonement. This is the potentially soul-transforming import of his music, the one that overwhelmingly threatens Chesnut's self-understanding as a righteous slaveholder.[38]

Though Nelson's effusions resonate at the level of emotion, the writer must claim to disregard them as noise in her account; any other interpretation, particularly that he has achieved personal transcendence, threatens Chesnut's metaphysical self-conception as a slaveholding Christian. That is, the alleged nontranslatability of black religious expression defaults to nonsense. But disavowal of slave religiosity is not quite the end of this story, as the narrating Chesnut tells it: for she completes her description of worship at the Negro church with a fascinating coda, a quotation from Chaucer that effectively constitutes a spiritual "response" to what we might term the black Methodist "call" emanating from Jim Nelson.

The passage is taken from the third stanza of Chaucer's "Truth," or the "Balade de Bon Conseyl," a lyric that became his third most popular work, if we judge from the evidence of existing numbers of manuscripts.[39] The third stanza unfolds:

> The wrestling of the world asketh a fall
> > Here is no home: here is a wildernesse.
> > Forth Pilgrim! Forth! Oh! Beast out of thy stall!
> Look up on high—And thank thy God for all! (214)

Against the description of slave spiritual ecstasy trumpeting the two-thousand-year old message of "good news" (Christ's atonement for the sin of man and his resurrection), amplified by the singing of a more contemporary, and heart-piercing, sorrow song, Chesnut juxtaposes Chaucer's verses. Black Christian music unfolds as prelude to white, early English poetry, though the verse is in ballad form, which somewhat blurs such distinctions between music and words. Despite the enduring power of Nelson's shout as part of the oral Christian tradition, Chesnut has argued that the driver's expressions leave no trace. In contrast, the Chaucer stanza has endured for over five hundred years, making its way from a volume in Mulberry's library to a quotation in the diarist's daybook and then into her 1880s narrative.

Ambiguity marks the content of the ballad stanza: it is unclear whether the writer is addressing herself as Chaucer's "beast," or whether she is putting the poet's apostrophe into the mouths of her slaves. Such antithetical meanings, given the complexity of the surrounding context, seem irresolvable, yet suffused with significance. In the first reading, Chesnut herself is the beast, a neat reversal of the very racist tropes she elsewhere articulates about African Americans. This analysis would be congruent with her (emotional if not intellectual) revelation during her account of the wartime worship service that as a slave mistress she perforce is a sinner. In the second interpretation, she is addressing her slaves both as beasts (untamed, wild creatures) and as domesticated animals (oxen or cows). Possessed of a double identity in their nonhumanness (dangerous yet tractable), which speaks more to her own ambivalence than to any inherent black nature, she enjoins them to rise up out of the bounds of slavery (their "stall") and look to God for strength as they begin their exodus (their "pilgrimage") out of bondage.

Such an injunction might be the 1880s writer's response to being moved deeply by Nelson's spiritual lament, music that perhaps has convinced the writer of the humanity of her slaves. Yet the first two lines of Chaucer suggest that in Chesnut's mind, any shift to freedom will be arduous; what her slaves can expect to face once emancipated is the harsh "wildernesse" of a world hostile to African Americans. Perhaps she is hinting that the wish for liberation may be more promising than the reality of economic hardship and "wandering." If so, she would not be the first slaveowner to argue that African Americans clearly would fare better under the paternalistic care of "good" masters than they would under the harsh realities of a free South.

Chesnut may be substituting Nelson's words that "leave no trace" with the more lasting refrain of the canonical early English poet. Most interesting is the fact that she does not quote the refrain, which would ordinarily follow and is based on St. John: "Ye shall know the truth and the truth shall make you free." It is as if the 1880s writer appreciates the danger of an injunction that would conflate the Christian promise of spiritual liberation with the political reality of freedom for the slave. To avoid this risk, she omits the gospel lines.[40]

Tellingly, the poem explicitly presents itself as advice. But it is not clear who is advising whom, or who is the model for the "true" spiritual stance. Nor do these verses make clear who is looking upward rather than at the earth below. We don't know if Chesnut recognizes that she is mired in the worldly by requiring the slave words to "leave a lasting trace" on the community. If Chaucer's words are surrogates for those of her bondspeople, she may be comparing them to the truth—the gesture of looking up. But she omits both the refrain from John and Chaucer's opening line: "That thee is sent, receive in buxumnesse [obedience]." Perhaps she omits the verse because it would comment severely on her own situation at the black church and her failure to understand the music

The deleted Chaucerian lines mandated the 1880s author's own obedience to a higher call, perhaps even God's requirement that she liberate her slaves. Read the other way, such verses could allow her to rationalize, with James Henry Hammond, George Fitzhugh, and other Southern slave apologists, that obedience redounds across the entire chain of being. Thus, the mistress owes fealty to God, and her slaves are enjoined to submit to her will by Southern law enforced through white power. Whatever the more likely reading, Chesnut obviates both by omitting the stanza's opening line—by offering this revised version of Chaucer in response to the haunting call of black religious worship. In deploying the language of the early English poet in reply to Jim Nelson and the slave sorrow song, the epic-minded Chesnut attempts to trump an overwhelming spiritual reality with the weight of classic literary tradition. That the quotation does not do its office, that it bears ironic rather than iconic weight, testifies to the power of African American religiosity to get under Chesnut's skin.

CHAPTER EIGHT

Masks

THEATRICALS IN WHITE

In this chapter I turn to the strangely inappropriate-seeming amateur theatricals mounted by the Richmond elite at the lowest point of the South's military prospects in 1864. Their frivolity impressed Chesnut's husband, recently promoted to brevet brigadier general, as fiddling while Rome burned. A less partisan onlooker might have understood the theatrical frenzy as the planter class's collective attempt at self-distraction from a political and military disaster over which they had no control. But there is another way of reading these frantic festivities: in Hegelian terms, as a desperate white elite's counterresponse to the unreadability of the bronze mask and the ventriloquized voice of the master class, that is, an instance of leisure unfolding in furious counterpoint to the terrifying prospect of African American resistance to white domination, whether through slave revolt, desertion, or emancipation in the aftermath of the looming Confederate defeat.

About two-thirds into the 1880s narrative, Chesnut represents the events her husband described as "hospitality run mad" (517). She labored over the pages she titled "The Bright Side of Richmond, 1864" more intensely in revision than she did on any other portion of the narrative; manuscript evidence shows that she hoped (and failed) to publish them as a free-standing essay, separate from the greater book. "The Bright Side of Richmond" shines a spotlight on the amateur theatricals mounted by Chesnut's social circle as a diversion for the "Kentucky Generals": Hood, Morgan, Breckinridge, and others posted to or furloughed in Richmond that winter. Evenings begun playing "charades" with elaborate costumes and sets ultimately gave way to still more highly orchestrated dramatic endeavors: the production of Richard Brinsley Sheridan's *The Rivals* (1775), an eighteenth-century English satire of sentimental conventions, including dueling; followed by the presentation of William Barnes Rhodes's *Bombastes Furioso* (1790), a parodic ballad opera, the songs to which, the 1880s writer notes, no one knew the words.[1]

So passionate was local ill feeling about these "theatricals" that the *Richmond Examiner* actually editorialized against Chesnut's friends for their extravagance. And similarly ambivalent accounts of the dramatic soirees appeared in at least three other important Southern memoirs of life during the war.[2] On the January, 9, 1864, the *Richmond Examiner* published an editorial response to the season of charades and amateur theatricals, which Mary Chesnut says was "down on us all" (535). The second paragraph of the article fulminates:

> There is no excuse for the absurd merriment which seems to be the tone in Richmond. If it is intended as a bravado, in order to show the Yankees that we are as irrepressible in the ball-room as on the battle-field, we opine that the moral effect will not make amends for the immorality of the means. Does Yankee merry-making strike terrour to our hearts? If it is a mere outburst of natural hilarity we can only wonder at the buoyancy which bears up under the enormous pressure of our misfortunes.—The sin of all this foolery does not lie, where some would put it, at the door of those who are mere lookers on, scions of "My Maryland," and Southern sympathizers from Northern latitudes. They may don the grinning mask and the thread-bare domino, if they have no bitter taste; but that true Southern people, whose liberties and fortunes are at stake, whose brothers have suffered or died for this cause, should allow themselves to be carried away by the silly example of these heartless creatures, is matter for both sorrow and anger. The farce is so bald; the "properties" so meager; the Elysian fields such unmistakable pasteboard; the rosy wine such indubitable ADAM'S ale; that we have been hoping for some time that the actors would weary of the play. As yet, however, we see no prospect of a speedy termination of the sickening phantasmagory. One reunion was, we learn, thinly attended because the arrival of the ambulance train had called off some of the ladies to nurse their wounded brothers; but after a while such little contretemps will not be permitted to interfere with the rights of youth and jollity. Impertinent kinsmen, who have been awkward enough to lose a leg, will not be suffered to trip up the fantastic toes of the fair dancers, and no one will peep out of the festive ark to see how the deluge of blood is rising.

Though the private theatricals were intended to offer carefree diversion to Richmond's officer class, they actually began with charades on historical subjects with tragic overtones, which were superseded by comedy and farce as the war news grew increasingly grim.[3] The first evening's activities were inaugurated with the acting out in charades of the word "suttee," the ritualized burning of widows in India, outlawed by the Raj in 1829.[4] Like those bereaved wives for whom suttee was created as a "solution" to the dilemma of remarriageability, Southern women between the ages of eighteen and forty found themselves far outnumbering the marriageable men of their own generation.[5] By the end of the war, an estimated one-quarter of the Southern male population between the ages of fifteen and fifty had been killed. Thus, as a topic for charades, the "barbaric" cultural practice of widow burning had resonance for the asymmetrical gender politics of the South.

Beyond the cross-cultural parallels at work sub rosa in this first charade, the example of "suttee" suggests that the Richmond theatricals found inspiration in recent international events, particularly the Indian Mutiny of 1857. This catastrophic episode of anticolonial violence abroad resonated with Southern fears of slave rebellion. In the 1880s narrative, the wartime Chesnut notes that she has read with great interest *My Diary in India in the Year 1858–1859* (1860), written by William Howard Russell, correspondent for the London *Times*.[6] She recurrently comments on the British treatment of the native sepoys who fought on behalf of the East India Company, until grievances against the company's army became overwhelming. In response, they rose up and massacred their British officers as well as these men's wives and children. As a member of the white American planter elite, the narrated self asserts she has feared that Southern slaves might do the same.

Chesnut alludes repeatedly to St. Domingo and the Indian Mutiny in her narrative. These two events, one past, one contemporary, serve as global analogues, shorthand for all she most fears about the potential for violence simmering under the surface of master-slave relations at home. The 1880s writer searched the globe for such examples, though the case of Virginia's Nat Turner had unfolded virtually in her own backyard. But that event had exploded when she was only eight years old, and rattled parents would likely have tried to protect their young children from knowledge of the trauma. Moreover, for the deeply Carolina-identified Miller family, Virginia really was another world.

Nevertheless, the adult Chesnut's disavowal of the Turner rising was not necessarily symptomatic of more than the central psychic mechanism enabling Southerners to carry on as slaveholders given the world's overwhelmingly negative opinion of their practice. After all, the British had abolished slavery on the mainland and in their colonial holdings by 1833, when Chesnut was ten years old. But the writer did not simply abjure the reality of racially fraught domestic unease. Unlike most of her peers, she saw her Southern world through a consistently comparative, international, perspective, and this made her somewhat unique even for a well-educated woman of her class. Across the narrative, she cites examples of racial conflict in imperial lands: the long-term fighting on St. Domingo between the French and various black and "colored" factions, the quarrels of the Russians and the Turks, the Russian struggle with the British for Afghanistan, and the British in India—all had lessons to teach about the combustible situation at home.

Chesnut's interests in international politics, significantly, had been piqued by the dramatic productions to which she was exposed in the years just before the war. In 1858 and 1859, her husband served in the Senate from South Carolina, and they lived in Washington, D.C. (Mr. Chesnut resigned in November of 1860, the first Southerner to do so following secession.) During this period, Mary Chesnut had attended a play on the subject of the Indian Mutiny, featuring a dramatization of the Siege of Lucknow. While in his voluminous footnotes to the 1981 edition of *Mary Chesnut's Civil War,* Woodward does not identify the name of this production, quite possibly it could have been *Jessie Brown; or, The Relief of Lucknow.* Written by Dion Boucicault, the drama was first presented at Wallack's Theatre in New York on February 22, 1858.[7] Boucicault, an Irish émigré, was the most popular playwright working in nineteenth-century America. It would make sense that his treatment of the subject, one of an outpouring of literary responses, poems, and pamphlets produced immediately after the Mutiny, might have been the version that traveled to Washington in the ensuing several years.

Ascertaining exactly which drama featuring the Siege of Lucknow Chesnut attended may be impossible. But she and her fellow spectators among the cohort of politicians, diplomats, and their wives would have constituted a captive audience for this highly fraught subject, particularly in the heated atmosphere of prewar Washington. In an 1880s entry for July 5, 1862, she reports:

> Read a book called *Wife and Ward* [by Edward Money, published in 1859]—scene laid at the siege of Cawnpore [where the British were overrun]. Who knows what similar horrors may lie in wait for us! When I saw the Siege of Lucknow dramatized in that little theater at Washington, what a thrill of terror ran through me as those black and yellow brutes came jumping over the parapets! These faces were like so many of the same sort at home. To be sure, John Brown had failed to fire their hearts, and they saw no cause to rise and burn and murder us all—like the women and children were treated in the Indian Mutiny. But how long would they resist the seductive and irresistible call "only rise, kill, and be free"? (409)[8]

Historians continue to argue about the causes of the Mutiny. Some scholars take the view that it was a conspiracy plotted against the background of festering Indian resentments, while others believe the uprising erupted spontaneously within the ranks of the British-led Army of the East India Company, whose officers were European but approximately 80 percent of whose troops were native Indian soldiers. One definite precursor to the full-blown rebellion of May 10, 1857, involved the actions of a sepoy called Mangal Pardy, who served at a military station in Barrackpore. For unknown reasons, Pardy went crazy and attacked his senior officers with swords while his fellow sepoys stood by, refusing to intervene in the violence. The mad sepoy then tried to commit suicide with his rifle on the parade ground, wounding himself severely but failing to end his life. Court-martialed for treason along with his senior native officer (who, though his immediate commander, ranked, as did all native officers, below the lowest member in the British chain of command), Pardy and his subahdar were hanged by the Army of the East India Company.

Less subject to debate than the origin of the Mutiny is what literary historian Christopher Herbert terms its "proximate cause": eighty-five sepoys refused to break with their teeth newly designed paper ammunition cartridges greased by lard from cattle and pigs.[9] Such an act would have violated the respective dietary taboos of Hindu and Muslim religious law. The Army of the East India Company construed this noncompliance as an act of intolerable insubordination. Far from pardoning the men's failure to cooperate on the grounds of respect for religious difference, they saw it as an instance of Indian defiance. Clapping the men in irons, the British court-martialed them to periods of long penal servitude, manacled them before their comrades, and put them in jail. The next day, the regiment mutinied: after liberating the prisoners, they massacred their British officers, dashed off to nearby Delhi, and persuaded native troops stationed there to join the uprising, while conducting a pogrom against English officers, their wives, and their children.

For Southern slaveholders after 1863, the Indian Mutiny became evocative for more than its earlier prognostication of slave rebellion. As of January of that year, former slaves newly emancipated by Lincoln's Proclamation (a legal document that went unrecognized in the South) began to join the Union army. Black martial resistance had become institutionalized. The wives and daughters of Richmond's elite, increasingly invested in creating theatrical distractions during the winter of 1864, did so just as masters in the Confederate ranks began to confront former bondsmen in the opposing army.

Thomas Wentworth Higginson, the New England minister and abolitionist who commanded the First South Carolina Volunteers as colonel of that all-black regiment of escaped slaves and freedmen, relates an extraordinarily moving account of one such racially charged meeting. On an expedition up the Edisto River in South Carolina, he and his troops encounter a plantation mistress (actually a Northern émigré) who deploys her adopted Southern belle charms in an attempt to manipulate him. Higginson will have none of it:

> However, I wished to present my credentials; so, calling up my companion, I said that I believed she had been previously acquainted with Corporal Robert Sutton? I never saw a finer bit of unutterable indignation than came over the face of my hostess, as she slowly recognized him. She drew herself up, and dropped out the monosyllables of her answer as if they were so many drops of nitric acid. "Ah," quoth my lady, "*we* called him Bob!"
>
> It was a group for a painter. The whole drama of the war seemed to reverse itself in an instant, and my tall, well-dressed, imposing, philosophic Corporal dropped down the immeasurable depth into a mere plantation "Bob" again. So at least in my imagination; not to that person himself. Too essentially dignified in his nature to be moved by words where substantial realities were in question, he simply turned from the lady, touched his hat to me, and asked if I would wish to see the slave-jail, as he had the keys in his possession.[10]

Slavery historian Leon Litwack cites another vivid example of this phenomenon, culled from the WPA oral history archive of interviews with former slaves. Recognizing the Rebel officer who recently had owned him body and soul, a black Union soldier is said to have shouted: "Hello Marster. Bottom rail on top dis time!"[11] So it was that at this period in the war such cross-racial encounters—with all their potential for ludicrousness and violence—were on everyone's mind. And, as the first amateur charade of "suttee" obliquely suggests, the reality of this fact was inescapable, whether one was on the battle lines or in Richmond.

Thus, responding to the city's palpable need for relief from martial strife, Mrs. Secretary of War Randolph, Miss Constance Cary, her famously beautiful cousin Miss Hetty Cary, and the leading matrons of their set (even Chesnut herself served as an unofficial wardrobe mistress) determined to mount ever more intricate theatrical productions. Moving from the politicized subject matter of the charade, they turned to the seemingly frivolous material of the eighteenth-century comedy in multiple acts. After Shakespeare's works, apparently Sheridan's lighthearted plays were more frequently performed in the antebellum South (Charleston and New Orleans) than the plays of any other, even nineteenth-century American, author.[12]

On first glance *The Rivals,* with its small cast and relatively inconsequential plot line, appears to be one of Sheridan's most purely frothy productions. That is, the stakes of whether Captain Adverse is betrothed to Lydia Languish by dint of his father's machinations or his own contrivances to disguise his identity hardly stand up to, say, King Lear's fate at the hands of daughters Goneril and Regan. And however one might read *The Rivals* politically, economically, and culturally, the play's substantive themes are incongruent with those of a charade about widow burning. Nevertheless, even a frivolous production could give displaced expression to the troubling cultural issues that resonated particularly for Mary Chesnut.

The Rivals justly was known for its savaging of maudlin Richardsonian and Rousseauian romantic conventions. Equally significant was its refusal to conclude on a moralistic, didactic note. Sheridan's assault in *The Rivals* on what he considered the inane conventions of eighteenth-century novelistic and dramatic romance must have gratified Chesnut's caustic sensibility, for her elaborate critique of sentimental ideology, particularly objections to the way a language of fellow feeling contributed to the mystification of white masters' sexual predation on slave women, is a central thread in the 1880s book. The figures of Lydia Languish and Faulkland, bound by sentimental codes so overdeveloped as to approach absurdity, offered just the note of relief she sought in invoking her preference for William Makepeace Thackeray and George Eliot over Susan Warner and Harriet Beecher Stowe.

Chesnut appreciated the imaginative power underwriting Sheridan's grandly ignorant creation in *The Rivals,* Mrs. Malaprop, whose famous butchering of the English language proved so culturally compelling that a term was coined in her honor: since the late eighteenth century, "malapropism" has meant a word garbled to the point of ridiculousness. "Exploded" instead of "exposed," "conjunctions" rather than "injunctions," "prepositions" for "propositions," and "hydrostatics" in place of "hysterics"—all expressions misspoken by Lydia Languish's aunt and guardian on the stage of *The Rivals*—have drawn gales of laughter from Sheridan's audiences, from his time, to the Richmond theatricals of 1864, into our own.[13]

Her comic relief aside, Mrs. Malaprop also may have piqued Chesnut's elitist and racist perceptions of uneducated or ill-educated linguistic ambitions (white as well as black): Chesnut comments haughtily in the 1880s narrative about various misuses of language by Yankees, social-climbing Southern whites, and African Americans. Perusal of her unfinished novel from the 1870s, "The Captain and the Colonel," suggests that as much as she abhorred the ways undereducated whites misused language, it was the slave "mangling" of English that most put her in mind of Mrs. Malaprop, though interestingly, such a connection is never overt in her 1880s epic. There, she avoids employing grotesque instances of African American vernacular in any of the minstrel modes exploited by plantation romancers of the period. Nor in the 1880s book does she model black language on the work of Harriet Beecher Stowe, whose use of racist idioms in moments of low comedy makes sections of *Uncle Tom's Cabin* painful to read. Particularly pointed is an example from near the end of that book: Long after her husband, Uncle Tom, has been sold to the trader Haley, Aunt Chloe, the Shelby's cook, travels to St. Louis to become trained as a "perfectioner" (614) — her term for a confectioner. Chloe's goal is to buy her own freedom and then to continue working to purchase her husband's liberty as well. It is crucial to remember that Chesnut's Molly and Laurence never sound like Stowe's Aunt Chloe; nor do they resemble her fictive Sam and Andy (both Shelby slaves) or Sambo and Quimbo (Simon Legree's slave enforcers).

However, in the novel fragment "The Captain and the Colonel," Chesnut's young female protagonist observes two slaves courting and says to her mammy: "They seemed dancing a black minuet, they flitted before each other so rapidly and so grandly. She said with a profound *reverence*, 'How does your corporosity seem to sagaciate, my Lord.' 'Quite abflout,' he answered. 'What do they mean?' I asked. Binkey Anne treated the whole thing with great scorn. She said they were 'playing ladies and gentlemen and talking dictionary.'... She ended by saying, 'Sambo's got no sediment.'"[14] We're once more in the company of Mrs. Malaprop, Sheridan's embodiment of linguistic absurdity, with whose garbled speech Chesnut had become well acquainted during rehearsals for the amateur theatricals.

To return to the larger issues suggested by the private production of *The Rivals,* it may seem peculiar that the Richmond matrons undertook elaborate amateur performances when the professional drama remained a cultural venue in 1864. A letter Chesnut wrote to Mrs. Louis T. Wigfall in January of 1863 makes clear that plays continued to serve as a refuge for her circle during the war. And work by W. Stanley Hoole, and also by Charles S. Watson, who study theatrical history in the antebellum, bellum, and postbellum South, supports the notion that what took place at Mrs. Randolph's and Mrs. Ives's in the winter of 1864 was far from the only theatrical entertainment in town.[15]

One explanation for the enthusiasm of Chesnut's circle for amateur drama involves the growing instability of what once had been thought of as a solid Southern class hierarchy. Formerly, planters from the oldest families of Virginia and South Carolina ranked on the top, while their most menial field slaves were positioned at the bottom. In between were all manner of people, starting on the low rungs with elite house slaves and freed blacks, then the poor white sandy-hillers just a step above, followed by white yeomen and artisans, and then the small planters and professional men of business (lawyers, doctors, bankers). The "national" crisis loosened these once clearly defined and stable rungs of status. Planters began to be ruined by the cooptation of their crops by the Confederate government, and the borrowing of black bondspeople to work on the defenses of the coasts deprived white elites of their agricultural labor. Ultimately, of course, it was the emancipation of the slaves, in whom inhered the core of their wealth, that put the final nail in the planters' coffin. Their fate had repercussions all the way down the economic chain. And by the winter of 1864, Mary Chesnut and her genteel friends were feeling the rumblings of what was to come.

Accordingly, to put on an eighteenth-century comedy in the midst of cultural chaos was to perform the fantasy that all was well, that leisure remained abundant, that the class hierarchy over which she and her friends presided remained intact. Historian Karen Halttunen and theater scholar Joseph Roach have written insightfully about the specific class inflection of amateur theatricals in nineteenth-century America and England. Notes Halttunen: "[M]iddle-class Americans were soon performing a wide variety of theatricals in their parlors, including acting charades, acting proverbs, burlesques and farces, *tableaux vivants* or living pictures, charades in *tableaux* and shadow pantomimes. The private theatrical had emerged as the most popular form of middle-class parlor entertainment."[16]

Clearly, the writer's cohort was not and never had been anything other than upper class. Not only did people like the Prestons and the senior Chesnuts possess vast wealth (though their riches would be lost by 1865), generations of Prestons and Chesnuts had been educated at the finest Northern schools, traveled across Europe, and immersed thoroughly in the study of fine arts, foreign languages, and cultures. Chesnut's circle seems to have taken their cue from Frank Vizetelly, the British artist and journalist who was sent to Boston by the *Illustrated London News* to cover the war, and who traveled on to Richmond for the Southern point of view. Vizetelly had popularized charades as an English parlor game.[17] His Richmond hostesses may or may not have been aware that instructions for such activities also had appeared in the 1850s in *Godey's Lady's Book,* perhaps the most influential middle-class Northern women's magazine.

Though genteel and aspiring Southern women of this period also read *Godey's,* they had their own, separate ladies' periodicals. But the magazines the 1880s Chesnut describes having loved were far more highbrow, intellectual, and English. Being Anglophiles of the highest order may have proved enough of an inspiration. That the plot of *The Rivals* stages romantic conflict across the classes and resolves with a suitably aristocratic marriage would have allowed the Richmond circle of Mrs. Randolph, Constance and Hetty Cary, Mary Chesnut, and others to indulge the fantasy that what was happening on stage held a mirror to their own lives, all the while that both their wealth and their status were undergoing complete upheaval.

Roach frames his analysis of private theatricals in the context of Anglo-European socioeconomic history in a way that resonates for Chesnut's friends: "In the limits of domestic space, the amateur theatrical production enunciates a high bourgeois reply to the court spectacles of Europe, which allegorized dynastic legitimacy and world-historical entitlements in canvas and gilt."[18] Consider the irony: in amusements like the "suttee" charade, the theatrical enactment of sacrifice is occurring as a great forfeiture of life, limb, and patrimony unfolds on Southern battlefields just outside Richmond. Put another way, through their form, the amateur theatricals express the wish to construct a world elsewhere for the Kentucky Generals and their minions, beyond the Civil War. But the content of these dramatic exercises, exemplified by the choice of the first evening charade, suggests that by 1864, all attempts to quarantine home front from battlefield have failed utterly.

Although General Hood, Buck Preston's high-ranking suitor, enjoyed a reputation for ferocity during the war, the 1880s Chesnut, transforming historical figure into literary character, dramatizes another, more vulnerable side of the man. Chesnut's Hood is a trauma survivor, a figure of pathos. Sporting only one healthy leg, a mangled arm, and a pair of crutches, he is featured sitting in the front rows at Mrs. Randolph's charades and at Mrs. Ives's theatricals—a big fish thrown out of his familiar, roiling waters and left thrashing for air. Disoriented by a social arena vastly different from the battlefield he knows, this simple warrior proves unable to distinguish dramatic characters on the stage from the soldiers he commands in combat, as shown in an episode from the evening on which *The Rivals* was performed. Hood's comrade General Breckinridge, tells Chesnut, "[W]atch Hood. He has not seen the play before, and Bob Acres [the wealthy rube in *The Rivals*] amazes him." Chesnut reports, amused, what she observes: "When he caught my eye, General Hood nodded to me and said emphatically, 'I believe that fellow Acres is a coward.' 'That's better than the play,' whispered Breckinridge" (February 5, 1864, 553).

According to Constance Cary's version of the incident in her *Recollections Grave and Gay,* Hood shouted out loud his disapproval of Bob Acres's spinelessness in the context of a dueling scene. Legally outlawed in the first quarter of the nineteenth century, but still practiced in South Carolina as late as the spring of 1861—elsewhere in the narrative Chesnut describes how she urged her husband to stop a duel in Camden[19]—the armed challenge had a long history in the Southern code of honor. But that a duel on an amateur stage (the fictive rehearsal of an always already dramatic event) could evoke Hood's martial passions would seem unbelievable, until we remember that the Kentuckian recently had suffered terrible wounds, including the loss of a leg, at Gettysburg and Chickamauga.

Moreover, Hood was lovesick and highly agitated over the precarious state of a wished-for engagement with Chesnut's protégée Buck Preston, an affair that had the entire community talking and that ultimately miscarried. On the evening in question, Buck Preston sat directly behind her fiancé in the audience, observing his first public performance in the role of genteel theater-viewer, an entirely new assignment, and far from the routine of a commanding general. While Buck surveyed Hood watching the play, one only can imagine his own anxiety as he awkwardly sat erect, fully aware that the object of all his desires was gazing at him as he viewed the production. According to Chesnut's account, a willing suspension of disbelief during the theatricals was not Hood's forte. In response to his shouts, his friends had to reassure Hood that the man in the role of Bob Acres only was pretending. If the playacting in Richmond constituted a kind of Southern cultural dreamwork, it apparently offered little refuge for the credulous John Bell Hood. For this mutilated veteran, and for others like him, the representations afoot on the parlor stages of the white elite were, in fact, symbolic elaborations of the military nightmare that stalked his waking life.[20]

James Chesnut Jr.'s unsettling comment on the last night of the theatricals sums up this troubled sense that distinctions between fantasy and reality had become blurred for his Confederate cohort. Walking home with her husband on this final evening (at 3 a.m. the next day, in fact), Mary Chesnut remarks that he has softened his earlier, hostile view of the theatricals. Weeks before, he had criticized Mrs. Chesnut's lightheartedness with the remark, "Senseless extravagance—stupid charades," and worked "himself up to such a pitch of wrath that he finally swore by all his gods that the play was not worth the candle" (528). Now, she tells him, "[Y]ou have spent a jolly evening," to which Mr. Chesnut replies, "I do not know. I have asked myself more than once tonight, 'Are you the same man who stood gazing down on the faces of the dead on that awful battlefield?' The soldiers lying there—they stare at you with their eyes wide open. Is this the same world? Here—and there—&c. &c." (February 5, 1864, 554).

The 1880s writer has remembered and envisioned a dreamlike setting for this perambulatory exchange. Describing a "moonlight" night "as light as day, almost," Chesnut evokes something like the eeriness of the background for Hawthorne's "Custom House" preface to *The Scarlet Letter*.[21] Possibly influenced by the weirdness of this atmosphere, Mr. Chesnut conjures harrowing images of those who have perished in the war. James's vision of his comrades in arms strikes a hideous contrast to the fictive apparitions on the parlor stage, precisely because the corporeality of death is all too real. This powerful memory of the open-eyed Confederate dead raises haunting questions for the general about how nearly inconceivable Confederate experience has become.

Mary Boykin Chesnut is the last person on whom the reality of this strange oscillation between fictional substitution and factual sacrifice is lost. Indeed, her earlier, lighter language in a passage describing the first round of theatricals consciously underscores the way in which in Richmond art has come to imitate Confederate life: "Mr. Hudson's mission is to substitute Halsey Wigfall for himself in the part of Sir Walter Raleigh" (January 12, 1864, 537), she reports. Elaborating the martial conceit in which the maneuverings before the footlights echo military machinations, she continues: "At Mrs. Randolph's Mr. Hudson came for me to congratulate him; his substitute, Halsey Wigfall, had done so well as Sir Walter Raleigh. He was quite satisfied he had made a good thing of changing places." Immediately following this remark she offers the thought: "In the spirit of the men who are so proud of the prowess of their substitutes in the army—actually, they say, put up monuments to them when they are killed!" (January 14, 1864, 538).

Roach argues that all performance involves the dynamic of surrogation: "[B]ecause collective memory works selectively, imaginatively, and often perversely, surrogation rarely if ever succeeds. . . . [T]he intended substitute either cannot fulfill expectations, creating a deficit, or actually exceed[s] them, creating a surplus." Furthermore, he adds, "in such dramas of sacrificial substitution, the derivation of the word *personality* from *mask* eerily doubles that of *tragedy* from *goat* [a sacrificial animal]. I believe that the process of trying out various candidates in different situations—the doomed search for originals by continually auditioning stand-ins—is the most important of the many meanings that users intend when they say the word *performance*."[22] We might conclude that, in all its theaters, from the battlefield on which Hood lost his leg to the parlor entertainment where he is distressed to the point of outburst, the Civil War's multiple dramas of substitutions have been equally ill-fated.

Two final episodes of "theatricals in white" form a short coda to this discussion. They take place in the 1880s narrative after the flurry of private dramatic performances of January and February 1864, the first in July of that year, the second one year later, July 1865, just three months following Lee's mid-April surrender. The narrative account of the earlier episode easily could have been inspired by Edgar Allan Poe's "The Masque of the Red Death," a story published in *Graham's Magazine* in 1842, when Chesnut, a passionate consumer of periodical literature, was nineteen years old. There is no conclusive evidence that she read this particular tale, though for many years she took the *Southern Literary Messenger,* in which Poe had made his reputation and of which he became editor in the 1830s. It is also the case, moreover, that during the war, in Richmond, Chesnut socialized with Mrs. John Allan, the second wife of Poe's adoptive father and patron.[23] This relationship makes it likely that Poe and his work remained vividly present for her, despite the fact that the popular writer of gothic horror had died more than fifteen years before the event she describes.

One can well imagine how the literary Chesnut, always informed by her ardent reading, might have envisaged the carnage of the Civil War as a latter-day version of "The Masque of the Red Death." This conceit helps illuminate her description of the manic maneuverings of Edmund Rhett, a contemporary in her elite circle, known for his imprudence.[24] The opening of Poe's ominous tale sets the scene:

> The "Red Death" had long devastated the country. No pestilence had ever been so fatal, or so hideous. Blood was its Avatar and its seal—the redness and the horror of blood....
> ... Prince Prospero was happy and dauntless and sagacious. When his dominions were half depopulated, he summoned to his presence a *thousand* hale and light-hearted friends from among the knights and dames of his court, and with these retired to the deep seclusion of one of his castellated abbeys.[25]

Prince Prospero orders that the walls of his fortress be welded shut after he has admitted one thousand healthy and carefree friends from among the elite of his domain. A mysterious stranger intrudes during the masquerade ball at the climax of the story. His face covered in blood and his form draped in the habiliments of the grave, the interloper is the Red Death personified. By the end of the evening, every reveler at the ball, starting with Prince Prospero himself, has fallen lifeless before his fatal gaze.

Chesnut's story for July 18 of 1864 similarly comingles celebration, morbidity, and mortality:

> At Mrs. Slocum's last night, the sensation of the evening, a frail young, invalid who had hemorrhages without number. The Confederacy is scant of clothes. We give that up. But this fair one was too thin. Peasant's waist [bodice] and

next to nothing under that. "Weak lungs! No wonder—so exposed!" She tottered as she walked, so weak was she. Not tottered—rolled and pitched. I accept the correction. But when the round dancing began, she was there. And Deadly Smooth «Edmund Rhett» her partner. Now he makes no concealment of the fact that he is dying of consumption. He sat by Mary P[reston] and myself. When the weak one danced up toward us, holding her dress— "Cancan," whispered Mary P—asked the invalid: "Why do you suppose I am so ill—why? I give it to you in a hundred guesses." "We give up." "Before I dressed to come here this evening I ate twelve eggs." "Dressed? Undressed you mean," in the same tone as "cancan," was whispered. Then: "Oh—ain't she common! At least she is unenclosed." How Edmund Rhett laughed—he who asserts he never feels inclined to smile at aught this world can do. (621)

In addition to its Poe-like atmosphere, the scene offers an uncanny counterpoint to James Chesnut Jr.'s invocation of his dead comrades, related to his wife in the February moonlight after the final theatrical. Now, in the height of summer, this female consumptive seems to embody the fate of the South itself, in a dance of death in tortured slow motion. Immediately after the ghastly encounter with the invalid belle, Chesnut herself declines Edmund Rhett's invitation to dance. Anxiously, he asks, "What depresses you so?" She replies: "'That carnival of death.' For our fevered one flew madly from right to left—holding the scanty skirts high. 'Poor thing! You can read her fate in her face. There is Gwin—worse—or at best, nearer his end. What a blunder, to bring us all together here. A reunion of consumptives—to dance and sing until almost one can hear the death rattle'" (620–21).

Several minutes later Edmund Rhett takes a leap that makes his verbal tableau of consumptives teetering at the edge of the grave all too real, a moment of horror Chesnut witnesses firsthand:

> Suddenly a black object sprang from a window beyond the piazza—and it fell fifteen feet or more to the ground. Somebody killed! My heart, as it has a way of doing, stood still.... There were shrieks, and the crowd poured out of doors. Edmund Rhett had picked himself up and was walking coolly up the steps. "What's the row?" he inquired. Nothing disturbs the equanimity of that ineffable dandy—not even a fall from fifteen feet. He said, looking round: "This is a mere porch. I took it for a piazza extending the whole front of the house—so I stepped out of a window in the game and fell to the ground." (622)

The consumptive dandy's defenestration marks the second time for 1864 that Chesnut has recounted a story of a fall from a great height. In her earlier report, the tragedy of Jefferson Davis's five-year-old son, the accident proved fatal. Rhett's reckless tumble and unlikely survival offer a grotesque contrast to the demise of the angelic little Joe, for the death of this child had struck the hearts of Southerners as a domestic disaster with terrible resonance for the national imaginary. Literally wasting away from the tubercular infection in his lungs when he plummeted out the window at Mrs. Slocum's, Edmund Rhett's embodiment of dissipation on the brink had a symbolic import for Chesnut and her project, and the theatrical scene he created in July 1864 did not bode well as a portent of the desperate straits in which the Confederacy found itself. It is no accident that Chesnut records this "carnival of death" on the home front only weeks before she tells how Willie Preston, beloved youngest son of Caroline Hampton and John Preston, and pampered little brother of Jack, Buck, Tudy, and Mamie, has his heart "shot away" (623).

The second example in the theatrical coda is equally emblematic, this time of the overripeness if not the corruption of a defeated South immediately after the war. Self-absorbed, disrespectful Harriet Grant, orphaned granddaughter and ward of old Colonel Chesnut, had proved a thorn in her family's side throughout a lifetime on Mulberry. Mary Chesnut called her Hecate in the 1860s diary, in entries which largely were devoted to venting her frustration over Harriet's nearly indescribable obnoxiousness. Rusticated in Camden during the war, and late to find a husband, given the near destruction of the marriageable male population, Harriet finally had become engaged to Dick Stockton in 1865. He was a Southern veteran who had determined to head North in the aftermath of Confederate defeat.

Vicissitudes of the surrender conspired to keep Harriet and Dick separated until July of 1865. In the 1880s entry for the day following his belated arrival in South Carolina—in Chesnut's dating, "Black" 4th of July—the writer describes how

> [the] bride-elect arrayed herself like a May queen—crown of natural flowers on her head and wreaths of flowers and evergreen looped up her dress on every side. Her uncle like a Goth took his knife and cut off the body garlands—left the wreaths of green flowing over the skirt of her gown. "You are not young enough for such nonsense. You will disgust the man. Dress like a Christian woman—not in masquerade." "A Christian woman—I would like to see that in her character." (833)

In this fantastic scene, Harriet Grant festoons herself with nearly every floral specimen available on the plantation, fashioning herself as pagan fertility goddess, a Maypole incarnate. In an absurd display of excess, Chesnut's loathsome niece would seem to be trumpeting sexual viability and the promise of

Northern renewal against her aunt's middle-aged childlessness and Southern rustication. Significantly, the episode is set in the closing moments of the 1880s narrative, the published version of which ends two pages after the description of Harriet's horticultural metamorphosis. All resolves comically when the vulgar Harriet is relieved of her flowers, so to speak, and de-garlanded by her "Goth" of an uncle who, even in the midst of poverty and defeat, remains determined to uphold Chesnut refinement with the wave of a knife blade.[26]

Most tellingly, James Jr. chastises his niece (with her unfortunate surname) for having outlived her Maypole days, and for approaching her nuptials as if they were a highly anticipated theatrical extravaganza rather than the consummation of a religious sacrament. Here, we might read Harriet Grant as a figure for the New South to be, in all its brassy, self-important disregard for history, but still subject to the (literal) dressing-down of an Old South that, while on its last legs, has not quite died and been buried. Though Harriet's origins are genteel, Chesnut sees her as well-born but ill-bred—or, perhaps, well-bred but ill-born? This scene and its protagonist evoke *Gone With the Wind*'s notorious white-trash character Emmie Slattery, mother to several illegitimate children by Jonas Wilkerson, the Northern overseer on Tara. Emmie marries this carpetbagging scoundrel after the war and fancies buying the O'Hara plantation when Scarlett and her family fail to raise cash enough to pay back-taxes, which have been inflated, impossibly, by a resentful Yankee government. In Margaret Mitchell's imagination, Emmie Wilkerson, née Slattery, is the New South rising from the hell of war.[27] For James Chesnut Jr., survival and endurance will entail far more than playacting in anticipation of a wedding long overdue. Committed to striking down the sentimental illusions signified by the flowers and garlands that have hampered his waning culture, we leave him at the end of the 1880s narrative, rejecting dramatic display and, knife in hand, ready to take up the arduous work ahead.

CHAPTER NINE

Revolt

FAMILY TROUBLES IN THE HOUSE DIVIDED

From the black comedy of July 1865, featuring James Chesnut Jr. wielding a knife over Harriet Grant's obscenely prolific nuptial garlands, we turn back to the early years of the war. Toward the beginning of the 1880s narrative, Mary Chesnut develops into a near novella an episode to which she had devoted brief but serious attention in the 1860s diary. Instead of the verbal threat of the 1865 scene, the 1861 account involves the real and brutal murder of an elderly white woman by her black bondspeople. Half suffocated at the hands of four of her house slaves, septuagenarian Betsey Witherspoon revived enough to address the quartet who, minutes later, would terminate her life. Quoting from the murderers' eventual confession, Chesnut's narrative records her cousin's final appeal: "She asked them what she had ever done that they should want to kill her?" (October 7, 1861, 211). Both a contemporary newspaper obituary and the 1880s writer noted that the deceased had been renowned as a "saint on earth" in her community of Society Hill, South Carolina (199). A self-attributed "indulgent mistress," who purportedly "spoiled" and "petted her slaves," Mrs. Witherspoon apparently had never believed it necessary to "discipline" them, as her son John vehemently wished (209). Nevertheless, the old woman's baffled question about "what she had ever done" to warrant being murdered by her "people" spoke to only one side of the double vision that enabled the white master class to hold nearly four million African Americans in bondage for more than two hundred years.[1] Mrs. Witherspoon had treated the blacks under her authority with comparative generosity and relative latitude. As owners went, she seems to have been better than most. But better than most did not change the fundamental truth of her existence: that she had held William, Rhody, Sylvie, Romeo, along with many others, in bondage for the duration of their lives. To borrow Hegel's formulation, her very position as mistress rendered them slaves, depriving them of legal status, education, economic agency, and social and domestic rights. What ever had she done, indeed? In this and the following chapter, I explore the Witherspoon murder as a limit case for insurrection. Featuring the slaying of an owner locally known for kindness, the incident put the white community on notice that no slaveholder—however "benevolent"—could be guaranteed immunity from the potential revenge of those held in bondage.

The killing of Mrs. Witherspoon was the only slave uprising to touch Chesnut personally during the four years of the Civil War. Twenty years after the fact, she devoted the longest recurring and most emotionally harrowing thematic cluster in her 1880s narrative to this episode, a personal tragedy with clear political significance. Exploring the case in detail affords us particular access to a palimpsest of Chesnut's racial unconscious: her wartime attitudes overlain with those of the post-Reconstruction era in which she revised and transformed her original diary. And studying the murder's impact on the enslaved men and women in the writer's purview (though of course, it was she, their white former mistress, who observed and recorded their responses) allows us to take some measure of black political sensibilities on the eve of emancipation.[2]

In order to appreciate Mary Chesnut's response to black on white bloodshed in her own South Carolina, it is helpful to understand her somewhat idiosyncratic ideas about the institution of African American bondage. Like many elite white Southerners on the eve of the Civil War, Chesnut worried about the looming prospect of "another St. Domingo" or a "second John Brown." Such terms constituted planters' shorthand for a number of apocalyptic racial fantasies: the slave caste rising up en masse against the masters and slaughtering them, eventually overturning the brutalities of the plantation system (as in Haiti) or an armed white visionary evangelizing enslaved blacks to end their subjugation through violent conflict (as had John Brown).

Details from Chesnut's 1880s narrative suggest that, although she shared many of the racist attitudes of her social class, she had come to conclude that slavery was wrong as early as the 1830s.[3] As discussed in the introduction, the teenaged Mary Boykin Miller was prescient enough to understand that the black families separated at auction after her father's untimely death were the blameless victims of Stephen Decatur Miller's unfitness for farming, his bad luck, and his tragic ill health. And any illusions she might have had about the benefits of white paternalism were shattered in this instant.

Recall the letter that the Chesnut of the narrative claims to have written to her husband early in their marriage on the subject of slavery's injustice. Despite the fact that this document had been lost by the time of the Civil War, the writer invokes its central ideas with some regularity, explaining how she had staked nearly "abolitionist" claims in that 1842 missive, when she was but nineteen. In fact, Chesnut loathed what she felt were intrusive Northern agitators. In the 1880s narrative, she accused abolitionists of knowing nothing about the reality of quotidian experiences shared by blacks and whites on the plantation, experiences that in her eyes went beyond the white mandate that blacks work without remuneration and in threat of punishment for resistance: the white nursing of ailing slaves; the collective celebrations of weddings, harvests, and New Year's Day; shared religious worship.[4]

Indeed, the 1880s Chesnut clearly stated that she had been convinced that slavery was near its death throes by the time of secession. But to put Chesnut's particular antislavery in historical and cultural context, it once again is useful to consider this comment by Chesnut overseer James Team: "In all my life I have only met one or two womenfolk who were not abolitionists in their hearts—and hot ones, too. [Old] Mrs. Chesnut is the worst. They have known that on her here for years. . . . all the ladies of this family hated slavery" (December 6, 1861, 255). His remark, recorded by the conscious artist of the 1880s, cut through the layers of "positive good" social ideology that saturated the attitudes of the planter elite, as well as any claim that life as a slave in America provided opportunities for Christian conversion and cultural uplift that freedom in Africa could not offer. Team suggested instead that any close observer who witnessed the travail of plantation slaves firsthand and over time invariably would turn against the institution, as he had come to do himself. By late 1861, he wanted to "free our negroes and put them in the army" (255), which seemed to Chesnut a progressive idea at the moment he uttered it to her.[5]

Even before her cousin was slain in 1861, Mary Chesnut may have known more about slave uprisings than most elite white wives in Camden. Not only had she lived on a Mississippi slave plantation, at a cosmopolitan girls' boarding school in Charleston run by refugees from St. Domingo, and in the heart of congressional Washington, D.C., Chesnut had traveled to Northern watering holes as well as to London. An avid reader of politics, history, and current affairs, she was fascinated by recent global instances of slaves rebelling against masters. Particularly compelling to Chesnut were the Haitian Revolution of 1793–1803 (successful), the horrors of which she had learned through the tales of her refugee teachers, mulatto and white, at Madame Talvande's School, and the Indian Mutiny of 1857–58 (ultimately quelled), about which she read in William Howard Russell's memoir of the concussion. Two years before the Witherspoon murder, she had worried over trouble unfolding in Virginia, with John Brown's raid on Harpers Ferry (1859). This failed scheme dominated the headlines during her brief career as a senator's wife, living in the District of Columbia.

These terrifying events—the first a decade-long imperial fiasco for French colonial whites that represented mass race-war to Chesnut; the second, an unexpectedly long-lived and gruesome native retort to British imperialism in India, which to Chesnut somehow personified a violation of the intimate relations between servant and mistress, as well as subaltern and gentleman-soldier; and the third, the ill-fated but powerfully publicized explosion of antislavery energies at home, which seemed to embody the maddest dimensions of abolitionism to Chesnut—became touchstones for her sense of the potentially precarious situation in her own South Carolina. Horrors once unimaginable on Southern soil could become possible if the black "family" writ large roused itself to throw off its white patriarchal oppressors.

Chesnut often turned to one of these three historical moments when writing about her own anxieties, sometimes to the effect of amplifying them. In her 1880s narrative for 1863, for example, as she contemplated the defection of South Carolina coastal slaves to Union gunboats, she pictured British women and children boarding rescue vessels after their purported release as hostages held by mutinying Indian sepoys. While the African American bondspeople, in the matter of an instant, became forever free, the expatriate Victorians only had moments to fathom the prospect of regaining their liberty before they were massacred nearly one and all.[6]

Thwarted Camden Slave Revolt, 1816

Mary Chesnut worried about the fragile state of Southern relations across the color line in 1861, developing the account of her anxiety in the 1880s narrative. But while Mrs. Witherspoon's murder may have seemed unprovoked, striking out of the blue, upcountry South Carolina had its own history of black rebellion. Slave insurrection was not simply an apocalyptic fantasy there in the years before the Civil War. Though Mary Boykin Chesnut never wrote a word about it, in keeping with her reluctance to countenance black rebellion in her narrative, slave revolt in fact had been averted, narrowly, in her own Camden at the beginning of the nineteenth century. In 1816, seven years before Mary Chesnut was born, a Camden bondsman revealed to his master that a black insurrection had been planned against the white community for July 4, 1816. His motivations for playing informant remain enigmatic, unrevealed in the few remaining court documents pertaining to the episode. Perhaps on basic humanitarian grounds, he felt enough attachment to his master and mistress to want to spare their lives. He also likely recognized that he would receive a significant reward for his trouble, given the danger such a revelation would pose for him among members of his own community. Or perhaps he was not convinced that the insurrection could succeed, and caught between two competing sets of allegiances, he sought to preserve his life. Regretfully, the documentary record is silent when it comes to the motivations of the slaves involved on both sides of the plot. Important enough to merit inclusion in Herbert Aptheker's groundbreaking 1943 analysis, *American Negro Slave Revolts,* the averted disaster was harrowing for the senior Chesnuts, who stood at the center of the storm because it was their slave, Scipio, who had revealed details that allowed the planter elite to preempt the massacre.

The few extant court records state that Colonel James Chesnut Sr. alerted other prominent Camden planters of the imminent peril. They devised a plan by which they could assemble without suspicion those who would be deputized to arrest the black conspirators, but who had not yet been apprised of the plot or their role in quashing it. The deputies were told to convene in the same place, allegedly for an impromptu fox hunt; there, two days before the plot was to unfold, they were instructed about which bondspeople to seek out and detain.[7] Local newspapers largely emphasized the positive side of the story: fifteen to twenty rebellious slaves with plans to "fire the town" and seize the arsenal had been identified, and five ringleaders would be punished by death. No names were published. The arraignments and trials of the implicated bondspeople were held in secret; though apparently the five resulting hangings were conducted outside the "gaol"—the jail—between the hours of 4 and 5 p.m.[8] Decades later, James Chesnut's diary-keeping wife apparently never referred to the events of 1816. In neither her 1860s jottings nor her 1880s narrative is there any hint of that troubled history and what must have been homicidal levels of hostility roiling the Camden slave community when James Jr. was an infant.

That the slave conspiracy thwarted at Camden in the summer of 1816 was planned for July Fourth, the most cherished national holiday in the post-revolutionary calendar, is no accident. Such timing signifies in two registers:

Revolt: Family Troubles in the House Divided 211

practical and symbolic. In the first regard, the insurgents had picked a date on which they knew the slaveowning community would be distracted with its own merrymaking. During the holiday celebrations, the slaves planned to set fires in the residential part of town farthest away from the Camden arsenal (built to store guns and ammunition in preparation for resisting the British during the Revolution). Their hope was that alerted citizens would flock to their homes to quench the flames, while the black rebels took possession of the arsenal. But beyond the pragmatic ingenuity of a plan to strike when the white community was absorbed in festivity, the political and philosophical significance of the Fourth was profound. A slave named Old Jack belonging to the Blanchard family quoted another bondsman named Spotswood, who belonged to the Mc Rae's, the elder James Chesnut's in-laws, summarizing the goal of the insurrection: the blacks "were going to rise and take the country." March, one of two of Captain Chapman Levy's slaves implicated in the plan, added that their mission was to "to fight this country—that the black people who would not join they would kill."[9]

As the rebels' language of "fighting a country suggests," the slaves of Camden understood the ways in which the rhetoric of the Founding—and particularly the Declaration of Independence—had not been fulfilled with the Revolution.[10] Implicated in the insurrection, for example, and tried, found guilty, and hanged, was the second of Captain Chapman Levy's slaves, Isaac, who forty years earlier had joined his master as a drummer boy when the latter fought the British during the War of Independence. Such exposure surely radicalized the bound black child, then only eleven years old. Indeed, following the revelation of the plot to which he was central, the town fathers became convinced that firsthand experience of the Revolutionary War had "tainted" the young Isaac's ideas about being a "contented" bondsperson. In response, they sought a legislative provision prohibiting slave youth from entering the army as musicians following their masters to battle.[11] As the former fugitive and abolitionist leader Frederick Douglass would say in Rochester some thirty-five years later in perhaps his most famous speech, "What to the American slave is your Fourth of July?" Apparently hoping to seize the freedoms that the nation had denied them, the African American people of Camden in 1816 might have offered quite a retort had their plan to "kill all the white people" come to fruition.

Largely lost to the historical record are the personal identities of the Camden conspirators, save for the fact that Isaac Chapman had gone to the Revolution as a drummer boy. In addition, the majority of the five slaves who were hanged as ringleaders had enjoyed excellent reputations for probity and religious feeling prior to the thwarted uprising. Meetings of the plotters apparently had taken place in Chapman Levy's brickyards, where at least two of the main conspirators labored. That Scipio also was a mason would have made a connection with these men unremarkable. Equally unexceptional was the fact that the uprising had been concocted among the slave artisan class: Gabriel Prosser, the leader of the Virginia slave uprisings thwarted in 1800, had been a blacksmith who hired his time in Richmond foundries; and Denmark Vesey, a former West Indian slave who purchased his freedom in Charleston after winning a windfall in the lottery and organized an insurrection foiled in 1822, had been by trade a carpenter.

Scipio

The slave Scipio, who died around the time that Mary Boykin Miller married James Chesnut Jr., may have had a son also called Scipio, given naming patterns among the Chesnut slaves. This latter Scipio served as the old Colonel's valet during the Civil War, and most likely well beforehand, and is one of the most intriguing figures in Chesnut's African American portrait gallery. Of all the relatively well-developed slave characters in Chesnut's unfinished epic—Laurence, Molly, Ellen, and Betsey Witherspoon's carriage driver and eventual murderer, William—Scipio the younger perhaps comes most dramatically to life, particularly in the twice-told tale of the Yankee's raid on Mulberry in the spring of 1865. In Chesnut's 1880s entry for May 18 of that year, he convinces the Federal officer in charge that old Colonel Chesnut, blind and deaf at ninety-three, must be treated with care: "The Yankees left Scipio unmolested. He told them he was absolutely essential to his old master, and they said, 'If you want to stay so bad, he must have been good to you always'" (815). (Note how the Federal officer speaks ungrammatically in Chesnut's accounting of an exchange she did not hear.) In an entry for June 1, Chesnut records Scipio's account of the experience in his own words: "Oh, I told them Marster couldn't do without me nohow, and then I carried them some nice hams that they never could have found, they were hid so good" (823).

It may be possible that Chesnut never knew that the very slave who rescued her father-in-law from being assaulted, and spared half of Mulberry House from being ransacked, may have had a familial connection to the Scipio instrumental in saving the day fifty years earlier by warning the old Colonel of the black insurgent plot. Most significant, Mary Chesnut does not record in any extant piece of writing that in 1816, it was the first slave Scipio who had testified against the conspirators in his own community, or that in 1817, he secretly had been manumitted by the State Legislature.[12] According to official documents in the State Archives of South Carolina, in addition to having been freed, a Chesnut slave called Scipio had been guaranteed an annual $50 pension, while his master was reimbursed $1,100 to compensate for the "loss" of this valuable bondsman.[13]

Family lore has it that despite having undergone a complete revolution in status, Scipio immediately returned to the Chesnut plantation and then to Mulberry House (the building of which was begun in 1818 and completed in 1820), where he resumed his life and his labors. Though he secretly was free and was slated to accrue relative affluence over time, state historians believe that this elder Scipio once again took up the role of one of Mulberry's slave masons after his own brief imprisonment and the trials of the insurrectionists.[14] (He had been jailed with the slave suspects in order to obscure the fact that he had served as informant.) Neither state historians nor family archivists have an explanation for why Scipio might have returned to the Chesnut plantation, though he may have sought to maintain family ties, or perhaps romantic attachments kept him rooted. Rapidly changing state laws during the antebellum period frequently mandated that free blacks leave their state of origin after one year of liberty; this was the case in 1820s Virginia, for example. Still enslaved, his friends and family would have had no ability to strike out with Scipio for the North or the West or even to a city with a free black population like Charleston. Conditions for slaves on Mulberry may also have seemed preferable to the perilous existence of many free blacks, who were restricted by law in where they could live, work, and what they could own.[15]

According to a different black political perspective, say, for example, that of William, the ringleader of Betsey Witherspoon's murder, Scipio would have played the villain rather than the hero of this story, a veritable race traitor. After all, William would argue, the first Scipio's actions protected not only the Chesnut family and other slaveholders. They actually abetted the institution of slavery itself. And, in an ironic twist, the elder Scipio's betrayal of his fellow slaves actually liberated him from permanent captivity without depriving his master of a cent. Only the State of South Carolina had to extend compensation to Colonel Chesnut, and the $1,100 it paid to match Scipio's market price certainly was worth the invaluable service he had performed in making possible the suppression of the planned insurrection. Another male slave might have understood this first Scipio's twenty-eight-year masquerade as the worst kind of cultural perfidy in which a free black man could engage; William, say, might have viewed Scipio as a kind of minstrel figure on Mulberry.

To those who believe that violent revolution is required for overarching social change, the sort of people the 1880s Chesnut derisively called the John Browns of the era, William's interpretation would have merit, politically; but such a viewpoint apprehends the conflict at the level of theory rather than on the ground. Scipio must have been relatively young at the time of the planned insurrection, and he might not yet have developed a political consciousness about slavery. Perhaps for him, maintaining kinship relations and even cross-racial attachments was paramount, above and beyond committing himself to revolutionary racial solidarity. Or he may have been fully aware of slavery's evils but perhaps viewed the planned insurrection as a suicide mission, a misguided effort by his black comrades against overwhelming white power.

In order to have been included in the plans of the plotters, at the time of the foiled 1816 insurrection, Scipio must have been at least in his late teens or early twenties, and possibly older. The dates for the events in which we know he participated suggests that he most likely was born between 1775, making him the same age as the old Colonel, and 1795, which would place him as a very young man at the moment of the threatened uprising. State treasury records reveal that a lifetime annuity ceased after 1842, suggesting that Scipio died during that year or early in 1843.[16]

With horrified disbelief, the *Camden Gazette* reported that the ringleaders of the 1816 plot were known for their religious sensibilities: several, apparently, were "class leaders" who conducted Sunday services, as Jim Nelson—the slave and driver who played a major role in Chesnut's 1880s epiphanic account of her wartime experience at Mulberry's black church—would do forty-five years later. It is important to remember, however, that while some whites believed that Christian practice could function as a mollifying force among bonds-people, others worried that it just as easily could take a revolutionary turn. Certainly this fear dogged the slaveholders who clamped down on black religious freedom in the wake of the Nat Turner rebellion quelled in Southampton, Virginia, in 1831, but not before fifty-seven white people had been killed. The Baptist Turner claimed that visions from God, which he had been receiving since childhood, had inspired him to lead fellow slaves in the massacre.

When the elderly James Chesnut Sr. passed away almost a year following the Confederate surrender, several sources note that at his former master's funeral, it was the valet Scipio who requested to be allowed to lead the final hymn, which was sung by Mulberry's freed people. Esther Davis, a granddaughter of the old Colonel, includes the text of that song in her "Memories of Mulberry," a family history of life before the war that she composed in the plantation-romance mode, which had become fashionable after Reconstruction. Ironically, this was one of the literary forms against which Chesnut implicitly railed in her attack on sentimentalism in the 1880s narrative. Davis's reminiscences nevertheless offer a treasure trove of sociological detail about Mulberry and its inhabitants, including the remarkable inclusion of Scipio the younger's final hymn at James Sr.'s interment. The second verse of his selection is particularly pertinent:

> One family, we dwell in Him,
> One Church above, beneath,
> Though now divided by the stream,
> The narrow stream of death.
> One army of the living God,
> To his commands we bow,
> Part of the host have crossed the flood
> And part are crossing now.[17]

Deeply involved at this point in the affairs of Mulberry's black church, the younger Scipio likely would have known a wide range of sacred songs from which to choose the service's final hymn. The ultimate selection could not have expressed more perfectly the complexities of his relationship with the old Colonel. Its lyrics adhere to traditional Protestant notions that the metaphysical body of God knows no distinctions of class, race, nation, wealth, or sex. The struggle to escape the slavery of the flesh, to be tried in the wilderness, to undergo a turning of the heart, and to enter into the kingdom of heaven constitute the ur-story of Christian conversion. But all of these stages also are congruent with a black celebration of emancipation, only a year into the constitutional abolition of slavery across the reunited nation.

Thus circa 1866, the hymn can be read on multiple levels: The Chesnuts, white and black, are "One family." Divisions involve the distance between the faithful in heaven and those striving on earth. But in this "army" of the living, *all* bow "to His commands." Having endured chattel slavery and achieved liberty, and having held blacks in bondage and then watched them become free, the Chesnut phalanx of believers, white as well as black, must heed God's orders. The human condition makes servants of everyone, not just those who have been slaves, but former masters as well. Thus, the hope expressed by this black chorus, serenading the old Colonel to his rest, is for a world in which all people will share the same challenges and blessings as they strive together for salvation. The redeemed are equals before God, and, the hymn hints, this message also applies to life on earth, a life forever freed from slavery.

If we consider the elderly and frail Colonel Chesnut at the end of the war, the old order completely overturned, it is imaginable that he might well have been done with the business of Mulberry. One might think it nearly impossible for the old man in his last year to be dealing with issues like labor contracts for recently freed slaves. But historian Christopher Williams Daniels, the great-grandson of Stephen Miller Williams, Chesnut's favorite nephew "Miller," notes that the old Colonel remained obsessed until the end of his life with the reconsolidation of all lands that once had been Chesnut property, despite overwhelming debts and mortgage payments. Given his emphasis on holding tight rather than letting go at every level (Daniels's characterization), a certain real estate transaction James Sr. made in the year prior to his death proves particularly fascinating.

The Wateree Mission Chapel, in which Methodist services had been held on Mulberry before and during the war, apparently had its own history as a scene of slave resistance in which Mary Chesnut herself participated. Daniels writes that it was there that "black children were taught to read when it was illegal in South Carolina before the war," and in her narrative Chesnut describes herself attempting to serve as teacher at the black Sunday school.[18] After the old Colonel's death, the free African American community apparently moved the building to a site eventually purchased from the Chesnut family in 1869, based on James Sr.'s agreement with former local slaves, which had been ratified in 1866. The old two-story edifice served as church and school until 1880. It was at that time that the building known as the Wesley African Methodist Episcopal Church was erected. To this day, African American congregants, some of whom apparently descend from Chesnut freed people, continue to journey to Mulberry and worship there, some 130 years after the building was consecrated.

The old Colonel clearly had a profound attachment to those of his former slaves who were inclined to religious practice, and this bond apparently made the idea of the sale a reality. Much nineteenth-century Southern slaveholding was based on a familial model, understood as a dynamic of mutual obligation and indebtedness informed by Christian principles, but distinctly inorganic in feeling. The documentary sources of this epoch suggest that what went on between old Colonel Chesnut and both the first Scipio (who had saved his life by informing) and the second (who protected him from potential Yankee violence) may have transcended paternalism's social constructedness. Then again, it is crucial to note that all of the remaining archival materials concerning both

Scipios have come down to us either through the legal record or through family or community lore.

Produced by former planters and their kin, who may have had an agenda in casting the master-bondsman relationship in a certain way, none of the evidence includes either the elder or the younger Scipio's actual voice. We only hear the valet Scipio by means of Mary Chesnut's ventriloquized 1880s account of what the slave she called "the black Hercules" had told her about his encounter with the Yankees on Mulberry. Filled with wit and confidence, Scipio's refracted account of protecting his master affords us our only flavor of his language or glimpse into his point of view. Despite the brevity of this material, Chesnut's inclusion of Scipio's voice is no trivial matter. In a few brief strokes, the writer transforms a high-ranking house slave into a hero and a believer. This picture offers a crucial example of the way in which her 1880s Civil War narrative differs almost completely from the memoirs composed by her peers, figures such as Constance Cary Harrison and T. C. DeLeon. The perspective on antebellum life Chesnut provides always constitutes a glass scarcely half filled. In contrast, her niece Esther Davis's portraits of her grandparents, the daily workings of their slave plantation, and Scipio the younger's loyalty to his master at the edge of the old Colonel's grave reveal a cup so full as to be overflowing.

Accordingly, as a gauge of the relationship between the old Colonel and Scipio, "Memories of Mulberry" actually may reveal more about Mrs. Davis's investments in the past than about the inner life and attachments of the valet who both outlived his master and his master's son. Thus, our scholarly ability to assess the sincerity of Scipio's bond to the old Colonel must be framed by important caveats about who is telling his story and to what ideological end the account is being put. On the subject of Scipio the informant's postinsurrection life on Mulberry, other than the fact that the younger man bearing his name did not follow him as a brickmaker, but held the more elevated post of personal valet, the record is silent.

The Power of Fire

From one bondsman's loyalty to his former master to a group of slaves' palpable rage against theirs, it is important to consider the methods of resistance that unfolded in the same community in 1816. Not surprisingly, arson was to have been the first step in the Camden blacks' "fight against the country." Various Southern states had passed laws prohibiting slaves from carrying guns of any kind. So in order for their small black militia to be prepared for the campaign ahead, Isaac, March, and company plotted to set a series of significant fires in the residential area of the town, as far as possible from the Camden arsenal, where they would seize enough guns and ammunition to initiate their war against the white people. Herbert Aptheker writes that arson was

> more frequent [than poisoning] and appears, indeed, to have been one of the greatest dangers to antebellum Southern society. While slaves generally would have had difficulty in getting hold of guns or knives [other than those working in a cane field with blades fifteen inches long], or poison, they had little trouble in creating fire.[19]

When the slaves rose up in St. Domingo, they used fire to decimate a landscape that C. L. R. James said had made their French colonial owners the richest planters in the world.[20] Fire also played a significant role in the Indian Mutiny, particularly during the notorious massacre of the boats. Well before the Civil War, suspicious blazes across the urban South almost always were attributed to disgruntled slaves. One of the more remarkable side effects of this climate of distrust involved the way that individual white Southern homeowners as well as businesspeople seemed willing to suffer economic penalties in order to perpetuate what they perceived as the benefits of living in a slaveholding society. Aptheker quotes a Georgia newspaper on the subject:

> Northern banks stopped issuing fire insurance to Southern customers; contemporary letters indicate that the prevalence of incendiarism in the slave area affected the policy of insurance companies. Thus, an official of the American Fire Insurance Company of Philadelphia told a gentleman in Savannah, Feb 17, 1820: "I have received your letter of the 7th instant respecting the insurance of your house and furniture, in Savannah. In answer thereto, I am to inform you, that this company, for the present, decline[s] making insurances in any of the slave states." (*Savannah Republican,* March 2, 1820)[21]

Consider the metaphorics of this financial position: by 1820, the slave states had become uninsurable; that is, they had come to bear a risk so high that it had put them beyond the pale of human guarantees. Expressed less philosophically, Southern applicants had failed to convince Northern insurers that their purportedly "happy" and "contented" slaves would stop setting fires. When the 1880s Chesnut takes up the subject of black incendiaries, she uses a curious aphorism, "The red cock crows in the barn."[22] For a period during 1862 when she stayed in Columbia, she records in the narrative: "Last night a house was set on fire, last week, two. 'The red cock crows in the barn.' Our troubles thicken indeed, if they ever begin to come from that dark quarter" (March 17, 1862, 309). The phrase comes from the third chapter of Walter Scott's novel *Guy Mannering:* "'We'll see if the red cock craw not in his bonnie barn-yard a morning.' 'What does she mean?' said Mannering... 'Fire-raising' answered the dominie." The passage suggests that by the 1880s, Chesnut had become aware that those in the very "dark quarter" to which she refers had been using fire for decades as a tool to resist slavery.

In the 1880s entries for March of 1864, Chesnut describes how the ethos of slave hostility about which she had been fretting has solidified into a serious menace, taking the very form feared most. In the company of Varina Davis, whose family has just survived an assault on the Confederate White House, perpetrated by their own hired bondspeople, Chesnut bears witness to the devastation wrought by a vengeful slave arsonist on the home of friends who have accused him of larceny and sent him to jail:

> Mrs. Davis took me to drive with her. We went to Laburnum to inquire of the Lyon[ses]'s welfare since the fire.
> It was really pitiful . . . smoke and ashes—nothing more. . . . They lost everything. Library filled with books and papers—&c&c. Even Mrs. Lyon[s]'s diamonds. Mr. Lyons, trying to save something, got a horrid fall and knocked out his front teeth.
> It was the work of an incendiary. A few weeks before, they accused a negro of theft. He was put in jail and bailed out just in time to do this thing. (March 15, 1864, 587)

The last straw here would seem to be Mr. Lyons's dreadful spill while trying to save some possession from the burning mansion. To lose one's front teeth not only was to be disfigured and deprived of one's bite—symbolically, it was to be unmanned. As a small detail of the Lyons's larger disaster, Mr. Lyons's injury in the face of homelessness offers an excruciating final flourish to Chesnut's literary narrative.

But the book's most politically significant arson scene involves the first family of the Confederacy and, accordingly, serves as an allegory for the nation. The 1880s Chesnut reports in an entry for January 21, 1864, the events of a gathering at the Davis's to which she and her husband were invited:

> Both of us too ill to attend Mrs. Davis's reception. It proved to be a very sensational one. First a fire in the house, then a robbery said to be an arranged plan of the usual bribed servants there and some escaped Yankee prisoners. Today the *Examiner* is lost in wonder at the stupidity of the fire-and-arson contingent. If they only had waited a few hours until everybody was asleep—*after* a recep-

tion the household would be so tired and so sound asleep. Thanks to his kind council, maybe they will wait and do better next time. (545)

Chesnut continues with an account for the following day:

> Went to see Mrs. Davis. It was sad enough. Fancy having always to be ready to have your servants set your house on fire—bribed to do it. Such constant robberies—such servants coming and going daily to the Yankees, carrying one's silver &c, does not conduce to make home happy. (547)

The Davises, apparently, have supplemented whatever slave force they brought from Mississippi with a retinue of Richmond bondspeople whose owners have allowed them to lease their time. Most hirelings, as John Hope Franklin calls this class of unfree blacks,[23] were house servants, skilled workers, and artisans, whose professional status suggests that they had risen from among the most intelligent and ambitious of the enslaved community. It is from such ranks that slave revolutionaries such as Gabriel and Denmark Vesey emerged.

Nevertheless, the 1880s Chesnut expresses naïve surprise over the "fire-and-arson" contingent, as well as the fact that the Davises have been deprived of their valuables. Her normally rigorous instinct for rejecting sentimental modes of thinking seems to have failed her here. Indeed, the language just quoted would suggest that the first couple functioned in her imagination as a form of Southern royalty, their crowns awarded on the basis of superior intellect and transcendent patriotism. (That they had enjoyed an elite status, while the masses were losing husbands, sons, and brothers and facing starvation, turned a majority of Southerners against the first couple well before the Rebel defeat of spring 1865.) What the writer failed to note is that this very idealization also made Jefferson and Varina Davis prime targets of disgruntled slaves and Yankee prisoners. Far from experiencing an expansion of self as the "people" of a celebrated Rebel family, the slaves who had been hired by the Davises well understood that their master and mistress were committed to perpetuating the servitude of African Americans. It is no wonder that they should have sought to burn down the house that stood for a nation in which they officially were dishonored and dehumanized.[24]

Prelude to the Witherspoon Murder

Dishonored and dehumanized—the status in the world's eye of even the most "fortunate" slave. It is with this paradox that I turn to Mary Chesnut's personal summa of black insurrection: the murder of her cousin Betsey

> This death unfolds a tale of horror and of woe—of crime most foul and unnatural.
>
> She died in the seventy-fifth year of her age, not from the slow and lingering exhaustion by which life is frequently extinguished at that advanced period of human existence—nor from the aches and pangs of acute incurable disease, but from violence, by the hand of the stealthy midnight murderer.
>
> On Monday, the 15th of September, 1861, she was in her usual health, and known to be in that condition until about 10 o'clock at night. On Tuesday morning she was found cold and lifeless in her bed. Marks of violence on the face showed that breathing through the mouth and nostrils had been obstructed by violent force and pressure, until life became extinct.
>
> On both arms at the elbows were purple discolorations, such as might be made by hands holding her down in bed by force. The jury of inquest set forth in their verdict that "Mrs. WITHERSPOON came to her death by violence, by smothering or suffocation, by some person or persons unknown."

FIGURE 9. *"Mrs. Elizabeth Witherspoon of Society Hill, S.C."* (clipping, Charleston Courier, *September 1861*). *After its initial obituary, the* Charleston Courier *published a follow-up story on Elizabeth Witherspoon's death. This second piece, whose author is identified only by the initials "T.S.," reveals that she was murdered. Courtesy of the South Caroliniana Library, University of South Carolina, Columbia.*

Witherspoon by her slaves. The tale of Mrs. Witherspoon's fate, which received multiparagraph coverage twice between mid-September and mid-October 1861 in the regional *Charleston Courier,* most likely endured in the community's oral tradition and family history, but it was lost to post–Civil War era readers until 1949. Then, novelist Ben Ames Williams restored in a second edition much of what Isabella Martin and Myrta Lockett Avary had sanitized or omitted from their inaugural 1905 version of Chesnut's narrative. Despite the passing of forty years, the crime whose monstrosity had rocked Society Hill, South Carolina, in the autumn of 1861 remained unspeakable to Chesnut's literary executor. Martin's ongoing disquietude over this material suggests that, even a half century after emancipation, privileged Southerners remembered African American bondage with emotions as varied as guilt, regret, ambivalence, and self-righteousness. Many of the planter elite indulged in a fantasy-driven nostalgia for an idyllic slaveholding paradise lost. And some, with the significant exception of Mary Chesnut, preferred not to remember slavery at all.

In the cut and bowdlerized first edition of Chesnut's book, the reader learns of Mrs. Witherspoon's death, ostensibly in her sleep. The text reports that the seventy-something widow had been found "dead in her bed," although the circumstances of the old woman's demise are never explained. The editors provide no information about the official inquiry that followed the family misfortune; nor do they describe the detective who ultimately revealed that what had seemed to be death from natural causes in fact was homicide by strangulation and battery; nor do they explain that Mrs. Witherspoon's own bondspeople—her "black family"—had beset and slain the old mistress ostensibly so good to them.

Working as the myth of the Lost Cause was peaking with Jim Crow segregation, legitimated by *Plessy v. Ferguson* (1896), the 1905 editors found the sordid realities of the murder unpalatable in the extreme.[25] Readers had to wait for the Williams edition, and then thirty some more years for the Woodward compendium of 1981, to gain a comprehensive understanding of the event Chesnut initially described in a phrase retained by all three editions in reporting Witherspoon's death: "killed, people say, by family troubles—contentions, wrangling, ill blood among those nearest and dearest to her" (September 19, 1861, 195).

In the antebellum South, the master class conventionally thought and spoke of the relationship between slaves and masters as those of the "black and the white families," or "our family, black and white." Accordingly, experiences such as Mrs. Witherspoon's violent death at the hand of her bondspeople raised disturbing questions about the efficacy of fictive kinship, the cornerstone, according to sociologist Orlando Patterson, of the institution of slavery, which both mystified gross inequality and rewrote plantation relations according to familial themes. Historians of African American bondage from Ira Berlin to Steven Hahn and beyond have shown that institutionalized bondage involved more than white oppression of blacks. It often was based on negotiations between compulsory labor and the guaranteed accessibility of provision gardens, visiting privileges, and Christian worship as well. The sturdiness of the social contract that slaves and masters purportedly shared depended on the relative balance or disequilibrium between black subjugation and white accommodation.

Death as a result of "family troubles," the writer's hypothetical speculation about the cause of her cousin's demise from a stress-induced heart attack or stroke, offers an attribution of blame more prophetic than Mary Chesnut could have imagined at the time she first noted her impressions of the case in the 1860s diary. Mrs. Witherspoon's local family comprised a grown son who lived nearby and was known for his bullying behavior to her slaves, his wife, Mary, and a "half-grown" grandson who lived with the elderly woman (209). The reality was that her "people" were the small group of black bondspeople who worked in the house. Slavery itself did not simply name a series of political and economic relationships. By the mid-nineteenth century and the heyday of paternalism, it described a domestic dynamic as well, one encapsulated in the term "family troubles." Across the 1880s narrative, Chesnut herself suggests that it was a rare plantation on which harmony across the color line prevailed.

Even Mulberry, which she depicts as a relatively serene establishment, had its "rascals," such as Claiborne, her maid Ellen's husband, and various members of the slave Methodist community who drank too much, or philandered, and had to account to the itinerant white minister for their infractions. And in the last pages of the 1880s book, Chesnut describes an episode in which her former maid Molly attacked another freedwoman with a red hot poker because she was wearing a calico frock that Molly's husband, Lige, apparently had expropriated from his wife and given to her: "She knocked the woman down on first blow and proceeded to burn the frock off her back with a red-hot poker, when help came and the victim was 'put out'" (June 4, 1865, 829).

Molly's use of fire is a remarkable choice in this episode. It recalls the modus operandi of insurrectionary slaves rather than the more predictable techniques traditional to scorned women: nails, fists, and household artifacts like brooms and feather dusters. A postbellum catfight, during which one freedwoman wields a red-hot poker against another is not trivial. And the fact that the guilty victim has to be "put out" recalls the crucial scene where Chesnut sits on a lighted chimney while viewing the firing on Fort Sumter and has to be "extinguished." At the end of the 1880s narrative, she presents Molly, only recently liberated from the status of chattel property herself, laying claim to what now is not just her frock, but her spouse, since all former slaves have been made to "remarry," officially, at the price of three dollars a marriage by the (white) religious authorities of South Carolina. Assuming an incendiary position in her efforts to repossess her husband, Molly rings a comic (if dangerous) change on African American resistance.[26]

To return to the "family" to whom Chesnut refers in her initial remarks about Mrs. Witherspoon's demise, the writer connotes an extended clan, beyond what contemporary sociologists call the "Oedipal" household. Such a group would include elders, aunts, uncles, cousins, and their kin. It would pertain, as well, to the slave mothers, fathers, children, grandparents, aunts, uncles, cousins, and their relations who toiled for such white families and lived intimately with them in both the plantation household and the quarters of the antebellum South.

Accordingly, family troubles could be code for intramural squabbles between whites in the big house, such as Chesnut's own low-level wrangling with niece-by-marriage Harriet Grant. The term could pertain as well to discord between members of the white planting family or its paid white retainers and individuals or groups of African Americans in their cabins. For example, Molly and Mrs. Team, the overseer's wife, had a terrible relationship, for Molly alleged that the white woman had commandeered excessive quantities of the Missis's meat and dairy provisions.[27] This sort of conflict across the color line could elicit punitive white discipline, but it also provoked acts of black resistance as small as feigned sickness to avoid work and as monumental as the killing of an aged mistress. In the case of the Witherspoon murder, Chesnut eventually learned, the crime had been committed to distract her sadistic son from fulfilling a threatened punishment of her slaves.[28]

The relevance of the transgression in question, along with the failed fugitive history of the instigator of the murder, only came to light after son John Witherspoon hired a detective from Charleston to investigate the case. Following the detective's disclosures, the 1880s Chesnut unfolded the chronology of revelations in the Witherspoon case piece by piece. In selecting this narrative strategy, she represented her own bafflement and growing elucidation in an echo of her historical 1861 experience. At the same time, she elaborated and transformed the episode into one of the imaginative highlights of her epic narrative. News that her cousin's death was not a result of natural causes came by letter, read aloud at Mulberry:

> [I]t was from Mary Witherspoon—and I broke down. Horror and amazement were too much for me. Cousin Betsey Witherspoon was murdered! She did not die peacefully, as we supposed, in her bed. Murdered by her own people. Her negroes. (September 21, 1861, 198)

Too anxious to offer an editorial response, the narrator leaps instead to another case in which a planter has been killed by his slaves: the brother of a political colleague of James Chesnut Jr., Dr. William Keitt. Alerted by a friend that what seems to be his chronic ill health in fact might not have an organic cause, Dr. Keitt discovers that his slaves have been putting white powdered calomel in his daily tea. A mercury compound used in tiny doses as a laxative or purgative, calomel, if swallowed in quantity, becomes fatal. Outraged and ever impetuous (the latter a problem he apparently shared with Betsey Witherspoon, according to Chesnut's narrative), Dr. Keitt dashes the hot liquid into the face of his cook, calls her an ungrateful beast, and accuses her of trying to poison him (October 18, 1861, 218). Having exposed his discovery of her scheme, the doctor believes that he is out of danger. But far from having quelled his bondspeople's homicidal urges, this "impulsive" master unwittingly has provoked the cook and her confederates to cut his throat that very night. William Porcher Miles, a mutual friend of Keitt and the Chesnuts, has told Mary this "dreadful story... horrible beyond words." Says he, "There goes Keitt, in the [House of Representatives] always declaiming about the 'beneficent institution' [of slavery]. How now?" (198). How now, indeed.

The narrating Chesnut attempts to convince herself that the circumstances that may have provoked her cousin's slaying do not apply to slave life at Mulberry. Mrs. Witherspoon's "household negroes were so insolent, so pampered, so insubordinate, that she lived alone and at home. She knew, she said, that none of her children would have the patience she had with these people who had been indulged and spoiled by her until they were like spoiled children. Simply intolerable" (198). The implication seems to be that Mrs. Witherspoon lived by herself because her ill-behaved, entitled slaves made it unbearable for her natal family to reside with her at Society Hill. While the writer has reflected to herself that the Chesnut slaves were indulged and spoiled as well, an important fact distinguishes them from Betsey Witherspoon's "people": the African Americans held on Mulberry were known widely for their superb training and exquisite manners. Such polished comportment did not, of course, guarantee that they plotted no violence against the white family. But Chesnut took comfort in their veneer of civility, contrasting it to the outright discourtesy Mrs. Witherspoon's slaves expressed to all.

It also appeared that the level of privilege Betsey's bondspeople enjoyed had made it impossible for the elderly woman to visit her children because her "simply intolerable" servants were not welcome traveling "abroad" with her. Accordingly, the so-called indulgence of her slaves—what the 1880s Chesnut ironically called having given them too much "freedom"—had isolated Mrs. Witherspoon from her blood kin. Such "indulgence" actually reversed the ideological dynamics of social death and natal alienation that were normative for African Americans under plantation slavery. In this extraordinary overturning, courtesy of Chesnut's authorial pen, Betsey Witherspoon had become a captive to her own bondspeople.

Operating in concert with the major motif of Mrs. Witherspoon's slaying by her slaves, the various items Chesnut places just before and after her intricately detailed denouement offer a wealth of examples of the seeming ubiquity of slave insurrection as a local theme that, though obliquely presented, is revealing and provocative. Chesnut unfolds her narrative fragments for September and October 1861 in the following order: She reveals that Witherspoon slaves have killed old Betsey. This provokes memories of Dr. Keitt's murder by his bondspeople. Chesnut then returns to the subject of Mrs. Witherspoon's indulgence of her slaves. Next, she describes the depression and gloom infusing the home of her neighbors, the Perkins. Middle-aged Priscilla is a widow, the daughter of a planter refugee from the slave rebellion in St. Domingo. Her own child, Callie (Caroline) Perkins, only seventeen, also has been widowed after an early marriage; since Callie's bereavement, Priscilla has kept her daughter in virtual seclusion in the family home. Chesnut worries over Priscilla's abiding hopelessness, which she fears will poison the life of lovely Callie.[29] She then notes that slaves William and Rhody, Betsey's old maid, are in jail, suspected of murder. Chesnut calls again at the Perkins's home and, once more, is prevented from visiting with Callie.

Soon after, the writer and her sister Kate discuss the Witherspoon case, wondering whether they should be "afraid of Negroes," and Chesnut's 1861 persona professes: "Two-thirds of my religion consists in trying to be good to negroes because they are so in my power; and it would be so easy to be the other thing" (199). The sisters conclude that "Mrs. Witherspoon is a saint on earth. And this is her reward." Kate's maid Betsey—with no comment from Chesnut on the echo of the dead white and live black women's names—responding to her mistress's fear, drags her mattress into Kate's bedroom and promises to serve as a human barricade against the threat of slave violence.[30]

Haunted by visions of "those black hands strangling and smothering Mrs. Witherspoon's gray head under the counterpane" (199), Kate cannot sleep, so she and her sister sit up all night, talking, while Betsey slumbers beside them. (The unspecified referent for "those black hands" is fascinating. Could they be attached not to William and Rhody, but to Kate's own maid Betsey, according to her insomniac fantasy?) Chesnut then dines with squabbling members of her mother's family, the Boykins, who throughout the 1880s book appear petty and obnoxious, a house ever divided. Finally, Chesnut reports that she has gone to visit with "that optimist, my mother-in-law," a veritable twin for Mrs. Witherspoon, devotedly tending to slave ailments and pregnancies on Mulberry, while her counterpart at Society Hill sleeps in the cemetery.

Try as she might, the narrating Chesnut seems unable to escape either the reality or the thought of slaves in murderous revolt as she describes the 1861 tragedy. Betsey Witherspoon puts her in mind of Dr. Keitt, who himself raises the question of what it means to have been a beneficent slaveholder. What is an apparent oxymoron to the twenty-first-century reader was a cultural ideal in the antebellum South, and Dr. Keitt's constant refrain about the nature of the institution emphasized its "beneficence." Both the doctor and the widow had been known for being "impulsive" in their slave management, a quality suggesting that their behavior toward their "people" may have been less than fully rational or well thought out, and decidedly un-saintlike. After learning the horrible truth about her cousin's death, the writer reports calling on a family whose dead patriarch had fled slave revolution in St. Domingo. Composed now of two widows—one, a chronically depressed matron, the other, a mere teen—the Perkins household hardly affords emotional respite from ideas of murderous slaves, massacred owners, death and destruction.

Chesnut then reports her marathon conversation with her beloved Kate on the subject of loyal "negroes" and white philanthropy. She reveals for the first time that though she enjoys attending the church services of various Protestant denominations, and has friends who are Catholics (Mrs. Munro, Bishop England) and Jews ("Mem" Cohen, Agnes DeLeon), her actual faith involves ameliorating black suffering. Many pages earlier, as I have discussed, Chesnut has confessed that she knows slavery is morally wrong, that she feels great guilt about being a party to it, even opining: "Slavery has to go, of course—and joy go with it" (June 29, 1861, 88). According to the calculation she has made above, her apportionment of one-third religious investment left over remains unspecified. Perhaps it involves her ecumenical worship attendance. She may be thinking of her work for various Confederate hospitals. Or perhaps Chesnut's strange use of fractions is meant to indicate simply that she is not consumed by philanthropy to the family's blacks, as is her saintly mother-in-law.

Rounding out the section with an unpleasant visit to her Boykin relatives, made out of obligation (Elizabeth Witherspoon was a Boykin), she notes in the wake of this encounter, as she does throughout her narrative, the Boykin "family troubles." This subject reprises the theme of divided houses, from the Chesnuts themselves (Mary Cox Chesnut versus Mary Boykin Chesnut; Mary Boykin Chesnut versus Harriet Grant; Mrs. Reynolds) to the Boykins (Mary Boykin versus her entire family), and the Witherspoons (John Witherspoon versus his mother's slaves), and on to the national level of a fractured Union. She concludes by paying a call to "that optimist, my mother-in-law," a doppelganger for Betsey Witherspoon. As I noted earlier, Chesnut believes that Mary Cox Chesnut "has been trying to make it up to the negroes for sixty years for being slaves" (September 24, 1861, 201). "Mrs. Chesnut, who is their good angel, is and has always been afraid of negroes. In her youth the St. Domingo stories were indelibly printed on her mind. She shows her dread now by treating everyone as if they were a black Prince Albert or Queen Victoria" (October 7, 1861, 211). This is not to mention, of course, the lingering traumatic effects she undoubtedly suffered in the wake of the averted 1816 Camden uprising forty-five years earlier.

Thus it is the elder Mrs. Chesnut, of all the family, who most is aware of the moral crisis of slaveholding, though she has never spoken out against the institution publically. Not surprisingly, the elder Mrs. Chesnut attempts to immunize herself from her terror of her own slaves, as much as anything else, to attain the kingdom of heaven with her good works toward them; and it is she alone who comes to express profound paranoia about her servants' loyalty in the wake of the Witherspoon murder. While the visiting Kate Miller Williams is haunted by images of "black hands" strangling old Betsey, it is the senior Mrs. Chesnut who believes in the real possibility that her own "people" could be poisoners. In an 1880s entry for October 18, 1861, Chesnut reports the following:

> Mrs. Witherspoon's death has clearly driven us all wild. Mrs. Chesnut this morning I found in great force . . . incessantly dwelling upon the innumerable negro women who swarm over this house. Mrs. Chesnut takes her meals in her own rooms. [Nearly disabled for many years by chronic arthritis, Mrs. Chesnut occupied a suite of rooms on Mulberry's first floor, across the hall from the dining room]. Today she came in while we were at dinner.
> "I warn you. Don't touch that soup. It is bitter. There is something wrong about it."
> The family answered her pleasantly but continued calmly to eat their soup.
> "Go back, mama, the soup is very nice—don't worry yourself—&c&c."
> The men who waited at table looked on without change of face.
> Kate whispered, "It is Cousin Betsey's fate. She is watching every trifle—and terrified." (217)

In fact, there is nothing "wrong about" Romeo's soup in 1861, or in any other year. On two other occasions, however, at least one of which does not involve mutinous slaves, Mary Chesnut the younger will survive poisonous doses of a drug given for illness during the course of the war. In the second, more serious episode, which Chesnut reports for March 1865 (one month prior to Lee's surrender), she is near death with fever. In response, her maid Ellen empties into the medicine glass what turns out to be an entire packet of opium. It has been prescribed to be parsed into individual doses, but Ellen, who probably cannot read, neither has studied the packet's words nor remembered to show her mistress the instructions as the doctor has ordered.

Examining Chesnut after forty-eight hours of continuous sleep, Dr. St. Julien Ravenal makes an ominous observation to both white mistress and black maid: "It was enough to last you a lifetime." And then to Chesnut alone: "It was murder" (March 12, 1865, 759). Notwithstanding the doctor's horror at nearly losing Chesnut to opium poisoning, the narrator makes light of Ellen's actions. She understands them as the product of sloppy administration of the physic rather than the scheming of a rebellious slave. And, she notes, the two days of unbroken sleep have afforded a better result than any professional intervention could have achieved. The refusal to imagine in retrospect that one of her own slaves could wish her dead reveals that despite her usual savvy when it comes to human nature, in the case of the mistress-slave relation, Chesnut sports a major blind spot.

Comically dismissing what her own physician initially misread as a failed poisoning, and identifying it correctly as an excessive dose innocently offered by an inexperienced but in no way murderous slave, Mary Chesnut reveals faith in the integrity of her own bondswoman as late as 1865. The entire tableau of the distracted Ellen nursing her mistress and the invalid's unexpected physical fortitude in the face of such rough handling is absurd: Chesnut endures what should have been a fatal dose of opium against all odds, while Ellen, Molly, and Laurence remain with the Chesnuts as their unpaid, unfree servants at a moment when emancipation has been in place for two years (though possibly, unbeknownst to them). This motley retinue continues to travel with the retreating writer, fleeing from Columbia on the heels of Sherman's invasion in March 1865, tattling on each other for drunkenness (Molly versus Laurence) and split loyalties (Ellen versus Molly), and scrounging to supplement a dwindling supply of food (Ellen alone).

In all this time, Chesnut neither hears nor overhears a word from Laurence, Molly, or Ellen about the war's probable outcome or the potential effect of defeat on Mulberry's "two" families, black and white. She clearly sees that in a matter of days or weeks, the South must surrender, a reality that eventually will carry with it the universal emancipation of all American slaves, with the Thirteenth Amendment to the Constitution. Nevertheless, none of these portentous prospects is discussed between members of Chesnut's racially mixed, refugee household. This nonacknowledgment of reality between the mistress and Laurence, Molly, and Ellen, their collective dance of denial, marks the fact that in some way, Mary Chesnut herself has donned the sphinx-like mask of inscrutability behind which, she had complained in 1861, her slaves hid *their* feelings about the war's potential significance.

CHAPTER TEN

Revolt

MORE FAMILY TROUBLES IN THE HOUSE DIVIDED

Far less comprehensible than slave reticence on the subject of the war is what might have led four seemingly contented house slaves who enjoyed unusual domestic latitude to commit murder. Staging the killing of their mistress as a natural death, they apparently hoped to avert a punishment threatened by John Witherspoon for the following day. Murder as a diversionary tactic would transform Witherspoon from an unmerciful disciplinarian to a grieving, distracted, son. Mrs. Witherspoon was in her seventies, an actuarial achievement for this moment in the nineteenth century (which made the nonagenarian senior Chesnuts veritable Methuselahs). Accordingly, Betsey Witherspoon's death could not be too far off. Her servants allegedly were "beyond control." Perhaps they had lost all respect for their mistress as a figure of authority, not to mention as a person with a soul. Or it may have been that these slaves imagined that any mistress was, by definition, soulless.

According to Chesnut's 1880s account, John Witherspoon's propensity for violence toward slaves was well known in the community. Chesnut suggests that to avoid his abuse, Betsey's bondspeople were willing to put their lives on the line. Perhaps their calculus was to sacrifice one elderly white person in order to preserve four African Americans in their prime. Chesnut implies that these slaves considered that in killing John's mother (but making it look as if she had died in her sleep, as indeed, had her niece), they offered a vicious blow to the white man they most despised, inflicting on him a loss that potentially would ruin or at least forever diminish his life. Assailing John Witherspoon directly would have extinguished the threatened violence at its source. But such a rebellious feat might have proved too difficult to accomplish, involving travel, an ambush, and a probable violent reaction from his slaves and members of his family. However delusional their plan, they were clearly in fear for their own lives, and killing Mrs. Witherspoon may have been the only way that they could imagine warding off her son's promised assault.

The historical record contains few solid answers to the questions posed by the case. Mary Chesnut's 1880s narrative, in fact, offers the most extensive reconstruction of the crime and its back story that remains. Initially, it was thought that the elderly mistress had passed away during the night: the *Charleston Courier* had announced the matron's death and rhapsodized over her angelic nature. A month following, the same paper tersely reported clinical details of the murder as revealed by the detective. Actually more forensic and dispassionate than the newspaper version, Chesnut's account of her cousin's slaying attempts to unfold the actions and possible motivations of the Witherspoon slaves, offering what Melville, writing about the mysteries of murder in another context, called "an inside narrative" of the psychology of the crime.[1]

Chesnut's work remains unique to both slave narratives and master's accounts of slaveholding from the mid-nineteenth century; she alone seems to want to get inside the minds of her slaves, to know what they are thinking, to attempt to understand their actions. Though her initial desire for this kind of psychological migration may have been defensive — the better to know what the slaves are planning so as to remain on guard — at some point her reasons shifted. The fully developed character studies of Laurence, Molly, and Ellen, which are absent from the 1860s diary jottings, afford her 1880s narrative its psychological realism and her politics a humanity that many other former mistresses never revealed, moving her closer to the action of profound sympathy described by Adam Smith in *The Theory of Moral Sentiments*.[2]

The English actress Fanny Kemble, for example, who married into a Georgia slaveholding family in the 1830s and published a journal of her life on the plantation at the beginning of the Civil War, related to her husband's slaves through a window of emotional distance and detachment. This could have been a function of the fact that she didn't think of Pierce Butler's slaves as "hers," or perhaps because her Englishness kept her aloof from those not from her class. Despite these possible rationales, Kemble evidently couldn't bear to experience a Smithian emotional migration: knowing what the slaves were feeling physically was obvious to her from her spirit-crushing work in the slave hospital she transformed; understanding what they were thinking simply was too unbearable.[3] Chesnut's house slaves, obviously far more privileged than the abject field hands on Pierce Butler's Georgia plantation, were, in her mind, worthy of "knowing." Accordingly, interpretation of the murder as a political event begins with the (scant) archival record. Supplementing the few extant nineteenth-century documents pertaining to the hanging of the four culpable slaves is the richer trove of literary evidence: the startling language Chesnut uses to portray the crime and its potential back story.

The writer begins her tale brilliantly: "And now it comes back on us that bloody story that haunts me night and day, Mrs. Witherspoon's murder" (October 7, 1861, 209). The words Chesnut chooses are telling. That this bloody tale comes "back on us" suggests the return of the repressed, as in Sigmund Freud's notion of the uncanny. In his famous essay of the same name, Freud delineates how the *unheimlich*—literally, un-home-like—involves the familiar simultaneously appearing strange. Consider how the house slaves who were intimate with Mrs. Witherspoon became the very figures who took her life. Her domestics became not only alien, but homicidal. Or perhaps Chesnut meant that the account of old Betsey's murder proved impossible to comprehend, to digest. Such a "bloody story," seemed to leave a stain on all who tried to contend with it.

The Master Spirit of the Gang

Still haunted by the episode twenty years after the fact, Chesnut opens the 1880s entry with one of the more subtle and literary characterizations of a slave by a mistress ever created. Not even abolition-minded Kemble, whose extraordinary published account of life on her husband's plantation employs Shakespearian analogies and picturesque tropes, can compare to Chesnut for her mix of staunch realism and poetic economy: "The man William, who was the master spirit of the gang, once ran away and was brought back from somewhere west. And then he and his master had a reconciliation, and the master henceforth made a pet of him" (209). Flouting the mid-nineteenth-century convention by which African American men of whatever age are referred to as boys, Chesnut acknowledges William's human dignity, what scholars of slavery call his "honor," with her attribution of manhood.[4] Not only is Chesnut's William a man; he actually is the "master spirit" of a collective, which follows both his will and his word.

In this act of bestowing both manhood and mastership on a bonded black man, the writer is reappropriating slavery's most basic vocabulary, inverting the institution's normative understanding of the relations between race and power. And by adding the term "spirit" to her description, she transports us from the debased world of human bondage to the ethereal realm of the romantic imagination, conjured by poets like Wordsworth, whom we know Chesnut read—a marked up copy of his complete poems, in her hand, with her signature, remains in the Mulberry library—Coleridge, and Keats.

For Anglo-American readers, "spirit" also evokes John Milton's depiction of Satan, a once-bright presence, now chief of fallen angels, reduced to acting as Adam's antagonist in *Paradise Lost*. In Milton's epic, the dark eminence ultimately is revealed as a complex and tragic figure, rather than as an allegorical personification of evil without dimension or substance. It is unlikely that Chesnut consciously meant to attribute such wasted nobility to William, a slave who escaped his master's home, was retaken, and later killed his mistress. Nevertheless, the Miltonic resonance seems unmistakable, complicating any attempt to read the ringleader of the murder in Manichean terms, as John Witherspoon clearly did. Without arguing outright that Chesnut had sympathy for William, perhaps one can read in her narrative a trace of admiration for this man as a political agent of sorts.

That Chesnut includes William's insurrectionary curriculum vitae in her saga of Betsey Witherspoon's murder is significant. On the one hand, Chesnut acts as good historian, offering the background details to flesh out her story. But it is equally the case that she is affording her reader a psychological rationale for what transpired in 1861, attempting to make sense of the crime as the final act in a long-running struggle over the nature of slavery. The impresario of the murder apparently had fled from the family many years before. On being captured somewhere "west" and returned, William was not sold farther south, the usual fate of male runaways in their prime; instead, he was "brought back . . . [a]nd then he and his master had a reconciliation."

In a penultimate twist, apparently denying the fact that William had rejected subjugation under his authority, Mr. Witherspoon anointed William as a favorite son of sorts.[5] Rare moments of disciplining slaves apparently devolved to the master's actual scion, John; and it was he who became a figure of menace to his mother's slaves and who inadvertently precipitated her murder by them many years later. The subtext of this one-sided Oedipal battle was not simply that a well-born white son may have felt negated by a certain black bondsman who ranked highly in his father's esteem. In the end, it became a political agon between slavery and freedom itself.

The elder Mr. Witherspoon's unwillingness to sell William and apparent favoring of the retaken fugitive reveal an extraordinary psychological vulnerability. William's flight seems to have created in Mr. Witherspoon what psychoanalysts call a "narcissistic injury" to his sense of himself as a benign slaveholder. No details exist concerning why William ran away: conditions may have been unbearable, though there is no evidence that the Witherspoons exacted arduous labor from their bondspeople. Perhaps William simply could not abide being a slave in any circumstance. Or maybe his situation was relatively benign and thus tempted the ambitious slave to seek his freedom. While history celebrates former fugitives of the nineteenth century (Frederick Douglass, Sojourner Truth, William and Ellen Craft, Harriet Jacobs), scholars have shown that as slave resistance went, escape was far less common than work stoppages, tool breaking, and short-term truancy. Successful flight to the north was rarer still.[6]

The fact that William ran west rather than north suggests either that he sought to reunite with separated family members or that he might have known something about new opportunities for land cultivation and American self-making across the Mississippi. He even may have been aware of the prospects for blacks in a relatively unsettled territory that had outlawed slavery, like Kansas post-1854. Characterizing his return to South Carolina, Chesnut calls whatever transpired between Mr. Witherspoon and the recaptured fugitive a "reconciliation." But this connotes a "resolution" and a "bringing together," both of which imply that parity exists between the parties in question. Most probably, William would have been bound or somehow restrained with chains or handcuffs in order to be brought back to South Carolina. And since his flight was an assertion of nonconsent to the prospect of forever remaining a slave, it seems very hard to believe that, on return, he was a willing participant in whatever his master was offering. Just as Mr. Witherspoon's "reconciliation" did not include the recaptured slave's compliance, so it had very little to do with William qua William at all. Instead, the rapprochement involved the master's attempt to repair his shattered self-conception as a beneficent slaveowner and to protect the patched-over injury by keeping William "contented"—making him a "pet" in a way that may have offered the veneer of favoritism but that also was dehumanizing.

Mr. Witherspoon's need to placate William inverted the principles of human parasitism and ideological reversal at the heart of institutionalized bondage, which said that slaves were nothing and masters were all. And his psychological investment in repairing his own image in William's eyes indicates that the master had crossed a line between "kind owner" into something more closely resembling an inappropriately attached father figure who had made it the psychic work of his slave "son" to mend his broken sense of self. Mr. Witherspoon had literalized the reality that white owners are dependent on their black slaves, all the while insisting—via ideological reversal—that without the master, the bondsperson would have and be nothing: no food, shelter, clothing, or position.

These details of Mr. Witherspoon's need to mollify William, all the while denying his humanity by keeping him enslaved, clarify the possibility that William may have felt long-simmering rage toward the Witherspoon family in general after his recapture. Whatever his intention in decamping from Society Hill, such animus most likely was reignited by John Witherspoon's threat of brutal punishment after an offence he saw as insufferable. It was then that William imagined that only the old woman's death would distract the menacing son from enacting his threats. Like William's belated petting by the master, Betsey's victimization in a sense may have had little to do with the old mistress herself. In killing her, William may have been striking a blow not only at son John, but also at John's father, his deceased master.

The "crime" for which John Witherspoon sought to give everyone (black) a "thrashing" involved "stealing and breaking glass and china and tablecloths." These were the accoutrements of a "ball" the Witherspoon slaves "had given," William ultimately reported, "fifteen miles away from Society Hill. To that place they had taken their mistress's china, silver, house linen &c&c" (October 7, 1861, 209). This "Negro ball," as such affairs were termed in the antebellum period, took place while Mrs. Witherspoon had been away from home. The elderly mistress's assertion, as reported by Chesnut, that she remained a prisoner in her own home was belied by the fact that it was her journey "abroad" that enabled the leisure time for her slaves to hold their ball fifteen miles from Society Hill. It is unclear how John Witherspoon discovered the extracurricular activities of his mother's slaves, though William's account of the articles damaged either in use or in transport (fifteen miles over bad country roads in the mid-nineteenth century was no small distance) suggests that Betsey's son was surveilling his mother's linen closet, silver chest, and crystal and china cabinets, as well as the quarters, and that he was looking for a fight. While American slave narrators have recorded numerous horror stories about sadistic masters, it is rare in nineteenth-century accounts of institutionalized bondage, black or white, to encounter a master-by-proxy like John Witherspoon seeking provocations for violence against slaves not his own whom he resented as if they were adversarial peers rather than his mother's human chattel.

The "Negro ball" held by his mother's "people," which apparently enraged John Witherspoon beyond imagination, constituted no petty flouting of the wretched status that being unfree entailed. Twenty-first-century scholars understand these events as elaborate acts of resistance featuring the black assumption of white culinary, sartorial, musical, and choreographic privilege. Such fetes involved multiple opportunities for creative self-expression: cooking delicacies served only in the big house; dressing elegantly, either by appropriating the mistress's finery, or by embellishing more humble garb with her ribbons, laces, jewelry, and other accessories; adopting the dances of the master class and embroidering them in parody; playing music for an all-black rather than an all-white audience, and adorning it with African rhythms.

In Cinderella-fashion, the bound black attendees at such affairs took up the entitlements of their white owners and, simultaneously, lampooned them. To invert Eric Lott's now classic formulation of white nineteenth-century performative culture's relation to African American traditions, arts, and mores, rather than "love and theft," the Negro ball materialized theft and love. Detecting such slave hubris, the white master or patroller would be outraged at the thievery—the assumption of the slaveowner's fine clothes, elaborate housewares, plentiful kitchen supplies, and delectable foodstuffs. And he would be wounded by the (twisted) love—the enactment of white entitlement in parodic fashion, whereby his slaves, for example, would do the minuet, but transform the steps and rework the accompanying melodies in ways that clearly passed judgment on the inadequacy or absurdity of white cultural practices.

Austin Steward provides one of the fullest representations of these often illicit parties in his *Twenty-two Years a Slave and Forty Years a Freeman* (1857).[7] Harriet Beecher Stowe also offers representations of slaves in *Uncle Tom's Cabin* preparing for a "Negro ball." The scene in question features Augustine St. Clare's elite mulatto house servants, the foppish valet Adolph and haughty maid Jane, arguing about what they will "borrow" from their master and mistress to wear. Their conversation, overhead by their darker-skinned peers who have not been invited to this exclusively mulatto affair, affords an illuminating example of intracultural prejudice and exclusion, all imagined by a free, white woman.

By contrast, and given the limited historiography on the subject, Steward's autobiography involves what is our most ethnographically detailed former-slave account of a "grand dance." He provides not only a description of the materials that were brought and the finery that was worn ("gaudy bandanna turbans and new calico dresses, of the gayest colors . . . bits of gauze ribbon and other fantastic finery"), but details about the kinds of meats that were prepared ("hogs, sheep, calves"), representations of the party itself, and of its tragic aftermath, in which frightened men and women fled just before the patrollers burst into the room.[8] During the course of fierce resistance from the black men who stood their ground, armed only with objects at hand, six slaves and three or four gun-toting white patrollers died. The slaveowner who had hosted the ball, Colonel Alexander (a near neighbor of Steward's master, William Helm), refused to give up any of his bondspeople for trial on charges of insurrection, arguing that the fete had had his blessing. This implied that the slaves had a natural right to defend themselves and that the patrollers may have been out of order in their assault. In the following days, instead of criminal court, Alexander attended all of the funerals held for his murdered slaves.

Apparently the affair, sanctioned by a planter held in disrespect by his Virginia neighbors for his solicitude toward his slaves, had raised the alert of the patrollers well in advance precisely because it was sponsored by a "benevolent" master.[9] Unlike any other Negro balls represented in both the historiographic and literary accounts of slavery, this fete featured written invitations, a remarkable testament to what must have been the unusual level of literacy in this bound black community. Colonel Alexander's "people" had, in turn, invited some twenty other bondspersons from surrounding plantations, some of whom apparently also could read the invitations they received. But these slaves did not have their masters' permission and the attendant passes that would have sanctioned their participation. Accordingly, the unauthorized cohort was vulnerable to the policing of the patrollers, who apparently determined to beset the cabin where the dance was being held and take as many passless prisoners as possible.

In considering the ambition that drove slave preparations for such a grand dance, Steward writes:

> [A]s slaves like on such occasions to pattern as much as possible after their master's family, the result was, to meet the emergency of the case, they *took*, without saying "by your leave, Sir," some property belonging to their master, reasoning among themselves, as slaves often do, that it cannot be *stealing*, because it belongs to master, and so do *we*, and we only use one part of his property to benefit another. Sure, "tis all massa's." And if they don't get detected in this removal of "massa's property" from one location to another, they think no more about it.[10]

An alternative slave rationale for this sort of "borrowing" entails a far less harmonious vision of supply, demand, and the circulation of goods on the plantation: it considers not who "owns" but who planted, cultivated, and harvested, say, the corn in question. To whom, in fact, should it belong, rightfully, if not the black folk who toiled to bring it into being? When the Witherspoon bondspeople set off on their fifteen-mile journey with the china, crystal, silver, and linen, it is unlikely that they told themselves that both they and their bounty "all belonged to old missis." They well knew that it was by the unrequited fruits of their hard labor that Mrs. Witherspoon had purchased such valuable, elegant goods, to the illicit use of which they were more than entitled.

Transporting in wagons over bad back roads the accoutrements necessary to create their fete, across a distance it would take a slave many hours to walk, the Witherspoon bondspeople faced enormous challenges of engineering and time-management. Would they not have been better served by forgetting the ball and turning their creative energy, rare leisure, and significant physical effort to running away en masse? Historians studying the rate of successful slave escapes even at this early point in the war suggest that they would not.[11] So perhaps as a more immediate amelioration of their bound existence, the Witherspoon slaves sought to release pent-up frustration in the sensual pleasures of eating, drinking, and dancing. Their behavior evoked the complex gratifications of ridiculing the master class by, as Austin Steward wrote of the "aristocratic slaves" at Colonel Alexander's grand dance, "swelling out and putting on airs in imitation of those they were forced to obey from day to day."[12]

Learning of their affront—the presumption, the audacity, the hubris of their Negro ball, any glory of which would have been impossible without his mother's heirlooms—apparently proved intolerable to John Witherspoon in September of 1861. Betsey's bondspeople's disrespect must have reached a tipping point in his mind. But perhaps what most of all incensed him was the flavor of rebellion he seemed to taste in this particular transgression, committed by a cohort of slaves with whom he long had taken issue.

This breech of the unspoken master-slave "code"—their convening the dance itself, not to mention damaging some of Betsey's finery—clearly marked an unprecedented, quasi-insurrectionary low point in the history of Witherspoon slaveholding. But John's menacing of serious violence took the Witherspoon master's response to a new nadir, particularly in the context of the family's many years of permissiveness toward their bound blacks. William articulated not simply his sense of entitlement but also his understanding of history and precedent under the Witherspoon regime, responding to news of the threatened thrashings by invoking the late Mr. Witherspoon: "If ole Marster was alive now, what would he say? Talk of whipping us a this time of day, &c&c" (210). White "indulgence" had forever disrupted the racial hierarchy that once may have organized Society Hill; and across the color line, the specter of white violence threatened to shatter the precarious equilibrium that had obtained since William's return from his attempted escape.

It might have made sense for John Witherspoon to challenge William and perhaps obviate the unimaginable tragedy that ensued, given that the tradition of dueling remained alive in antebellum Southern culture, albeit less robustly since the passage of laws against it. But of course, white gentleman did not invite black slaves to a contest of equals. Accordingly, the provocation, in the form of promised whippings, was issued to everyone involved, which assured the enraged white man that power, once more, would reside in his hands. Most unfortunately, the old mistress, who had decided to interdict her son's violence on the morrow, had no opportunity to inform him in time to head off disaster that she would not abide his "disciplinary scheme." The white folks were atomized by their different visions of "the family black and white," not to mention the geography of the two separate plantations on which they lived, and which divided them. Meanwhile, Mrs. Witherspoon's slaves banded together to deflect the threatened assault.

It is astounding to consider that the slaves' diversion of John Witherspoon from his appointed rendezvous with the cowhide had to be accomplished at the cost of Mrs. Witherspoon's life. William and company must have imagined that their lives were at stake as they never had been before (or at least since his recapture). Perhaps beatings never occurred at Society Hill; perhaps the prospect of either the psychic humiliation or the physical agony was intolerable. The other side of the equation, involving the value of the old lady's life, is harder to equilibrate. Mrs. Witherspoon's slaves may have rationalized that she was past her earthly time in terms of years lived, or there may have been some latent hostility driving them, perhaps connected with William's escape and return.

Or it may have been even more simple than that: John Locke, father of Anglo-American political philosophy, understood slavery as a state of war.[13] According to the logic of Locke's account, bondspeople were embroiled in a deadly struggle in which they could take no prisoners, spare no one, which in the Witherspoon case meant not even a septuagenarian mistress. Paternalism was all very nice when brutality played no part in the relation between master and slave. But when vindictive aggression incommensurate with whatever had provoked it threatened to enter the mix, then the "proprieties" of the "peculiar institution" were up for grabs. Once the Witherspoon blacks were threatened by John's violence, it seems that their understanding of their existence shifted. Without the privilege of literacy, much less the sort of education that involved the reading of thinkers like John Locke (i.e., the kind of intellectual training enjoyed by James Chesnut Jr. and John Witherspoon himself), William, at least, apparently came to feel that he had reached a state in which the only choice was to kill or be killed.

Little could he have imagined that both mandates would ultimately prevail. William and company failed to think through the fact that with the death of the old lady—assuming they were never charged with her murder, that their scheme to make her demise look natural proved successful—the slave property would be dispersed to her heirs. Most likely, they would be bequeathed to the very brute they were trying to disarm, though this possibility seems not to have crossed their minds. William and his companions were focused exclusively on the here and now, which blinded them to the inevitability that their fate would involve John Witherspoon or death, no matter the outcome.

Whatever the philosophical motivations of these slaves, the fact that they had a "rale fine supper and a heap of laughing at the way dey's all look tomorrow," before carrying out William's plan gives pause. Having been threatened to be thrashed for creating an elaborate affair modeled on white forms of hospitality, it would seem extraordinary that the very next thing Mrs. Witherspoon's slaves did was to convene another festive meal, a last supper of sorts. Certainly either the old lady herself or her maddened son, were he to have returned to the plantation that evening, easily might have walked in on this laughter-punctuated dinner in one of the cabins and wondered what reason in the world a group of blameworthy slaves on the eve of their punishment should have had to be celebrating. Enacting a gallows' sensibility, the behavior of Chesnut's renegade characters suggests that despite the apparent bravado with which they approached their scheme, William and company well understood the grimness of the murder to come.

Thinking they could craft the slaying to appear as a death by natural causes, Mrs. Witherspoon's slaves unwittingly revealed a fatal ignorance. They seemed unaware that their beating and suffocation of the old woman would with time register as bruises of black, blue, and purple on her pale body.[14] Surely the remains of both white and black people felled by "old age," as Betsey was to look, whose hearts had stopped or whose organs had failed, were unmarked by blood or gore; they appeared as if asleep rather than transformed into a painter's palette of chartreuse and violet. Unexceptional deaths did not entail contusions. Nor did those who died in their sleep besmirch bedside furniture with bloody handprints. In hoping to dispatch Mrs. Witherspoon quickly, her bondspeople apparently underestimated her vitality and capacity for resistance. This returns us to the quotation with which this chapter began, in which old Betsey begged for her life, promised never to report her enslaved attackers, and asked what ever had she done to them to make them want to kill her.

Before September of 1861, the institution of slavery did not appear to be taking a noticeable toll on Betsey Witherspoon's black folk. Her indulgence seemed to make the effects of bondage look less deadly than they might have done, say, on Dr. Keitt's Florida plantation, where Chesnut suggests that the slave retinue wore sour, disgruntled expressions. But the writing of slavery's hideous reality was on the wall once the septuagenarian's stiff black and blue body was examined in the light of day. Just as there was no such thing as benign slaveholding, so there was no such thing as a natural-appearing murder victim.

As much as William, Rhody, and company fancied they could stage their crime to look organic, in this particular exercise, their hubris got the best of them. Bodies soil themselves en route to death, particularly when the journey is a violent one. It is unclear whether Rhody and her son and daughter, (another) Romeo and Sylvie, understood or expected this. Perhaps they did not. And in the process of killing their mistress, the slaves "spoiled the [nightgown] she had on," Chesnut's euphemistic reference to the tell-tale excremental stains that mottled her linen, putting her killers in a state of panic.

In an improvised response to this disruption of the plan, Rhody remembered the precise location of a hidden, locked trunk, fully packed and featuring a set of "new and very fine nightgowns" the old woman apparently never had worn (210). (It also included a stash of gold, which the bondswoman pocketed.) But in her haste and anxiety over having to clean up Mrs. Witherspoon's corpse, Rhody failed to remember the quixotic way in which the old lady had made use of this particular trunk: as a cache for hoarding finery and money rather than as a repository for the clothes that actively circulated in her wardrobe. Despite being thrown off by the gruesome setback, Rhody found the keys and extracted a clean gown to substitute for the one her mistress had soiled in the course of expiring so horribly. In Rhody's mind, it could have made no sense for a rich white lady to own beautiful things and not use them. As a slave, most likely provisioned with only one or two dresses a year, but witness to the finery worn in the big house, she could not conceive that someone could possess gorgeous garments and leave them locked away unworn.

This understandable imaginative failure, the effect of slavery's limiting vistas, explains how the quartet's otherwise careful scheme broke down: Rhody, the mistress's closest slave intimate, failed to fathom the significance of the white woman's hoarding. Dazzled by the luxury of new lingerie (later and tellingly identified by the matron's daughters as never-before-worn), she grabbed the "wrong" nightgown, a garment the pristine whiteness of which, ironically, would expose that human malevolence had caused Mrs. Witherspoon's demise. With the white nightgown as a red flag, both Betsey's daughters and the detective who had arrived at Society Hill, growing increasingly distrustful, moved on to the mystery of the gory handprints that besmirched the victim's bedroom candlesticks and extra counterpane. The slaves came under suspicion, and young Romeo, Rhody's son, isolated from his fellows by the professional from Charleston and goaded by the detective's highly effective interrogation techniques, began to talk. Rhody's cabin was searched, and there the detective found the gold, the stained sheets, and the incriminating nightgown, the latter two of which in her thrift she had preserved for her own future use.

Whose Bloody Hands?

As the Witherspoon case unfolded several decades before the development of fingerprint technology, not even the investigator from Charleston could identify the bloody handprints on the candlesticks and counterpane. Were they William's? Rhody's? Mrs. Witherspoon's? or did they belong to John or Mary Witherspoon themselves, or perhaps the unnamed Witherspoon daughters so knowledgeable about their mother's nighttime sartorial habits? Or did the bloody handprints belong to all of the above: bondsperson and master, murderer, victim, and survivor, black and white, all together. What was the institution of slavery itself if not the work of bloody hands? Not just the bodily effusions of field worker and house slave, toiling for naught and beaten more often than rewarded. Were not the hands of the masters, traders, brokers, breakers, patrollers, and factors even more besmirched? What of the owners of and workers at Northern banks, insurance companies, shipping firms, and railroad lines? Wasn't American slavery the ultimate drama of bloody hands, like Betsey Witherspoon's gruesome story, the stain of which continues to flow all the way into the twenty-first century?

For Chesnut, the Witherspoon murder was inexplicable, in spite of the full report of who did what, where, and when, which the detective managed to reconstruct. The horror and unprecedented nature of the event exposed what was possible, even in comparatively benign conditions, when one set of human beings held another as their permanent captives. What did it mean to cosset, pet, and pamper one's bondspeople when, in fact, they remained forever unfree? What Mary Chesnut vaguely but also deeply understood, which she expressed in her metaphors of William as master spirit and characterizations of Betsey as impulsive, was that there was no such thing as a spoiled slave, nor any such thing as a generous master. Her literary narrative reveals that she knew, somehow, her own "benevolent" hands were themselves besmirched, if not bloodied, for her participation in the institution she for over thirty years, at least in theory, had been convinced was wrong.

Some haunting remarks sum up how the slaves who killed old Betsey called into question the racial hierarchy of Society Hill in ways that proved prophetic of the eventual unmaking of Southern slaveholding. Mary Chesnut records in the 1860s diary but tellingly deletes from the 1880s book words overheard and reported by Mary Witherspoon, John's wife: "Mary W. repeated what she heard her negroes say «showing they know we are afraid of them.» ... 'Let us go to that hanging. It's a warning to us all'" (*TPMC*, October 27, 1861; *MCCW*, October 25, 1861, 224). This statement's manifest content seems to be something along the lines of "We, John Witherspoon's black bondspeople, understand that Betsey's murder was horrific, the work of deviant monsters. We assure you that we never could commit such an act. We are and will remain loyal to our master."

Latent within this, however, lies an altogether different, extremely ominous message: "We intend to go to that hanging in solidarity with and in honor of our martyred slave brothers and sisters. But the warning in question is not for us or for any black bondspeople. In fact, it is an admonition to you white folks, who think this execution has cut the head off the spirit of insurrection. Don't rest too easily. . . . If you are paying attention, you never should sleep soundly again." We have no explicit rationale for Chesnut's motivation in excising the powerful lines. But her deletion of the overheard retort is in keeping with her overall impulses in the narrative concerning the representation of slave agency and menace: elide all traces of both.

In short, however unconsciously, John Witherspoon's slaves' assertion that "those hangings are a warning to us all" represents the laying down of a gauntlet. Only sixteen months later, their escaped, freed, and free peers would take up the challenge as Union soldiers. Commencing at that moment, in January of 1863, President Lincoln began to transform what for over two hundred years had been an unspoken state of war into a righteous, nation-redeeming, cause.

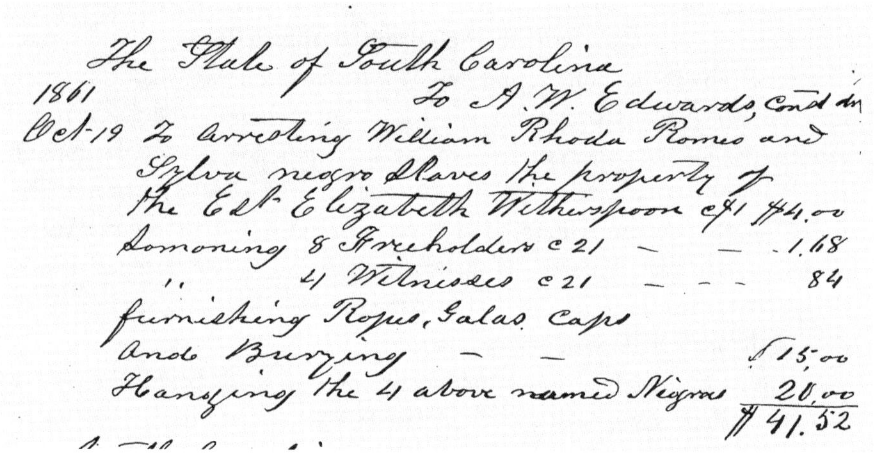
The State of South Carolina
1861 To A. W. Edwards, Cond in
Oct-19 To arresting William Rhoda Romeo and
Sylva negro Slaves the property of
the Est Elizabeth Witherspoon @1 $4.00
Summoning 8 Freeholders @ 21 — — 1.68
" 4 Witnesses @ 21 — — — 84
furnishing Ropes, Galas Caps
And Burying — — $15.00
Hanging the 4 above named Negroes 20.00
$41.52

FIGURE 10. *Gallows bill for hanging Elizabeth Witherspoon's murderers (manuscript, 1861). This bill itemizes charges for the use of the gallows, the hoods covering the killers' heads, and the rope used for the execution of the four slaves who murdered Elizabeth Witherspoon. Courtesy of the Darlington County Archives, Darlington, South Carolina.*

Coda: Laurence's Gold Pencil Case and Slave Resistance in a Tonic Key

The international examples of slave rebellion fascinated Chesnut in the years leading up to and including the Civil War. Servile insurrection nearly exploded in Camden in 1816. Arson was central to slave revolts: Consider the case of the slave thief's revenge for incarceration, his burning down of the Lyons family's Richmond estate. Consider, too, the attempted blaze and successful robbery and slave defection at the Confederate White House inhabited by Jefferson and Varina Davis. Betsey Witherspoon's murder by her slaves constitutes the centerpiece of this analysis. In every example, whether disaster has been averted (Camden) or endured (the Witherspoon murder, the Lyons fire), the writer has treated the subject with appropriate grimness and irony. Only in the example in which she describes how her mother-in-law authorized a hunt for fire that yielded only the smoldering ashes of a slave family's soap-making does potential catastrophe gently yield to a sense of the absurd.

Nevertheless, one other story in the comic vein remains to be told about black resistance, this time among the Chesnut slaves themselves. It features behavior far less overt than the stealing of corn and pilfering of provisions that apparently occurred with regularity during the war, according to Molly, her mistress's self-appointed informant on such matters, and it involves Laurence, General Chesnut's heretofore devoted slave valet. Laurence traveled with the couple across the South, from Montgomery to Richmond to Columbia and back and to and from Mulberry, a figure of relative privilege until his bad behavior got him rusticated to Camden in the late winter of 1865. The writer describes Laurence as plump and very distinguished, like a "gold colored" Count Fosco, the Italian secret agent and villain of Wilkie Collins's 1856 sensation novel *The Woman in White*. Beyond physical similarities between the fictive Count and the corpulent Laurence—both men are well-dressed and fond of sensual pleasures—the reference remains puzzling. Fosco, in fact, is Collins's malefactor, an unscrupulous, gold-obsessed international spy, working against the revolutionaries in Italy who seek a nationalist government and unification of their country.

In this case literary allusion doesn't seem to serve the writer as she intended, unless of course, the parallel is meant to indicate either that she actually believes that Laurence—if he indeed understands his enslaved situation as being a state of war—could come to betray or harm the Chesnut family or that she suspects Laurence's intimate proximity to General Chesnut affords him access to secret information about the doings of the Confederate cabinet or the strategy of the Rebel cavalry in South Carolina. Despite the dramatic possibilities evoked by such connections, Laurence, as painted in the narrative, is far too phlegmatic and pleasure-seeking to become a likely murderer of his master and mistress.

Laurence is most recognizable in the 1880s book sitting outside his master's chamber door and looking impassive. He registers what Mary Chesnut so memorably calls a sphinx-like blankness in nonresponse to outside indications (such as canon fire) that the dangers of war surround him. Throughout the narrative, particularly as the Chesnuts spend long periods away from home in rented Richmond quarters and a cottage let in Columbia, Laurence's primary role shifts from valet and tailor to the genius of procurement, specializing in hard-to-find supplies for the kitchen and the liquor cabinet. Chesnut proudly boasts that he is able to track down from mysterious sources (the Confederate black market) even the most obscure delicacies on her shopping list. He and his mistress do tangle over the fact that such delectable fare has become prohibitively expensive in Richmond. Indeed, the prices he quotes consistently prove far higher than what she expects. Nevertheless she gives Laurence absolute authority over the family pocketbook, relieved not to have to be acquiring on her own the obscure food and blockaded drink she desires for her ongoing salons and fetes.

During the final year of the war, Laurence begins to behave in ways utterly out of character for the heretofore dignified "gentleman's gentleman" of Mulberry, his small but real protest against having to remain in slavery as the war moves to its inevitable end. In a series of episodes beginning in the winter of 1863, Laurence attempts to perform his duties for the Chesnuts while intoxicated, though nowhere in the 1880s narrative for 1861 or 1862 does Chesnut indicate that he has ever had a drinking problem.

Stringent laws across the antebellum South prohibited slaves from using alcohol, carrying firearms, learning to read and write, and traveling without a pass. Scholars of slave resistance such as Ariela Gross and Stephanie Camp discuss the significance of slave drunkenness as one of the more benign versions of protest in which certain bondspeople, particularly men, engaged. Like truancy, among other activities, inebriation stood in lieu of more monumental acts of dissent, such as running away or murdering one's master. According to Gross, "laws against selling spirituous liquors to slaves or free blacks accomplished the same goal of dishonoring blacks by denying them access to these cultural rituals."[15]

Achieving a state of drunkenness, accordingly, had a triple significance: It indicated that the black man in question had reclaimed his honor (which he then squandered with intemperance). It medicated his sorrow and or rage over being enslaved, numbing the despair. And it allowed the intoxicated bondsperson to express otherwise unspeakable recriminations against the planter elite. Never one for chatter, unlike Molly, Laurence as a drunkard is in no way more voluble. Instead, in the narrative, drink prompts him to run off from the Chesnuts and disappear for a day or two, or get himself arrested. And in the final episode his mistress records, he damages a landlord's property in North Carolina and so enrages James Chesnut Jr. that Mary has to send him back to Mulberry.

In the first scenario in which Laurence gets into trouble, his peccadillo seems innocent enough, ironically the result of possessing a better wardrobe than most of his bound peers. The 1880s narrator sets the scene in an undated entry from the 1862–63 "Memoirs" section:

> At negro balls in Richmond they were required to carry "passes"—and in changing his coat Laurence forgot his. Next day Laurence was missing, and Molly came to me laughing *to tears*. "Come and look. Here is the fine gentleman, tied between two black niggers and marched off to jail." She laughed and cheered so, she could not stand without holding onto the window. Laurence disregarded her and called to me at the top of his voice. "Please, ma'am—ask Mr. Jeems to come take me out of this. I ain't done nothing." As soon as Mr. C. came home, I told him of Laurence's sad fall, and he went at once to his rescue. There had been a fight and a disturbance at the ball. Police [were] called in—every man made to show his "pass"—and so Laurence was taken up as having none. He was terribly chopfallen when he came home, walking behind Mr. C. He is always so *respectable* and well behaved and stands on his dignity. (457–58)

Note from the writer's tone that the accessibility of Laurence's pass is not an issue; apparently, the Chesnuts put no restrictions on the social freedom of Laurence, Molly, and Ellen in Richmond and Columbia during the war, itself a remarkable extension of autonomy on the part of master to slave. (As a devout Methodist, Molly preferred staying home and ironing to attending the dances of which she disapproved. Thus the Chesnuts' relative liberality was lost on her.) That Laurence had more than one dress jacket reveals that the family slaves were well provided for, sartorially speaking. Comparatively privileged, bound to an elite family, and always possessing the necessary pass, the Laurence of the narrative is wounded and mortified over being misrecognized for the sort of slave rabble who would crash a Negro ball in the capital city. Seeming not to have suffered at the hands of James Chesnut Jr. the dishonor that scholars from Wyatt-Brown to Patterson have described as fundamental to the master class's "breaking" of the spirits of the enslaved, Laurence first experiences it at the hands of the Richmond police.

It was soon after this ruinous public humiliation, witnessed by the pedestrians of Richmond, his white mistress, and his compatriot and rival Molly, that Laurence's drinking problem seemed to emerge. The narrator describes her wartime persona's absolute incredulity over the following incident for January 4, 1864:

> [D]ay of disasters. Laurence drunk! And the kitchen stove fallen in. Molly and Laurence had a grand row. He will have a fire in his room. And as he keeps the key to the coal cellar—that is as *he* pleases. Molly says, "As master dresses without fire to economize—and he taking a cold bath, reg'lar as the day comes—you might."
>
> "Oh," says Laurence. "Have I got anybody to rub me with a towel till I am red hot?"
>
> "Who's Laurence, I like to know?" cries Molly. "He can't set by the kitchen fire like the rest of us. You watch your coal hole—that's all." (526)

The implication is that this morning dawned with a drunken Laurence and an irate Molly facing off in the kitchen of the Chesnuts' rented Richmond quarters. Though it is not clear that Laurence has had anything to do with the collapse of the kitchen stove, it does seem like a bizarre turn of events and he was, in fact, intoxicated. Then comes the extraordinary exchange about Laurence's apparently pervasive sense of entitlement, on the one hand, and on the other, Molly's rejection of such grandiosity, and her stalwart identification with the group of bound Chesnut blacks whom she describes as "the rest of us." The sparring ends with Molly's less than subtle charge to her mistress that, not only is Laurence indulging himself with a coal fire, but he may be pilfering excessive amounts of fuel for his own purposes.

Across the narrative, Chesnut has painted Molly as a snitch when it comes to fellow slaves acting dishonestly or imperiously. The writer dramatizes her maid's outrage over the shenanigans of the overseer's wife, a white woman who is stealing poultry, eggs, and ham before Molly's eyes. There, her indignation is not merely as Mrs. Chesnut's proxy; these comestibles actually belong to her and Mrs. Chesnut, via the butter-and-egg business in which Molly serves as a partner, working on shares. While Molly's tendencies toward tattletaling may be a result of her rigorous Methodism, she also is a self-righteous woman who loves lording it over her peers, an impulse that may have mitigated the oppressiveness of being a slave.

Laurence in Richmond, apparently, gives her plenty to snitch about. During another morning binge, Laurence's intoxication moves beyond mere mischief and embarrassment, actually damaging someone else's property. For the sake of the family's reputation, Mary Chesnut determines that he must be treated with rigor. As her narrative records for February 12, 1864:

> Laurence has gone back ignominiously to South Carolina. At breakfast already, in some inscrutable way he became intoxicated. He was told to move a chair, and he raised it high over his head, smashing Mrs. Grundy's chandelier. J.C. said: "Mary—do tell Laurence to go home. I am too angry to speak to him." So Laurence went with[out] another word said. He will soon be back, and when he comes will say, "Shoo! I knew Mars Jeems could not do without me." And indeed he cannot. (564)

Laurence's drunkenness on two separate mornings indicates either that he has partaken for an entire night and staggered home and back to work or that he has taken up drinking continuously, imbibing all day long. We have no evidence, of course, but it is telling that whatever is ailing Laurence is being "treated" with alcohol, leading to chronic arguments with Molly and, in this final example, carelessness on the job that has caused serious material destruction. Imagine the sound of a chandelier being smashed by a chair and the shards of glass flying about a small space filled with servants. Though the narrator's description suggests an unfortunate accident, it certainly comes off as a spectacular event. Laurence largely remains silent throughout Chesnut's narrative, but his actions eloquently suggest that he has lost Molly's level of commitment to remaining a Chesnut slave.[16]

I close with a scene that takes place nearly a year after Laurence's banishment to Mulberry after the chandelier shattering. The valet has been back in Richmond for months, and he now must accompany the refugee Chesnut and Ellen to "off the track" Lincolnton, North Carolina, in flight from what the writer calls "Sherman's bugles" in the winter of 1865. A remarkable scene occurs as the Chesnut party arrive at their first North Carolina lodgings:

> At the door—before I was out of the hack—the woman of the house packed Laurence back, neck, and heels. She would not have him at any price.... She said his clothes were too fine for a nigger—"his airs indeed"—and poor Laurence was as humble—and silent. He said at last, "Miss Mary, send me back to Mars Jeems." I began to look for a pencil to write a note to my husband. In the flurry could not find it. "Here is one," said Laurence, producing a gold pencil case. "Go away," she shouted. "I wants no niggers here with pencils—and airs." So Laurence fled before the storm—not before he begged me to go back. He thought, "If Mars Jeems knew how you was treated he'd never be willing for you to stay here." (February 16, 1865, 718)

The first and last straws for this white woman are what she perceives as Laurence's "fine clothes." That anyone, white, black, free, enslaved, once aristocratic, or even once humble, could, in the winter of 1865, be wearing intact, much less elegant, garb, seems impossible. But apparently, the landlady recognizes that Laurence's jacket and trousers, however threadbare, once were fine; and she resents what she believes they still communicate of privilege.

And Chesnut, turning to borrow a writing implement from Laurence, who for his sartorial hubris has been ejected by the landlady from their intended residence ("she won't have him at any price"), adds fuel to the fire by revealing to their incensed hostess Laurence's advanced literacy. (The ability to write was far more rare among slaves at this period than was the ability to read.) Vividly underscoring his intellectual prowess is his possession not only of a pencil, but of a container to hold it, *made of gold.* At this point all bets are off.[17] Chesnut immediately realizes that her innocent slave's actions have created such agitation in their hostess that she herself risks being sent back on the road. So, once again, the writer dispatches Laurence to Camden, neither intoxicated nor physically menacing, but clearly disturbing enough to the landlady to jeopardize Chesnut's comfort. It is debatable whether the landlady finds Laurence's so-called airs or the gold pencil case more threatening.

Laurence's quickness for reading and writing may have been encouraged and rewarded by the gift of this gold pencil case. Mary Chesnut boasted early in the 1880s narrative that she had taught all of her parents' slaves to read. But surely the presentation of this particular gift would not be the obvious reward offered to most of the family's bondspeople. Such an artifact conveyed that its bearer was cultivated, genteel, a kind of man of letters. It makes complete sense that the gold box had driven the landlady to distraction: it was an index of her comparatively lower status and potentially inferior education, despite the fact that fair skin automatically should have promoted her well above a slave. Nothing made relatively poor whites more anxious at this historical moment than the presence of elevated blacks, even those in bondage.

Accordingly, as a mark of slave resistance, the golden pencil case ultimately may have been more significant than a haughty demeanor or a once elegant jacket. After all, at the end of the day it was Molly, skilled only as a domestic and agricultural laborer, who remained with her former mistress as a loyal servant, though no longer a slave, and also a partner in the butter-and-egg business. The literate, cultured, and polished Laurence, on the other hand, disappeared from the record, presumably having left Mulberry for a life of freedom elsewhere.

But to complicate this seemingly bifurcated picture of the Chesnut slaves postemancipation, consider the former slave informant, Scipio the first. His affords the clearest, if ironically, the most highly classified case, of how "family troubles" across the color line did not ineluctably mandate deadly resistance. Whether in maintaining the ruse of his continued bondage to avoid losing connections with his enslaved kin or to prevent disharmony in the Mulberry quarters, he built a meaningful life.[18] And through the man whom Chesnut suggests was his son, Scipio the valet, he created a black worship community on the plantation that lived well beyond slavery into the Reconstruction era and the twenty-first century. The Witherspoon slaves, on the other hand, took a more aggressive path and wound up tried and hanged for their trouble. Out of that catastrophe, the upcountry community, black and white, was offered a lasting message about slavery's hidden costs, which the myth of paternalism so tragically had obscured. In a state of war, people die. Whether everyone involved could decipher this tragic truth—before the end of the fighting and the Thirteenth Amendment changed the story—was another question altogether.

CHAPTER ELEVEN

Recognition
LOOKING DEFEAT IN THE FACE

Black bondspeople in Chesnut's purview reacted variously as the peculiar institution began to loosen its grip at the onset of the Civil War. But rebels such as the Witherspoon's William and Rhody, as well as quietists like the Chesnuts' first Scipio, were not representative. A range of African Americans in South Carolina had changed or would change their station during this epoch just prior to attaining freedom in 1865. To white observers paying close attention, this unexpected mutability seemed to suggest that movement on the chain of being could become a prospect for Southerners of *all* colors. Mary Boykin Chesnut was nothing if not an observant witness to her times, and in this final chapter I explore through two key episodes her own transformations of status, as the energies of war swept her from Camden to Montgomery to Richmond to Columbia and again toward home in late spring of 1865. In each instance, Mary Boykin Chesnut went unidentified in her proper persona and was shaken to the core by the misrecognition. Crafted in the 1880s along Homeric lines, but laced with distinctive black humor, these episodes offer a war-spanning summa of Chesnut's struggle for self against a social world disintegrating under her feet.

The first episode expands a comic debacle that took place in a Richmond hotel in 1861, when a Confederate officer burst into Chesnut's room, mistaking the middle-aged matron for his trysting partner. From a mere kernel in the 1860s diary, the 1880s writer develops one of the most dazzling set pieces of her entire narrative, a scene that raises vital questions about what, beyond the outer trappings of self, constitutes identity. The second tableau, recorded for the spring of 1864, occurs when a servantless Chesnut goes unrecognized at a South Carolina railroad station. Not only is she snubbed: she is mistaken by a telegraph man for a woman of the lower classes and ill-treated by a haughty, heavily made-up white hostess of dubious rank. In a moment of near self-erasure, the narrator reports how her persona has to remind her oblivious interlocutor that as girls in Camden, nearly thirty years before, the two had attended school together. Though their early education has clearly failed to elevate the "Speckled Peach"—Mr. Chesnut's name for this woman, who had flirted with him in inappropriate ways—it affords Mary Chesnut her only advantage during an excruciating contretemps that marks a nadir of her wartime encounters.

Both of these scenes conjure the experience of Odysseus's homecoming. In book 22 of the *Odyssey,* the once and future king of Ithaca, disguised as an aging beggar, enacts his revenge against the rapacious horde courting Penelope. Odysseus's disguise proves so convincing that the suitors fail to identify the nonentity with whom they think they are contending. The tattered stranger prevails in a contest to string the enormous bow that, twenty years earlier, of all his countrymen, Odysseus alone had proved that he could wield. Nevertheless, the suitors remain without a clue. Not until he strips off his rags to assail them for their exploitation of Penelope's hospitality does Odysseus stand revealed before the incredulous throng, which he proceeds to destroy.

Such dramas of recognition have come to constitute central components of epic literature from Homer to the present. Chesnut's confrontation with the Confederate officer and her distressing wrangle with the Speckled Peach uncover an important and heretofore inexpressible truth about her evolving selfhood. In her 1880s narrative of war and wandering, Chesnut's descriptions of these profound encounters reveal the writer's very identity as up for grabs. These tableaux thus afford us access to the ways in which a devastating national conflict transformed a childless, bibliophilic, Southern matron into the nation's most searching chronicler of the disaster.

The episodes are linked by an important philosophical concept that I have touched upon before but that is worth rehearsing here in more detail: each instance of (mis)identification or (non)recognition in Chesnut's narrative arises during a "facing scene," in which the literary representation of the self is confirmed, denied, or rerouted as the result of a face-to-face exchange with another. Taking this paradigm from Hegel's account of lord and bondsman, literary scholar Kimberly Benston uses it to analyze such dynamics in works of twentieth-century African American literature. It also proves illuminating for nineteenth-century novels and memoirs that deal with slavery.[1] In *The Phenomenology of Spirit,* Hegel stages the confrontation of lord and bondsman in order to explore the mutual dependency underwriting what ostensibly seems a one-way power relation. Without the slave's servitude and homage, the master cannot expropriate the labor, accrue the possessions, or obtain the authority that install him as dominant. Conversely, without the lord to commandeer the fruit of the bondsman's labor, the slave would come to recognize his own value as a creator. Accordingly, he would not be dependent on the lord to endow him with the merit that marks his being. Exegetes of Hegel theorize that it is imperative for the master to mystify his own dependence on the slave, never to let on that his superiority rests on the bondsman's maintenance of his subordinate position.

Considering Hegel in a sociological light, Orlando Patterson argues that the master performs an ideological reversal, in which his slave is made to believe that he is nothing without the master. In fact, however, it is the lord who depends on the bondsman's submission to sustain his superior status. The scenes of facing that Mary Chesnut undergoes across the narrative put into stark relief what becomes of the master class when conditions conspire to tear off the veil of mystification buttressing the institution of slavery. What happens, the writer asks in an elided diary entry, when "ole missis" must "«look defeat in the face»" (August 13, 1861, 142)?[2]

Crazy Jane

Chesnut's two most profound glimpses of "defeat" concerned the social rather than the martial arena. The first, involving a case of mistaken identity worthy of the French stage, rattled her otherwise strong self-conception. The writer transformed an unseemly event that had earned a telegraphic entry into the diary into one of the most memorable scenes of the 1880s book. Any other well-born Southern matron would have wished to forget such an opportunity for meditating on the nature of identity itself. Here is her 1860s entry:

> Was seated in my rocking chair in petticoat & sack—hair plaited & screwed up & disheveled like a Crazy Jane, when in walked Captain Page—stared wildly— stood still—& rushed out. I am such an object I do not think he will recognize me in decent attire. (*TPMC,* August 25, 1861, 138)

Clad only in her petticoat and a loose jacket (a sack / saque), hair unkempt, in her mind's eye looking like the tragic, mad, seduced, and abandoned heroine of Matthew G. "Monk" Lewis's eponymous 1830 ballad, Chesnut sat in repose. A familiar Confederate officer (Woodward and Muhlenfeld speculate that he was Captain Robert Lucien Page, of the Rebel navy) suddenly entered the room. Midway across the floor, he stopped, gawking ferociously, then dashed from the chamber. Chesnut noted in response that far from looking like herself, she had proved an alien presence to the interloper's apprehension. Thus, she described herself as resembling an "object," indicating something unfamiliar presented to the senses, a term employed by empiricist philosophers in the eighteenth-century. Translated into less technical language, she reckoned that her appearance had been so distorted by the absence of proper garments that her unexpected visitor would not be able to distinguish her from any other lady once she had resumed the attire in which genteel women present themselves.

In the expanded, literary 1880s version, Chesnut has transformed this episode into a miniature novella:

> So I came up, tired to death, took down my hair, had it hanging over me in Crazy Jane fashion. Sat still, hands over my head, half-undressed, but too lazy and sleepy to move. I was in a rocking chair by an open window, taking my ease—and the cool night air.
>
> Suddenly the door opened, and Captain ——— walked in. He was in the middle of the room before he saw his mistake.
>
> He stared—transfixed, as the novels say. I daresay I looked an ancient Gorgon.
>
> Then, with a more frantic glare, he turned and fled without a word.
>
> I got up and bolted the door after him. And then I looked in the glass and laughed myself into hysterics. I will never forget to lock the door again.
>
> It does not matter. I looked totally unlike the person bearing my name who, covered with lace caps, &c&c, frequents the drawing room. I doubt if he knows me again. (*MCCW,* August 25, 1861, 162)

While the 1860s account of the scene features one literary allusion, its reworked counterpart sports three references to poetry, fiction, and epic: the revising Chesnut speaks again of the gothic madwoman from Monk's nineteenth-century ballad; she also mentions novel writers in general and refers to Homer's mythic Gorgon. But in the elaborated episode, Chesnut structures the story as dramatic tableau. She sets the stage with her persona-protagonist at the window, in dishabille, sitting still. Suddenly, into the room charges a naval officer (now unnamed), unaware of his gaffe—this is the wrong room—until he is halfway across the floor. In an extraordinary use of metaphor, the 1880s writer describes her intruder as held captive by the gaze of whomever it is he sees. Adding a metaliterary touch, she notes that his mesmerized attitude reminds her of the way in which fiction writers portray such moments of visual fascination. Here, as Chesnut imagines it, life literally is imitating art.

Meanwhile, her use of "I daresay" sarcastically conveys outrage—if not hurt—over being viewed with such a look of horror. Chesnut's invocation of the classical tradition of female monstrosity offers another way for us to understand the epic nature of the writer's ambitions for her book. And though she doesn't specify herself as Medusa—the only mortal Gorgon of the three monster sisters—the hysterical laughter that follows her gaze into the looking glass uncannily conjures for twenty-first-century readers an important turn in French feminist thinking. Pioneered by Hélène Cixous in her famous essay, *The Laugh of the Medusa* (1983), the call was for a new women's writing in which the body and its functions, particularly laughter, inform creative expression.

But it is not necessary to look to Cixous in order to understand Mary Chesnut or her maniacal hilarity at this moment. Remember that before fleeing, the captain bestows a "more frantic glare" on the recipient of his intrusion. The writer implies that after recovering from his shocked trance, the man has assumed an expression both crazed (which is appropriate in the circumstances) and hostile (which decidedly is not) and then amplifies it to an even higher level of antipathy. In this facing scene, the instigator not only blames the injured party but makes her feel monstrous by projecting onto the innocent matron his own horror and humiliation over violating the sanctity of her chamber. In this gendered division of emotional labor, the woman is made to do the man's psychic work: thus the ogre in the piece is not the libertine officer but the semiclad, disheveled, middle-aged Chesnut. Recasting her treatment of the event twenty years after the fact, Mary Chesnut the writer may have identified more closely with the unrecognizable Gorgon in dishabille in Richmond circa 1861 than she did with the narrated self who bore her name and sported caps and laces.

Over twenty years of mulling, Chesnut attempted to make literary sense of what had happened. One reading of the episode would unfold according to the generic rules of farce: a group of illicit couples all quartered at the same country house clandestinely manage to locate the wrong bedrooms in a series of ridiculous conjunctions. Ultimately, the best-suited twosomes are sorted out and reunited at drama's end. But nineteenth-century Civil War Richmond is hardly eighteenth-century stage-Versailles, and the genre into which the 1880s Chesnut transforms this episode is not farce but ontology. Checking her image in the looking glass once she safely is alone and locked inside, the persona mirroring the captain's initial stare becomes for a fleeting moment the intruder herself. But in assuming the man's gaze, she who peers at the reflection in the mirror also becomes the Gorgon. However one reads the encounter, the narrator is not turned to stone, perhaps her escape afforded by the release of hysterical laughter.

The 1880s narrative contains several key instances in which the laughter of Chesnut's wartime persona has drawn social condemnation. In an entry preceding First Manassas, the writer quotes the critical words of her young cousin Mary Hammy (Boykin): "You are like Cousin Mary. She laughs at everything. She laughs at General Washington" (July 9, 1861, 94). In the context of the Witherspoon murder, the narrator notes, "It is encouraging when one hears a piece of fun, however broad. If one can afford to laugh, things are mending" (September 9, 1861, 191). For later in the war, Chesnut represents her persona's deep wounding by the following remark: "It seems Miss Sarah Parker said, 'The reason I cannot bear Mrs. Chesnut is that she laughs at everything and everybody.' If she saw me now, she would give me credit for some pretty hearty crying as well as laughing" (June 16, 1862, 392). In the epoch just after little Joe Davis's death and the encounter with the Speckled Peach, during her sad visit to Mulberry after her mother-in-law's passing, the narrator reports having gone to church: "A capital sermon. It made me cry, and I have no gift that way. Laughing is my forte" (May 8, 1864, 607). Then, as the war moves to its final phase, she notes, "Sherman marches always—all RRs smashed up. And if I laugh at any mortal thing, it is that I may not weep" (January 16, 1865, 705).

During her travails, laughter was connected to survival for Chesnut. She writes in the 1880s book of the near overdose of opium administered by Ellen as they are in flight from Sherman in Lincolnton: "The comic side of my being able to stand that horse's dose has since given us both some hearty laughs. [The doctor] says I will die hard, that it is not easy to kill me, and that I have a sturdy constitution" (March 12, 1865, 759). Considering the possibility that Ellen's excessive use of medication *could* have been construed as a murder attempt, Chesnut's subsequent laughter may have expressed denial as much as relief. In this moment, the reader can imagine that she herself displays the very blind spots that in the 1860s diary she faults in mistresses who seem to believe that mulatto children have no white fathers but simply drop from the clouds.

Chesnut's propensity to laugh through horror was well known to her friends: "Miss Middleton says Mrs. Chesnut will laugh when the time to laugh comes, with no respect whatever to fatal consequences. Witness—when the irate landlady took fright at Laurence's gold pencil case. 'Look again,' said Mrs. C. 'It is only a pencil—not a rifled canon'" (March 27, 1865, 766). Such pleasantries punctuate the writer's depiction of her flight from Sherman's troops. But unbeknownst to Chesnut's wartime persona and her refugee cohort holing up in Chester, South Carolina, by mid-April 1865, Lee has surrendered and Lincoln has been assassinated. To be sure, the intimations of Southern collapse have been evident for some time: "With this storm of woe impending, we snatched a moment of reckless gaiety ... patriots supposed to be sunk in gloomy despondency. We played cards. Then the stories told were so amusing I confess I laughed to the point of tears. I knew the trouble was all out there, but we put it off, kept it out one evening—let it bang at the door as it would" (April 15, 1865, 784–85). In her account for several days later, now aware of the loss of the war, the murder of the president, and the demise of her former way of life, Chesnut notes: "The plucky way our men bear up is beyond praise. No howling—our poverty is made a matter of laughing. We deride our own penury. Of the country we try not to speak at all" (April 19, 1865, 790).

The seemingly incongruous outburst of horrified mirth recorded in the Crazy Jane tableau in fact may have represented a mode of psychic compensation that had cultural precedent in the intense trauma many Americans suffered during the war. Such hysteria was not a part of the original account for the August 1861 hotel room episode. But the 1880s version may have been inflected with a backlog of the feeling that had begun to accrue as the miseries of the war unfolded. And it may have accelerated after 1865, during the two grueling decades in which Chesnut meditated her Confederate experiences. That is, belated emotion could have amplified her memory of the encounter. Confederate defeat merely proved the tip of the iceberg of loss for Chesnut. That devastation was made even more unbearable by the unexpected and premature deaths of the "Cool Captain," beloved nephew Johnny Chesnut, in 1868, and of treasured sister Kate Williams, as well as Kate's daughter Serena, "Princess Bright Eyes," in 1877. This accumulated heartache might well have informed her narrative expansion of the hysterical outburst at the looking glass.

Indeed, there seems to be an important connection between the writer's Gorgon allusion, her description of uncontrolled laughter both in the Crazy Jane scene and across her book, and her recognition that psychic ossification could be the emotional cost of survival. Consider the following portrait of gallows humor she draws for the summer of 1864:

> At dinner, a soldier on crutches,—from typhoid fever, however, no wound. He could not be hurt in his heart—he has none. He fancies himself a mimic and a humorist. His idea was to amuse the dinner table by the variety of fixed grins on the faces of the dead found on the battlefield. Can the hardening process of war go further than that? (July 26, 1864, 626)

The fact that typhoid rather than a bullet has made an invalid of this Rebel may help explain his callousness: perhaps he is ashamed that it is disease rather than a wound that has propelled him from the field of battle to a dinner among the elite of Columbia. But Chesnut, herself a chronic sufferer of typhoid, points to something beyond shame as motivating his ghoulish humor. In a more profound psychic transformation, the horrors of war, rather than her Gorgon's stare, may have turned his heart to stone. Thus attempts at mirth remain his exclusive social gambit. In the midst of genteel company, this unfortunate soldier shows how war has unfit him to mix with those who once constituted his community. That the elaborating writer situates this anecdote featuring the sick man's heartlessness immediately following her report of the tragic artillery death of the Prestons' favorite child, young Willie, "his heart literally shot away" (July 25, 1864, 623), adds to its irony and ghastliness. Soldiers' hearts constitute the organs most vulnerable to the physical and emotional horrors of war.[3]

Perhaps Chesnut's inclusion of the invalid soldier's gruesome anecdote allowed the writer to express her own wartime anxieties about her husband's and nephew's potential death or dismemberment. That the most condemnatory critics of Chesnut's gallows humor in the narrative are members of the Boykin-Chesnut family, itself a house divided, should prove no surprise to the reader: not only friendly cousin Mary Hammy Boykin, but also the hostile Reynolds nieces (mouthpieces for their mother, Mary Cox Chesnut Reynolds, James Jr.'s censorious sister), all chime in disapproval over Aunt Mary's unseemly wit. Clearly, dark comedy constitutes a dominant thread in the affective texture of Chesnut's 1880s work. But far from impairing her faculties, her capacious range of feeling, shifting from sorrow to mirth and back again, seems to have enabled the creative process itself: such intense emotions apparently stoked her imaginative energies and focused them in a narrative direction.

And, indeed, it is only after her eruption of hysterical laughter in the Crazy Jane tableau that the writer's wartime persona seems to have had her epiphany of self. She draws a distinction between the woman spied in her petticoat and sack and "the person bearing my name, who covered with lace caps . . . frequents the drawing room."[4] This is the moment in which Chesnut reveals her understanding that the Southern belle is socially constructed, created from the hoopskirt up.[5] Far from being a natural effusion of the South Carolina landscape, like any number of magnolias and azaleas, the historical women on whom such figures as Scarlett O'Hara were based were trained in etiquette, music, dancing, drawing, riding, and foreign languages. Indeed, they were cultivated as assiduously as were the hothouse flowers nurtured for the adornment of their mothers' exquisite interiors. It might have taken the loss of the Civil

War to lead the writer to such a prescient insight, a century ahead of her time. But the episode in the Richmond hotel room in 1861 offered a provocative point of departure for her meditation on the issue.

"For the first time in my life, I was nobody"

Describing a wedding she attended in Camden in late 1864, Mary Chesnut reports feeling ill-treated and practically shunned by rising Camden youth: "For the first time in my life," the writer complains, "I was nobody" (December 27, 1864, 696). Her words also could stand as a caption for her most devastating experience of misrecognition, an encounter at a Kingsville, South Carolina, railroad station recorded in an entry dated seven months earlier. The writer sandwiches her account of the episode between the shattering tale of the death of Joe Davis and one of only two reflections of feeling on the loss of her mother-in-law: "Sad enough at Mulberry without Mrs. Chesnut, who was the good genius of the place" (May 8, 1864, 606).

It is no accident that Chesnut strategically places the scene marking a painful passage of identity in suspension between two tragic stories involving death: one brutal and unexpected at the start of a young life and the other after more than ninety rich years. If the writer is caught between identifications with the intrusive Captain Page and a Gorgon evil-twin in her Richmond hotel looking glass, she shows herself even more vulnerable at the Kingsville railroad station, sans male escort (her husband delayed on another train) or slave attendants (returned to Mulberry in the wake of the senior Mrs. Chesnut's passing). If the Southern belle can be said to have been constructed socially, of lace caps, flounces, and hoops, waited on by bound black maids and escorted by multiple beaux or a dashing husband, the social rank of the drawn, exhausted, and ailing woman in the torn dress and Balmoral petticoat is particularly murky:

> My maid belonged to the Prestons. She was only traveling home with me and would go straight on to Columbia. So without fear I stepped off at Kingsville. My old Confederate silk, like most Confederate dresses, had seen better days. And I noticed, like Oliver Wendell Holmes's famous shay, it had gone to pieces suddenly and all over. It was literally in strips. I became painfully aware of my forlorn aspect when I asked the telegraph man the way to the hotel, and he was by no means respectful. I was a *lone* and not too respectable-looking old woman. It was my first experience in the character, and I laughed out loud. A very haughty and highly painted dame greeted me at the hotel.
>
> "No room. Who are you?" I gave my name.

"Try something else. Mrs. Chesnut don't travel round by herself no servants, no nothing." I looked down. There I was—dusty, tired, tattered, and torn.

"Where do you come from?"

"My home is in Camden."

"Come, now. I know everybody in Camden." I sat down meekly on the bench in the piazza that was free to all wayfarers.

"Which Mrs. Chesnut, I say?" (sharply) "I know both."

"I am now the only one. And now what is the matter with you? Do you take me for a spy? I know you perfectly well. I went to school with you at Miss Henrietta DeLeon's—and my name was Mary Miller."

"Lord sakes alive—and to think you are her. Now I see—dear! me! Heaven sakes woman, but you are broke! . . .

"Now, you know, you do look funny, that bright Balmoral petticoat grinning through all these tears, and you see we are *'bliged* to be pertickler here—and respectable."

"You look like it," I *thought,* looking her straight in the face—and wiping my own.

"Molly and Laurence both went by a month ago. They said you'd an English lady for a maid. Where is she?"

"I never had a lady for a maid in my life."

"They said she was white as anybody. You know, lots come here, call themselves any name they think we know, and then slip away on a train and don't pay. . . . We—don't take no imposters now. We mean to reform this house. No stray ladies with no servants and no protectors. But then, I made an awful mistake not to know you."

"It was not pleasant. At any rate, it is a new experience," said I coolly, but I was inwardly raging. (May 8, 1864, 604–5)[6]

Looking frayed in a tattered four-year-old dress with her petticoat winking through, Chesnut's wartime persona believes she has been mistaken for a woman of much lower status. Or so the rude and dismissive comportment of the telegraph man seems to suggest. But surely Mary Boykin Chesnut was not the first woman of the planter aristocracy to reveal her diminished circumstances at the Kingsville railroad station. In fact, over the course of the war, ladies of the plantation elite were precisely the class that had no ready money and could not renovate their exhausted attire, other than by "turning" dresses to display the less worn inside, and trimming them with different ribbons, buttons, and bows, which they rotated from one garment to anther. Whatever the telegraph man may have been thinking, his rude behavior causes the writer to report that it has made her feel disreputable, "my first time in the character." As if in a scene to be played, she recognizes that her pitiful costume has cast her into an entirely new "part."

The encounter with the railway hostess whom she describes as a "highly painted dame"—what the Puritans would have called a type of fallen woman— reinforces the realization that she herself embodies a vagabond, or a stout, dark-haired sandy-hiller trying her luck in the city. Appearances being all, Chesnut's refugee persona is denied accommodation. Indeed, only after being summarily dismissed is she even asked her name. In response to the answer "Mrs. Chesnut," the painted woman expresses incredulity, because "Mrs. Chesnut don't travel round by herself [with] no servants."

Thus ensues an elaborate exchange, in which the dame interrogates Chesnut about just who she might be. In the most ludicrous moment of the entire conversation, her interlocutor demands that the matron state precisely "which" Mrs. Chesnut she is, apparently oblivious to the fact that the elder Mary Chesnut would be in her early nineties, while the woman standing before her clearly is nowhere near that age. And though the difference of fifty years should have been hard to mistake (particularly in the nineteenth century, when most people died by sixty), the Speckled Peach seems to have had little clue about who it is, if "anyone," she is dealing with. Even more significant, the painted dame reveals her ignorance of the fact that the elder woman has been dead for over two months. (The Speckled Peach's nonawareness of the senior Mrs. Chesnut's demise is particularly bizarre, since she immediately thereafter reveals that she has seen and spoken with Laurence and Molly when they last passed through, most likely on their way to Mulberry to aid the grieving Colonel James Chesnut Sr.)

It is at this point that the narrated Chesnut has had quite enough and turns the conversational tables on the florid and officious hostess. "Do you take me for a spy?" she queries, in tones ever polite, though she silently grows livid. "I know you perfectly well. I went to school with you . . . and my name was Mary Miller." Suddenly, the Speckled Peach seems to recognize her former Camden classmate and feels compelled to defend her insensibility by rendering judgment on Chesnut's evident economic distress, materialized in her unraveling garments. Suppressing her wrath and her words, the narrator describes herself thinking hateful thoughts about the woman's nonrespectability as she looks her "straight in the face." And, as if this mirroring scene actually has the power to befoul her own countenance with cheap rouge and bad powder, the narrator recalls herself "wiping [her] own."

However, the railroad hostess remains undeterred in her battle against aristocracy in pauper's guise. She attempts to turn Laurence and Molly's information about the purported English maid—Mrs. Charlotte Bones, who arrived at the end of March 1864 and worked for Chesnut for six weeks, during Laurence and Molly's return to Camden—against a mistress so obviously reduced in her fortunes: "They said she was as white as anybody," opines the Speckled Peach. "I never had a lady for a maid in my life," retorts Chesnut, her wrath mounting. Implicit in the writer's words is the verdict that this painted (that is, less than pure, thus not quite white) dame will never herself achieve the status of gentlewoman. The two women get into a verbal scuffle over the fact that someone as downtrodden-looking as Chesnut is the type that could and likely would "slip away on the train and don't pay." And then the Speckled Peach's coup de grace: "Yes—we don't take in no imposters now. We mean to reform this house. No stray ladies with no servants and no protectors. But then, I made an awful mistake not to know you."

The writer describes her emotions as "inwardly raging," indicating that this remembered encounter had provoked more anger than she records anywhere else in the narrative. Chesnut's wrath in this scene is far worse than that aroused by her ongoing conflict with impossible niece Harriet Grant, by her quarrels with the at times too reticent and emotionally buttoned-down James Jr. (mostly elided from the 1880s account), by her frustration over being judged wanting by her in-laws, or by her society contretemps with Mrs. Lydia Johnston. (Mrs. General Joseph E. Johnston loathed Chesnut's beloved Jefferson Davis almost as much as did her retreat-prone defense-minded husband, the major-general. Davis appointed, relieved, and reappointed Joe Johnston across four years of war.)[7] All of these chronic thorns in her side had peeved and saddened the writer. But nothing could compare with the quality of exposure, vulnerability, and rejection she had experienced alone at an isolated railroad station, with only a thoughtless, negligent woman on whom to depend for aid.

Ever the well-born lady, even if she no longer looks it, Chesnut's refugee persona "coolly" tells her interlocutor regarding her "awful mistake not to know" her: "It was not pleasant. At any rate, it was a new experience." Like the lower portions of the ruined dress bespeaking her poverty, Chesnut's identity is in tatters. Indeed, in a vulgar turn of phrase, the highly painted dame observes that the matron's Balmoral petticoat (typically a fine woolen underskirt worn in lieu of a crinoline cage, or hoops) is "grinning through the tears." Though the hostess is clearly referring to the rents in Chesnut's outer garment, the heteronym of "tears"—the fluid testament to strong feelings of sorrow, anger, and joy—underscores the emotional power of the scene. Grinning through the tears, through the rents and the weeping, the narrator has limned an astonishing Odyssean moment of apparent invisibility, balancing it between two representations of significant deaths: one in her own family, the other bereaving an entire society.

Once an elite Southern matron from a first family of Carolina, the Mary Boykin Chesnut of the narrative has become "no body."[8] The Homeric epithet emphasizes how far she has descended: from having been one of the Confederacy's celebrated intellectuals, she goes unrecognized at the late 1864 Camden wedding from which the title of this section derives. For over three years, the narrated Chesnut has traveled to and fro between her hometown, thirty miles northeast of Columbia, and the various urban locales hosting the Confederate cabinet. Now, for the first time, the matron has found herself socially invisible to the smart set of her tiny hamlet. And this deflating reality only amplifies the animus she has always felt about her Camden neighbors, of whom she writes: "[T]hese people have grown accustomed to dullness. They were born and bred in it. They like it as well as anything else" (November 30, 1861, 250).

The writer's identification with Odysseus in his "nemo" persona, however, cuts in more than one direction. Southern defeat in the spring of 1865 would mean more than two decades of grueling poverty, familial loss, and personal disappointment. Three untimely deaths, the financial ruin and suicide of niece Mary Williams's first husband, and the realization that nephew David Williams, whom she helped to raise post-1865, was profoundly deaf constituted ongoing, devastating, blows. Chesnut's chronic invalidism, the ways in which her physical self grew increasingly incapable of the activity and enterprise she continued to imagine even in the last phase of her life, worsened with age. Thus, the notion of being "no body"—without corporeal extension—proved both devastating and liberatory. Despite being and having "no body," she still could create, and her mind always had been her most valued part.

So it was that a once-casual female scribbler transformed herself into a writer of consummate skill. From diary jottings in the 1860s, she developed an encyclopedic narrative, featuring her culture in formation: its divinities and theological figures; Northern and Southern politicians; domestic workers slave and free, black, white, and Irish; oral traditions from Mozart's *Requiem,* the "Dead March" from Handel's *Saul,* and Scottish ballads to slave spirituals and Stephen Foster's plantation odes; two trips to the underworld; and her own deconstruction of the epic universe, through descriptions of the burning of letters and diary pages themselves.

Chesnut crafted catalogues of dead warriors, living flowers, fresh foods, and reading material from newspapers such as the *New York Herald* and the *Richmond Examiner* to novels by Thackeray, Eliot, and of course, Stowe. She created epithets to conjure Rebel generals such as Beauregard the "melancholy retreater," family members such as "Princess Bright Eyes" Serena Williams, and friends such as "Mother of the Gracchi," Louisa McCord. And she punctuated her achievement with important scenes of recognition. Built of fragments, her book drew its particular animation, its tartness and bite, from her acuity for seeing the dramatic in the mundane and for culling the quotidian from the epochal. These pieces of her achievement, like brightly colored mosaics, became the material of her luminous reconstruction.

If encounters like the one at Kingsville in 1864 had battered her, the blow proved less enduring than was her imaginative resilience. This elasticity enabled Chesnut to draw on such moments of vulnerability as she invented her panoply of characters, figures absurd, stalwart, and triumphant. The rending of the self afforded by her 1860s experiences, and the reweaving of her being through the work of creation decades later, suggested that an aesthetic redemption remained possible. Ever a survivor, Mary Boykin Chesnut could gaze into the mirror and see the Gorgon grinning through the tears, turning no one into stone, but transforming the fragments of her Civil War diary into an epic work of art.

NOTES

Chapter One

1. *Mary Chesnut's Civil War,* ed. C. Vann Woodward (New Haven: Yale University Press, 1981), August 13, 1861, 143. All further references to this edition of Chesnut's "book" appear parenthetically in the text and include the 1860s date under which the revising Chesnut of the 1880s included the material I have quoted. Where it is necessary to distinguish quotations from this edition from other versions of her diary, I use the abbreviation *MCCW.*

   Diary entry for March 29, 1861, *The Private Mary Chesnut: The Unpublished Civil War Diaries,* ed. Elisabeth Muhlenfeld and C. Vann Woodward (New York: Oxford University Press, 1984), 50. All future references to this edition will appear parenthetically in the text as *TPMC,* and include the 1860s date and page number. Where Woodward has imported quotations from the original diary into his 1981 edition of *Mary Chesnut's Civil War,* I cite that edition and provide the 1860s date he included, distinguishing the imported diary material in the double, angled brackets—« »—he has adopted in his editorial apparatus.

   Born in South Carolina in 1823, Mary Boykin Miller was the daughter of self-made lawyer, congressman, and later failed planter Stephen Decatur Miller, who rose to governor of South Carolina during Mary Chesnut's childhood, congressman soon after, and who died when she was only fifteen. Her mother, Mary Boykin, was the daughter of an elite Camden planting family. All biographical details come from Elisabeth Muhlenfeld's superb *Mary Boykin Chesnut: A Biography* (Baton Rouge: Louisiana State University Press, 1981).

2. It was estimated at the opening of the Civil War that Colonel James Chesnut, Sr. was the third richest planter in the Palmetto State, owning more than 430 slaves, as well as several plantations: Mulberry, Sandy Hill, Knight's Hill, and Bloomsbury, in Camden.

3. MBC to Varina Davis, June 18, 1883. All letters quoted here, unless noted otherwise, come from Allie Patricia Wall, "The Letters of Mary Boykin Chesnut," M.A. thesis, University of South Carolina, 1977, 83. Additional letters come from the private archives of Mulberry Plantation, Camden, South Carolina, and are quoted with permission.

4. These were volumes for January 28, February 4, 11, 18, 25, 1905.

5. Thanks to Elisabeth Muhlenfeld for this insight.

6. After the war, Chesnut made notes toward a portrait of her husband, which she intended for publication. Elisabeth Muhlenfeld writes that the sketch never achieved coherence, nor did it ever appear in print. The manuscript for this piece is in the Williams-Chesnut-Manning Collection at the Caroliniana Library, University of South Carolina; Muhlenfeld also appends it to her doctoral dissertation, "Mary Boykin Chesnut: The Writer and Her Work," University of South Carolina, 1977. See also Muhlenfeld's *Mary Boykin Chesnut,* 232 n. 39.

7. Scholars estimate that at the end of the war, four million African Americans were emancipated from slavery in the South.

8. My thanks to Professor James Kibbler of the University of Georgia Department of English for sharing with me his knowledge of Chesnut's 1880s narrative, her life, and the surrounding Southern literary context.
9. See *A Diary from Dixie*, ed. Ben Ames Williams (Boston: Houghton Mifflin, 1949).
10. My understanding of the editorial complexity of Chesnut's work is completely indebted to C. Vann Woodward's introductory editorial apparatus in *Mary Chesnut's Civil War* and to Elisabeth Muhlenfeld, Chesnut's distinguished biographer and the coeditor with Woodward of *The Private Mary Chesnut*, as well as editor of *Two Novels by Mary Chesnut* (Charlottesville: University of Virginia Press, 2002).
11. In his review essay of the Woodward Yale edition, historian Michael P. Johnson argues that

> by the 1880s [Chesnut's] racism had deepened, and she gave it freer rein. In the original she wrote of her father-in-law's estate as "one profitless plantation, where the black man must be kept as dark and unenlightened as his skin." In the 1880s narrative this became, "the swamplands only are utilized now for the black man—a creature whose mind is as dark and unenlightened as his skin." Another 1880s entry ascribed a slave woman's infanticide and suicide to laziness. The Chesnut overseer James Team said that slavery "'does not make good mothers—teaches them to expect other people to take care of their children.' Then told a tale of a woman so lazy she tied her child to her back and jumped in the river. She said 'she did not mean to work—nor should her child after her.'" In the original [1860s diary] Team told of one of a neighbor's "'Negroes driven to despair by the driver tying her baby on her back & walking into the river—found drowned—baby still strapped to her back'—& said Team—'the man who caused it was not hung! Ho for honest poverty!'"

See Johnson, "Mary Boykin Chesnut's Autobiography and Biography: A Review Essay," *Journal of Southern History* 47, no. 4 (November 1981): 589; Johnson quotes the following passages: *TPMC*, December 8, 1861, 214; *MCCW*, October 4, 1861, 208, and December 6, 1861, 256.

12. See Edmund Wilson, *Patriotic Gore: Studies in the Literature of the American Civil War* (New York: W. W. Norton, 1962); Daniel Aaron, *The Unwritten War: American Writers and the Civil War* (Madison: University of Wisconsin Press, 1973); Eugene Genovese, *Roll, Jordan, Roll: The World the Slaves Made* (New York: Vintage, 1976); and Elizabeth Fox-Genovese, *In the Plantation Household: Black and White Women of the Old South* (Chapel Hill: University of North Carolina Press, 1988).
13. That General Hood had a mangled, unusable arm (from wounds at Gettysburg) and had lost a leg (just before Chickamauga) transformed him into something of a marvel and celebrity among the population of Richmond. And, indeed, he joked of being a centaur (an allusion in keeping with Chesnut's epic project) when on horseback with his prosthetic leg.
14. Hood went on to marry after the war, fathering numerous children, all of whom died with him and his wife during a yellow fever epidemic in the 1870s. Buck turned to suitor Rawdie

Lowndes after breaking her engagement to Hood and ultimately married him, giving birth to three children before dying at thirty-eight as a result of complications from surgery. My thanks to Mr. John Sherrer, director of Collections and Interpretation at the Historic Columbia (South Carolina) Association, as well as to Elisabeth Muhlenfeld, for sharing information on Buck's postwar fate.

15. In a remarkable moment in her narrative, Chesnut reports having heard the Stephen Foster ode "Massa in the Cold, Cold Ground" being sung on the occasion of the raising of the Confederate flag. In an entry pertaining to April 1861 but dated February 18, 1865, the writer notes:

> "Dixie"—"I'll take my stand by Dixie land" was mere prosaic truth. It never moved me a jot. In Montgomery, when the band played "Massa is in the cold, cold ground," it sent a cold chill to the marrow of my bones. Nothing could they contrive to play but that—when Miss Tyler first ran up the Confederate flag.
> And yet I am not superstitious. (722)

Foster's song is composed in the voice of an adult slave, grieving over the death and burial of his beloved, benevolent master. The lyrics suggest that the bound black community on this plantation may be in for a precipitous drop in their quality of life now that "Massa" is in the cold, cold ground. Emphasizing the paternal benefits and purported philanthropic dimensions of the system that had made the South the region it was, this song could have been used in the propaganda wars waged by figures such as George Fitzhugh and his proslavery minions in the 1850s.

At the end of Chesnut's 1880s narrative for the winter of 1865, the writer describes her maid Ellen, her sole companion during her refugee flight from Columbia, South Carolina, in advance of Sherman's march, singing this very song; Chesnut tells her to hush and also records the dry comment of Isabella Martin:

> "Stop, Ellen! No more 'Massa in the Cold, Cold Ground.' Sing something else."
> "Well, so they are, most of them," says Isabella. "Time's revenge." (724)

Here Chesnut brilliantly invokes the lyrics of a proslavery spiritual to "signify" on the reality of the end of African American bondage and the demise of the paternalistic planter as master. This entry also marks an example of the way her epic deconstructs not only its own textual materiality (through the burning of pages of prose), but the very world of the Old South as it unravels.

16. It certainly is my intuition that Margaret Mitchell read the *Diary from Dixie,* given that Chesnut describes an outrageous costume worn during the war by a peer, featuring a green velvet dress trimmed with golden sheaves of wheat worn in her hair: "Such extraordinary-dressing «comical people there»—a grass green dress with a gold belt and gold wheat sheaves in the fair one's hair" (August 24, 1861, 159).

17. In *The Feminization of American Culture* (New York: Avon Books, 1977), Ann Douglas reads Margaret Fuller as the nineteenth-century's last best hope for an authentic American romanticism, a contracultural prospect extinguished by Fuller's untimely death by drowning.

I want to argue that Chesnut constitutes an alternative figure of contracultural power, unfeminized because of a unique constellation of variables, among them her superb and unusually rigorous education, her continued curiosity and autodidacticism throughout adulthood, her antipathy to her husband's very conventional, aristocratic Southern family, and her childlessness. An eyewitness to historical disaster, Chesnut was suited by her ironic temperament and driving energy (despite a life of semi-invalidism) to work in the tragic and epic modes as was no other nineteenth-century American woman writer, other, perhaps, than Rebecca Harding Davis or Elizabeth Stoddard.

18. See Harold Bloom, *The Anxiety of Influence: A Theory of Poetry* (New York: Oxford University Press, 1973).

19. See also historian Thavolia Glymph's "African American Women in the Literary Imagination of Mary Boykin Chesnut," in *Slavery, Secession, and Southern History,* ed. Robert Louis Paquette and Lois A. Ferleger (Charlottesville: University of Virginia Press, 2000), 140–59. Glymph argues that figures like Chesnut's maid Molly function as comic foils to the unfolding dark fate of white Confederate characters facing the defeat of their "revolution." While comparative study of the 1860s diary against the 1880s narrative reveals that Chesnut developed the portraits of her former slaves Laurence, Molly, and Ellen from mere kernels in the 1860s to rich dramatis personae in the revisions, Glymph reads these representations as projections of Chesnut's racist fantasies. My sense of Laurence, Molly, and Ellen's individuality and agency is more complicated.

For explicitly feminist treatments of the 1880s narrative, see also Clara Juncker, "Writing Herstory: Mary Chesnut's Civil War," *Southern Studies* 26, no. 1 (spring 1987): 18–27; Suzy Clark Holstein, "'Offering Up Her Life': Confederate Women on the Altars of Sacrifice," *Southern Studies* 22, no. 2 (summer 1991): 113–30; and Melissa Mentzer, "Rewriting Herself: Mary Chesnut's Narrative Strategies," *Connecticut Review* 14, no. 1 (spring 1992): 49–55.

What follows is a list of the dissertations focusing on Chesnut, listed in chronological order: Melissa Mentzer, "Rewriting the Unwritten: The Fictions of Autobiography in the Civil War Journal of Mary Chesnut," Ph.D. diss., University of Oregon, 1989; Wendy Ann Kurant, "Mary Chesnut's Civil War: Formulations of Femininity in the Novels and the Diary," Ph.D. diss., University of Georgia, 1990; Catherine Ross Nickerson, "The Domestic Detective Novel: Gothicism, Domesticity, and Investigation in American Women's Writing, 1865–1920," Ph.D. diss., Yale University, 1991; Karen Sue Nultan, "The Social Civil War," Ph.D. diss., Rutgers University, 1992; Kendra Lynne McDonald, "The Creation of History and Myth in Mary Chesnut's Civil War Narrative," Ph.D. diss., Ohio State University, 1996; Lynn Marie Romina, "Ain't I an American? Women's Autobiographical Narratives and the Construction of National Identity," Ph.D. diss., State University of New York, Stony Brook, 1997; Joan Elizabeth Dell, "When Mammy Left Missus: The Southern Lady in the House Divided," Ph.D. diss., University of Texas, Austin, 2003; and Kristina Pope Key, "Rehistoricizing the Civil War: Notions of Self-Representation and Southern Loyalty in the Diaries of Mary Boykin Chesnut and Kaye Gibbons' *On the Occasion of My Last Afternoon,* and Alice Randall's *The Wind Done Gone,*" Ph.D. diss., University of Louisiana, Lafayette, 2003.

20. Michael O'Brien compares Chesnut to Virginia Woolf. See O'Brien, "The Flight down the Middle Walk: Mary Chesnut and the Forms of Observance," in *Haunted Bodies: Gender and Southern Texts,* ed. Anne Goodwin Jones and Susan V. Donaldson (Charlottesville: University of Virginia Press, 1998), 113, 121.
21. Ibid., 125.
22. Ibid., 123–24.
23. See G. Thomas Couser, *Altered Egos: Authority in American Autobiography* (New York: Oxford University Press, 1989), 156–88.
24. See Joel Fineman, "The History of the Anecdote: Fiction and Fiction," in *The New Historicism,* ed. H. Aram Veeser (New York: Routledge, 1989), 49–76; Jane Gallop, *Anecdotal Theory* (Durham: Duke University Press, 2002); Helen Deutsch, *Loving Doctor Johnson* (Chicago: University of Chicago Press, 2005); and Leah Price, *The Anthology and the Rise of the Novel* (Cambridge: Cambridge University Press, 2000).
25. See Susan Stewart, *On Longing: Narratives of the Miniature, the Gigantic, the Souvenir, the Collection* (1984; repr., Durham: Duke University Press, 1993), 135, 136, 139.
26. I am grateful to Kathleen Diffley for coining this formulation to describe the postwar experience for formerly privileged white elites and the freed people whose hopes rose and fell so precipitously by the end of Reconstruction.
27. Civil War historian Drew Gilpin Faust estimates the Southern death toll at something like 20 percent of all males between the ages of twenty-eight and forty. See her *Republic of Suffering: Death and the American Civil War* (Cambridge: Harvard University Press, 2007), 250–65.
28. So, too, in the last days of the war, Chesnut gave her maid Ellen her diamonds for safekeeping, which Ellen promptly returned when they were reunited at Mulberry. Chesnut marveled that the black woman seemed as unmoved by the burden she handed over to her former mistress than had she been looking after a bag of peas.
29. Sociologist Orlando Patterson's notions of slavery producing social death in its victims and human parasitism in its perpetrators have been central influences on my thinking about African American bondage in the antebellum South. See *Slavery and Social Death: A Comparative Study* (Cambridge: Harvard University Press, 1982).
30. For Chesnut's modern readers, these words may call to mind Dylan Thomas's villanelle contra the death of his father, "Do Not Go Gentle into That Good Night."
31. See James McPherson, *Battle Cry of Freedom: The Civil War Era* (New York: Ballantine, 1988), 829.

Chapter Two

1. The term comes from Paul de Man's essay, "Autobiography as Defacement," *MLN* 94, no. 5 (1979): 919–30, which has been vital to my thinking about genre.
2. The writer describes the behavior of a highly-strung, socially impossible Irish woman, with whom she shares a railroad car toward the end of the war. Holding a huge mirror as she enters the train, the woman places it on the seat next to hers, despite the fact that soldiers are standing because the cars are so packed. While she is sleeping, an exhausted recruit

sits down next to her, not seeing the mirror on the seat cushion. Inadvertently shattering the looking glass and severely lacerating his own hindquarters, he cries out in pain; but the ire of the outraged Celtic lady trumps his howls of agony, and she lambastes him for his carelessness (November 28, 1863, 490). Chesnut portrays another equally memorable and terrible story of little Joe Davis's Irish nurse, Catherine, whom she tacitly blames for leaving the boy untended before his fall to his death from a second-story piazza. Chesnut disparages her lying on the floor and "howling" over the little boy's corpse (May 27, 1864, 609). Female Irishness, in the writer's judgment, is tantamount to excessive emotionality that endangers the innocent.

Two Jewish women appear in Chesnut's narrative: Miriam "Mem" Cohen and Phoebe Yates Levy Pember. Cohen was a dear friend, and her affection and companionship prove particularly important in the middle of the work, provoking Chesnut to pen the following effusion, the philo- or anti-Semitic nature of which is not fully clear to me: "Elsewhere Jews may be tolerated. Here they are the haute vole. Everybody here has their own Jew exceptions. I have two—Mem Cohen, Agnes DeLeon" (January 22, 1864, 547). (DeLeon actually converted to Christianity on her marriage.) Pember was a celebrity of sorts because she ran a major ward of Chimborazo Military Hospital in Richmond. In the narrative, she crosses Chesnut's radar, so to speak, during one of her very rare days off in the company of British artist, illustrator, journalist, and amateur theatrical booster Frank Vizetelly during the amateur theatrical craze mounted by Chesnut's female circle.

3. Classicist Richard Sacks points out that Homer characteristically deploys this simile with its attendant linguistic formulae to describe death on the battlefield. Yet here, the poet is invoking "dark mists" to represent Andromache's traumatized swoon; the fact that the subject of the simile is a female civilian rather than a male warrior and that she is not dead but only unconscious constitute two ways in which the phrasing marks a significant departure from Homeric convention, one worthy of literary critical attention.

4. When Chesnut records military events she often is motivated by direct connections, such as the involvement of her husband or personal friends in a particular battle or theater of war.

5. The 1880s Chesnut details how the Confederate army created Homeric, epithetic, nicknames for its most prominent generals. Thus, like swift-footed Achilles or rosy-fingered Dawn, Beauregard was known as "Engine" (because he was an artillery instructor); Johnston was the "Marlboro" of the engagement; and most significantly, Thomas J. Jackson became known forever more as "Stonewall" Jackson, because his men "stood so stock-still under fire" (July 24, 1861, 108).

Chesnut's keenness as a historian is remarkable, illustrated in the following entry in her narrative for February 16, 1864: "General Johnston writes that the governor of Georgia refuses him provisions and the use of his roads. The governor of Georgia writes, 'The roads are open to him and in capital condition,' and that he has furnished him abundantly with provisions from time to time, as he desired them. *I suppose both of these letters are placed side by side in our archives*" (569, my emphasis).

6. Elisabeth Muhlenfeld reports a wonderful detail about Chesnut's postwar reaccessioning of her husband's clothing when she describes a neighbor viewing that strange old lady gardening in pants decades after the surrender. See Muhlenfeld, *Mary Boykin Chesnut,* 5.
7. One might argue that when, in Richmond, Chesnut encounters the ghastly faces of paroled Confederate prisoners who are unable to look her in the eye, she is passing through another version of the underworld: "[T]hese men were so forlorn, so dried up, shrunken, such a strange look in some of their eyes. Others so restless and wild looking—others again, placidly vacant, as if they had been dead to this world for years" (March 24, 1864, 591). My focus in this chapter, however, is Chesnut's personal experience of undertaking the journey to the land of the dead; in this case, its ghosts have escaped to the upper regions where they continue to haunt the living.
8. See Kathleen Diffley, ed., *To Live and Die: Collected Stories of the Civil War, 1861–1876* (Durham: Duke University Press, 2002), 1.
9. Historian Alice Fahs offers readings of *Harper's Weekly* in *The Imagined Civil War: Popular Literature of North and South, 1861–1865* (Chapel Hill: University of North Carolina Press, 2001). In addition to Diffley's *To Live and Die,* see her monograph *Where My Heart Is Turning Ever: Civil War Stories and Constitutional Reform, 1861–1876* (Athens: University of Georgia Press, 1992).
10. The abolitionist Thomas Wentworth Higginson, a colonel in the Union army, describes the following very close call during his expedition up the Edisto River of South Carolina in the summer of 1863: "As my orderly stood leaning on a comrade's shoulder, the head of the latter was shot off." See Higginson, *Army Life in a Black Regiment* (1870), in *Army Life in a Black Regiment and Other Writings,* ed. R. D. Madison (Harmondsworth: Penguin Books, 1997), 136. In a narrative one might mistake for the work of Mark Twain, but in which humor is reserved for nonfatal episodes, Sam Watkins recalls with horror four different instances during his service as a private in the Army of Tennessee in which a man standing next to him in battle has his head shot off before his eyes. He also describes having his own hat and cartridge box shot up, and he is shot through the ankle, foot, and finger before war's end. See Watkins, *Company Atych: A Memoir of the Southern Confederacy* (New York: Plume, 1999).
11. Could Chesnut here be alluding to the scene in book 10 of *Paradise Lost* in which Sin and Death bite into what they think are apples and taste only ashes and wormwood? Milton writes: "There stood / A Grove hard by, sprung up with this thir change, / His will who reigns above, to aggravate / Thir penance, laden with fair Fruit, like that / Which grew in Paradise, the bait of *Eve* / Us'd by the Tempter" (lines 546–52). And then, "greedily they pluck'd / The Fruitage fair to sight, like that which grew / Near that bituminous Lake where *Sodom* flam'd; / This more delusive, not the touch, but taste / Deceiv'd, they fondly thinking to allay / Their appetite with gust, instead of Fruit / Chew'd bitter Ashes, which th' offended taste / With spattering noise rejected: Oft they assay'd, / Hunger and thirst constraining, drugg'd as oft, / With hatefullest disrelish writh'd thir jaws / With soot and cinders fill'd" (lines 561–70). See *John Milton: Complete Poems and Major Prose,* ed. Merritt Y. Hughes (Indianapolis: Bobbs-Merrill, 1957), 419–20.

12. In a situation worthy of Jane Austen, but with results far more dire for Mary Chesnut in the absence of a rescuer, an American Mr. Darcy, Colonel James Chesnut Sr.'s obsession with patrimony and patrilineage will prove his heirs' economic ruin.
13. In that regard, Sally is not unlike Odysseus, transformed by Athena into an old man for his initial return to Ithaca.
14. In his three-volume historical account of the conflict, *The Civil War: A Narrative* (New York: Vintage, 1986), Shelby Foote is particularly interested in noting those cases in which brothers or fathers and sons serve as military and naval officers on opposite sides of the conflict. I am thinking particularly of General J. E. B. Stuart, the Confederate cavalry phenomenon, whose father-in-law was the Union cavalry commander Brigadier General Philip St. George Cooke, whom Stuart actually faced in his famous "ride around McClellan" in 1862. Additionally, George Bibb Crittenden was a general for the Confederate army, while his brother, Thomas Leonidas Crittenden, served as a general in the Union army. The men were sons of John Crittenden, U.S. senator for the border state of Kentucky.
15. That a woman should report the death of her own children as if she were reading from a book surely is not the expected reaction to such loss. "As if reading it" suggests a profound shutting down of feeling. This moment relates to the writer's antisentimental project and her own ideas about the appropriate place and use of emotion. Apropos of her loathing of affective display, it is strange that an emotional eruption is exactly what she sees as missing in her sister's response. It is crucial to note that soon after this moment, Sally breaks down in hysterics; her stoicism ultimately masks a deferral of feeling rather than a lack of it. Perhaps the "reading of books" constitutes a prelude to real emotional experience.
16. Ironically, Achilles goes on to contradict this sentiment when he queries Odysseus about his son's fate and glories upon learning of Neoptolemos's heroic fame.
17. Or, perhaps, it would have made great sense. The function of the epic simile is to open out the scope of the object to which it refers by comparison with an altogether other realm of existence; such figures enlarge the scope of the epic universe. In Chesnut's 1880s narrative, associative digressions do much of the work of the similes that are building blocks of the epic, extending the range of connection between seemingly disparate realms analogically.
18. Such jobs were sinecures for which white men applied to the state legislature; often they then would hire out the actual labor to poor whites or blacks (slaves or freed people) for an hourly wage.

Chapter Three

1. See Gillian Brown's *Domestic Individualism: Imaging Self in Nineteenth-Century America* (Berkeley and Los Angeles: University of California Press, 1990), particularly the reading of various kitchen scenes in chapter 1 (13–38). Consider Stowe's own Eucharistic-Christic language as she describes the way the chicken parts frying in Rachel Halliday's pan have sacrificed their lives so that the fugitive family can share them with their Quaker hosts. Stowe's narrator observes: "[E]ven the knives and forks had a social clatter as they went on to the table; and the chicken and ham had a cheerful and joyous fizzle in the pan, as if

they rather enjoyed being cooked than otherwise." See *Uncle Tom's Cabin; or, Life among the Lowly,* ed. Ann Douglas (1852; Harmondsworth: Penguin Books, 1981), 223. All subsequent references to Stowe's work are to this edition.

2. *MCCW,* 190 n. 6. See also Muhlenfeld, *Mary Boykin Chesnut.*

3. In an entry from her diary of the 1860s, elided in the narrative and restored by Woodward, Chesnut writes: "«[These people] remind me of dogs, with eager eyes watching a man eating, with mouths open, watching to catch any bone, and snapping and quarreling at every other dog who comes near, for fear he should get anything. The miserable, degraded, money-loving, grasping spirit these poor people have from dogging this poor old man for forty years for his money»" (October 24, 1861, 223–24). Here we see the human parasitism that Patterson characterizes as operating at the heart of master-slave relations take on a white-on-white, intrafamilial form. In a Dantesque maneuver, Chesnut figures her niece Harriet Grant and other young Chesnut cousins as animals, eager to devour the flesh of their own. The 1860s diarist performs her own ideological reversal in describing white people as the subhuman, bestial, monstrous, stereotypes usually deployed by slaveholders to talk about African American bondspeople.

4. Buchanan wrote to the American minister to Great Britain, Louis McLane, "Mr. James Chesnut, junior, of South Carolina, who in pursuance of medical advice, has suddenly left our country for Europe accompanied by his lady & child." Buchanan misspoke, of course, in indicating that the Chesnuts were traveling with their child, as they were childless. See Muhlenfeld, *Mary Boykin Chesnut,* 56 n. 20, 234.

5. For Mary Cox Chesnut to "My dear children," August 29, 1845, see the Williams-Chesnut-Manning Collection, Caroliniana Library, University of South Carolina.

6. Ironically, the field itself developed from experiments that Dr. J. Marion Simms performed on slave women he culled from plantations near his Montgomery, Alabama, medical practice. He established a makeshift hospital in his yard for slaves afflicted with vesico-vaginal fistula and, through a protracted process of experimentation on them—with their consent and cooperation—he eventually developed a surgical technique to cure what previously had been understood as an intractable and life-destroying medical condition. Some of these slave women underwent up to fifty operations over the course of several years in order to secure a final "cure." Simms credits them as collaborators in his discovery, praising their heroic fortitude in enduring nearly unimaginable pain during surgery without anesthesia. Of course, only their first names—Betsey, Anarchia, Lucy, etc.—are preserved in his account. See J. Marion Simms, *The Story of My Life* (1884; New York: De Capo Press, 1968), 223–46.

7. See Charles M. McLane, M.D., and Midy McLane, "Half Century of Sterility," *Fertility and Sterility* 20, no. 6 (1969): 857.

8. There is little if any data on positive outcomes—pregnancies carried to term—as a result of these procedures. See Elaine Tyler May, *Barren in the Promised Land: Childless Americans and the Pursuit of Happiness* (New York: Basic Books, 1995), and Margaret Marsch and Wanda Ronner, *The Empty Cradle: Infertility in America from Colonial Times to the Present* (Baltimore: Johns Hopkins University Press, 1996).

9. In 1864, as I will discuss at length, little Joe Davis fell off an upper story piazza at the Confederate White House in Richmond and died. Langdon Cheves McCord, Louisa McCord's only son, was wounded badly at the battle of Second Manassas in 1862. Removed from the field and taken to Richmond to recover in the home of a family friend, he perished when a bullet that had lodged in his brain shifted positions unexpectedly.

10. While Chesnut experiences their comments as thoughtless and even cruel, it could be that what drives the older couple is grief over what they consider their *real* family line stopping with James's death. Although the estates would then devolve to Johnny Chesnut, eldest son of the late John Chesnut Jr., who died in 1838, the default heirs are his siblings in Florida for whom the old Colonel has little fondness. Thus, Mary Boykin Chesnut is wounded by the reminder of reproductive failure, but she may not see that her in-laws experience it not only as the loss of potential relationships but also as a dynastic disaster.

11. Old Mrs. Chesnut's language can be compared, usefully, to that of those sentimental women novelists and memoirists whose narratives are underwritten by gothic rage, figures such as Harriet E. Wilson, Harriet Jacobs, and Louisa May Alcott. That an aristocratic, slaveholding white woman in her nineties should share a sensibility with a former slave like Jacobs should seem unlikely, but it is in fact the case that the elder Mrs. Chesnut sympathizes with slave mothers wronged by an institution that looks the other way at the sexual abuse of bondswomen by white men.

12. Lucia Stanton, "Report on the Research Committee on Thomas Jefferson and Sally Hemings: Appendix H, Sally Hemings and Her Children, Information from Documentary Sources," January 2000 report from the Thomas Jefferson Foundation, Thomas Jefferson's Monticello (http://www.monticello.org/plantation/hemingscontro/appendixh.html - top).

13. While Colonel James Chesnut Sr.'s will mentions several Rachels in bequests of slaves to his three surviving children (James Chesnut Jr., Sarah "Sally" Chesnut, and Mrs. George [Mary Cox Chesnut] Reynolds), it is unclear whether any of these women is the "Rachel" of the 1860s diary's accusation. In the will a Chesnut slave "mantua maker" (dressmaker) called Tenah or Tena, whose mother and sister both are named Rachel, has been singled out with a small group of other slaves: James Sr. stipulates that they are never to be sold "for profit," even in the eventuality that family estates need to be broken up. Neither of these two related Rachels, nor any other slaves by that name, constitutes part of this special cohort. The will of James Chesnut Sr., drafted 1864, is held in the archives of the Kershaw County Probate Records, Kershaw County Court House, Camden, South Carolina.

14. See Hammond's extraordinarily incriminating autobiography, *Secret and Sacred: The Diaries of James Henry Hammond, Southern Slaveholder*, ed. Carol K. Blesser (New York: Oxford University Press, 1988), in which he confesses all of the above mentioned crimes, including miscegenation and incest.

15. In an attempt to answer this question, I have examined the pertinent holdings in the Caroliniana Library, University of South Carolina, the South Carolina State Archives, the Camden Archives and Historical Museum, and the Mulberry Plantation Archives, which have provided all of the primary source material used in this study.

16. Will of Colonel John Chesnut (1743–1818), 1816, privately owned; copy at the South Carolina State Department of Archives and History, South Carolina Will Transcripts, 1782–1868 (microcopy no. 9), series no. S108093, reel 0014, frame 00741, item 00, date 1818 / 04.
17. See Lennard J. Davis, "Dr. Johnson, Amelia, and the Discourse of Disability in the Eighteenth Century," in *Defects: Engendering the Modern Body,* ed. Helen Deutsch and Felicity Nussbaum (Ann Arbor: University of Michigan Press, 2000), 54–74, 74 n. 60. See also Virginia Woolf, *On Being Ill* (1926; Paris: Paris Press, 2002). I am grateful to Carole Slade for sharing this essay with me.
18. See Timothy O'Sullivan, "Harvest of Death, Gettysburg," in *Harpers' Weekly Magazine,* July 1863. This image is included as plate 36 in Alexander Gardner's *Photographic Sketch Book of the War* (1866; New York: Dover, 1959). See also Franny Nudelman, *John Brown's Body: Slavery, Violence, and the Culture of War* (Chapel Hill: University of North Carolina Press, 2004), particularly her discussion of "the grim reaper."
19. The fact that war-based anxiety appears to dull Decca's maternal impulses would have been particularly disturbing to Chesnut, given her heightened sensitivity to relations between mothers and children. In that regard, the scene evokes a literary counterpart from Susanna Haswell Rowson's best-selling novel, *Charlotte Temple,* which in its American incarnation (1794), inaugurated the sentimental novel tradition in the new republic. I am thinking of the titular heroine's deathbed ravings and her nonrecognition of her own newborn daughter. We know that Chesnut was familiar with Rowson's book from several entries in the 1880s narrative in which she conjures "Charlotte Temple" as a pseudonym for a seduced and abandoned woman in Camden whose fate compels old Mrs. Chesnut to the point of obsession.
20. Speaking of her kinswoman, Mary Boykin, whose husband has been wounded and whose son, Tom, has been captured (and will die in a Yankee prison), the writer notes: "Weeping, wailing women are pitiful enough—but save me, good Lord, from such cold, hard stony faces as Mary Boykin. She sits by her wounded husband, her eyes fixed, dead eyes, to all seemingly" (June 28, 1864, 618).
21. The fact that Robert Barnwell's death is recorded in the "Memoirs" section of the 1880s narrative makes precise dating within the thirteen-month range of September 1862–October 1863 impossible from internal evidence.
22. In an article about Civil War photography in the *New York Times,* July 21, 1862, the anonymous writer comments: "There is one side of the picture that the sun did not catch, one phase that escaped photographic skill. It is the background of widows and orphans, torn from the bosom of their natural protectors by the red remorseless hand of Battle. . . . All of this desolation imagination must paint—broken hearts cannot be photographed" (quoted in Timothy Sweet, *Traces of War: Poetry, Photography, and the Crisis of the Union* [Baltimore: Johns Hopkins University Press, 1990, 116]). See also Nudelman, *John Brown's Body.*
23. As Chesnut would have it, Sally Baxter Hampton has her doubts about the viability of the Confederacy; she is "wanting in faith of our ultimate success" (351).
24. See Elaine Scarry, *The Body in Pain: The Making and Unmaking of the World* (New York: Oxford University Press, 1985).

25. Jackson's body had been mutilated by the amputation of his left arm, surgery that should have saved his life after the battle of Chancellorsville, had he not then succumbed to pneumonia during the period of recovery. The manner in which he suffered his wound was itself novel-worthy: riding through the Chancellorsville battlefield immediately after sunset to scout the possibility of reprising the fighting later that night, Stonewall Jackson was mistaken for a Union officer and shot by pickets from a North Carolina regiment. Though his surgeon, Dr. Macguire, believed that removal of the destroyed left arm would enable him to survive the injury, he had not factored in postoperative vulnerability to infection, which apparently killed more Civil War soldiers than gunshot wounds themselves.

A report from the front page of the *Richmond Daily Dispatch,* Wednesday, May 13, 1863, describing the rituals attending Jackson's funeral offers a fascinating glimpse of Confederate protocol, including the fact that though the coffin was metallic, there was a glass door placed over the face, to facilitate final viewing:

> For hours after the coffin had been placed in the large hall thousands continued to crowd in and around the Capitol, awaiting their turn for a last look at the features fixed in death.—The coffin which contained the remains of the deceased was a metallic one, with glass door over the face.

26. In philosophical terms, this is a Hegelian encounter in which identity and difference meet on primal ground. Understood according to Lacanian psychoanalytic theory, the gaze into the mirror affords a nascent infantile self the (delusional but convincing) experience of totality and wholeness. And in the work of deconstructive literary theorist Paul de Man, such moments of face-to-face connection speak to the way in which autobiographical writing itself marks a defacement of identity: the narrating self and its narrated counterpart never can realign, since language itself (the signifier) stands in for the loss of presence, totality, and full meaning (the signified).

27. Cuthbert, only in his twenties, became another Confederate casualty after being shot leading his men at the battle of Chancellorsville in early May 1863. The plan was apparently for him to recover at the Chesnuts':

> [T]he surgeon did not think [Cuthbert] mortally wounded. He sent a message that he was coming at once to our house. He knew he would soon get well there. Also that I need not be alarmed; those Yankees could not kill him.
>
> He asked one of his friends to write a letter to his mother. Afterward he said he had another letter to write but that he wished to sleep first—he felt so exhausted. At his request they then turned his face away from the light and left him. When they came again to look after him, they found him dead. He had been dead for a long time. It was so bitter cold—and the wounded who had lost so much blood weakened in that way. ("Memoirs," September 23, 1863, 425)

28. See Adam Smith, *The Theory of Moral Sentiments,* ed. D. D. Raphael and A. L Macfie (1759; Indianapolis: Liberty Classics, 1982).

29. Sweet, *Traces of War,* 112.
30. Ibid., 117–18.
31. Ibid., 120–28.
32. See Gardner, *Photographic Sketch Book of the War,* plates 36, 37, and 4, respectively.
33. Scouring a vast array of late-eighteenth- through mid-nineteenth-century "sentimental flower books" from France, England, and the United States, Seaton has produced the most comprehensive treatment of this subject to date. See *The Language of Flowers: A History* (Charlottesville: University of Virginia Press, 1995); see also Marina Heilmeyer, *The Language of Flowers: Symbols and Myth,* trans. Stephen Telfer (Munich and Berlin: Prestel Verlag, 2006).
34. Seaton, *The Language of Flowers,* 180–81 (ivy), 184–85 (magnolias), 190–91 (roses).
35. Ibid., 180–81 (yellow jasmine), 184–85 (mulberry); 186–87 (oaks), 190–91 (roses), 196–97 (violets).
36. Of course, contemporary abolitionists and twenty-first-century critics alike would argue that the introduction of slavery onto the North American mainland denoted the advent of Satan into the New World garden; the Civil War simply brought the crisis to a culmination. Chesnut scholars would add that Mary Cox Chesnut—such an advocate for the human rights of her husband's slaves—obviously had as little power (or perhaps, inclination) to free her husbands' bondspeople as she did to prevent "the fall" that was the onset of the Civil War in 1861.
37. Here, of course, I echo not only *Hamlet* but *Lear,* the play that Chesnut herself returns to again and again as she writes the fate of the Confederacy.
38. Seaton, *The Language of Flowers,* 194–95.
39. Ibid., 174–75 (green boughs). While the Davises are no strangers to loss, Joe is the only one of their children to die accidentally. After years of failing to conceive, Varina Davis apparently underwent at least two miscarriages. She finally gave birth to a living child, a boy named Samuel, seven years after her marriage, who perished from measles before his second birthday. Then followed Maggie, Jeff Jr., Joe, William, and Varina Anne. William died of diphtheria at ten; Jeff Jr. lived to young adulthood but was killed by yellow fever; this left only Maggie and "Winnie" (the nickname of the Davises' youngest and most famous child, the so-called "Daughter of the Confederacy"). Throughout her entire life her mother's constant companion, Winnie broke an engagement to a Northern man she adored (and of whom her father's former constituency disapproved on regional grounds) after his home mysteriously burned and he went bankrupt. Winnie became the living and working surrogate for Jefferson Davis after his death, embodying the "Lost Cause" about which she remembered nothing (she was born in 1864) and the region in which she had not lived (she was educated in Germany). At thirty-three, during a Daughters of the Confederacy engagement in Rhode Island, Winnie caught a terrible cold and, soon afterward, died of pneumonia. Varina never forgave the DOC for what she considered their role in Winnie's death. Only Maggie Davis Hayes outlived her parents. See Joan Cashin, *First Lady of the Confederacy: Varina Davis's Civil War* (Cambridge: Harvard University Press, 2006).
40. See Seaton, *The Language of Flowers,* 180.

41. See Nina Silber, *The Romance of Reunion: Northerners and the South, 1865–1900* (Chapel Hill: University of North Carolina Press, 1993).
42. Woodward explains: "Anticipating more than one 'defeat,' M.B.C. has in mind J.C.'s approaching contest in the S.C. legislature for the Confederate Senate, as well as her hopes for the Paris or London [Confederate diplomatic] appointments" (for deleted passage «August 13, 1861», *MCCW,* 142 n. 5). James Chesnut's campaign adviser, Mary Chesnut's uncle Alexander Hamilton Boykin, apparently out of touch with the shifting political winds, failed to realize that the center of power in the state had shifted away from the northeast counties that James Jr. had represented and, accordingly, overlooked doing what would have been necessary to assure his election. In this defeat, as in the case of the various other career disappointments her husband underwent during the war years, including not being chosen as minister to either England or France, her real heart's desire, Mary Chesnut experienced the setback much more viscerally and emotionally than did he.

Chapter Four

1. Mary Chesnut never was in danger of real starvation during and immediately after the Civil War. In the fall of 1864, had she been willing to return to Mulberry, with its abundant gardens and livestock remaining in nearly full supply, the problem of sufficient provisions would not have been an issue. But shortages were a real concern in the cities of the South, where Chesnut chose to remain until the eleventh hour. Even then, elites managed to obtain and share food, just as Chesnut was rescued by the unknown Mrs. McDonald. Most severely affected were the urban poor, who had no provision gardens on which to rely. And the greatest suffering was experienced by recently emancipated impoverished blacks who had not yet been paid for their now (free) labor and who found sky-high prices for what little produce and staple goods there were in the stores.
2. Indeed, after the war, the Prestons returned to Europe, their fortunes shattered with the loss of their Louisiana sugar plantations after the fall of New Orleans in 1862.
3. Among his various commissions, Powers sculpted a portrait bust of Buck Preston, Chesnut's favorite among the Preston family's daughters, who plays an important supporting role in the 1880s narrative. The mutilated bust is held by the Columbia Historical Foundation, and Woodward includes a photograph of the piece in his edition, following page 156.
4. Sociologist and French scholar Priscilla Parkhurst Ferguson explores the ways in which Parisian cuisine became a universal language for "culture" in her *Accounting for Taste: The Triumph of French Cuisine* (Chicago: University of Chicago Press, 2005). Ferguson notes in passing that *dindon aux truffes* was a standard of the nineteenth-century repertoire.
5. For material on Chesnut's various medical conditions, I have consulted the following works: Charles F. Wooley, *The Irritable Heart of Soldiers and the Origins of Anglo-American Cardiology: The U.S. Civil War (1861) to World War I (1918)* (London: Ashgate, 2002); James Bradley and A. McGee Harvey, *Two Centuries of American Medicine: 1776–1976* (Philadelphia: W. B. Sanders Company, 1976), particularly chap. 23, "Cardiovascular Diseases";

Science and Medicine in the Old South, ed. Ronald L. Numbers and Todd L. Savitt (Baton Rouge: Louisiana State University Press, 1989). I am grateful to Megan Glick for identifying these important sources from the history of medicine.

6. Muhlenfeld, *Mary Boykin Chesnut,* 55.
7. See Karen Hess, *The Carolina Rice Kitchen: The African Connection* (Columbia: University of South Carolina Press, 1998); see also Judith Carney, *Black Rice: The African Origins of Rice Cultivation in the Americas* (Cambridge: Harvard University Press, 2001); and for what scholars believe is the first cookbook published by a black woman (dictated to white amanuenses, as the author could not read or write), see Abby Fisher, *What Mrs. Fisher Knows about Southern Cooking,* ed. Karen Hess ([Carlisle, MA]: Applewood Books, 1993).
8. The cultural diversity Chesnut reports among the mistress class is wider than one would imagine: for every Louisa McCord or Varina Davis there is also the sort of mistress whose calling for her slaves across three fields from her veranda constitutes a sort of local scandal.
9. See Ira Berlin, *Many Thousands Gone: The First Two Centuries of Slavery in North America* (Cambridge: Harvard University Press, 2000), 232.
10. I read this as a fantasy in which the senior Mrs. Chesnut's thwarts the apparition of pure whiteness at table in favor of blending the pallid rice or hominy with tints of red or green (tomato or cucumber relishes were the most common such flavor enhancers served at the Southern table in the second half of the nineteenth century). By so doing, the Northerner who spends her entire adult life wanting to "make it up to the negroes for being slaves" also obviates the Manichean color palette of the peculiar institution. Abby Fisher actually was famous for the sale of her relishes and preserves, developed during her time as a slave cook on a South Carolina plantation before the War; see *What Mrs. Fisher Knows.* See also E. Merton Coulter, *The Confederate Receipt Book* (Athens: University of Georgia Press, 1981).
11. See Lydia Maria Child, *The American Frugal Housewife* (1844; repr. from 29th ed., New York: Dover, 1999), "Common Cakes," 70–76, and "Breads, Yeast, &c," 76–80. Child includes only two recipes for what I would call savory cakes—pancakes and Indian cakes—her closest cognate to Southern buttered biscuits. Her list of breads is even more terse, containing only brown bread, flour bread, dyspepsia bread, and rice bread.

    Child mentions nothing resembling what became known as Parker House rolls, which originated during the 1870s at Boston's Parker House Hotel. These breadstuffs "are made by folding a butter-brushed round of dough in half; when baked, the roll has a pleasing abundance of crusty surface. Recipes for Parker House rolls first appeared in cookbooks during the 1880s" (*Oxford Encyclopedia of Food and Drink in America,* vol. 1, ed. Andrew F. Smith [New York: Oxford University Press, 2004], 117).
12. Rice first was brought to the North American mainland from Africa. Geographer Judith Carney notes that slave laborers kidnapped and transported in the charter generations actually taught white planters the secrets of the grain's successful cultivation across a variety of "microenvironments" such as swamp paddies and tidewater plots, and eventually in the creation of complexly engineered irrigation gates, sluices, and embankments. Carney's

Black Rice constitutes the first detailed history of what she calls the "African knowledge system" that transformed the agricultural fate of South Carolina from the seventeenth century to the 1930s. Sweet potatoes (and not yams, for which they often are mistaken) were introduced in a similar fashion, with African slaves transmitting the agricultural techniques of their home lands to the very people who held them in bondage. See also Berlin, *Many Thousands Gone.*

13. See Patterson, *Slavery and Social Death.*
14. Early in the 1880s narrative, Chesnut notes that though Johnny has had two blacks arrested for selling liquor and stolen corn to the slaves on his plantation, he is a "pretty softhearted slave-owner." She continues: "The culprits in jail sent for him. He found them (this snowy weather) lying in the cold on a bare floor. And he thought they had punishment enough, they having had weeks of it. But they were not satisfied to evade justice and slip away. They begged him (and got it) for five dollars to buy shoes to run away in. I said, 'Why, that is compounding a felony!' And Johnny put his hands in the armholes of his waistcoat and stalked majestically before me. 'Woman, what do you know about law?'" (March 19, 1861, 32).
15. Entire studies have been devoted to Southern food shortages during the Civil War. Particularly illuminating are Mary Elizabeth Massey, *Ersatz in the Confederacy: Shortages and Substitutes on the Southern Home Front* (Columbia: University of South Carolina Press, 1993), and Coulter, *The Confederate Receipt Book,* both of which detail the ways in which people coped with deprivation by substituting unexpected commodities for the luxuries of yore, such as corn for coffee.
16. In his exploration of the biology of starvation, scientist Ancel Keyes reports that the same phenomenon occurred in World War II prisoners who underwent severe food deprivation. See Keyes, *The Biology of Human Starvation* (Minneapolis: University of Minnesota Press, 1950).
17. See Dr. Nathaniel Chapman, "Remarks on the Chronic Fluxes of the Bowels," reprinted in *Medical America in the Nineteenth Century: Readings From Literature,* ed. Gert H. Brieger (Baltimore: Johns Hopkins University Press, 1972): 107–14; for calomel and Dover's pills as therapy, see 112. Calomel is a purgative and was the powder used by slaves to slowly murder Dr. Keitt, a miniature instance of slave uprising discussed in chapter 9.
18. Ibid., 113. Chapman's remark about the use of blackberries to combat diarrhea helps make sense of why it would have been the case that Chesnut's surviving niece associated the eating of this fruit with her sister's death; the ailing Katie, I hypothesize, had been consuming the berries to treat her stomach disease.
19. See John Hammond Moore, *The Confederate Housewife: Receipts and Suggestions, Together with Sundry Suggestions for Garden, Farm & Plantation* (Columbia: Summerhouse Press, 1977), 103.
20. Ibid., 104
21. Professor Richard Wallace, lecture on Renaissance painting and iconography, "Introduction to Western Art, II," Wellesley College, spring semester, 1978. The language of flowers also associates the peach blossom with constancy (Seaton, *The Language of Flowers,* 188).

22. See Susan Williams, *Savory Suppers and Fashionable Feasts: Dining in Victorian America* (Knoxville: University of Tennessee Press, 1996), 113. In regard to the gentlemen's responsibilities for dressing the salad, Williams is quoting cookbook author Eliza Leslie, *The Ladies' Guide to True Politeness and Perfect Manners* (Philadelphia: T. B. Peterson & Brothers, 1864), 128; cited in Williams, 113 n. 37.
23. Moore, *The Confederate Housewife*, 103.
24. Brought to North from South America during what geographer Judith Carney calls the "Columbian Exchange," her field's hypothetical term for how seeds were dispersed in the fifteenth century, tomatoes became a new world staple. See Carney, *Black Rice*, 12.
25. See Hess, *The Carolina Rice Kitchen*, afterword.
26. Civil War literary scholar Jane E. Schultz has called this a "deus ex cuchina," emphasizing the ways in which Chesnut's epic is attuned to the world of domesticity within the universe of war.
27. Letter from Mary Boykin Miller Chesnut to her niece-in-law, Jane Pettigrew Williams, Princeton, Indiana, August 16, 1885, unpublished, quoted by permission of the Mulberry Plantation Archives, Camden, South Carolina.
28. Only twenty years earlier, slaveowners like Chesnut worried that they might die at the hands of their servants, and poisoning was a particular threat in which they imagined unsatisfied black bondspeople conspiring. St. Domingo's first, inchoate slave conspiracy, concocted by MacIndal in the eighteenth century, involved a plan to poison the well water of every white family in a certain area of the island. Days before the plot was to have commenced, the ringleader got drunk and blurted out his plans, upon which, he was captured, tried and executed. See C. L. R. James, *The Black Jacobins* (1937; New York: Vintage, 1963), 21.
29. Chesnut will bequeath Olly and another Jersey cow, Flora, to niece Serena Chesnut Williams Harrison, daughter of Kate's daughter Mary Williams Harrison Ames (Mamie of the 1880s narrative). Chesnut's 1886 will is filed in the Kershaw County Courthouse, Camden, South Carolina.
30. Parkinson's *The Complete Confectioner, Pastry Cook, and Baker* (Philadelphia: J. B. Lippincott, 1864) provides the following recipes:

> *Macaroon:* Prepare your mixture as for almond cakes (but do not cut your almonds), and add two spoonfuls of orange-flower water, in an oval shape; sift sugar over them, and bake them in a rather brisk oven; when lightly coloured over, they are done. (114)

> *Almond Cakes.*—Take one pound of sweet Valentia, or Provence almonds—cover them with boiling water, and rub them out of their skins; cut about two ounces of them into thin slices; put the rest into a mortar, with one pound and a half of loaf sugar, the whites of six eggs, and one table-spoon full of orange-flower water; pound it fine; lay your wafer-paper on the tin, and drop your almond cakes on it about the size of a walnut—then drop a few of your cut almonds on each of them, and bake them in a slow oven. (110–11)

31. And in a moment of historical double vision, perhaps the 1880s writer amplified the self-punitive effects of a gastronomic act from the 1860s that symbolically reenacted the way she had devoured the labor of her slaves before and during the war. Her sick stomach represented the inability to swallow the reality of her complicity.

Chapter Five

1. Chesnut calls this unnamed author "Mrs. Saxon" in the 1860s diary—itself an almost allegorical appellation for a writer working in English—but excises the name in the 1880s. This move accords with her overall practice: where in the jottings of the 1860s she names names, in the 1880s, she bestows anonymity on those figures whom she represents negatively. The 1880s narrative assiduously avoids even minor slights to the reputations of her former Confederate peers, much less cruelty or revenge.
2. Indeed, just as distortions of language in minstrel performances offer a critique of conventional assumptions about the relation of race and class, so Mary Chesnut's satire exposes pretensions of class and education in the Southern white elite of which she is a member.
3. The 1860s diary reveals that the woman is Mary Lang Boykin, Chesnut's cousin on her mother's side.
4. Though these remarks were intended to represent Chesnut's feelings at age thirty-nine, she actually penned them in the last years of her life, when she was in her early sixties. Despite the double vision produced by the process of imaginatively reworking her 1860s Civil War diary twenty years after Confederate defeat, it was also the case that Chesnut *felt* old in her forties, immersed in a cultural milieu that elevated female youth and beauty to the ultimate status and rendered nearly invisible those older and less blessed.
5. This is one of the rare remarks Chesnut makes in any of her writings suggesting that she believed that her family's blacks felt that a war fought and won for the welfare of African Americans need not have been waged at all.
6. Thomas's actions are described by Drew Gilpin Faust in her introduction to the late-twentieth-century edition of the book. See Augusta Jane Evans, *Macaria; or, Altars of Sacrifice,* ed. Drew Gilpin Faust (1864; Baton Rouge: Louisiana State University Press, 1992), x.
7. Muhlenfeld has identified several essay drafts on the subject of Stowe's book that she believes Chesnut composed well after the war in rehearsal for the pervasive anti-Stowe thematic of the literary manuscript of the 1880s. The most comprehensive holdings of Chesnut's major and miscellaneous works can be found in the Caroliniana Library at the University of South Carolina, Columbia.
8. See Douglas, *The Feminization of American Culture.* In subsequent essays of the early 1980s, particularly her introductions for the Penguin editions of *Uncle Tom's Cabin* and *Charlotte Temple and Lucy Temple,* Douglas tempers her earlier, skeptical view of what Jane Tompkins has called "sentimental power" (see *Sensational Designs: The Cultural Work of American Fiction, 1790–1860* [New York: Oxford University Press, 1985]), and instead argues that the sentimental work of best sellers like Stowe's and Susanna Rowson's did have the cultural authority to transform women's minds.

9. Chesnut also had read the novels of William Gilmore Simms, the tall tales of Augustus Longstreet, and the poetry of Southern laureates Henry Timrod and Paul Hayne and expressed no bias against writers hailing from her native region. I believe that it was Evans's sentimentalism and her ability to generate huge sales that turned Chesnut against her work.
10. It is significant to note, however, that nothing she cites in the 1880s manuscript was published after 1865. Indeed, the latest George Eliot novel that we know she has read (for a second time!) is *Romola,* published in 1863, and "all the rage" abroad; apparently, Lucius Quintus Lamar gives her a life of radical monk Savonarola to get her "tuned up" for *Romola*'s fifteenth-century Florentine religious context.
11. Consider the way in which Isabella Martin barely figures in the 1860s diary but becomes a major character in the second half of the 1880s narrative, often articulating the somewhat unspeakable material that Chesnut herself was thinking or expressing in the Civil War era jottings.
12. See Kenneth S. Lynn's review of Woodward's then new edition of Chesnut, "The Masterpiece That Became a Hoax," chap. 6 of *The Airline to Seattle: Studies in Literary and Historical Writing about America* (Chicago: University of Chicago Press, 1981), 50–59.
13. It is challenging for the reader to reconcile the fact that Chesnut called for realism in her 1880s narrative but also cut the infamous "dropped from the clouds" passage that made her 1860s diary famous—in large part as a result of documentarian Ken Burns's significant use of the quotation in *The Civil War.* (In reediting the passage to suit his narrative purposes, Burns himself elided some crucially subtle sentences, though his bowdlerization lies beyond the scope of this argument). In the 1860s diary, Chesnut says that "only nasty women" like Stowe, whose story of Cassy's sexual servitude to Simon Legree particularly horrifies her, discuss slavery's sexual politics. This principle may constitute another reason that Chesnut is unwilling to write more explicitly about which white man or men she has in mind as "visiting the quarters." In the 1880s text, Chesnut continues to write about sex, particularly interracial intercourse, as "nasty and coarse." Accordingly, perhaps excising the "dropped from the clouds" passage had less to do with concealing a particular white patriarchal offender than preserving her authorial integrity in a work she meant for publication. In defining herself against Mrs. Stowe, perhaps the genteel Chesnut did not want to present herself as nasty and coarse as she imagined the vulgar and economically grasping author of *Uncle Tom's Cabin* to be. In a final irony, Chesnut's lineal descendant Martha Williams Daniels reports that portraits of Stowe and Chesnut hang in close proximity in a space devoted to prominent nineteenth-century American women in the National Gallery of Art in Washington, D.C. Curatorial history for some time has achieved what literary history only now attempts.
14. *Adam Bede* (1859) is the story of stalwart and decent British carpenter in love with a dairymaid who is seduced and abandoned by a member of the local gentry, has his illegitimate baby, exposes it to the elements, is tried for infanticide, and has her death sentence commuted to transportation when the baby's father returns from the army and testifies on her behalf. Hetty Sorrel is aided in prison by the love and faith of itinerant female Methodist

preacher, Dinah, who had lived on the farm where they both had labored as nieces of the family. Adam realizes that he loves Dinah, who secretly has been enamored of him for years; they marry and have a child, also called Adam, and she is forced to give up itinerant preaching when the Methodist Conference rescinds the privileges it once had afforded women.

The Mill on the Floss (1860) recounts the economic disaster of a mill-owning family in a small English town, whose patriarch comes to be ruined as a result of his obsession with entering lawsuits over petty matters. George Eliot traces the fate of his two children, Tom Tulliver, who self-sacrificially takes up his father's cause, goes to work, and eventually restores the mill; and Maggie Tulliver, intellectually superior to and better educated than any woman in the community, who loves her brother devotedly but comes to be emotionally involved with his father's enemy's disabled son, Philip Wakem. Tom has forbidden Maggie and Philip's connection just as a second suitor appears: Stephen Guest, son of the richest man in town. Maggie is tricked into eloping with Guest (after several days trapped on a barge, she is sent back home unscathed, but the townspeople will not believe she is not ruined). In the novel's denouement, the river begins to flood, catastrophically, and in their attempt to escape in a small boat, Maggie and Tom are drowned, clutching each other in a quasi incestuous embrace.

15. The idea that none other than Mrs. Stowe herself served as the chief muckraker in the affair in which Byron was accused of incest in his romance with his half sister was enough for Chesnut to throw the matter out without a second thought.

16. When William Tecumseh Sherman telegraphed to Lieutenant General Grant to request permission to continue the campaign through the Carolinas, he concluded, "I can make this march, and make Georgia howl!" Telegram dated Oct. 9, 1864, quoted in William Tecumseh Sherman, *Personal Memoirs of Gen'l W. T. Sherman*, 4th ed. (Charles L. Webster: New York, 1892), 2:152.

17. In the final hundred pages of what becomes the printed version of her 1880s manuscript, Chesnut records a litany of "howling" activity: of slave children; inhabitants of Columbia; and herself (641, 642, 734, 750, 752). In the penultimate entry of this series, for March 8, 1865, she writes: "Without any warning the band crashed out in a thunder of military music. I sprang into the floor as if I was shot and gave a howl of agony worthy of an Irish wake." The last notation in the 1880s narrative is for April 15, 1865, the day that Abraham Lincoln died, though Chesnut was unaware of the fact. In this final howl, Chesnut seems to be identifying with a soldier wounded on the field of battle as well as with Catherine, the Irish nursemaid who was supposed to have been attending little Joe Davis when he fell to his death. It is at this moment that Mary Boykin Chesnut becomes King Lear himself—a bare forked animal. She will, of course, recover and go on to create her epic Civil War narrative.

18. The theory that the king had "two bodies," that of the mortal man and a second self that stood for the state and was immortal, via the divine right of kings, was developed by Ernst H. Kantorowitz, *The King's Two Bodies* (1957; repr., Princeton: Princeton University Press, 1997).

Chapter Six

1. I borrow these terms from Bloom, who describes the struggle of younger poets with their larger-than-life precursors as poetic "agons," the Greek term for a contest for a prize, often between a protagonist and an antagonist, in a literary drama.

    It is also a convention of the epic form that it revise a precursor: thus, in the *Iliad*, Homer engages the oral tradition of Greek mythology and tales of the Trojan War; in the *Odyssey*, he revises Odysseus's fate at Troy into an entirely other narrative of wandering and homecoming; and in the *Aeneid*, Virgil takes up the *Odyssey* in his first six books, and the *Iliad* in his second, transforming his Homeric precursors in profound and fascinating ways. The principle extends to Dante's numerous epic borrowings from Virgil in the *Divine Comedy* and to Milton's use of both the Roman and the Italian motifs in *Paradise Lost*. One of the most important characteristics of the epic is its cannibalistic use and transformation of the prior poetic, or in Chesnut's use of Stowe, the narrative, tradition to which it aspires.

2. See Cindy Weinstein, "Stowe and the South," in *The Cambridge Companion to Harriet Beecher Stowe*, ed. Cindy Weinstein (New York: Oxford University Press, 2004), 39–57; see also her superb chronology xi–xiv. Stowe became most familiar with the Deep South after buying property in Florida in 1868, on which she developed an orange plantation. She had encouraged her n'er-do-well, alcoholic son Fred, who had suffered a head wound during the Civil War from which he never recovered, to take up farming there in a cooperative venture; and she became so enchanted with the climate and the freedom of uncultivated land that she threw in herself with some of the profits from her writing. She and her husband, Calvin, would winter there for over a decade.

3. Hedrick calls Stowe's book a work of "literary realism." I would characterize the novel as a sentimental epic built variously of comic satire, local color, political and evangelical polemic, and Christian tragedy. Realism was a term used by Stowe's contemporaries to describe the effect of her critique of slavery and American quietude on the subject. On Stowe, see Joan Hedrick, *Harriet Beecher Stowe: A Life* (New York: Oxford University Press, 1994), 81.

4. Hedrick's biography, my central source for historical material about Stowe's life, does not elaborate on the way in which the writer worked out wages for potential domestic employees who were hirelings. It is not clear whether Stowe paid the slave-workers directly, or whether she remunerated their masters, who then were expected to give their bondspeople a proportion of the wage. But the fugitive who worked for the family for a time and then was aided in flight by Calvin Stowe and Henry Ward Beecher obviously received her earnings directly from Mrs. Stowe.

5. See Hedrick, *Harriet Beecher Stowe*, 121.

6. In an entry for March 17, 1862 (311), Chesnut refers to Wade Hampton III's tales of his aunt Camilla, whose treatment of her slaves leads him to describe her as "beStowed."

7. See McCord, "*Uncle Tom's Cabin*," in the *Southern Quarterly Review*, n.s. 7 (Jan. 1853): 81–120, reprinted in *Louisa S. McCord: Political and Social Essays*, ed. Richard C. Lounsbury (Charlottesville: University of Virginia Press, 1995), 244–80.

8. Judge John Belton O'Neall, a justice of the South Carolina State Supreme Court, published comments in refutation of *Uncle Tom's Cabin* in 1853, the same year that Louisa McCord published her review of the book in the *Southern Quarterly Review*. He writes: "Generally slaves at the south are treated with more kindness, have more comforts and more money of their own than free servants at the north or in Europe. This may be denied. I have only to say to Mrs. Stowe and all who think as she does, come and see. Visit Charleston, Columbia, Camden, Governor Aiken's plantation, at Jehossee; Colonel Hampton's near Columbia; *Colonel Chesnut's near Camden,* and the whole upper part of the state, and see if the institution of slavery be as depicted in 'Uncle Tom' or the 'key,' make it known far and wide. But if not, do us justice. We ask no more" (Springfield, S.C, July 1853). These comments about Stowe's novel were later included in his book, *The Annals of Newberry* (1858). Thomas H. Pope reprinted them in his own *History of Newberry County, S.C.* (Columbia: University of South Carolina Press, 1973), my emphasis.
9. See Tompkins, *Sensational Designs*.
10. This tradition famously begins with James Baldwin's "Everybody's Protest Novel," and is summarized by Kenneth Warren in his essay "The Afterlife of *Uncle Tom's Cabin*," in Weinstein, *The Cambridge Companion to Harriet Beecher Stowe*, 219–34.
11. See Jefferson Davis, *The Rise and Fall of the Confederate Government,* foreword by James M. McPherson (1881; repr., New York: Da Capo Press, 1990), 2, part 4: 161–62.
12. McPherson, foreword to Davis's *The Rise and Fall of the Confederate Government,* iii–iv, quoted in David W. Blight, *Race and Reunion: The Civil War in American Memory* (Cambridge: Harvard University Press, 2001), 259.
13. The phrase was coined in 1866 by Pollard, in a book called *The Lost Cause: A New Southern History of the Confederates,* and promulgated in the articles on the subject written by former Confederate general Jubal Early. For one of the topic's more recent exegetes, who offers a good bibliography on the subject, see Blight, *Race and Reunion*. See also essays in the collection edited by Gary W. Gallagher and Alan T. Nolan, *The Myth of the Lost Cause and Civil War History* (Bloomington: Indiana University Press, 2000).
14. Blight, *Race and Reunion,* 259.
15. See Douglas, *The Feminization of American Culture,* 307.
16. See Cindy Weinstein, *Family, Kinship, and Sympathy in Nineteenth-Century American Fiction* (New York: Cambridge University Press, 2004), and Sarah Mesle, "Sentimental Literature in Proslavery America," dissertation in progress, Department of English, Northwestern University.
17. Janice Carlisle, *Common Scents: Comparative Encounters in High-Victorian Fiction* (New York: Oxford University Press, 2004), 4, 27, and 43. Carlisle is quoting from Freud's 1917 essay "Mourning and Melancholia," though I believe that she has confused incorporation with introjection.
18. See Julie Saville, *The Work of Reconstruction: From Slave to Wage Laborer in South Carolina, 1860–1870* (New York: Cambridge University Press, 1994); for the case of southwest Georgia, where newly freed blacks possibly fared worst of all, see Susan O'Donovan, *Becoming Free in the Cotton South* (Cambridge: Harvard University Press, 2007).

19. See Linda Kerber, *Women of the Republic: Intellect and Ideology in Revolutionary America* (Chapel Hill: University of North Carolina Press, 1980). See also Rosemarie Zagarri, "Morals, Manners, and the Republican Mother," *American Quarterly* 44, no. 2 (Jun. 1992): 192–215.
20. *Gazette of the United States,* Wednesday, April 22–Saturday, April 25, 1789, issue 4; p. 15. In this and the following quotation, minor typographical errors have been corrected and archaic orthography eliminated.
21. *Gazette of the United States,* Saturday, April 25–Wedesday, April 29, 1789, issue 5, p. 19.
22. See Tom Hester, "The Great Man Returns," *Star-Ledger,* April 23, 1789 [September 9, 2001], 1–3, part 22 of *The Center of the Storm,* a series of articles published in 2001 by the *Star-Ledger,* in conjunction with the New Jersey Historical Society and New Jersey Network Public Television, in honor of the 225 anniversary of the signing of the Declaration of Independence (http://www.nj.com/specialprojects/index.ssf?/specialprojects/revwar/rev22.html).
23. Letter 732, [Stockton], Harriet Chesnut Grant to Mary Boykin Chesnut, April 3, 1864, privately held, Mulberry Plantation.
24. The death of Abraham and Mary Lincoln's eleven-year-old son Willie from typhoid fever in 1862 makes an apt counterpoint here. Consider the following newspaper account of the national void left by his death: "The White House has been thrown into mourning and grief by the death of the second eldest son of the President, William Wallace Lincoln, an exceedingly intelligent and lovely youth of eleven years, whose bright though brief example is worthy of imitation by all the youth of our land" ("Decease of the President's Son," *Farmer's Cabinet* [Amherst, N.H.], February 27, 1862, issue 31, p. 2).

Popular magazine writer Nathaniel Parker Willis, brother of Sara Willis Payton (Fanny Fern), composed a touching eulogy of Willie Lincoln, published in the *Home Journal* and extracted in the *Farmer's Cabinet* for one month later (March 27, 1862, vol. 60, issue 35, p. 1): "He was his father's favorite. They were intimates—often seen hand in hand. And there sat the man, with a burden on his brain at which the world marvels—but now with the load at both brain and heart—staggering under a blow like the taking from him this child!" Not only did North and South "read the same bible and pray to the same God," as Lincoln noted in his Second Inaugural Address, two years after losing Willie; both looked to their respective first families as living symbols of the republic; thus, the loss of these well-loved little boys tugged on national, as a well as domestic, heartstrings.

Chapter Seven

1. Historians of slavery continue to argue over the political efficacy of daily slave practice. Is resistance the opposite of survival? Do the terms exist on a continuum? For more on the issue of slave challenges to white power, see Philip Morgan, *Slave Counterpoint: Black Culture in the Eighteenth-Century Chesapeake and Low-Country* (Chapel Hill: University of North Carolina Press, 1998).
2. The issue of Confederate nationalism has a lengthy and complex scholarly history, which lies beyond the scope of this chapter. For important recent treatments of this subject, see

Drew Gilpin Faust, *The Creation of Confederate Nationalism: Ideology and Identity in the Civil War South; The Walter Lynwood Fleming Lectures in Southern History* (Baton Rouge: Louisiana State University Press, 1990); Gallagher and Nolan, *The Myth of the Lost Cause;* and Blight, *Race and Reunion.*

3. My discussion of Civil War theatricals in black and white is inspired by the work of dramatic historian and theorist Joseph Roach, who defines performance as "'restored behavior' or 'twice-behaved behavior,' behavior that must be reinvented the second time . . . because it cannot happen exactly the same way twice." In that regard, Chesnut's reworkings of her 1860s diary into the narrative of the 1880s must themselves be understood as textual performances. "Performance," Roach continues, "offers a substitution for something else that pre-exists it. Performance, in other words, stands in for an elusive entity that it is not that it must vainly aspire both to embody and to replace." See Roach, *Cities of the Dead: Circum Atlantic Performance* (New York: Columbia University Press, 1996), 3.

4. Saidiya V. Hartman writes: "How does one determine the difference between 'putting on ole massa'—the simulation of compliance for covert aims—and the grins and gesticulations of Sambo indicating the repressive construction of contented subjection? At the level of appearance, these contending performances often differed little. At the level of effect, however, they diverged radically. One performance aimed to reproduce and secure the relations of domination and the other to manipulate appearances in order to challenge these relations and create a space for action not generally available." See Hartman, *Scenes of Subjection: Terror, Slavery, and Self-Making in Nineteenth-Century America* (New York: Oxford University Press, 1997), 12.

5. Chesnut's father, Stephen Decatur Miller, was chosen as governor of South Carolina in 1828 and elected to the United States Senate in 1830; he resigned his Senate seat in 1833 as the result of ill health.

6. Eugene Genovese remarks: "[T]he political danger to the whites became apparent. 'The negroes are in every family,' said David Bard of Pennsylvania in 1804 while leading a fight to tax slave imports in order to restrict the size of the slave population. 'They are waiting on every table; they are present on numerous occasions when the conversation turns on political subjects, and cannot fail to catch ideas that will excite discontentment with their condition.'" Genovese concludes: "The desertions to the Union lines could never have proceeded so far had the field slaves not been well informed by the house servants about the course of the war and the shifting battle lines." See Genovese, *Roll, Jordan, Roll,* 341–42, quoting Bard, *Annals of Congress,* 8th Cong., 1st sess., 995–96, quoted in Winthrop Jordan, *White Over Black: American Attitudes Toward the Negro, 1550–1812* (New York: W. W. Norton, 1968), 388.

7. See Eric J. Sundquist, *To Wake the Nations: Race in the Making of American Literature* (Cambridge: Harvard University Press, Belknap Press, 1993), 40–42; also Patterson, *Slavery and Social Death,* 97–100, 336–37. And, see as well Hegel's *Phenomenology of Spirit,* trans. A.V. Miller (Oxford: Oxford University Press, 1977), B.iv.a, "Interdependence and dependence of self-consciousness: Lordship and bondage," 111–19.

8. Bertram Wyatt-Brown writes, "Behind the mask of docility, the male slave was still himself and gave the lie to southern claims of 'knowing' their blacks. As W. J. Cash pointed out,

'even the most unreflecting must sometimes feel suddenly, in dealing with him, that they were looking at a blank wall, that behind that grinning face a veil was drawn which no white man might certainly know he had penetrated.'" See Wyatt-Brown, "The Mask of Obedience: Male Slave Psychology in the Old South," *American Historical Review* 93, no. 5 (Dec. 1988): 1242, quoting Cash, *The Mind of the South* (New York: Alfred Knopf, 1941), 319.

9. For information on Soulouque, see David Nicholls, *From Dessalines to Duvalier: Race, Colour, and National Independence in Haiti* (New Brunswick: Rutgers University Press, 1979), and Michel-Rolph Trouillot, *Haiti: State against Nation; The Origins and Legacy of Duvalierism* (New York: Monthly Review Press, 1990).

10. Thus we see the ongoing articulation, in the story the Chesnuts tell themselves about their practices as slaveowners, of what Orlando Patterson calls slavery's human parasitism and ideological reversal: examples of James Chesnut Jr.'s refrain can be found in the narrative on pages 249, 261, 464, and 679.

11. The following passage from *Uncle Tom's Cabin* bears an uncanny relation to Chesnut's meditation on the slave's double status as property and person: "It is one of the bitterest apportionments of a lot of slavery, that the negro, sympathetic and assimilative, after acquiring, in a refined family, the tastes and feelings which form the atmosphere of such a place, is not the less liable to become the bond-slave of the coarsest and most brutal,—just as a chair or table, which once decorated the superb saloon, comes, at last, battered and defaced, to the bar-room of some filthy tavern, or some low haunt of vulgar debauchery. The great difference is, that the table and chair cannot feel, and the *man* can; for even a legal enactment that he shall be 'taken, reputed, adjudged in law, to be a chattel personal,' cannot blot out his soul, with its own private little world of memories, hopes, loves, fears, and desires" (480–81).

12. Genovese makes a similar observation when he notes, "The house servants' inclination to identify with their masters constantly ran into limits, which reminded even the most caste-conscious that they too were slaves. Their masters resembled other employers of household labor in at least one important respect: they acted as if their house servants had neither eyes nor ears—as if they hardly existed at all. Just as many parents will speak between themselves and with their guests about the qualities and deportment of their children as if the children were not present, so the slaveholders, in the words of Frances Trollope, talked of their slaves, 'of their condition, of their faculties, of their conduct, exactly as if they were incapable of hearing.'" See Genovese, *Roll, Jordan, Roll*, 341, quoting Frances Trollope, *Domestic Manners of the Americans* (1832; n.p.: Reprint Services Corporation, 1901), 249.

13. Karl Marx, *Capital*, trans. Ben Fowkes (1867; London: Penguin Books, 1976), 1:163–64. To different ends, Helen Deutsch offers an astute reading of this passage from Marx in her chapter on commodities in Pope's "The Rape of the Lock." See Deutsch, *Resemblance and Disgrace: Alexander Pope and the Deformation of Culture* (Cambridge: Harvard University Press, 1996), 75.

14. A Georgia Supreme Court Case in 1861 ruled on whether a slave who had been killed while traveling on a train was to be viewed as a passenger (for whom a fare would have

to be paid) or as a commodity (in this case, attached to a military company also riding in the cars). The court concluded that since no fare had been paid for the victim, he was not legally a passenger, and thus, no restitution had to be paid to his owner. See *Muscogee Railroad Company v. Redd* in, *Reports of Cases in Law and Equity decided by the Georgia Supreme Court in the Year . . . 1847–1890* (n.p.: Edward Jenkins, 1867), 1:34–36.

15. See Sundquist's chapters on *The Confessions of Nat Turner* and *Benito Cereno*, in *To Wake the Nations*, 27–224. See also Roach *Cities of the Dead*. For work on the origins of the motif of masking in African American literary history, see Rafia Zafar, *We Wear the Mask: African Americans Write American Literature, 1760–1870* (New York: Columbia University Press, 1997).

16. See Morgan, *Slave Counterpoint*, 284.

17. In an episode that is resonant with this passage from Chesnut's narrative, Harriet Jacobs devotes an entire chapter of her autobiography to the exposé of an illiterate white mob. Titled "Fear of Insurrection," it details the spectacularly theatrical rather than physical way in which Jacobs and her grandmother orchestrate resistance to the white rabble militia of Edenton, North Carolina, authorized to search the quarters of all slaves in the wake of Nat Turner's rebellion. Jacobs adorns her grandmother's house with wildflowers, makes the beds with their best white quilts, and conspicuously displays every piece of finery in the family's possession to make a comparative statement about the relation of race and class. Just as Jacobs and her grandmother have predicted, their flamboyant exhibition of nearly-middle-class domestic status enflames the resentment of the lower-class white mob. One outraged member yells: "[W]here'd dis damn nigger git all dese sheets and table clarf?" while a compatriot announces lividly, "[D]is 'ere yaller gal's got letters!" See Harriet Jacobs, *Incidents in the Life of a Slave Girl Written by Herself*, ed. Jean Fagin Yellin (Cambridge: Harvard University Press, 1987), 65. See also Genovese, who surmises that the term "poor white trash" was coined by slaves (probably the relatively privileged class of house servants) rather than by elite whites (*Roll, Jordan, Roll*, 25 n. 72).

18. The 1880s writer describes a remarkable episode that can be seen as the near-tragic inversion of the burlesque that is Simon's ventriloquism at Sumter, an incident from her mother's past in a community called Shelby, "a white man's country where Negroes are hated" (473). While on a visit to their brother, who temporarily leaves them alone with some of his male slaves in a largely unfinished house on the frontier (Shelby County), Mrs. Miller and her sister Charlotte Boykin hear the clamor of white men and dogs hunting what appears to be a lone black man. Amid the commotion of the chase, the slave in question, John, running for his life, makes it into the Boykin house. Chesnut writes:

> [T]here was a loud knocking at the door—men swearing, dogs tearing round, sniffing, like mad, &c.&c. Aunt C. was sure she heard the panting of the negro as he ran in a few moments before. What could have become of him? Where could he have hid? The men shook the doors and windows and loudly threatened vengeance. My aunt pitied her sister, so feeble, so cut off in that room [locked in across

the hall from Aunt Charlotte's chamber]. The fright might kill her. The cursing and shouting continued. A man's voice in harshest accents made itself heard over all. "Leave my house, you rascals! If you are not gone in two seconds I'll shoot." There was a dead silence except the noise of the dogs. Quietly, the men slipped away. Once out of gunshot, they began to call for their dogs. After it was all over, my aunt crept across. "Sister, what man was it scared them away?" My mother laughed aloud in her triumph. "*I am the man.*" "But where is John?" Out crept John from a pile of rubbish in the corner of the room my mother had thrown over him. "Lord bless you, Miss Mary opened de door for me and dey was right behind running me." Aunt C. says mother is awfully proud of her prowess and she showed some moral courage, too.

Here we have an elite white woman mimicking the voice of mastery for the purpose of saving the life of a slave who has become the object of racist thugs. But in the entire 835-page space of the published 1880s narrative, we do not hear the voice of a white man ventriloquizing the words of a slave. That is, in Chesnut's epic, mimicry and ventriloquism are black modes of speaking truth to power by other means. For theorizations of mimicry, see Homi Bhabha, *The Location of Culture* (London: Routledge, 1994).

19. The 1880s Chesnut writes, "[T]hese old gray-haired darkies and their automatic noiseless perfection of training—one does miss that sort of thing. Your own servants think for you, they know your ways and your wants; they save you all responsibility, even in matters of your own ease and well-doing" ("Memoirs," September 1863, 488).

20. Indeed, according to Benedict Anderson's formulations in *Imagined Communities: Reflections on the Origins and Spread of Nationalism* (London: Verso, 1991), Molly would be exhibiting a protonationalist consciousness. Though the 1880s writer notes that she has attempted to teach all her slaves to read, it is not clear that Molly benefited from this pedagogical "philanthropy" as a bondswoman on Mulberry before the war, when Chesnut lived in her own homes and then in Washington, unless, of course, she learned the skill under the tutelage of Mary Cox Chesnut or Sally Chesnut.

21. In a slightly different context, Bertram Wyatt-Brown notes, "masters, for instance, liked to hear their slaves singing in the fields; silence was too ominous" ("The Mask of Obedience," 1239).

22. Stowe creates, for example, seemingly stock Sambo characters in the slaves Sam and Andy in *Uncle Tom's Cabin* who, in performing slave "slowness," "senselessness," and "foolishness" in the most exaggeratedly clownlike manner, strategically divert the slave trader Haley from capturing the runaway Eliza (95–102). I would argue that in these portraits, Stowe's romantic racialism breaks lose from authorial constraints to do a kind of latent subversive work, a version of Hartman's "putting on ole massa—the simulation of compliance for covert aims" (*Scenes of Subjection,* 12).

23. For the curriculum at Madame Talvande's French School for Young Ladies, see Muhlenfeld, *Mary Boykin Chesnut,* 29. See also Richard Green and Eric Handley, *Images of the Greek Theater* (Austin: University of Texas Press, 1995).

24. The original title for the first section of the chapter was to have been "Black Skin, Bronze Masks," after Frantz Fanon's *Black Skin, White Masks* (1952; repr., New York: Grove Press, 1991), the classic text of what is now known as postcolonial theory in literary studies.
25. Again, in proposing Chesnut's contrast to Stowe, I am thinking of the latter's caricatures Sam and Andy, "cutting the monkey for the white folk." The phrase is Zora Neale Hurston's, *Their Eyes Were Watching God* (1937; Urbana: University of Illinois Press, 1978), 210. See also note 22 above.
26. Melville made revisions of the novella for its inclusion in his *Piazza Tales* (1856).
27. See Wilson Jeremiah Moses, *Afrotopia: The Roots of African American Cultural History* (Cambridge: Cambridge University Press, 1998), 6 n. 14, quoting Constantin Francois Volney, *The Ruins; or, Meditations on the Revolutions of Empires* (Paris, 1791; 2nd American ed., 1890; repr., Baltimore: Black Classic Press, 1991). John Cullen Gruesser notes that in his book, *The Star of Ethiopia,* pioneering black sociologist W. E. B. Du Bois "linked the origins of human civilization, the achievements of ancient Egypt, and the greatness of more recent African empires to the experiences of black people in the United States." See Greusser, *Black on Black: Twentieth-Century African American Writing about Africa* (Lexington: University of Kentucky Press, 2000), 61.

    Moses also explains that "[b]lack Egyptocentrists believe that ancient Egyptian culture was ... profoundly influenced by black Africa.... Their project, therefore, is simply to prove that the basic elements of Egyptian culture are historically intermeshed with the cultures of other regions of Africa. The glorification and romanticism of ancient Egypt is clearly only a part of what we call Afrocentrism today. It is to be admitted that since the early nineteenth century some black authors have desired to identify with the land of the pharaohs. It is important to note, however, that many black nationalists—especially those with a strong sense of class consciousness—are disinclined to romanticize pharaonic dominion" (*Afrotopia*, 4–5).
28. Chesnut first mentions what she calls her abolitionist letter in an 1880s entry for November 27, 1861: "I have before me a letter I wrote to Mr. C while he was on our plantation in Mississippi in 1842. It is the most fervid abolition document I have ever read. I came across it, burning letters the other day. That letter I did not burn. I kept it—as showing how we were not as much of heathens down here as our enlightened enemies think. Their philanthropy is cheap. There are as noble, pure lives here as there—and a great deal more of self-sacrifice" (246). Woodward and Muhlenfeld both note that this letter has been lost.
29. For Chesnut's references to herself as Cassandra, see 171, 182, 298, 650, 652, 654, 655, 683, 688, 768, and 809.
30. See Northrop Frye, *Anatomy of Criticism: Four Essays* (1957; updated ed., Princeton: Princeton University Press, 2000).
31. Frederick Douglass uses the metaphor of the circle to delineate those of his fellow slaves who understood the meaning of the sorrow songs while still in bondage, and those, like himself (or so he claims), who did not. In my many years of teaching the 1845 *Narrative of the Life of Frederick Douglass,* it remains unclear to me whether Douglass means his readers to understand this claim literally or figuratively.

32. Prior to the Southampton rebellion, certain white Methodist class meetings ordained and licensed free blacks to serve as preachers and exhorters; influential members of slave communities, such as drivers, often functioned as class leaders during religious services. Because Nat Turner had gathered his co-conspirators in the context of Christian worship (in his case, a Baptist meeting), authorities in Virginia and the deeper South immediately cracked down on freedom of both slave and free black religious assembly as a way to minimize future uprisings thought to be fomented as a result of African American religious millennialism. The following studies of Protestantism in the antebellum period, which include standard histories and monographs on slave and free black religious experience, from the African "sacred cosmos" (the phrase is Mechal Sobel's) to syncretic African Christian experience to African American Baptist and Methodist practices, have been vital to my understanding of the issues of race and sect: see Donald G. Mathews, *Religion in the Old South* (Chicago: University of Chicago Press, 1977); Mechal Sobel, *Trablen' On: The Slave Journey to An Afro-Baptist Faith* (Princeton: Princeton University Press, 1977); Ann Taves, *Fits, Trances, and Visions: Experiencing Religion and Explaining Experience from Wesley to James* (Princeton: Princeton University Press, 1999); Sylvia R. Frey and Betty Wood, *Come Shouting to Zion: African American Protestantism in the American South and British Caribbean to 1830* (Chapel Hill: University of North Carolina Press, 1998); and Jon Butler, *Awash in a Sea of Faith: Christianizing the American People* (Cambridge: Harvard University Press, 1990).
33. See Muhlenfeld, *Mary Boykin Chesnut*, 27.
34. Mathews, *Religion in the Old South*, 215.
35. In a chapter on the ancient foundations of modern slavery in his study of the rise and fall of New World bondage, David Brion Davis notes, "Augustine and other church fathers had already provided an answer by drawing a profound and influential connection between slavery and original sin." See Davis, *Inhuman Bondage: The Rise and Fall of New World Slavery* (New York: Oxford University Press, 2006), 44.
36. Mathews writes, "[A] universal phenomenon of revivals in England, Wales, Ireland, New England, and colonies to the south, the conversion experience with its various forms of hysteria, ecstasy, and psychological transformation seemed to the Africans to be very much like the vitality of their own religion. Evangelical 'experience' seemed very much like African 'possession' of the devout by spirits 'whom they favored,' a phenomenon which was a 'vital part of African traditional religion,' and which was an 'experience greatly sought after.'" See Mathews, *Religion in the Old South*, 190, quoting Leonard F. Barrett, *Soul-Force: African Heritage in Afro-American Religion* (Garden City: Doubleday, Anchor Books, 1974), 25.
37. Mathews, *Religion in the Old South*, 214, my emphasis.
38. Chesnut opines that "two-thirds of [her] religion consists in being good to Negroes" (199).
39. "Look up on high" is a variant reading from "Truth" or the "Balade de Bon Conseyle"; by the number of surviving manuscripts, it was Chaucer's third most popular work (after the *Canterbury Tales* and *A Treatise on the Astrolabe*). In one manuscript it is associated with the figure of the Parson from the *Canterbury Tales* (the one who brings the tale-telling to an end, telling a "tale" that's really a treatise on penitence). In other words, the ballad comes

from a part of the Chaucer canon as distant as possible from, say, the "Miller's Tale," and quite distant as well from straightforward literary canonicity.

40. Chesnut had omitted Chaucer's next line, influenced by the Gospel of John, about the liberating nature of truth. Chesnut performed her own editorial work on Chaucer's ballad.

Chapter Eight

1. For the best recent book on eighteenth-century ballad opera, see Diane Dugaw, *Deep Play: John Gay and the Invention of Modernity* (London: Associated University Presses, 2001). Thanks to Professor Dugaw, the leading expert on this genre, for email exchange about *Bombastes,* as well as to Professor Steven Newman, whose work on the ballad begins in the early eighteenth century and extends through the romantic period. Though I have read an 1829 Philadelphia reprint of this one-act play, first published in 1790, there exists no extant secondary material about its provenance, its author, or its cultural significance. Featuring a classicized king of "Utopia," his loyal minister of state, his chief general, and a poor dairymaid of easy virtue, the story takes place in the wake of successful military conquest (a phantasmagoric analogue, for the Richmonders, for the outcome of the Civil War). Artaxominus, the king, who is already married, meets and falls in love with Distaffina, not knowing that the dairymaid is the beloved of his chief general, Bombastes. Confronting the king in his mistress's cottage, the general and the king fight over Distaffina; the general slays the king and then is himself killed by the chief minister, Fusbos, leaving Distaffina abandoned, without a patron.

The Richmond audience would have interpreted these individual male armed encounters as duels, thus reprising one of the themes of *The Rivals,* which itself encapsulated perceptions and roles transformed by the realities of the Civil War. In this light, it is crucial to add that Mary Boykin Chesnut found herself a dairymaid of sorts, running a butter-and-egg business on shares from 1862 until the end of her life—a humbling parallel, but a resonant one as well.

Also perhaps telling, the only musical line anyone in Chesnut's set can remember from the opera involves a song entitled "Hope Told a Flattering Tale," which comes at the end of the first scene. Sung by the general, it unfolds in the following manner:

> Hope told a flattering tale
> Much longer than my arm.
> That love and pots of ale,
> In peace would keep me warm:
> The flatterer is not gone,
> She visits number one;
> In love I'm monstrous deep,
> Love, odds bobs destroys my sleep.
> Hope told a flattering tale,
> Lest love should soon grow cool;
> A tub thrown to a whale,
> To make the fish a fool:
> Should Distaffina frown,

Then love's gone out of town,
And when love's dark dream is o'er
Then we wake and dream no more.

According to the stage directions, "The King evinces strong emotions during the song, and at the conclusion starts up." See Thomas [William] Barnes Rhodes, "Bombastes Furioso: A Tragic Burlesque Opera in One Act" (1790), in *Fisher's Edition of Standard Farces* (New York: Turner and Fisher, 1829; repr., Chicago: T. S. Denison, n.d.). Thanks to Melvin Pena.

Woodward has argued convincingly that Chesnut cites the first verse of this song to allude to a miscarriage she had suffered early in her marriage; in September of 1861, she writes of her father-in-law's offspring and grandchildren, "At one time they seemed all in all with him. That is, before they developed exactly what material they were made of, and hope told a flattering tale. We had no children. They were to carry on his line and inherit the estates he loves so well." In a footnote here, Woodward quotes the Rhodes opera's song lyrics and then adds: "M.B.C. could have been referring to an otherwise unmentioned miscarriage—in view of the sentence following" (*MCCW,* 190 n. 6). No offspring from any of the royal, martial, rural couplings in the *Bombastes* appear at the end of the opera, either. Both Rhodes's fictional and Chesnut's historical worlds are full of milk and eggs, but there are no children.

2. Additional accounts of the amateur theatricals appeared in various important Southern civilian and military memoirs of the war years, written during the period roughly contemporary with that of Chesnut's reworking of her "book" in the 1880s: particularly interesting is Phoebe Yates Pember's *A Southern Woman's Story* (1879; repr., Columbia: University of South Carolina Press, 2002). In chapter 15 of her memoir, "Collapse of the Confederacy," Pember writes: "All this winter of '64, the city had been unusually gay. Besides parties, private theatricals and tableaux were constantly exhibited. Wise and thoughtful men disapproved openly of this mad gayety. There was certainly a painful discrepancy between the excitement of dancing and the rumbling of ambulances that could be heard in the momentary lull of the music, carrying the wounded to the different hospitals. Young men advocated this state of affairs, arguing that after the fatigues and dangers of a campaign in the field, some relaxation was necessary on their visits to the capital. To thinking people, this recklessness was ominous" (77).

Mrs. Burton Harrison also writes extensively of the dramatic evenings in her own memoir, *Recollections Grave and Gay* (New York: Charles Scribner's Sons, 1911), 166–76. A twenty-something belle during the war, the then Constance Cary was deputized by the wife of the secretary of war, Mrs. George Randolph, to orchestrate the theatricals. Finally, T. C. DeLeon, the nephew of Chesnut's great friend Miriam Cohen, also wrote a memoir in which the theatricals are described. DeLeon tellingly begins his two chapters on the dramatic evenings with the following remark: "The whole South was one great stage. From opening overture at Sumter to final curtain at Appomattox, the men and women played in endless tragedy of battlefield and hospital, or in comedies of statecraft, intrigue, and love-making. And there were plays within plays. Richmond was to the rest of the South what the Comedie Francaise was to the world of art." See his *Belles, Beaux, and Brains of the 60s* (1909; New York: Arno Press, 1974), 213 for the quotation, and 215–31 for his account of private theatricals in Richmond during the winter of 1864. DeLeon was another member of the Jewish "haute volee" with whom Chesnut socialized.

3. Across the entire archive of Chesnut's extant writing, there is only one instance in which she refuses an opportunity to attend the theater: it occurs in 1863, during the period immediately following the death from a head wound of Cheves McCord, the only child of her beloved friend Louisa McCord. In a letter to Mrs. Louis T. Wigfall, dated late January 1863, Chesnut writes: "My dear Mrs. Wigfall, My heart is heavier today than it has been since this murderous war began—I dare say I have told you over & over as I always talk what is uppermost that my *cronies* in Columbia my bosom friends were Mrs. Preston Mrs. McCord & Mrs. Izard—Capt Cheves McCord—only *son* of my friend lies dead—at a Mr. Myers only a few doors below us—I did not know he was here—Mr. C had a letter from him yesterday—dated Fredericksburg. He was wounded at the Second Manassas—two balls in his leg and one in his head—Contrary to the advice of his Doctors he has rejoined his Company—& this is the *end*—he died in convulsions—from a pressure in the brain—his Mother is expected by every train—poor thing—I could not sleep for thinking of her—She seemed to have but one thought in this world—'My Son' he is barely twenty one—is married—his wife a beautiful girl—unfortunate & miserable & wretched is it all—She is on the eve of her confinement—I will try & see you as soon as possible—do not pay calls without me—as I want to take the hack with you—but I will not as I had hoped take the box with you—this unhappy boy lying dead so near me—makes the thought of Theaters hateful to me just now" (MS, Library of Congress, 4 pages quoted in Wall, "The Letters of Mary Boykin Chesnut," 67).

4. Scholars of Indian religion note that orthodox Hinduism never condoned the practice, developed by a heretical sect in the sixth century A.D., which sought to limit the growing number of widowed females who had lost husbands in the Muslim wars. The *OED* defines *suttee* from the Hindi or Urdu as, "faithful or virtuous wife"; also, "widow who immolates herself on the funeral pyre of her husband's body."

5. See in Chesnut's narrative Isabella Martin's lamentation that she will never meet her intended husband because he already has been killed on the battlefield: "Here we are, and our possible husbands and lovers killed before we so much as knew them. Oh! The widows and old maids of this cruel war" (523).

6. Russell's sympathies in *My Diary in India,* interestingly, do not always lie with the British East India Company Army. In fact, he reports with horror the episodes of "blowing away" sepoy mutineers at the mouths of British canon, or their being hanged in trees by the score. It makes sense that Russell, having been born in Ireland, though working for an English newspaper, possessed allegiances that were catholic, small "c," and often sympathetic to the underdog in a conflict.

Russell also traveled across the United States during the first year of the war as a *Times* correspondent; in the midst of the war, he collected the essays he had produced as a volume entitled *My Diary North and South.* Chesnut actually socialized with Russell in 1861, during his tour of South Carolina. She remained ambivalent about him: admiring of his intellect, but wounded when he was critical of the South. O'Brien nevertheless sees *My Diary in India* as an inspiration for Chesnut's narrative form ("The Flight down the Middle Walk," 109–25).

7. Chesnut describes "black and yellow brutes . . . jumping over the parapet" (409), while Boucicault includes this stage direction in the first scene of act 1: "Achmet [Mrs. Campbell's Indian servant] drops his knife and leaps over the parapet" (8). Mrs. Campbell, the widowed Scottish wife of an officer of the British in India, refers to Indians as "blacks." See *Dick's Standard Plays,* no. 473, cited in Richard Fawkes, *Dion Boucicault: A Biography* (London: Quartet, 1979), 98–101.

8. Chesnut was using language loosely here, for far from being overrun, the British surrendered under promise of safe passage out of Cawnpore, were led to the river and waiting boats, and then massacred brutally.

9. Christopher Herbert was kind enough to discuss his understanding of the Mutiny in a long and fruitful conversation as I was completing this book. Since then, he has published *War of No Pity: The Indian Mutiny and Victorian Trauma* (Princeton: Princeton University Press, 2008).

10. See Thomas Wentworth Higginson, *Army Life in a Black Regiment and Other Writings,* ed. R. D. Mardsen (1870; repr., Harmondsworth: Penguin Books, 1997), 66.

11. See Leon F. Litwack, *Been in the Storm So Long: The Aftermath of Slavery* (New York: Vintage, 1980), 102. The First Carolina Volunteers, the initial black Union regiment, lead by the Massachusetts abolitionist Colonel Thomas Wentworth Higginson and made up largely of former slaves, affords what might have been an uncanny example for Chesnut's Columbia "cronies." It is altogether possible that among her closest friends, a man such as General John Preston himself could have found himself face to face with his own former slaves, though Chesnut never makes mention of such a confrontation.

12. See David Grimstead, *Melodrama Unveiled: American Theater and Culture, 1800–1850* (Chicago: University of Chicago Press, 1968), 254. I have consulted the following sources on nineteenth-century American theater: Lawrence Levine, *High Brow/Low Brow: The Emergence of Cultural Hierarchy in America* (Cambridge: Harvard University Press, 1990); *When They Weren't Doing Shakespeare: Essays on Nineteenth-Century British and American Theatre,* ed. Judith L. Fisher and Stephen Watt (Athens: University of Georgia Press, 1989); and Bruce A. McConachie, *Melodramatic Formations: American Theater and Society, 1820–1870* (Iowa City: University of Iowa Press, 1982).

13. See Richard Brinsley Sheridan, *The Rivals,* ed. Vincent F. Hopper and Gerald B. Lahey (New York: Barron's Educational Series, 1958), 112 (act 3, scene 3).

14. See "The Captain and the Colonel," in Muhlenfeld, *Two Novels by Mary Chesnut,* 72.

15. For the text of the Wigfall letter, see note 4 above. In "Charleston Theatricals during the Tragic Decade, 1860–1869," W. Stanley Hoole catalogues the comic, dramatic, and musical entertainment available to Charlestonians during the Civil War and in the early years of Reconstruction. During the first years of the crisis, the Charleston Theater remained open, vetting benefit performances by various military regiments such as the French Zouaves and the Charleston Volunteers, as well as short dramas on martial subjects. On

December 11, 1863, the Charleston Theater was destroyed by a tragic (and accidental fire) that consumed a third of the city. In response to public demand for theatricals, the Hibernian Hall was reconfigured as a theater, hosting largely what appear to have been musical performances, minstrel shows, and burlesque troupes. By 1864, Hoole writes, with the city besieged, "the Hibernian remained open, offering miscellaneous diversions for the stricken citizens. . . . And there were many showings of panoramic war views, band concerts, several dress balls, and 'music festivals.'" See Hoole's essay in the *Journal of Southern History*, "Notes and Documents," 11, no. 4 (Nov. 1945): 541. In the chapter entitled "Drama Goes to War" in Charles S. Watson's *The History of Southern Drama* (Louisville: University Press of Kentucky, 1976), we learn that "the demand for partisan drama reached its peak." He continues: "[W]hen Union troops occupied active theatrical centers such as New Orleans, adjustments were rapidly made: actors transferred to more secure locations such as middle Georgia. As new companies developed and southern 'stars' began to rise in the theatrical firmament, Richmond, the capital of the new nation, became the 'Broadway of the South.' During the 1862–1863 season the city had two theaters always open and sometimes four. When the Richmond Theatre burned, the decision was made immediately to construct a replacement, and on February 9, 1863, a gala opened the New Richmond Theatre. On that occasion, Henry Timrod's 'Inaugural Poem,' which won a prize of $300, preceded *As You Like It*" (75).

16. Karen Halttunen, *Confidence Men and Painted Women: A Study of Middle-Class Culture in America, 1830–1870* (New Haven: Yale University Press, 1982), 175.

17. See W. Stanley Hoole, *Vizetelly Covers the Confederacy* ([Wilmington, N.C.]: Broadfoot Publishing, 2000).

18. Roach, *Cities of the Dead,* 152. To invoke the best-known nineteenth-century American example, in Louisa May Alcott's *Little Women,* the amateur theatrical mounted by the March sisters is a gothic seduction thriller penned by Jo; it features unrighteous political authority taking sexually predatory form. In Alcott's protodemocratic case, and in Chesnut's more haute-bourgeois private dramatic production—where the class structure represented in the play is far narrower than that in Alcott, spanning only the distance between Sir Anthony Adverse and the wealthy Mrs. Malaprop to the servant class (Bob Acres, though a rube, is also a landholder)—class and politics have always played a part. It is important to distinguish, however, that in the Richmond theatricals, the discourse of race and class must be read figuratively. I understand the Richmond version of Mrs. Malaprop as reverberating white racist fantasies about slave misappropriations of English.

19. Mr. Chesnut apparently dissuaded the parties to the threatened duel from coming to blows, the disagreement possibly prompted in the wake of a "negro trial" (31–32). This episode, however, involves one of the very few examples in which Woodward, ordinarily a crackerjack sleuth in unpacking the back stories in the 1880s narrative, is silent. Perhaps no accounts of the affair exist beyond Chesnut's.

20. Woodward, almost always loathe to editorialize in his footnotes, actually goes so far as to write in the reference annotating "The Bright Side of Richmond": "MBC believed that by 1864, Confederate defense had become a charade" (528 n. 4).

21. The writer nowhere records whether or not she is familiar with *The Scarlet Letter;* we do know, however, that she read *The Blithedale Romance* in March of 1864, immediately following the period detailed in "The Bright Side of Richmond, Winter 1864," some twelve years after its initial publication. It is interesting to consider the fact that of all Hawthorne's romances, she chose (or reported choosing) his satirical-tragic portrait of a failed New England utopian community, rather than a story about Puritan Boston (*The Scarlet Letter*), industrializing Salem, daguerrotypy, and mesmerism (*The House of the Seven Gables*), or nineteenth-century American artists in Rome (*The Marble Faun*). Although abolitionism is not an overt object of Hawthorne's critique of 1840s-era reform in *The Blithedale Romance,* perhaps Chesnut had hoped it would be. Significantly, she hated the book: "Today read *Blithedale. Blithedale* leaves such an unpleasant impression. I like pleasant, kindly stories now. We are so harrowed by real life. Tragedy is for hours of ease" (March 11, 1864, 581).

22. Roach, *Cities of the Dead,* 2, 3.

23. For November 26, 1863, Chesnut writes, "Mrs. Scotch Allan sent me cream and Lady Cheek apples from her farm" (493).

24. Woodward informs us in the early pages of the narrative that Edmund Rhett's attack on Edward Magrath's brother in the *Charleston Mercury,* the Rhett family-owned newspaper, precipitated a fatal duel fought by relatives of each man. William Taber lost his life; and Edmund Rhett's brother, Robert Barnwell Rhett Jr., assumed the editorship of the newspaper (35 n. 3).

25. "The Masque of the Red Death" (1842), in *Poe: Poetry and Tales,* ed. Patrick F. Quinn (New York: Library of America, 1984), 485.

26. In literary terms, we might view James Jr.'s actions as an episode of ritual antifertility marking the South's destruction, as well as a putting in her place of his niece, whose competition with her childless aunt was an ongoing source of friction. Moreover, the menace of sexual or, at very least, gendered violence pervades the scene. James Jr. can be seen as asserting patriarchal power in the wake of a particularly emasculating moment for Southern men, who have experienced military defeat. Chesnut also may be telegraphing cultural anxiety about incest in the postemancipation South. In the defeated Confederacy, the pool of appropriate white partners may have become reduced either to a figurative notion of white family (elite relatives and friends) or to a more interdicted, because literal, one. James may be expressing his disapproval of North-South reunion accomplished through exactly such a marriage as this, which also became a literary trope in postwar fiction. While Mr. Chesnut may be playing the defender of family refinement, this moment also works through the fantasy that he somehow is the villain responsible for the barrenness of his own marriage. Mary Chesnut's choice to cast her husband in such violent terms constitutes a fascinating penultimate tableau in her 1880s narrative.

27. The important distinction, of course, is that Mitchell's novel epitomizes the historical distortions plaguing the plantation romance, where slaves are happy and contented and on the same political page as the master class when it comes to assaults by the Yankees. While Chesnut does create the valet Scipio as a figure who remains loyal to his master—not

unlike, say, Mitchell's portrait of Mammy, she rarely indulges in the nostalgic fantasies that pervade *Gone With the Wind* and is willing to reveal the "seamy side" of slavery's horrors.

Chapter Nine

1. W. E. B. Du Bois's concept of "double-consciousness" is anachronistic for describing the paradoxical thinking of white slaveholders about their slaves at the beginning of the Civil War; he coined the term in 1903. Perhaps Freud's notion of disavowal offers a more trenchant way of understanding how masters could "know" that their "people" were fully human and yet still treat them as if they were not.
2. Steven Hahn observes that political consciousness under slavery was beginning to be expressed through what he calls the community's "grapevine telegraph," which carried news from plantation to plantation. See Hahn, *A Nation under Our Feet: Black Political Struggles in the Rural South from Slavery to the Great Migration* (Cambridge: Harvard University Press, 2005). Following Woodward's assessment in his 1981 introduction, I have found Chesnut to be a remarkably accurate historian. While the 1880s narrative is full of testimonials to her former slaves' devotion to her and to Mulberry, which may evoke skepticism in some readers that she indulges in plantation romance mythology, she provides many counter-examples of former bondspeople of the Camden and Charleston communities who spurn any trappings of slavery and issue ultimatums to former owners about the rights of loved ones left behind. Consider this extraordinary vignette from the "Memoirs" section for 1862–63:

   > Mrs. Lewis of Audley was stripped by the Yankees of all her earthly possessions. It began by degrees.
   >
   > One day a card was brought her—"Mr. John Washington." Now the name of the father of his country opened all doors at Audley [Lorenzo Lewis had been a grand-nephew of Washington], so the gentleman was promptly asked into the drawing room. He proved to be a crow black negro—black beyond the usual darkness allowed them by nature, and glossy withal. He produced a letter from Milroy [U.S. Brigadier General Robert Hurston Milroy, who would have authorized the emancipations of slaves in regions where the enemy was in rebellion, like Richmond in the winter of 1862–63].
   >
   > Now the wife of Mr. John Washington was one of Mrs. Lewis's women, and the order ran thus: "Mrs. Lewis must send John Washington's family in one of her carriages. She also must send a white driver if she wants her horses returned to her, for her slaves are all freed by Lincoln's proclamation—consequently would not return to her." (435–6)

   It is important to add that Chesnut concludes the anecdote by noting, "Many of the negroes refused to leave [Mrs. Lewis] of course" (436). But the force of the story still weighs on the side of former bondspeople striking out for freedom.
3. To unpack the stereotypes to which she subscribed: Chesnut believed most African Americans were lazy, unclean, and delighted by bright, gaudy colors and clothes. The so-called

evidence grounding these notions came largely from her experience on Mulberry. Laziness, of course, is in the eyes of the beholder, and what Mary Chesnut so described may have coded resistance to laboring without remuneration. Her complaints about dirtiness most likely pertained to slaves who toiled in the fields without sufficient bathing facilities (she never complains in the narrative about the smell of house slaves, for example). Finally, the characterization of African Americans' taste in colors and garments most likely reflects Chesnut's ignorance of African aesthetic and ritual tradition, traces of which lived on in South Carolina well into the nineteenth century. Hannah Crafts discusses black taste and aesthetic preferences in her unpublished 1850s novel, *The Bondswoman's Narrative,* ed. Henry Louis Gates Jr. (New York: Warner Books, 2002), largely set in Virginia and North Carolina. There, the heroine, also named Hannah, describes her preferences in fabrics and colors (6, 26). Unlike her firmly proslavery peers, such as Louisa McCord and Jefferson Davis, Chesnut suspected that the qualities she criticizes were produced by the environment slavery created. That is, far from believing that white supremacy had been ordained as a function of the natural order of things, much less by God, Chesnut understood the fact that slavery was sustained by force, ideology, and tradition alone.

4. Scholars have identified these experiences as examples of white paternalism. But from my reading of primary source accounts of slavery and the historiography, from Eugene Genovese through Philip Morgan through David Brion Davis, Ira Berlin, Steven Hahn, and beyond, it seems clear that any given example of raw paternalism could also have included genuine affective attachment. Paternalistic motives do not cancel the emotional experience of cross-racial community at ritual times and places.

Clearly, the official sources—legal documents, court records, wills, and petitions—afford scholars the most unbiased accounts from which to speculate about the motives of historical actors, white and black, though of course, the scribes for such materials were often white elites or yeomen. For example, the record of Colonel James Chesnut Sr.'s agreement to sell land to a collective of black former slaves may be more clinically objective than Chesnut granddaughter Esther Davis's account in her "Memories of Mulberry" of Scipio the younger leading the black freedmen in the final hymn sung at the old Colonel's funeral in 1866. Nevertheless, as nostalgic and romanticized as Davis's reminiscence about her own family may be, the text of the hymn she includes constitutes its own, independent sort of evidence that, once interpreted in a literary fashion, affords fascinating insight into Scipio's expressive agency. Though its meaning(s) are coded in religious figures, they are decipherable to the reader trained in the analysis of poetry. Accordingly, even documents marked by explicit ideological predispositions unexpectedly can yield rich, valuable, information.

5. Chesnut records her husband's ideas on this subject: "[JC's] negroes offered to fight for him if he would arm them. He pretended not to believe them. He says one man cannot do it. The whole country must agree to it. He could trust such as he would select. And he would give so many acres of land and his freedom to each one he enlisted" (March 18, 1862, 313). Historian Bruce Levine has remarked that certain slaveowners who advocated freeing their bondspeople and arming them to fight the Union were by no means antislavery

in any larger sense. Instead, they were willing to sacrifice a small fraction of their own "people" to the Rebel army and emancipation if it meant that the South would win the war and thus be able to keep the majority of African Americans in bondage. See Levine, *Confederate Emancipation: Southern Plans to Free and Arm Slaves during the Civil War* (New York: Oxford University Press, 2006).

6. Once put onto the boats, these released hostage women and children were hacked to death with long knives by Indian mutineers who had lain in wait for them. The Union navy, on the other hand, was eager to give asylum to the runaway slaves in order to put them to work, unless they were women and children, who were regarded as obstructions to the military endeavor at hand and often treated badly.

Perhaps the episode most cognate with the Indian massacre at the boats involved runaway slave woman and children trying to join Sherman's March through Georgia in December 1864. On the ninth of that month, at Ebenezer Creek, a young Union general, uncannily named Jefferson C. Davis, ordered his men to cut away the pontoon bridges that had enabled the army and male slave runaways to cross a deep river. Of the approximately 670 fugitives, something like 180 slave women and children, as well as the slower men, drowned in the wake of this brutal decision. Confederate cavalry general Joseph Wheeler and his men soon arrived on the near bank, shooting down many of the remaining former slaves. Later, after finding another way to cross the river in pursuit of Sherman's army, a rear guard came back and captured surviving black stragglers. E. L. Doctorow brilliantly dramatizes this horrendous event in *The March,* his 2005 novel exploring Sherman's trek from multiple viewpoints: slave, Southern civilian, Union military, and Rebel deserter.

The 1880s Chesnut marveled, as well, over the horror of British reprisals against their sepoy enemies, strapping Indian men to the mouths of canons and firing, which resulted in their immediate decapitation and dismemberment. As Hindu religious law enjoins that the dead must be burned or buried intact, the dismemberment unfit these dead for sacred interment, something the British clearly understood. Another horrifying mode of execution involved the hanging of as many as nineteen sepoy guerillas from one tree, which became a rood of terror as each prisoner was brought forward to his death. These acts were breathtaking exercises in excessive cruelty; certainly they would have been considered unimaginably barbaric had they been perpetrated by the Indian rebels against the British soldiers of the East India Company.

7. The elder man also insisted that his son write down an account of Mrs. Witherspoon's murder for his ninety-year-old mother. The younger Mary Chesnut observes: "Old Mr. Chesnut and his wife must know everything: 'I want her to know.' So my husband had to write several sheets of paper filled with poor Mrs. Witherspoon's tragedy. We thought it could so easily have been kept from Mrs. Chesnut's ears—she is so deaf. But he ordered it otherwise" (October 20, 1861, 218).

8. See the *Camden Gazette* for July 4, 1816, vol. 1, issue 14, p. 2; also for July 11, 1816, vol. 1, issue 15, p. 3; and for July 18, 1816, vol. 1, issue 16, p. 3. For an "Extract of a Letter from a Gentleman in Camden, S.C., to his Friend in Philadelphia, dated July 4, 1816" (possibly

Colonel Chesnut writing to one of his brothers-in-law, Mr. Cox or Mr. Binney), see the *Reporter* vol. 12, issue 693, p. 1.

9. Records of the Court of Magistrates and Freeholders (Kershaw County), L28225, Trial Papers, 1802–1861, held in the South Carolina Department of Archives and History. These records also are available on the department's Web site (http://www.state.sc.us/scdah/guide/rg0028.htm). See also Glenn Inabinet's 1973 paper "The July Fourth Incident 1816: An Insurrection Plotted by Slaves in Camden, South Carolina," Camden Historical Society, Black History File, 6.

10. In a rare compendium of Negro insurrectionary behavior in South Carolina that includes "analysis" of the thwarted Fourth of July uprising in Camden, white chronicler Edwin C. Holland noted that "two brothers engaged in this rebellion could read and write, and were hitherto of exceptional characters. They were *religious,* and had always been regarded in the light of faithful servants. . . . [M]ost of them [have been actuated by] wild and frantic ideas of the rights of man, and *the misconceived injunctions and examples of Holy writ.*" See Holland, *A refutation of the calumnies circulated against the southern and western states, respecting the institution and existence of slavery among them; To which is added, a minute and particular account of the actual state and condition of their Negro population; Together with historical notices of all the insurrections that have taken place since the settlement of the country; By a South-Carolinian* (Charleston: A. E. Miller, 1822), 76.

Eric Sundquist's *To Wake the Nations* offers the finest account of the way in which the American Revolution was incomplete when it came to the human rights of the nation's blacks, both slave and free.

11. Soon after the thwarted rebellion in Camden, the South Carolina General Assembly passed a series of laws in response to the near disaster: legislation prohibiting slaves from serving as musicians in the army; an extra guard for the Camden arsenal (for which see S165000, year 1816, item 00056, South Carolina Department of Archives and History, Columbia, South Carolina); stricter curfews for slaves; prohibitions against slaves trading with whites; making it illegal to teach bondspeople to read and write; and the prohibiting of manumission of slaves in the state by anyone other than the state legislature. Most remarkably, a small group of those masters whose slaves were executed for conspiring to rise petitioned for compensation. Mrs. Sarah Lang, for example, actually received approximately a hundred dollars for her executed slave, although he probably was valued at least six times this amount on the market in the early nineteenth century. For these petitions, see Document Number: ND 1816, and ND 1661, Records of the General Assembly, South Carolina Department of Archives and History, Columbia, South Carolina.

12. Chesnut does, however, note that a slave named "Dick," whom I have identified via guardianship papers taken out by the first John Chesnut—the old Colonel's father and James Jr.'s grandfather—"was set free fifty years ago or more for faithful services rendered Mr. Chesnut's grandfather" (November 5, 1861, 243). The "faithful services" of this aforementioned "Richard Chesnut" were not elaborated in the will. Under the apparent sponsorship of "guardian" John Chesnut I, he apparently lived in Camden and worked as a barber. Later that year, manumission was outlawed in South Carolina.

13. For the trial records, and for documentation of Scipio's role as witness for the state, see *Records of Trial of Slaves for Attempted Insurrection* (July 3–17, 1816), Thursday July 4, 1816, Item A-786, in the Caroliniana Library, University of South Carolina.
14. Bruce Brown, present-day owner of Bloomsbury, the Chesnut family "town" home in Camden, identifies informant Scipio the elder as the "slave" in charge of the brickworks on Mulberry. Brown explained that Bloomsbury's foundation was built with materials produced by Scipio and his team on the Chesnut plantation.
15. See testimonial comments to this effect in *Historic Camden,* Part 2, *Nineteenth Century,* ed. Thomas J. Kirkland and Robert M. Kennedy (Columbia: The State Company, 1926), 187–90. See also Christopher Williams Daniels, "Colonel James Chesnut, II: His Life and Economic Circumstance," master's thesis, Department of History, University of Colorado, 1995.
16. Thanks to Marion C. Chandler of the South Carolina Department of History and Archives.
17. Esther Davis, "Memories of Mulberry," 18–19, in appendices to Daniels, "Colonel James Chesnut, II"; also held in the Williams-Chesnut-Manning Collection, Caroliniana Library, University of South Carolina.
18. See Daniels, "Colonel James Chesnut, II," 290. The 1880s narrator describes her failed attempts to teach Sunday school to the slave children on Mulberry: "I know how hard it is to teach them, for I have tried it, and I soon let my Sunday school all drift into singing hymns—which all parties did well" (December 8, 1861, 260).
19. Herbert Aptheker, *American Negro Slave Revolts,* 50th anniversary ed. (1943; New York: International Publishers, 1993), 142.
20. See C. L. R. James, *The Black Jacobins: Toussaint L'Ouverture and the San Domingo Revolution* (1938; New York: Vintage, 1989).
21. Aptheker, *American Negro Slave Revolts,* 145.
22. The aphorism is quoted in E. Cobham Brewer, *Dictionary of Phrase and Fable* (Philadelphia: Henry Altemus, 1898), which Brewer traces to Walter Scott.
23. See John Hope Franklin and Loren Schweninger's *Runaway Slaves: Rebels on the Plantation* (New York: Oxford University Press, 1999).
24. Elizabeth Bowser, a free woman who worked for Elizabeth Van Lew, Grant's foremost Union spy in Richmond, might have had something to do with the episode Chesnut decries. Bowser took on the role of a hired slave, found employment in the Confederate White House, and overheard important information while serving President Davis his dinners. As an operative of Van Lew's, Bowser would have access to the Yankee prisoners that her mentor cared for, officially, in her home; occasionally, such prisoners would "escape" and collaborate with local slaves in acts of espionage and insurrection. My information on Bowser comes from a CIA Web site, of all places, entitled "Black Dispatches," a term coined by Union officers for a special file created to contain valuable pieces of intelligence provided by slaves and contrabands (http://www.cia.gov/library/publications/additional-publications/civil-war/p20.htm).
25. These social and juridical impediments to black civil rights took root in the 1890s. The myth of the Lost Cause is defined by historian David Blight as involving remembrance of

the Civil War that includes the following three components: (1) female guardianship of the mythology and the memorializing of the war, via the creation of voluntary organizations such as the United Daughters of the Confederacy; (2) the sentimental mythologizing of the causes of the war and the sacrifices of both soldiers and their women on the home front; (3) the denial that the war was fought over slavery. See Blight, *Race and Reunion*.

26. Remember that the 1880s Chesnut puts into Molly's mouth the words that the "missis" should burn her diary to keep it from the Yankees. That is, some of the most significant incendiary associations in Chesnut's narrative involve the experiences of slaves.

27. Molly reports that overseer Mr. Team's wife "has grown so fat she has to go through the big gate—the little one too narrow for her now. No wonder Sundays 'they puts two of yo' hams on their dinner table.'" And she concludes: "Yourn, Missis. Yourn overseer takes yo' things" (November 30, 1861, 248).

28. Among the brutal "punishments" meted out by whites for black "infractions" we find the example of "Dr. Flint," the proxy-master of "Linda Brent," punished her for her refusal to consent to his sexual demands, pushing her down a flight of stairs while pregnant, giving her a viciously violent haircut, putting her children in jail. See Jacobs, *Incidents in the Life of a Slave Girl*.

29. In one of the great ironies of Chesnut's life, Callie Perkins not only survives her mother's despondency but lives to nurse Chesnut herself in her final illness in 1886. In fact, it is Caroline Perkins who writes to S. Miller Williams the letter announcing the details of Chesnut's death. One of Chesnut's two most beloved nephews (and Johnny sadly has been dead for nearly twenty years), Miller was the industrious child equestrian who saved the Williams's family's horses during a retreat at the end of the war. Unpublished, and dated November 1886, the letter is held in the archives of Mulberry Plantation.

30. The 1880s Chesnut records for May 29, 1862, that the Williams's have sold Betsey to a telegraph man. This information is extraordinary, since Kate's husband, David R. Williams, a grandchild of the old Colonel, was raised in an ethos that frowned on the buying and selling of blacks. Accordingly, Betsey must have caused quite a problem, despite her protestations of loyalty in 1861. Chesnut paraphrases her own maid Molly on the subject: "My Molly thinks her mistress very lucky in getting rid of her. She was a dangerous inmate. But she will be a good cook, a good chamber maid, a good dairy maid, a beautiful clear starcher (and the most thoroughly good-for-nothing woman I know), to her new owners, if she chooses. Molly evidently hates her but thinks it is her duty to stand *by her color*" (May 29, 1862, 350).

Chapter Ten

1. I am thinking of Melville's subtitle for the novella *Billy Budd, Sailor: An Inside Narrative*. His *Benito Cereno* also features (mass) murder, when the slaves held as cargo on the San Dominick (evoking St. Domingo and the slave revolution there) rise up and murder the captain. They also hold the owner, Cereno, hostage when they take over the ship. The narrator is obsessed with gaining access to the thought processes of Babo, the diminutive and innocuous-looking slave mastermind of the revolt. But the tale's narrative form never

allows the reader an "inside" view of the black rebel chief's intellectual and emotional machinations.

2. See above, chap. 3, note 28.
3. Frances Kemble, *Journal of a Residence on a Georgia Plantation, 1838–1839*, ed. John A. Scott (Athens: University of Georgia Press, 1984).
4. See Patterson, *Slavery and Social Death,* and Wyatt-Brown, "The Mask of Obedience."
5. There is no evidence that the late senior Mr. Witherspoon was William's biological father. But Chesnut's romantic metaphors suggest that something beyond what was common knowledge may have been at work in William's relationship with the younger Mr. Witherspoon. One possible motive for the old master's willingness not only to "forgive" his runaway, but to retain him on the property and actually favor him before all his other slaves could have involved some sort of kinship tie. Surely there is something extraordinary about William's attempted escape and old Mr. Witherspoon's highly idiosyncratic response. And the fact that the black bondsman resorts to murdering his late master's widow to avoid the wrath of his late master's son, whose jealousy smacks of sibling rivalry, amplifies the sense that whatever went on at the Witherspoon plantation in the decade prior to the Civil War went beyond simple paternalism, transcending the cultural conventions that plantation patriarchs must tend to their slaves as fathers do to their children.
6. "Few set out for the north, as distances were far too great." See Franklin and Schweninger, *Runaway Slaves,* 42. See also Stephanie Camp, *Closer to Freedom: Enslaved Women and Everyday Resistance in the Plantation South* (Chapel Hill: University of North Carolina Press, 2005).
7. See Austin Steward, *Twenty-two Years a Slave and Forty Years a Freeman* (Rochester: William Alling, 1857); also available in an electronic edition as part of "Documenting the American South," a digital publishing initiative sponsored by the University Library at the University of North Carolina, Chapel Hill (http://docsouth.unc.edu/fpn/steward/steward.html).
8. Ibid., 30.
9. Ibid., 28.
10. Ibid., 29.
11. See Franklin and Schweninger, *Runaway Slaves.*
12. Steward, *Twenty-two Years a Slave,* 30.
13. See John Locke, *Second Treatise on Government,* ed. C. D. McPherson (Indianapolis: Hackett Publishing, 1980), 17.
14. While nineteenth-century death ways were such that the dead of rural communities were often attended by a local white woman connected with midwifery or, perhaps, on a large plantation, by a female slave healer, the funeral industry as we understand it did not come into its own until early in the Civil War, with the perfection of embalming. See Ashley Byock, "Embalming in Memory: Mourning, Narrativity, and Historiography in Nineteenth-Century America," Ph.D. diss., Northwestern University, 2008, chap. 5.
15. See Ariela J. Gross, *Double Character: Slavery and Mastery in the Antebellum Courtroom* (Princeton: Princeton University Press, 2000), 144.

16. One could argue, of course, that Molly had significant, guaranteed motivation for remaining that Laurence obviously did not: her butter-and-egg business with Mary Chesnut continued at least through 1871. Laurence's postwar whereabouts, on the contrary, have not materialized in lists of freedmen working the Mulberry fields or in Chesnut's daybook for wages paid to black domestics. Laurence's only wartime income came from what he skimmed from the Chesnut grocery bill during periods of their urban life. While dwelling on the plantation, of course, everything they ate came from their own fields, flocks, and herds.
17. To imagine such a tableau in contemporary terms, think of a homeowner asking the illegal immigrant cutting his lawn to borrow a pencil and paper, and then being handed a Mont Blanc pen and an extra blank sheet from the gardener's handy *Oxford English Dictionary* to write on. How would not his biases about the immigration crisis and the skill or lack of skill of Hispanic workers be turned on its head?
18. See chapter 9 for the later history of Scipio the elder according to the oral traditions of the Chesnut-Williams family, as rehearsed by Bruce Brown, contemporary owner of Bloomsbury, the senior Chesnut's town home in Camden.

Chapter Eleven

1. See Kimberly W. Benston, "Facing Tradition: Revisionary Scenes in African American Literature," *PMLA* 105 (Jan. 1990): 98–109.
2. I am intrigued by what the face of defeat might look like. This fascinating personification evokes some of Emily Dickinson's most difficult conceits; it calls to mind, particularly, the figure from "There's a certain slant of light": "'tis like the distance / On the look of death." In this poem, death takes mortal form, complete with a human visage, which allows it to manifest facial expressions such as looks. As Dickinson's death wears a human face, so, too, does Chesnut's defeat. But for Chesnut, the aspect of defeat is most accurately glimpsed in a mirror, as the projected face of the self who has lost everything.
3. This ailing soldier with deficient heart evokes Chesnut's portrait of her stony-faced cousin, Mary (Mrs. Edward Mortimer) Boykin, whose apparent lack of response to the news of her husband's battlefield wounding and her son's capture by the Yankees deeply disturbs the 1880s writer. See the entry quoted above in chap. 3, n. 20.
4. It also is possible that the captain actually recognized Mrs. Chesnut and did not want to embarrass her. If so, his flight could have signaled an unwillingness to acknowledge that ladies occasionally stepped down from the pedestal on which Southern men sought to keep them.
5. Chesnut most likely would have admired Constance Fennimore Woolson, a Northern writer who migrated to the South, and who rejected the dominant women's narrative mode, sentimentalism. Her greatest work, a novella titled *For the Major* published in 1883, the year we think Chesnut put down her pen, uncannily dramatizes the very ways in which the Southern belle had been socially constructed. The work's protagonist, the devoted second wife of a veteran Confederate officer suffering significant physical decline after the war, uses various prosthetics and articles of costume to convince her husband, and the

attendant community, that she is still young, and thus that the past has been preserved. A brilliant tale the denouement of which is not unreminiscent of Poe's "The Man Who Was Used Up," Woolson's work would have delighted Chesnut, never one for the denial of history.

6. In her reference to Oliver Wendell Holmes's shay "gone to pieces and all over," Chesnut quotes Holmes' tale, "The Deacon's Masterpiece; or, The Wonderful 'One Hoss Shay,'" in *The Autocrat of the Breakfast Table* (1858).

7. Across the 1880s narrative, Chesnut provides elaborate details of the feud between Davis and Johnston, whose initial emotional injury came when Jefferson Davis preferred Robert E. Lee as ranking commander of the Confederate Army of Northern Virginia, despite the fact that before secession, Johnston had held the highest rank among the five top Southern generals to leave the U.S. Army. Johnston had been brigadier quartermaster general; perhaps Davis did not consider this post on a par with that of commanding officers in the field. Johnston never forgave Davis for this perceived disrespect, and the two men hated each other for the entire war. Chesnut documents throughout her narrative the ways this feud registered among wives and other officers; and this small chapter of the larger text of the war is a story that could comprise an entire book in itself.

8. When Odysseus finds himself trapped in the cave of the murderous Cyclops, he concocts a brilliant plan to enable an escape that will defy pursuit: he tells the one-eyed monster that his name is "nemo," no one (*Odyssey* 10.408, 416).

INDEX

The abbreviation MBC is used throughout the index for Mary Boykin Chesnut; MCC, for Mary Cox Chesnut; and JC, for James Chesnut Jr. Page numbers in italics refer to illustrations and captions.

Aaron, Daniel, 10, 11, 13, 268n12
Abram (Grandfather Abram) (Chesnut slave), 140
Achilles, 13, 29, 32, 44, 46, 274n16
Adam Bede (George Eliot), 120, 122, 124, 125, 126; Adam (character), 286–87n14; Dinah (character), 125, 286n14; Hetty (character), 125, 285n14; as morally superior George Eliot novel, 121; plot of, 285–86n14
Aeneas, 46
Aeneid, 29, 287n1; book 6, 34
African Americans: four million emancipated from slavery, 267n7; political consciousness of, circa 1861, 208; political progress of, 180; restricted condition of in South Carolina, 214; stereotypes of, 181; violence against, 6. *See also* Chesnut, Mary Boykin, views of: African Americans; Chesnut, Mary Boykin, views of: slaves; slaves
Agamemnon, 44
Ajax, 44
Alcott, Louisa May, 276n11; *Little Women,* 145, 300n18
Alexander, Colonel, 237–38
Allan, Mrs. John ("Scotch"), 203, 301n23
Allston, Washington, 151
almond cakes, 104, 283n30
amateur theatricals, Richmond, 1864: and changing Southern class hierarchy, 198–99; charades as component of, 192–93, 200; local hostility toward, 192; as white self-medication, 167–68, 191–206
American Revolution, 154; incompletion of, 212, 305n10
Ames, Mary Williams Harrison, 265, 283n29
Anderson, Benedict, 293n20
Anderson, Mrs. Richard Heron, 175–76
Anderson, Robert, 34–35, 95
Anderson family, 175; relative privilege of slaves, 175
Andromache, 31–32, 272n3
Apollo, 5
apricots, 49, 91–92, 93, 94
Aptheker, Herbert, 211, 219, 306n19
Arabian Nights, 128
arrowroot, 92, 93
Astyanax, 31
Athena, 274n13
Atlantic Monthly, 117
Austen, Jane, 18, 51, 274n12; *Pride and Prejudice,* 51
Avary, Myrta Lockett, 3, 117, 222. *See also* Chesnut, Mary Boykin, 1880s narrative: Martin-Avary edition

Baldwin, James: critique of *Uncle Tom's Cabin,* 142, 288n10
Balzac, Honoré de, 114, 119; *Comédie humaine,* 119; *Cousine Bette,* 119; *La Peau de chagrin,* 119

Bard, David, 290n6
Barnwell, Mrs. Robert Woodward (Mary), 62–63, 65
Barnwell, Robert Woodward, 62–63, 65, 277n21
Barnwell family, 61, 62
Barrett, Leonard F., 295n36
Bartow, Francis Stebbins, 59
Bartow, Mrs. Francis Stebbins, 52, 119
battles, Civil War: Appomattox, 46, 89, 143, 183, 258; Atlanta, 32; Brandy Station, 65, 154; Chancellorsville, 4, 5, 32, 278n25, 278n26; Chickamauga, 25, 32, 201; Cold Harbor, 124; First Manassas (First Bull Run), 14, 25, 32, 59, 104, 109, 168; Fort Sumter, 14, 32, 34–35, 37–38, 123, 147, 167, 169, 180; Franklin, 32; Gettysburg, 32, 59, 201; Second Manassas (Second Bull Run), 276n9, 298n3; Sharpsburg (Antietam), 63, 68; Shiloh (Pittsburg Landing), 32, 183; Spotsylvania, 124; the Wilderness, 32, 124
Beaumarchais, Pierre-Augustin Caron de: *Le Barbier de Seville*, 118; *Le Mariage de Figaro*, 118
Beauregard, Pierre Gustave Toutant, 14, 35, 141, 148, 266; as "Engine," 272n5; failure to pursue Union troops after First Manassas, 32–33
Beecher, Henry Ward, 135, 287n4
Benito Cereno (Herman Melville), 181, 185, 307–8n1; Atufal (character), 185; Babo (character), 307n1; Benito Cereno (character), 181, 307n1. *See also* Melville, Herman
Benston, Kimberly, 254, 309n1
Berlin, Ira, 223, 281n9
Bethesda Presbyterian Church (Camden), 183
Betsey (slave nurse of JC), 146

Betsey (Williams slave): performs loyalty, 227; sold, 307n30
Bhabha, Homi, 293n18
Bible: Exodus, 127; Genesis, 54, 127; John, 189; Mark, 27; Matthew, 24
blackberries, 49, 92, 93, 282n18
black church, on Mulberry, 216. *See also* Wateree Mission Chapel
Blackwood's, 113, 117
Blight, David, 143, 288n12, 306–7n25
blockade, Northern naval control of Charleston, Norfolk, Savannah, and Wilmington, 118
Bloom, Harold, 39, 270n18, 287n1
Bloomsbury (Chesnut home in Camden), 57, 267n2
Bombastes Furioso (William Barnes Rhodes), 98, 192; plot of, 296–97n1
Bones, Charlotte, 264
Boucicault, Dion: *Jessie Brown; or, The Relief of Lucknow*, 194, 299n7
Bowser, Elizabeth, 306n24
Boykin, Alexander Hamilton, 103–4, 280n42
Boykin, Burwell (uncle of MBC), death of, 42–43
Boykin, Charlotte (aunt of MBC), 43, 292–93n18
Boykin, Katherine (Katie) (daughter of Sally Amelia Miller Boykin), 43
Boykin, Mary (Mamie) (daughter of Sally Amelia Miller Boykin), 43
Boykin, Mary Lang, 284n3
Boykin, Mary Whitaker (Mary Hammy), 258, 260
Boykin, Mrs. Edward Mortimer, affect of, 277n20, 309n3
Boykin, Sally Amelia Miller (sister of MBC), 5, 41, 42, 274n13; grief of, 43–44, 274n15
Boykin, Thomas Lang, 277n20

Boykin family: as house divided, 227, 228, 260; religious affiliation of, 183
Bradley, James, 280n5
bread, 95–96, 281n11
Breckinridge, John Cabell, 191, 200
Brewer, E. Cobham, 306n22
Brown, Bruce, 306n14
Brown, Gillian, 274n1
Brown, John, 172, 194
Brown, Manning, 184
Browne, Mrs. William Montague, 53
Browne, Thomas, 128
Browning, Elizabeth Barrett, 115
Buchanan, James, 51, 275n4
Butler, Jon, 295n32
Butler, Pierce Mease, 232, 233
Byock, Ashley, 308n14
Byron, George Gordon, Lord, 13, 112, 125, 286n15

Camden, South Carolina, slave uprising thwarted in 1816, 149, 210–15, 229, 245, 305nn10–11
Camden Confederate, 93
Camden Gazette, 215, 304n8
Camp, Stephanie, 246, 308n6
Cantey, Camilla, 287n6
Carlisle, Janice, 146, 288n17
Carlyle, Thomas, 127
Carney, Judith, 281n7, 281–82n12, 283n24
Cary, Constance (Mrs. Burton Harrison), 196, 200, 218, 297n2; *Recollections Grave and Gay,* 200, 297n2
Cary, Hetty, 89, 196, 200
Cash, W. J., 290–91n8
Cashin, Joan, 279n39
Catherine (Davis nurse), 272n2, 286n17
census, Camden, Kershaw County, South Carolina: 1850s, 55, 150; 1860s, 55

Chandler, Marion C., 306n16
Chapman, Dr. Nathaniel, "Remarks on the Chronic Fluxes of the Bowels," 92, 282nn17–18
Charleston, South Carolina, MBC witnesses attack on Fort Sumter from hotel roof in, 32
Charleston Courier, 222, 232
Charleston Mercury, 301n24
Charleston Theater, 299–300n15
Charleston *Weekly News and Courier,* 114
Charon, 46
Chaucer, Geoffrey, "Balade de Bon Conseyl" ("Truth"), 188–90, 295–96nn39–40
Chesnut, James, Jr. (JC), 1, 18, 29, 32–33, 41, 46, 48, 89, 129, 137, 158, 204, 240, 245, 247, 249; chastises Harriet Grant, 205–6, 301n26; death of, 2–3; disapproval of amateur theatricals, 167, 168, 191, 201–2; emphasized in MBC's 1880s narrative, 4; hires out slaves to Camden hotel, 82; jealousy toward MBC's potential "suitors," 13; political career of, 194, 280n42; response to mother's death, 159, 161; on his slaves, 86–87, 173, 291n10, 303n5
Chesnut, James, Sr. (father of JC), 1, 34, 45–46, 51, 53–54, 58, 141, 147, 148, 158, 164, 169, 263, 267n2, 274n12; alerts Camden planters of peril in 1816, 211; declines after wife's death, 160; emphasized in MBC's 1880s narrative, 3; estate of, 276n10; funeral of, 215–17; insularity of, 82; memorizes JC's letters, 160; possible sexual impropriety with slaves, 54–56; response to wife's death, 159–60, 161–62; sells land for black church, 217, 303n4; tyrannical personality of, 134; will of, 276n13

Chesnut, John, Sr. (grandfather of JC): possible mixed-race children of, 58; possible sexual impropriety with slaves, 150; will of, 58, 277n16

Chesnut, John, III (Johnny, the Cool Captain) (nephew of JC), 27, 51, 86, 137; accuses slaves of theft, 87–88; death of, 129, 259; dream of postwar chicken farm, 97; emphasized in MBC's 1880s narrative, 4; failure to restore Mulberry fields after war, 97; response to death of MCC, 159, 161; treatment of slaves, 282n14

Chesnut, Mary Boykin (MBC), biography, 1, 267n1, 270n17; accidental overdose of opium, 229–30; adopts special diet of milk, rice, and stoned and seeded fruits to combat illness, 92, 94; angina pectoris of, 2, 81; "Annual Expense Book," 98, *99, 100, 101*; beneficiary of slave labor, 10, 134; bibliophilia of, 112; borrowed children of, 18, 52; buries 1860s diary pages, 25; burns portion of 1860s diary, 4; chronic anxious depression of, 16–17, 42; complains she is "nobody," 261; cosmopolitan vision of, 194; croup (diphtheria or pneumonia) of, 81; dairy business of, 17–18, 98; danger of psychic ossification for, 259; death of, 2–3; different roles assumed by, 112; does not write in 1863–64, 4; dress catches on fire on Charleston rooftop, 39–40; dyspepsia of, 80–81; education of, 137, 181; faith in literature, 128; familial loss suffered post war, 259; "gastric fever" (typhoid) of, 2, 16, 67, 81, 92, 260; gustatory pleasures of, 103, 284n31; illness in August of 1862, 4; illnesses enable writing, 58–59, 265; infertility of, 15, 22, 40–41, 42, 50, 51–53, 58, 102, 122, 150, 152, 297n1; intense emotions of, 260; knowledge of slave uprisings, 209–10; laughter as mode of survival for, 258–60; letter to Jane Pettigrew Williams about dairy herd, 98, 102; life in Washington, 83; literary ambition of, 134; lost abolitionist letter, 182, 209, 294n28; marriage to JC, 12–13; medications of, 92; mistaken for Confederate officer's trysting partner, 253, 255–56; mistaken for lower class woman, 254, 261–62; money belt of, 20, 22–23; possible miscarriage, 51–52, 148, 297n1; post-Reconstruction bitterness of, 153; racism of, 133–34, 208, 268n11, 302–3n3; refuses theater invitation, 298n3; relation between diary writing and dairy business, 98; religious tolerance of, 183, 228; returns to Camden at end of war, 45–47; robust appetite of, 92; rusticated in Camden, 122; self-medication with opium, 16–17, 92; sends bread to Mrs. Rutledge, 96; social regime of, 115–16; teaches slaves to read, 217, 293n20, 306n18; trip to visit ill mother, 41–45; understanding of slavery as social construction, 303n3; wears JC's clothes, 273n6; will of, 283n29; witnesses sale of Miller plantation slaves as a youth, 10

Chesnut, Mary Boykin, 1860s diary: declares "My subjective days are over" in, 130; "mama smells a smell" kernel in, 147; mulatto children dropping "from the clouds" passage in, 56–58, 151; no entries for 1864 in, 159; "Rachel and her brood" remark in, 54–57; religious references in, 113

Chesnut, Mary Boykin, 1880s narrative: avoids grotesque instances of African American vernacular in, 198;

black incendiaries in, 219–21; "The Bright Side of Richmond, 1864," 191; catalogues of barren women in, 52; catalogues of words in, 107; as "countermemory," 144; culinary catalogues in, 80; as epic, 13–14, 17, 20, 26–27, 29–47, 50, 64, 88–89, 107, 254, 265–66, 269n15, 272n3, 273n7, 274n17; death of Joe Davis in, 162–65, 261; death of MCC described in, 159–65, 261; MBC's declaration of kindness to "negroes" in, 227; elision of slave agency in, 244; episodes of misrecognition in, 253–66; explorations of slave consciousness in, 232; the face of defeat in, 309n2; fall of Richmond described in, 161; generic classification of, 9, 10–11, 14, 16, 17, 109, 129; "howling" references in, 286n17; incendiary thematics in, 39; journeys to the underworld in, 5, 14, 30, 33–34, 41–47, 273n7; juxtaposition of the domestic and the political in, 110, 149, 200; keen historical sense in, 272n5, 302n2; laughter in, 257–60; literary criticism in, 130–31; as literary work of art, 2, 5–6, 8, 10–11, 16–17, 18, 131; Martin-Avary edition, 3, 6–7; metanarrative episodes in, 23, 25, 27, 178; the miniature as structural unit of, 17, 18, 19, 20; Odyssean moment of invisibility in, 265; MBC's organization of, 3–4; provides documentation for Beauregard's battle plan, 24, 32–33; poultry motif in, 96–98; reappropriation of vocabulary of slavery in, 233–34, 243; MBC's revisions to, 2, 4, 7–9, 12, 115–17, 207, 243–44, 284n31, 284n1, 285n11; satirical account of original sin in, 184; scholarly treatment of, 10–12, 12–13, 16; slave resistance as theme in, 227, 245; social roles in, 169; use of phrase "The red cock crows in the barn" in, 219–20; use of phrase "sword of Damocles" in, 173; visit to Mulberry black church in, 183–90; Williams edition, 7, 268n9; women on the walls in, 30, 34–39; Woodward Yale edition, 7, 8–9, 11

Chesnut, Mary Boykin, fictive personae, 23; Andromache, 39; Cassandra, 5, 44, 182, 294n29; Crazy Jane, 255–56; Gorgon, 256–57, 266; King Lear, 128, 286n17; Lord Nelson, 68; scribbling Confederate matron, 4, 6

Chesnut, Mary Boykin, other writings, 11, 267n6, 268n10, 284n7; "The Arrest of a Spy," 114; "The Captain and the Colonel," 8, 197–98; "Manassas," 8; "Two Years; or, The Way We Lived Then," 8

Chesnut, Mary Boykin, reading of. *See individual authors and works*

Chesnut, Mary Boykin, relationships with: family-in-law, 13, 27, 148, 264; Harriet Grant, 205, 225, 264; JC, 264; MCC, 84, 136, 141–42; Molly, 179; unnamed niece, 43–44, 282n18

Chesnut, Mary Boykin, views of: African Americans, 9–11, 15, 133–34, 140, 152–53, 185, 189; death, 42–45, 60–68, 74–76; "Dixie," 3, 269n15; domestic sphere, 15, 27, 149; female slave fertility, 15, 50; the Irish, 271–72n2; Jewish friends, 272n2, 298n2; life in Camden, 16, 45; marriage as form of slavery, 13; miscegenation, 84, 136, 149–51; misuse of language, 109–11, 197; her narrative's value, 23–24; New England abolitionists, 145; Northern schools, 110, 111; photographic portrait taken in March 1861, 1–2; professional writers, 108; Sandy Hill, 148; sentimentalism, 12, 15, 77, 115,

INDEX 315

Chesnut, Mary Boykin, views of (*cont.*) 131, 133–34, 140–41, 142, 186, 216, 274n15; slave religion, 182–90; slavery, 10, 18, 77, 84, 133–34, 136, 142, 143–44, 152–53, 173–74, 182, 185, 208–9, 228, 269n15, 293n19; slavery as cause of Civil War, 77, 142; slaves, 20–21, 169, 170–71, 173–74, 181, 184, 189, 230, 232–34, 245–51, 284n5; Southern male sexual impropriety with slaves, 56, 57–58, 285n13; Southern schools, 110; women's degraded legal status, 15

Chesnut, Mary Cox (MCC), 34, 51, 53–54, 72–73, 126, 169, 209, 245, 263, 293n20; angelic personality of, 134; bibliophilia of, 112, 151; biography of, 85, 149, 154, 158, 172; compared to Eva (*Uncle Tom's Cabin*), 136, 137, 164–65; deafness of, 150–51, 152; death of, 138, 159; as doppelganger for Betsey Witherspoon, 227; gustatory preferences of, 79, 84–86, 281n10; hypersensitivity to scents, 145–49, 152; insularity of, 82; interaction with slaves, 146; literary preferences of, 118–19; "mama smells a smell," 137; member of "white-robed choir" serenading Washington in Trenton in 1789, 137, 154–58, *157;* on miscegenation, 136; moral paradoxes of, 127; passive-aggressive streak of, 84; reaction to Witherspoon murder, 229; relationship with MBC, 84, 137; sentimentality of, 141–42; view of female slaves, 151, 276n11; views of slavery, 84–86, 136, 149, 152, 228–29, 279n36

Chesnut, Richard (Dick) (manumitted Chesnut slave), 305n12

Chesnut, Sarah (Miss Sally), 147, 148, 158, 160, 293n20

Chesnut family: as house divided, 148, 228, 260; religious affiliation of, 183
Chesnut's Ferry, 45
Chester, South Carolina, 45
Cheves, Langdon, Sr., 62
Child, Lydia Maria, 281n11
Chimborazo Military Hospital (Richmond), 272n2
Cicero: *De officiis,* 181; *De oratore,* 181
Civil War: aftermath of, 46; death of Southern men in, 20, 69–70, 193, 271n27; enduring legacy of, 6; psychic costs of, 259–60; Southern social transformation in wake of, 253, 262. *See also* battles, Civil War
Cixous, Hélène, *The Laugh of the Medusa,* 257
Claiborne (Chesnut slave), 224
Cohen, Miriam (Mem), 60, 183, 228, 272n2, 297n2
Coleridge, Samuel Taylor, 234
Collins, Wilkie, 245. *See also Woman in White, The*
Columbia, South Carolina: food shortage in, 89, 95–96; Union army's destruction of, 45, 88
Commodity, defined by Marx, 174
Complete Confectioner, Pastry Cook, and Baker, The (Parkinson), 283n30
Confederate government: impresses slave labor, 199; requisitions crops, 199
Confederate White House, 74, 220, 245
Congaree House (Columbia), 24, 94
Cooke, Philip St. George, 274n14
corn, 85–86
cornbread, 84, 85–86
Cornhill Magazine, 117
Coulter, E. Merton, 281n10, 282n15
Couser, G. Thomas, 17, 271n23
Cox, John (father of MCC): manumitted slaves, 85; served on George Washington's staff, 85

Craft, Ellen, 235
Craft, William, 235
Crafts, Hannah, *The Bondswoman's Narrative,* 303n3
Crittenden, George Bibb, 274n14
Crittenden, John, 274n14
Crittenden, Thomas Leonidas, 274n14
Cromwell, Oliver, 73
Cummins, Maria, 50
Currier and Ives, 137, 158; "Washington's reception by the ladies . . . ," *157*
Custis family, relatives of Martha Washington, 149, 154
Cuthbert, George, 67, 278n27
Cyclops, 54, 310n8

Dahlgren, Ulric, failed cavalry raid on Richmond, March 1864, 123–24
Daily South Carolinian, 70, 71
Daniels, Christopher Williams, 217, 306n15
Dante Alighieri, 13, 88, 275n3; *Divine Comedy,* 287n1
Daughters of the Confederacy, 76–77, 279n39, 307n25
Davis, David Brion, 295n35
Davis, Esther, 215–16, 218; "Memories of Mulberry," 216, 218, 303n4
Davis, Jefferson, 14, 24, 27, 29, 32–33, 34, 74, 77, 97, 124, 138, 163, 264, 303n3, 306n24, 310n7; disavows slavery as cause of Civil War, 142–43; *The Rise and Fall of the Confederate Government,* 143, 288n11
Davis, Jefferson, Jr. (Jeff), 163, 279n39
Davis, Jefferson C., 304n6
Davis, Joseph Evan (little Joe): children behave badly at funeral of, 164; compared to Eva (*Uncle Tom's Cabin*), 138, 164–65; crowds of children attend funeral service of, 76; death of, 74–76, 138, 162–65, 204–5, 276n9, 279n39; mourned by unnamed child, 74–76; tableau of prayer saying, 138
Davis, Lennard, 58–59, 277n17
Davis, Margaret Howell (Maggie), 163, 279n39
Davis, Rebecca Harding, 270n17
Davis, Samuel Emory, 279n39
Davis, Varina Anne (Winnie), 163; biography of, 279n39
Davis, Varina Howell, 41, 52, 74, 138, 162, 220–21; children of, 163, 279n39
Davis, William Howell, 279n39
Davis family, 128; Confederate people begin to turn on, 221; MBC's idealization of, 221; religious affiliation of, 183
Deas, Margaret Chesnut, 58
Declaration of Independence, 212
DeLeon, Agnes, 228, 272n2
DeLeon, Henrietta, 262
DeLeon, Thomas Cooper (T. C.), 218; *Belles, Beaux, and Brains of the 60s,* 297–98n2
Dell, Joan Elizabeth, 270n19
Delphic Oracle, 6, 75
de Man, Paul, 271n1, 278n26
DeSaussure, Wilmot Gibbes, salad dressing of, 94
DeSaussure mansion (Columbia), 71–72
Deutsch, Helen, 19, 271n24, 291n13
diarrhea (symptom of "gastric fever"), nineteenth-century treatment for, 92–93, 95, 282nn17–18
Diary from Dixie, A, 3, 117; excerpted in *Saturday Evening Post,* 3, 6; Southern readership of, 6. *See also* Chesnut, Mary Boykin, 1880s narrative: Martin-Avary edition
Dick (Miller slave), 170–72, 174, 175–77, 182; position as elite Miller slave, 176; refuses to face MBC, 170; as sphinx, 171–72, 180
Dickens, Charles, 113, 118

Dickinson, Emily, 8; "There's a certain slant of light," 309n2
Diffley, Kathleen, 16, 19, 36, 271n26, 273nn8–9
Doctorow, E. L., *The March,* 304n6
double consciousness: of MBC, 2, 6, 19, 60, 284n31; W. E. B. Du Bois on, 302n1
Douglas, Ann, 114, 144–45, 269n17, 284n8
Douglass, Frederick, 235; eloquence of, 177; *Narrative of the Life of Frederick Douglass,* 294n31; "What to the American slave is your Fourth of July?," 212
Du Bois, W. E. B., 294n27; concept of double consciousness, 302n1
dueling, 200–201
Dugaw, Diane, 296n1

Early, Jubal, 77, 288n13
East India Company, 193, 195, 298n6, 304n6
Eastman, Mary Henderson: *Aunt Phyllis's Cabin,* 139
Edgefield Adviser, 93
Edward Burke (mulatto manumitted by John Chesnut Sr.), 58
Eliot, George, 113, 114, 115, 117, 119–22, 131, 142, 197, 265; born Mary Anne Evans, 119; character development technique of, 179; idolized by MBC, 4; reputation as fallen woman, 124–27. *See also individual works*
Eliot, T. S., *The Waste Land,* 19–20, 50
Ellen (slave maid of MBC), 21, 22, 91, 146, 213, 224, 230, 269n15, 271n28; administers overdose of opium to MBC, 229–30; relative autonomy of, 247; warns of no food in 1865, 96
Elpenor, 44
Emaeus, 89

Emancipation Proclamation, 170, 171, 195, 244, 302n2
Emerson, Ralph Waldo, 113, 145
England, 51
England, John, 183, 228
epic, defined, 13–14, 29, 50, 254, 274n17, 287n1. *See also* Chesnut, Mary Boykin, 1880s narrative: as epic
epistolarity, 25–26
Evans, Augusta Jane: absent from MBC's 1880s narrative, 113–15, 285n9; *Beulah,* 113, 115; *Macaria,* 113, 115, 284n6
Eyck, Jan van, 94

facing scene, defined, 66, 254
Fahs, Alice, 273n9
Fanon, Frantz, 181, 294n24
Farmer's Cabinet, 289n24
Faulkner, William: insights in *Absalom, Absalom!* anticipated by MBC, 15; possible reading of *A Diary From Dixie,* 15
Faust, Drew Gilpin, 271n27, 284n6, 290n2
Fawkes, Richard, 299n7
Ferguson, Priscilla Parkhurst, 280n4
Feydeau, Ernest-Amié: *Fanny,* 115, 118
fictive kinship, defined, 223
Fineman, Joel, 18–19, 271n24
fire insurance, denied in slave states, 219
Fisher, Abby, 281n7, 281n10
Fisher, Judith L., 299n12
Fitzhugh, George, 190, 269n15
Flat Rock, North Carolina, 67
Flaxman, John, "Andromache Fainting on the Wall," 37–39, *38*
Flora (MBC's cow), 283n29
flowers, 72–77. *See also specific flowers*
food. *See specific foods*
Foote, Shelby, 274n14
Fort Moultrie: bread episode, 95
Foster, Stephen, 265; "Massa in the Cold, Cold Ground," 269n15

Fox-Genovese, Elizabeth, 10, 268n12
Franklin, John Hope, 221, 306n23
Freeland, Rose, 74
Freud, Sigmund: on disavowal, 302n1; "Mourning and Melancholia," 160, 288n17; on the uncanny, 233
Frey, Sylvia R., 295n32
fruit, 79; MBC's emphasis on stoned and seeded fruits, 91–92. *See also individual fruit types*
Frye, Northrop, on the comic unfolding of Christianity, 182, 294n30
Fuller, Margaret, 269n17

Gallagher, Gary W., 288n13
Gallop, Jane, 19, 271n24
Gardner, Alexander: *Photographic Sketch Book of the War*, 69, 70–71, 277n18; "A Sharpshooter's Final Sleep," 71; "Where General Reynolds Fell," 71. *See also* O'Sullivan, Timothy: "A Harvest of Death, Gettysburg, Pennsylvania"
Garrison, William Lloyd, 135
Gazette of the United States (New York), account of George Washington at Trenton in 1789, 155–56, 158, 289nn20–21
Genovese, Eugene, 10, 268n12, 290n6, 291n12, 292n17
Glover, Mrs. Thomas Worth, story of "infair," 90
Glymph, Thavolia, 270n19
Godey's Lady's Book, 199
Goethe, Johann Wolfgang von, *Elective Affinities*, 126
Gone With the Wind (Margaret Mitchell), 143; Emmie Slattery (character), 206; Jonas Wilkerson (character), 206; Mammy (character), 302n27; as plantation romance, 301–2n27; Scarlett O'Hara (character), 206, 260

Gorgon, 256–57
Graham's Magazine, 203
Grant, Harriet, 27, 148, 159–60, 161, 205–6, 275n3; called "Hecate" in MBC's 1860s diary, 205
Grant, Ulysses Simpson, 69, 71, 89, 138, 286n16, 306n24
Greece: ancient burial rituals, 46; popularity of cultural themes of in nineteenth-century America, 37; theatrical tradition of masking, 181; United States of America as, 38
Greeley, Horace, 145
Green, Richard, 293n23
Grimstead, David, 299n12
Gross, Ariela, 246, 308n15
Gruesser, John Cullen, 294n27
Grundy, Mrs. Thomas Billop, 123, 249
Guignard, Mrs. James Sanders, Jr., 93
Gwin, Captain, 204
gynecology, pioneered on slave women, 275n6. *See also* infertility

Hahn, Steven, 223, 302n2
Haiti, 172, 208; Haitian Revolution of 1793–1804, 210. *See also* slave resistance: at St. Domingo
Halttunen, Karen, 199, 300n16
ham, 91
Hamilton, Louisa, 40
Hammond, James Henry, 57, 190, 276n14
Hampton, Frank, 5, 61, 79; death of, 64–67; as doppelganger for MBC, 66–68
Hampton, Mrs. Frank (Sally Baxter), 64–65, 79, 277n23; identified in death by MBC as Sally Baxter, 65
Hampton, Wade, III, 51, 61, 62, 287n6; commanding general of Confederate cavalry, 57; governor of South Carolina, 57; wound of, 110–11

INDEX 319

Hampton family, 61, 64–65
Handel, George Frederick, *Saul,* 14, 265
Handley, Eric, 293n23
Harper's Weekly, 35–38, 71, 117; pro-Union sentiments of, 36. See also "Housetops in Charleston during the Bombardment of Fort Sumter, The"
Harrison, Serena Chesnut Williams, 283n29
Harrison, Thomas, suicide of, 265
Hartman, Saidiya V., 290n4, 293n22
Harvey, A. McGee, 280n5
Haskell, Alexander, 61, 64
Haskell family, 61
Hathaway, Anne, 130
Hawthorne, Nathaniel: *The Blithedale Romance,* 114–15, 125, 301n21; *The House of Seven Gables,* 301n21; *The Marble Faun,* 80, 301n21; *The Scarlet Letter,* 187–88, 301n21. See also *Scarlet Letter, The*
Hayne, Paul, 285n9
Hector, 31–32, 37
Hedrick, Joan, 135, 287n3
Hegel, Georg Wilhelm Friedrich, 170–71, 181, 191, 208, 254–55, 278n26; on mutual dependence of lord and bondsman, 255; *The Phenomenology of Spirit,* 255, 290n7
Heilmeyer, Marina, 279n33
Helm, William, 237
Hemings, Easton, 56–57; as cameo-copy of Thomas Jefferson, 57
Hemings, Madison, 56–57
Hemings, Sally, 56–57; possible sexual relationship with Thomas Jefferson, 56
Herbert, Christopher, 195, 299n9
Hermitage, the, 86
Hess, Karen, 96, 281n7
Hester, Tom, 289n22
Hetty (slave maid of Mary Boykin Miller), 43, 175

Hibernian Hall, 300n15
Higginson, Thomas Wentworth, 195–96, 299n11; *Army Life in a Black Regiment,* 273n10
Holland, Edwin C., 305n10
Holmes, Oliver Wendell, 261; "The Deacon's Masterpiece, or, the Wonderful 'One Hoss Shay,'" 310n6
Holstein, Suzy Clark, 270n19
Home Journal, 289n24
Homer, 13, 17, 31–32, 44, 46, 131, 254, 256, 265, 272n3, 287n1
hominy, 85
Hood, John Bell (Sam), 29, 191; as centaur, 268n13; postwar biography of, 268n14; response to performance of *The Rivals,* 200–201, 202; romance with Buck Preston, 12, 14, 201; wounded at Chickamauga, 25, 201, 268n13; wounded at Gettysburg, 201, 268n13
Hoole, W. Stanley, 198, 299–300n15, 300n17
Horwitz, Tony, 6, 143
house divided theme, 12–13, 15, 26–27, 228
"Housetops in Charleston during the Bombardment of Fort Sumter, The" 35–39, 40; as frontispiece of *The Private Mary Chesnut,* 35. See also *Harper's Weekly*
Howell, Margaret Graham (Maggie), 162–63
Hudson, Edward M., 202
human parasitism: defined, 87; exemplified, 275n3. See also slaves: as human parasites
Hurston, Zora Neale, 294n25

ideological reversal: defined, 87; exemplified, 226, 235–36, 275n3
Iliad, 14, 29, 30, 37, 38, 287n1; book 6,

31; book 22, 32. *See also individual characters*
Illustrated London News, 199
Inabinet, Glenn, 305n9
incest, anxiety about in postwar South, 301n26
Indian Mutiny of 1857–58, 193–95, 210, 219; causes of, 195; fear of slave rebellion provoked by, 193; massacre of the boats, 210, 219, 304n6; parallels with slave rebellion, 195; siege of Cawnpore, 194, 299n8; siege of Lucknow, 194
infertility, nineteenth-century medical understanding of, 41, 52. *See also* Chesnut, Mary Boykin (MBC), biography: infertility of
Isaac (slave of Chapman Levy), 212, 219
Ives, Mrs. Joseph Christmas, 198, 200
Izard, Mrs. Walter, 298n3

Jackson, Thomas J. ("Stonewall"), 5, 29, 39, 59; death of, 65–66, 183, 278n25; as "Stonewall," 272n5
Jacobs, Harriet, 235, 276n11; *Incidents in the Life of a Slave Girl,* 145, 292n17, 307n28
James, C. L. R., 219, 283n28, 306n20
Janin, Jules, 118
Jefferson, Thomas, 56–57; *Notes on the State of Virginia,* 181; possible sexual relationship with Sally Hemings, 56
Jesus Christ, 165, 188
Jim Crow segregation, 223
Johnson, Michael P., 268n11
Johnston, Albert Sidney, 39, 59
Johnston, Joseph Eggleston, 14, 264, 272n5, 310n7; as "Marlboro," 272n5
Johnston, Mrs. Joseph Eggleston, 264
Jordan, Winthrop, 290n6
Juliana (mulatto manumitted by John Chesnut Sr.), 58
Juncker, Clara, 270n19

Kansas, 235
Kantorowitz, Ernst H., 286n18
Keats, John, 234
Keitt, William J., 225–26, 241; murdered by slaves, 226, 227–28, 282n17
Kemble, Fanny, 232–33, 308n3
Kennedy, Robert M., 306n15
"Kentucky Generals" (Breckinridge, Hood, Morgan), in Richmond in 1864, 191, 200
Kerber, Linda, 289n19
Key, Kristina Pope, 270n19
Keyes, Ancel, 282n16
Kibbler, James, 6, 15, 268n8
King Lear (William Shakespeare), 15, 127–29, 279n37; called "the tragedy of the world" by MBC, 128; Cordelia (character), 128; Edgar (character), 129; Goneril (character), 128, 197; King Lear (character), 128, 197; Regan (character), 128, 197. *See also* Shakespeare, William
Kirkland, Thomas J., 306n15
Knight's Hill, 267n2
Kurant, Wendy Ann, 270n19

Laburnum (Lyons home), 220
Lacan, Jacques, 278n26
Lamar, Lucius Quintus Cincinnatus (L. Q.), 121, 124, 126, 127, 285n10
Laurence (slave valet of JC), 20–22, 92, 134, 140, 159, 160, 169, 182, 198, 213, 230, 245–50, 262, 263, 264; "bronze mask" of, 20, 22, 174; caught without pass, 247; compared to Count Fosco (*The Woman in White*), 245–46; disappears after war, 250, 309n16; emergent drinking problem of, 246–49; expelled from North Carolina lodging on account of finery and gold pencil case, 249–50; intimate proximity to JC, 245–46; literacy of, 250;

Laurence (slave valet of JC) (*cont.*)
personality changes, 246; relative autonomy of, 22–23, 246–47
Lee, Mary Ann Randolph Custis, 92
Lee, Mrs. Robert E., 154
Lee, Robert E., 27, 29, 69, 71, 138, 169, 310n7; fantasy of unlimited fried chicken, 97
Leslie, Eliza, 283n22
Levine, Bruce, 303–4n5
Levine, Lawrence, 299n12
Lewes, George Henry, 124–25, 126
Lewis, Matthew G. (Monk), 255–56
Lewis, Mrs. Lawrence (Aunt Nelly Custis), 154, 302n2
Lige (Chesnut slave), 224
Lincoln, Abraham, 27, 34, 68, 244; assassinated, 259, 287n17; Second Inaugural Address, 289n24
Lincoln, William Wallace (Willie), death of, 289n24
Lincoln family, 128
Lincolnton, North Carolina, 45, 89, 90, 249
"literary lady" (Southern periodical writer MBC meets in Alabama in 1861), 108
Litwack, Leon F., 196, 299n11
Locke, John, 308n13; on slavery as state of war, 240
London, England, 52, 181
Longstreet, Augustus, 285n9
"Lost Cause," 77, 223; defined, 143, 306–7n25
Lott, Eric, 237
Lowndes, Rawlins (Rawdie), 268–69n14
Lynn, Kenneth, 117, 285n12
Lyons, Mrs., 178, 180, 220
Lyons family, 82, 245

macaroons, 103–4, 283n30
Macguire, Dr., 278n25
MacIndal, 283n28
madness, Southern view of, 63
Magrath, Edward, 301n24
Manning, John Laurence, 169
March (slave of Captain Chapman Levy), 212, 219
Marsch, Margaret, 275n8
Martin, Isabella, 5, 74, 117, 183, 222, 269n15, 298n5; becomes character in MBC's 1880s narrative, 285n11; intellectual accomplishments of, 109; as MBC's literary executor, 3. *See also* Chesnut, Mary Boykin, 1880s narrative: Martin-Avary edition
Martin family, 74
Marx, Karl, 174, 291n13
Massey, Mary Elizabeth, 282n15
Mathews, Donald G., 185, 186, 187, 295n32, 295n36
May, Elaine Tyler, 275n8
McConachie, Bruce A., 299n12
McCord, Langdon Cheves, 5; death of, 139, 276n9, 298n3
McCord, Louisa Susannah Cheves, 5, 26, 52, 59, 61, 74, 266, 298n3, 303n3; review of *Uncle Tom's Cabin,* 114, 134, 138–39, 287n7, 288n8
McDonald, Kendra Lynne, 270n19
McDonald, Mrs., as deus ex machina, 96, 280n1
McLane, Charles M., 275n7
McLane, Midy, 275n7
McMahon's lodging house (Columbia), 74, 80
McPherson, James, 143, 271n31
Means, Emma, 63–64
Means, John Hugh, 63–64
Means, Mrs. John Hugh, 63–64
Means, Robert Stark, 63–64
Means family, 61, 63
Medusa, 62; only mortal of three Gorgons, 257

Melville, Herman: *Benito Cereno,* 181, 185, 232; *Billy Budd, Sailor,* 307n1; *Piazza Tales,* 294n26. See also *Benito Cereno* (Herman Melville)
Mentzer, Melissa, 270n19
Mesle, Sarah, 288n16
Middleton, John Izard, Jr. (Jack), 89
Middleton, Miss Susan Matilda, 26, 60, 90, 258
Middleton, Mrs. Oliver Hering, Sr., 95–96
Middleton, Oliver Hering, Jr., 60
Miles, William Porcher, 226
milk, 92, 93
Miller, Mrs. Stephen Decatur, Sr. (Mary Boykin Miller) (mother of MBC), 41–42, 171, 267n1, 292–93n18; death of, 3
Miller, Stephen Decatur, Sr. (father of MBC), 170, 176, 177, 209, 267n1; political career of, 290n5
Miller family, religious affiliation of, 183
Miller slaves, relative privilege of, 175
Mill on the Floss, The (George Eliot), 120; plot of, 286n14
Milroy, Robert Hurston, 302n2
Milton, John, 13, 73, 107, 129–31, 234, 287n1. See also *Paradise Lost* (John Milton)
mimicry, 180, 293n18
minstrelsy, 109, 181, 198, 284n2
Mitchell, Margaret, 206; possible reading of *A Diary from Dixie,* 269n16. See also *Gone With the Wind* (Margaret Mitchell)
Moliere, 128
Molly (slave maid of MBC), 21, 22, 42, 91, 92, 134, 146, 159, 198, 213, 225, 230, 245, 249, 262, 263, 264, 293n20; accuses Laurence of superiority complex, 248; assaults romantic rival with hot poker, 224; color loyalty of, 307n30; MBC's dairy business partner, 18, 98, 248, 250, 309n16; disapproval of Negro balls, 247; MBC's fantasy construction of, 178–80; mimicry of Mrs. Lyons, 178, 180; and Mrs. Team, 225, 307n27; potential political consciousness of, 178–80; relative autonomy of, 247; a snitch, 230, 248; warns MBC to burn diary in Stoneman's raid, 178
Money, Edward, *The Wife and the Ward; or, A Life's Error,* 194
Montgomery Hall, 80–81, 94
moonshines, 103–4, 107
Moore, John Hammond: *The Confederate Housewife,* 93, 95, 282n19
More, Thomas, 112–13
Morgan, John Hunt, 191
Morgan, Philip, 176, 289n24
Moses (Sarsfield freedman), 102
Moses, Wilson Jeremiah, 294n27
Mozart, Wolfgang Amadeus: *Requiem,* 265
Mulberry (Chesnut plantation), 57, 71–73, 82–83, 217, 267n2; Union troops raid in spring of 1865, 25, 213
Muhlenfeld, Elisabeth, 4, 16, 51, 52, 53, 81, 117, 172, 183, 256, 267n5–6, 269n14, 273n6, 284n7; on James Chesnut Sr.'s possible sexual impropriety with slaves, 54; *Mary Boykin Chesnut,* 267n1; *The Private Mary Chesnut* (editor), 9, 35, 54, 267n1, 268n10; *Two Novels by Mary Chesnut* (editor), 268n10
Mundt, Klara: *Joseph II and His Court* (*Joseph II*), 127
Munford, William Preston (Willie), 65
Munro, Mrs., 90–91, 228
Muscogee Railroad Company v. Redd (1861), 292n14

Negro ball, 23; as act of slave resistance, 236–37; as theft and love, 237; Witherspoon slaves hold, 236–39
Nelson, Horatio, 68, 137
Nelson, Jim (Chesnut slave), 185–90, 215; effect of singing on MBC, 186–90
Neoptolemos, 274n16
Newman, Steven, 296n1
Newport, Rhode Island, 51, 52
New York Herald, 265
New York Times, 70, 277n22
Nicholls, David, 291n9
Nickerson, Catherine Ross, 270n19
Nolan, Alan T., 288n13
North, mythologized as Puritan wilderness, 71
Nudelman, Franny, 277n18
Nultan, Karen Sue, 270n19
Numbers, Ronald L., 281n5

O'Brien, Michael, 16–17, 53, 271n20, 299n6
O'Donovan, Susan, 288n18
Odysseus, 44, 46, 88–89, 274n13, 274n16, 287n1; homecoming of, 254; as "nemo," 265, 310n8
Odyssey, 30, 50, 287n1; book 11, 44; book 12, 34; book 22, 254. *See also* individual characters
Old Jack (Blanchard slave), 212
Olly (MBC's cow), 102, 283n29
O'Neall, John Belton: refutation of *Uncle Tom's Cabin,* 288n8
O'Sullivan, Timothy, 59; "A Harvest of Death, Gettysburg, Pennsylvania," *69,* 70–71, 277n18. *See also* Gardner, Alexander: *Photographic Sketch Book of the War*
Owen, William Miller, 92

Page, Robert Lucien, 253, 255–56, 261
Paradise Lost (John Milton): Adam (character), 73; book 6, 73; book 9, 130; book 10, 273n11; Eve (character), 73, 130; Satan (character), 73, 234
Pardy, Mangal, 195
Parker, Sarah, 258
Pascal, Blaise, 128
pastoralism, 70–74
pastry, 91
paternalism, 87, 269n15; and affect, 303n4; defined, 217; nineteenth-century development of, 176
Patterson, Orlando, 87, 223, 247, 255, 271n29, 275n3, 290n7, 291n10
Payton, Sara Willis (Fanny Fern), 289n24
peaches, 49, 91, 93, 107; as symbol for fidelity in art, 93–94
Pember, Phoebe Yates Levy, 272n2; *A Southern Woman's Story,* 297n2
Penelope, 254
Perkins, Caroline (Callie), 227–28, 307n29; vulnerable to mother's poisoned affect, 227
Perkins, Mrs. Priscilla Bryan, 227–28
Peter (Sarsfield freedman), 102
Pettigrew, James Johnston, drawings of scenes from the *Iliad, 30, 31*
pharaohs, 181
photographic portraits, 1
Pickens, Francis Wilkinson, 116
plantation romance genre, Reconstruction era, 46, 180, 198, 216, 301–2n27, 302n2
Poe, Edgar Allan, 203; "The Man Who Was Used Up," 310n5; "The Masque of the Red Death," 203
Plessy v. Ferguson (1896), 223
Pollard, Edward, 143, 288n13
Pope, Alexander, as translator of the *Iliad,* 37, 38, 39
Pope, Thomas H., 288n8
Powers, Hiram, 80, 280n3

Preston, Caroline Hampton, 12, 61, 66, 80–81, 97, 169, 205, 298n3
Preston, John Smith, 12, 80–81, 205, 299n11; as gourmet, 81; participation in Confederate cause, 80, 169
Preston, John, Jr. (Jack), 205
Preston, Mary Cantey (Mamie), 204, 205
Preston, Sally Campbell Buchanan (Buck), 103, 146, 200–201, 205, 280n3; engagement to Hood as social allegory, 12; postwar biography of, 268–69n14; romance with Hood, 12, 14, 201
Preston, Susan Frances Hampton (Tudie), 205
Preston, William Campbell, Jr. (Willie): death of, 205, 260
Preston family, 74, 118, 119, 280n2; French haute cuisine of, 80–81, 94; intellectual accomplishments of Preston daughters, 109
Price, Leah, 19, 271n24
Pride, Mrs., 74
Prosser, Gabriel, 221. *See also* slave resistance: of Gabriel Prosser
Putnam's Monthly Magazine, 181

race: and class, 250, 284n2, 292n17; as performance, 153, 167–90
"Rachel" (unknown slave woman), 54–55, 57, 276n13
Raleigh, Walter, 202
Randolph, Mrs. George Wythe, 92, 196, 198, 200, 202, 297n2
Ravenel, Mrs. St. Julien, 26
Ravenel, St. Julien, 230
recipes, recited to staunch hunger, 90
Reconstruction, 6
Redemption, 6
Renee (MBC's calf), 102
Rex (MBC's bull), 102; MBC suspects poisoning of, 102–3

Reynolds, Mary Cox Chesnut, 27, 141, 158, 260
Rhett, Edmund, Jr., 203–5; falls out of window, 204–5; scandalous history of, 301n24
Rhett, Robert Barnwell, Jr., 301n24
Rhody (Witherspoon slave), 208, 227, 242–43, 253
rice, 85, 86, 93; North American origins of in slavery, 281n12
Richardson, Samuel, 197; *Clarissa,* 15
Richmond: fall of, 14
Richmond Daily Dispatch, 278n25
Richmond Examiner, 52, 265; editorializes against amateur theatricals, 192
Rivals, The (Richard Brinsley Sheridan), 12, 108, 192, 196–97, 198, 200, 296n1; Bob Acres (character), 200, 300n18; Captain Adverse (character), 197, 300n18; Faulkland (character), 197; lampooning of sentimentalism in, 197; Lydia Languish (character), 197; Mrs. Malaprop (character), 108, 197–98, 300n18; plot of, 197, 200
Roach, Joseph, 183, 199, 200; definition of performance, 290n3; theory of surrogation, 202
Roman models, popularity in eighteenth-century America, 37
Rome, 29
Romeo (Chesnut slave cook), 82–83, 229; culinary training of, 82
Romeo (Witherspoon slave), 208, 242
Romina, Lynn Marie, 270n19
Romola (George Eliot), 121–27, 285n10; plot of, 120–21; resonance of for MBC, 122; Romola (character), 120–21, 24; Savonarola (character), 119, 120–21; Tito (character), 120–21, 24
Ronner, Wanda, 275n8
roses, 46, 72–73

Rousseau, Jean-Jacques, 197
Rowson, Susanna: *Charlotte Temple,* 144, 277n19; title as pseudonym for seduced and abandoned woman, 151, 277n19
Russell, William Howard: *My Diary in India in the Year 1858–1859,* 193, 210, 298–99n6; *My Diary North and South,* 298n6
Rutledge, Mrs. Benjamin Huger, 95–96
Rutledge, Sarah Henrietta (Sally), 25

Sacks, Richard, 13, 32, 272n3
Saint Paul's Episcopal Church (Richmond), 97
Sandy Hill (Chesnut summer plantation), 57, 141, 147, 267n2; as possible scene of MBC's miscarriage, 148
Saratoga, New York, 51, 52
Sarsfield (home of MBC), 18, 98
Saturday Evening Post, 3, 6
Savannah Republican, 219
Saville, Julie, 288n18
Savitt, Todd L., 281n5
Scarlet Letter, The (Nathaniel Hawthorne): Arthur Dimmesdale (character), 188; "Custom House" preface to, 202; Hester Prynne (character), 187–88. See also Hawthorne, Nathaniel
Scarry, Elaine, 65, 277n24
Schlegel, Friedrich von, 181
Schultz, Jane E., 283n26
Schweninger, Loren, 306n23
Scipio the elder (Chesnut slave), 213–15, 217–18, 306n14; legacy of, 251; as minstrel, 215; as race traitor, 214; thwarts slave uprising in Camden in 1816, 149, 211
Scipio the younger (Chesnut slave), 215–18, 253, 301n27; called "the Black Hercules" in MBC's 1880s narrative,

218; legacy of, 251; loyalty to James Chesnut, Sr., 25, 46, 213; sings hymn at funeral of James Chesnut, Sr., 215–16, 303n4
Scott, Walter: *Guy Mannering,* 220
Scribe, Augustin Eugène, 118
Seaton, Beverly, 72, 76, 279n33, 282n21
seeds, 50, 79. See also Chesnut, Mary Boykin (MBC), biography: infertility of; flowers; fruit; *and individual flower, food, and fruit types*
Semmes, Mrs. Thomas Jenkins, 163
sentimentalism: examples of genre, 145. See also Chesnut, Mary Boykin, views of: sentimentalism; Stowe, Harriet Beecher; *Uncle Tom's Cabin* (Harriet Beecher Stowe)
Serenola (MBC's cow), 102
Shakespeare, William, 108, 113, 121, 127, 129–31, 196; *As You Like It,* 154; *Hamlet,* 128, 279n37; *King Lear,* 15, 127–29, 279n37; *Macbeth,* 113, 128; *A Midsummer Night's Dream,* 154. See also *King Lear* (William Shakespeare)
Shand, Peter J., 62
Sheridan, Richard Brinsley, 196. See also *Rivals, The* (Richard Brinsley Sheridan)
Sherman, William Tecumseh, 127–28, 168, 286n16; capture of Atlanta, September 1864, 115; march to sea, 25–26, 89
Silas Marner (George Eliot), 116, 121, 124, 125, 127; as morally superior Eliot novel, 121
Silber, Nina, 280n41
Simms, J. Marion, 275n6
Simms, William Gilmore, 71, 285n9
Simon (Miller slave): episode at Sumter, 177, 292n18; mimicry of Stephen Decatur Miller, Sr., 175–77
Singleton, Mrs. John Coles, 61–63, 65

Singleton, Rebecca (Decca), 61, 64, 277n19
Singleton family, 61
Slade, Carole, 277n17
slave religion, 295n32; as Afro-Christian synthesis, 186; practiced on Mulberry, 182–90; rejection of original sin in, 185; restricted post-1831, 182
slave resistance: via arson, 218–21, 245; and Christianity, 215; defined, 86; of Denmark Vesey, 213; escape as unsuccessful form of, 239; of Gabriel Prosser, 213; at Harpers Ferry in 1859, 172, 208, 210; on the Hermitage, 86; often initiated by artisans, 213; via intoxication, 246–47; against the Jefferson Davis family, 220–21, 245; at the Lyons home, 220, 245; via mimicry, 180; on Mulberry, 86, 152; of Nat Turner, 182, 193, 215, 292n17, 295n32; Negro ball as act of, 236–37; opium overdose administered to MBC by Ellen as possible form of, 230; MBC participates in form of, 217; via poisoning, 283n28; potential for, 177; prospect of in 1864, 191; and survival, 289n1; at St. Domingo, 149, 172, 193, 208, 219, 283n28; thwarted in Camden in 1816, 149, 210–15, 229, 245, 305n10–11; via theft of foodstuffs, 245; white fear of, 148, 208. *See also* Witherspoon murder
slavery: abolished by the British in 1833, 193; as advent of Satan into New World garden, 279n36; based on negotiations between accommodation and demand, 223; class hierarchy under, 176; defined, 173; as drama of bloody hands, 243; as original sin, 185, 295n35; as performance, 167–90; "positive good" rationale for, 209; and Protestant theology, 216; and social death, 173; as tragedy, 182; white ideological fiction undergirding, 173–74, 228; white Southern cultural memory of, circa 1905, 222–23
slaves: agency of, 7, 23, 173, 244; consciousness of, 7, 168, 174; as dishonored persons, 247; dissimulation of, 167–68; Egyptian origin of, 181, 294n27; forced to remarry after emancipation, 224; as human parasites, 88, 152; legal restraints on, 179, 218, 246, 305n11; problematic access to voices of, 218; of South Carolina defect to Union gunboats, 210
slave women, leave babies behind at Mulberry when emancipated in 1865, 116
Slocum, Mrs. Cuthbert H., 203, 205
smell, at bottom of hierarchy of senses, 146
Smith, Adam, 68; *The Theory of Moral Sentiments*, 232, 278n28
Smith, Andrew F., 281n11
Sobel, Mechal, 186, 295n32
Society Hill, South Carolina, 207, 222
"Sonata," performed by "white-robed choir" for George Washington at Trenton in 1789, 155, 156
Sophocles, 33, 171, 181, 182
Soulouque, Faustin, 172, 291n9
South, mythologized as cavalier Eden, 71
South Carolina, secession of, 34
Southern belle, social construction of, 260, 309n5
Southern cuisine: created by slaves, 82; influenced by Caribbean and West African flavors, 82
Southern Federal Union, 95
Southern Literary Messenger, 71, 113, 203
Southern Quarterly Review, 138
Sparta, 13
"Speckled Peach," 261–64; flirts with JC, 254; obliviousness of, 263

INDEX 327

Spenser, Edmund, *Faerie Queene,* 154
Sphinx, 171; Egyptian, 181
Spotswood (McRae slave), 212
Spotswood Hotel (Richmond), 81, 94
Stanard, Mrs. Martha, 97
Stanton, Lucia, 276n12
Stark, Mary Sophia, 63
Star-Ledger, 289n22
Stevens, Mary, 83
Steward, Austin, 308n7; account of Negro ball in *Twenty-two Years a Slave and Forty Years a Freeman,* 237–39
Stewart, Susan, 271n25; notion of the souvenir, 19
stickies, 103–5
Stockton, Richard (Dick), 205
Stoneman, George: Richmond raid, 4, 178
Stowe, Calvin, 135, 287n2, 287n4
Stowe, Harriet Beecher, 50, 116, 118, 119, 144–45, 181, 197, 265, 286n15; aided fugitive slave, 135, 285n4; biography of, 287n2, 287n4; Calvinism of, 165; knowledge of African Americans, 135; MBC's hatred of, 113–14, 131, 133–36, 285n13; MBC's obsession with, 15, 135, 138–40. See also *Uncle Tom's Cabin* (Harriet Beecher Stowe)
Stuart, J. E. B., 39, 51, 57, 59, 274n14
Sue (slave of John Chesnut Sr.), 58, 152
Sue, Eugene, 151
sugar, 91, 103–4; associated with slave labor in Deep South, 103
Sumner, Charles, 145
Sundquist, Eric J., 290n7, 305n10
suttee, 193, 298n4
Sutton, Robert, 196
Sweet, Timothy, 70, 71, 277n22
sweet potatoes, 84, 85; North American origins of in slavery, 282n12
Sylvie (Witherspoon slave), 208, 242

Taber, William, 301n24
Talvande, Ann Marsan (Madame Talvande), 172
Taves, Anne, 295n32
Taylor, Jeremy, 112
Team, James, 140, 146, 268n11; believes all women are abolitionists, 209; wants to free slaves and put in army, 209
Team, Mrs. James, 225, 307n27
Tennyson, Alfred, 112
Thackeray, William Makepeace, 113, 114, 118, 127, 128, 131, 197, 265; *Vanity Fair,* 116, 119
Thebes, 171
Therese (French cook of MBC), 83
Thirteenth Amendment, 230, 251
Thomas, Dylan, "Do Not Go Gentle into That Good Night," 271n30
Thomas, Lorenzo, bans *Macaria* from Union ranks, 114
Thompson, John R., 71, 113, 121, 124
Thoreau, Henry David, 37, 145
Times (London), 193, 298n6
Timrod, Henry, 285n9, 300n15
Tiresias, 44
tomatoes, 50, 91, 94, 95; nineteenth-century belief in curative powers of, 95; North American origins of, 283n24
Tompkins, Jane, 142, 144, 284n8
Trenton, New Jersey, 137, 155
Trojans, 29, 37
Trollope, Anthony, 113, 118, 137
Trollope, Frances, 291n12
Troy, 13; Confederate States of America as, 38
Trouillot, Michel-Rolph, 291n9
Truth, Sojourner, 235
Turner, Nat, 188; biography of, 215. See also slave resistance: of Nat Turner

Twain, Mark, 273n10
Tyler, Letitia Christian, 269n15

Ulysses, 13, 44. *See also* Odysseus
Uncle Tom's Cabin (Harriet Beecher Stowe), 50, 76, 118–19, 133–45, 142, 144–45, 164–65, 186, 274–75n1; Adolph (character), 140, 237; Andy (character), 198, 293n22, 294n25; Augustine St. Clare (character), 139; Aunt Chloe (character), 198; Aunt Ophelia (character), 165; MBC's critique of, 12; Eliza (character), 135, 293n22; Eva (character), 134, 164–65; generic classification of, 287n3; Haley (character), 198, 293n22; influence on MBC's 1880s narrative, 15, 116, 139–40, 287n1; Jane (character), 237; Negro ball in, 237; obliquely mentioned in 1860s diary, 116, 139; MBC's obsession with, 15, 135, 138–40; Quimbo (character), 198; Rachel Halliday (character), 274n1; racist idioms in, 198; MBC reads five times during the war, 113, 116; Sam (character), 198, 293n22, 294n25; Sambo (character), 198; Simon Legree (character), 134, 139, 140, 142, 198; slaves as objects in, 291n11; Tom (character), 134, 198; Topsy (character), 134, 165
Union army: blacks begin to join in 1863, 195

Van Lew, Elizabeth, 306n24
Van Zandt, John, 135
Vesey, Denmark, 221. *See also* slave resistance: of Denmark Vesey
Villari, Pasquale, *The History of Girolamo Savonarola and of His Times (Life of Savonarola)*, 121
Virgil, 17, 44, 287n1
Virginia Dare (MBC's cow), 102

Vizetelly, Frank, 199, 272n2
Volney, Constantin Francois, 181, 294n27

Wall, Allie Patricia, 267n3
Wallace, Richard, 282n21
Warner, Susan, 50, 142, 197; *Say and Seal,* 140; *The Wide, Wide World,* 50, 141, 145
Warren, Kenneth, 288n10
Washington, George, 37, 85, 149, 154; composes "Card" for "white-robed choir," 154, 156, 158; at Trenton en route to inauguration in 1789, 137, 154–58, *157*
Washington, John, 302n2
Wateree Mission Chapel, 217. *See also* black church, on Mulberry
Wateree River, 45
watermelon, 84, 85, 86, 92
Watkins, Sam, *Company Aytch,* 273n10
Watson, Charles S., 198, 300n15
Watt, Stephen, 299n12
Webster, Daniel, 37
Weinstein, Cindy, 287n2, 288n16
Wesley African Methodist Episcopal Church (Camden), 217
Westminster Abbey, 68, 98
Wheeler, Joseph, 304n6
Whitaker, Maria (Chesnut slave), 146
white men in the quarters, 56, 86, 140, 150. *See also* Chesnut, Mary Boykin, views of: miscegenation
Wigfall, Francis Halsey, 202
Wigfall, Louis Trezevant, 29
Wigfall, Mrs. Louis Trezevant, 198, 298n3
William (Witherspoon slave), 208, 213, 214–15, 227, 233–36, 239–43, 253, 308n5; MBC's dignified portrait of, 233–34; favorite slave of Mr. Witherspoon, 234

Williams, Ben Ames, 7, 117, 222. *See also* Chesnut, Mary Boykin, 1880s narrative: Williams edition

Williams, David Rogerson, Jr., 97, 307n30

Williams, David Rogerson, III, 18, 103; deafness of, 265

Williams, Jane Pettigrew, 102

Williams, Katherine Miller (Kate) (sister of MBC), 4, 52; death of, 129, 259; response to Witherspoon murder, 227, 229

Williams, Serena (Princess Bright Eyes), 266; death of, 129, 259

Williams, Stephen Miller (Miller) (nephew of MBC), 102, 217

Williams, Susan, 94, 283n22

Willis, Nathaniel Parker, 289n24

Wilson, Edmund, 10, 11, 13, 33, 268n12

Wilson, Harriet E., 276n11

Witherspoon, Elizabeth Boykin (Betsey), 169, 228, 231, 241–43; death of as murder, 207–8, 225; family of, 224; objects to son's threats to slaves, 240; as prisoner of own slaves, 226; treatment of slaves, 207–8, 226, 239. *See also* Witherspoon murder

Witherspoon, John (son of Betsey Witherspoon), 225, 234, 239–41, 243, 308n5; effect of mother's murder on, 231; sadistic to slaves, 207, 231–32, 234, 236, 239

Witherspoon, John Dick (husband of Betsey Witherspoon), 239; as indulgent master, 239; relationship with William, 234–36, 308n5

Witherspoon, Mrs. John (Mary), 225, 243

Witherspoon murder, 7, 83, 172, 221–29, 231–45; accounts of published in *Charleston Courier, 222,* 232; as act of revenge, 236; bloody handprints at scene of, 242–43; gallows bill for slaves convicted of, *244;* goriness of unanticipated by Witherspoon slaves, 242; indicts all slaveholders, 243; restored in Williams edition, 217, 222–23; sanitized in Avary-Martin edition, 222–23; as slave insurrection, 208; slaves' potential rationale for, 240; staged as a natural death, 231; uncanniness of, 233. *See also* Witherspoon, Elizabeth Boykin (Betsey)

Woman in White, The (Wilkie Collins), Count Fosco (character), 245

Wood, Betty, 295n32

Woodward, C. Vann, 3, 4, 13, 16, 23, 33, 51, 53, 54, 60, 114, 117, 194, 256, 280n42, 297n1, 300n20; on James Chesnut Sr.'s possible sexual impropriety with slaves, 54; *Mary Chesnut's Civil War* (editor), 267n1, 268n10; *The Private Mary Chesnut* (editor), 9, 35, 267n1. *See also* Chesnut, Mary Boykin, 1880s narrative: Woodward Yale edition

Wooley, Charles F., 280n5

Woolf, Virginia, 18, 277n17

Woolson, Constance Fennimore, *For the Major,* 309–10n5

Wordsworth, William, 112, 234

Wyatt-Brown, Bertram, 247, 290–91n8, 293n21

Wyeth, N. C.: "Washington's Procession into Trenton," 158

Yankee spies, in Lincolnton, North Carolina, 111

Zafar, Rafia, 292n15
Zagarri, Rosemarie, 289n19